DIXONIA

DIXONIA

A Bio-Discography of Bill Dixon

Compiled by **Ben Young**

Discographies, Number 77
Michael Gray, *Series Editor*

Greenwood Press
Westport, Connecticut • London

Library of Congress Cataloging-in-Publication Data

Young, Ben, 1971–
    Dixonia : a Bio-discography of Bill Dixon / compiled by
Ben Young.
        p.   cm.—(Discographies, ISSN 0192–334X ; no. 77)
    Includes bibliographical references and index.
    ISBN 0–313–30275–8 (alk. paper)
    1. Dixon, Bill, 1925- —Discography. I. Title. II. Series.
ML156.7.D59Y68   1998
781.65′092
[B]—DC21   98–14756
                    MN

British Library Cataloguing in Publication Data is available.

Library of Congress Catalog Card Number: 98–14756
ISBN: 0–313–30275–8
ISSN: 0192–334X

First published in 1998

Greenwood Press, 88 Post Road West, Westport, CT 06881
An imprint of Greenwood Publishing Group, Inc.

Printed in the United States of America

The paper used in this book complies with the
Permanent Paper Standard issued by the National
Information Standards Organization (Z39.48–1984).

10 9 8 7 6 5 4 3 2 1

This work is above all for Bill Dixon;

for my parents;
Dr. Sue Gilmore and Mary Catherine Bradshaw; and
Janie Iadipaolo--

without whose art,
example,
inspiration, and
understanding
it might only have been a fancy.

Contents

Preface

I. Why Bill Dixon?

Bill Dixon has made essential contributions to all phases of creative Black
Music since he first made a full-time committment to music. An unbiased
assessment of his work, though, has heretofore been thwarted by the unusual
course of his career: Dixon first made an impact as an organizer in the
pioneering efforts toward self-determination for working musicians and a broader
awareness of the musical spectrum of 1959-65. In the public view, the profile
of these involvements--with the United Nations Jazz Society and his Jazz
Composers' Guild--has masked the import and seriousness of his later activities
as a composer and musician.

This stream began in the early Sixties, as Dixon evolved a thoroughly original
music for orchestra that, reaching its apex a decade later, had almost no wide-
spread representation on records or the greater world stage. At the same time, he
developed a constant collaborative partnership with dancer/choreographer Judith
Dunn. Both of these endeavors and their procedures were crystallized within the
educational program that he created and sustained as the premier (the only?)
institution in the world to take up the mission of producing work while

equipping a next generation of players technically and aesthetically to embrace the vanguard thinking in the art form and advance it to the next level. Of all his accomplishments, Bill Dixon's personal acumen as an improvising brass player has probably been recognized most recently, with the zenith that encompasses his trio, quartet, and sextet recordings of the 1980s.

The task of accounting for these achievements must in 1998 carry with it the observation that while many of Dixon's works of even a quarter-century ago still represent the most advanced refinements of art, craft, and theory in the music, the importance of his forward steps has gone unabsorbed by nearly all of the current practitioners and spectators in creative music. Nonetheless, he continues to work. Dixon's latest musical works for large and small ensembles are masterpieces of his kinetic approach to the orchestral displacement of sound. Those compositions and two decades of unaccompanied trumpet pieces testify to the timeless marvels of Dixon's pantonal conception on the instrument and his extension to the catalog of available trumpet sounds.

It is to Bill Dixon's credit that his musical identity in both orchestration and instrumental practice can be seen as "singular"; to have a distinctive musical voice has, after all, been one of the measurements of genius in this music throughout its history. But for that musical vision to have remained unique to him, undigested by others, and merely "legendary" in the canon is an error for the culture, one made all the more ironic by his own superior qualifications to demystify its inner workings. A forthright, articulate analyst, Dixon has also been eyewitness to the entire development of the so-called *avantgarde* in Black Music.

Dixonia is fundamentally a book of facts. While the proper understanding of Bill Dixon's music will show that future volumes of musical analysis, biography, critical assessment, and record guides are warranted, this volume concerns itself only tangentially with these matters, but primarily with cataloging Dixon's works, as an indispensable step for all perspectives of analysis.
The purpose of this research is to identify every known episode of Bill Dixon making music, adding relevant information about these events and their relationship to the entire trajectory of his career to date.

A. Issued Recordings

Dixonia contains an exhaustive list of Bill Dixon's published (i.e., commercially available) recordings. A digest of these issued records is presented on page xxi, to be used as a quick reference tool for identifying their component parts. As they are generally the definitive and most tangible presentations of Dixon's work (and often milestones in his career as well) the sessions are described in detail and often referred to in the body of this work, but the entries for them comprise only a fraction of the entire text.

Dixonia is greatly indebted to the example of Walter C. Allen's treatises on King Oliver and Fletcher Henderson, which set the standard for bio-discography in Black Music, and also the works of Laurie Wright and Chris Sheridan on Jelly Roll Morton and Count Basie, respectively.[1] These studies were compiled with the wise view that comprehending an artist's career starts with rigorous disc-documentation, supplemented by information about the artist's day-to-day activities and the turning points that fall between recording dates. As a "bio-discography," this volume has the same mission but somewhat different proportions, owing primarily to the uncharacteristic pattern of Bill Dixon's musical activities.

B. Unissued Recordings

Contrary to the general opportunism of the Jazz music industry, Bill Dixon has resolutely accepted offers to make records only when respectable terms have coincided with an original concept worthy of presentation. (A quick glance at the last thirty years show that the terms were lacking more often than new ideas.) Consequently, unlike the recorded histories of Oliver, Henderson, Morton, and Basie, Bill Dixon's commercially released discs are dwarfed in number and scope by a myriad of little-documented "private recordings," so listing the latter becomes even more critical to a comprehensive study. Obviously, his career has also occupied an era when recording technology is readily available to musicians themselves and not just institutions or record companies.

According to Dixon's outlook on performance, formal or even public concert situations are not necessary for the making of significant music. Most of the definitive statements in his area of music have emerged separate from the considerations of "audience" or "market". With this view that recording is primarily useful as a reference tool--or even "notation"--for the players themselves, Bill Dixon evolved a policy of recording everything he did in music--concerts, lecture-demonstrations, workshops, rehearsals, classes, closed sessions, and the gamut of informal playing situations--however possible for later re-examination. *Dixonia* applies a corollary to that theorem in trying

---

[1] Walter C. Allen, *Hendersonia* (Highland Park, NJ: Jazz Monographs No. 4, 1973); Walter C. Allen and Brian Rust, *King Joe Oliver* (London: Sidgwick & Jackson, 1957?); Laurie Wright, *Mister Jelly Lord* (London: Chigwell, 1980); Chris Sheridan, *Count Basie* (Westport,CT: Greenwood Press, 1986).

to account for all tapes of Dixon's music with equal thoroughness. <u>Unissued tape recordings are cited alongside and among the issued records in chronological order, and all are weighted in terms of their musical importance, rather than the breadth of their dissemination.</u> It will be noted, however, that many of the running tapes from Dixon's regular classes and ensemble meetings remain unexplored. In order to acknowledge their existence, these have been listed in tables as Appendix Two of this volume. Whereas many of the public concerts that culminated a term's work at the University of Wisconsin/Madison or Bennington College have been given individual entries in the main text, the developmental readings in which these pieces were assembled are submerged chronologically into the tables. More information on this aspect of Dixon's philosophy and performance practice may be found on pages 174 and 182.

C. Unrecorded Performances

Dixonia <u>attempts to complete the picture by listing every discrete and verifiable Bill Dixon performance--whether recorded or not--</u>in order to give appropriate emphasis to segments of his career that apparently were not illuminated by any sort of recording. This additional information will be of most value relative to the extremely active New York period 1958-68 in which a large number of crucial episodes seem to have gone undocumented. It may also be useful to future researchers of Dixon's work, as tapes for some events that were certainly recorded are not currently evident but may someday come to light. *Dixonia* <u>therefore cites all known performances that can be specifically identified by venue, date, personnel, title of a work, or other factors.</u> Rehearsals prior to 1971 are mentioned if known and also given individual item numbers if recordings still exist. Many other occurrences, such as having played with a certain musician or at a certain venue on an indefinite occasion, have been submerged into relevant or adjacent entries; items pertaining to the Archie Shepp-Bill Dixon Quartet, the Cellar Cafe, and the Bill Dixon-Judith Dunn collaborations are three of the most common areas of the text where this occurs.

Any creative artist faces prospective working situations or collaborations that--for whatever reason--fail to materialize. Dixon's steadfast professional ethics has resulted in a multitude of such designs--planned but never realized. Most of these are not mentioned in *Dixonia*. Some that bear directly on the scope or intended direction of Dixon's work are mentioned. Events that were advertised and cancelled, or those inaccurately described in print are reported here in an effort to rectify existing misperceptions. In all cases, these "phantom" episodes have been attached to relevant entries for actual performances, and they are not listed independently. Some examples are shown in **R68-0000**, **67-0802** and **64-1030**.

D. Bill Dixon's Epoch

Lastly, this volume demonstrates the breadth of Dixon's artistic spectrum in sections covering (respectively): his music performed by others (Chapter 11-- which also enumerates instances where Dixon's recordings have been applied *ex post facto* to live dance, theater, or film events); concerts or recording dates held under Dixon's *aegis* as organizer, without his participation as a player (Chapter 12); and, other involvements in the music (mainly speaking and teaching engagements) that have not included his music (Chapter 13).

Dixonia also has a tertiary mission to describe the artistic environment in which Bill Dixon has worked. In the painful absence of any comprehensive research on the new music that emerged in the 1960s, the Jazz Composers' Guild, the *oeuvre* of Judith Dunn, or the contemporary ensemble programs at the University of Wisconsin at Madison and Bennington College, this volume has been prepared with a maximalistic approach, adding details that perhaps overlap these domains though they may not be integral to Dixon's path. It is hoped that students dealing with these topics will benefit from the wide scope of information gathered here.

Many details shown may seem irrelevant to Bill Dixon's history or outright meaningless; on the contrary, they have been specifically included in order that future researchers might have as many clues as possible (and not have to retrace paths already traveled) in identifying recordings or recollections that will be uncovered in the future.

II. Methodology

Information contained in this volume has been substantiated or corroborated by Bill Dixon. He provided much of the background information directly and has been consulted on its appropriate placement within the text. Interviews with Dixon have been quoted copiously to elucidate the details of each entry. All unattributed quotes are Dixon's words, drawn from one or more of the following sources, most in the span 1990-97:

a. On-air and pre-recorded discussions with Dixon undertaken for the *Bill Dixon Radio* series on WKCR-FM radio
b. Other fact-checking and explanatory discussions with the author
c. Dixon's written corrections to various drafts of this text
d. Correspondence with the author
e. Recorded or printed lectures and concert introductions since 1971
f. Telephone and face-to-face discussions with the author

Information from other parties--including the artists and researchers named below--was drawn from a similar panoply of sources; published ones are noted.

In addition to scrupulously documenting his own music, Dixon maintains an unequalled archive of printed materials relating to that work, including letters, concert programs, scores, schedules, posters, newspaper advertisements, feature articles, reviews, contracts, receipts, payrolls, and various informal notations. His *curricula vitae*, resumés, and lists of BMI-registered compositions have been consulted, and wherever possible, supplemented by references in periodicals of the time (advertisements, announcements, press reviews, and the like). Facts from all of these are incorporated into *Dixonia* to establish the specifics for each event.

All other relevant secondary sources known and available to the author-- including artist and label discographies, biographical monographs, and articles-- have been consulted.

This project has also been considerably assisted by direct communications with many of Dixon's colleagues and collaborators in music, dance, drama, film, and various organizations. The following are among the musicians and artists who have contributed their time, recollections, and resources to the effort that produced *Dixonia*:

Rashied Ali, Helen Alkire, Jay Ash, Thais Barry, Chris Billias, Carla Bley, John Blum, Karen Borca, Arthur Brooks, John Benson and Peggy Brooks, Don Calfa, Penny Campbell, the late Denis Charles, Warren Chiasson, Bill Cole, Laurence Cook, Bob Cunningham, Dr. Art Davis, Joe DiCarlo, Hal Dodson, Ehran Elisha, Marco Eneidi, Barbara Ensley, Susan Feiner, Crystal Field, Joe Fonda, Joel Freedman, Gary William Friedman, Gene Friedman, Vinnie Gerard, Hugh Glover, Herb Golzmane, William Greaves, Burton Greene, John Hagen, Paul Haines, Maxine [Marlene] Haleff, Stephen Haynes, Don Heckman, Mark Hennen, Baird Hersey, Stephen Horenstein, Jeff Hoyer, Howard Johnson, Howie Kadison, Franz Koglmann, Jackson Krall, Byard Lancaster, Henry Letcher, Rod Levitt, Cheryl and Dan Lilienstein, Glynis Lomon, the late Sid MacKay, Michael Mantler, Carlo Mazzone, Butch McAden, Makanda Ken McIntyre, Molly McQuarrie, the late Charles Moffett, Sr., Don Moore, Michael Moss, Paul Motian, Daniel Nagrin, Al Neese, Tony Oxley, Gary Peacock, Justin Perdue, Fausto Pollicino, Mara Purl, Perry Robinson, Roswell Rudd, Peter Sabino, Lawrence Sacharow, Susan Sgorbati, Elaine Shipman, Alan Silva, Syd Smart, Lisa Sokolov, Edith Stephen, Ed Summerlin, Steve Swallow, Aldo Tambellini, Linda Tarnay, John Tchicai, Jim Tifft, Steve Tintweiss, John Voigt, the late Marzette Watts, Valdo Williams, Leslie Winston, Leopanar Witlarge, Lewis Worrell, Jason Zappa, Ralph Zeitlin, Eric Zinman.

Many researchers, reporters, and eyewitnesses have also contributed in one capacity or another, including:

Chris Albertson, Larry Applebaum, Chris Bakriges, Daniel Bergér, Samantha Black, Tony Carruthers, Marc Chaloin, Terry Creach, Scott Currie, John D'Agostino, Steve Dalachinsky, Les Davis, Jeanne Dixon, Maia Garrison, Kris

Gilliland, John Gray, Phil Greene, Carlos Kase, Theodora Kuslan, Robert Levin, Francesco Martinelli, Brad McCuen, Dan Morgenstern, Cliff Preiss, Peter Pullman, Ann Resch, Bob Rusch, Laura Schandelmeier, Rick Schussel, Ethan Singer, Ken Thomson, Thierry Trombert, Sharon Vogel, Cynthia Walters, Anton Young, Eric Ziarko, Anonymous, and the staff and administration of WKCR-FM, New York City.

A special note of appreciation is due to Phil Schaap, who first showed me the value of Black Music research involving the primary participants, and, by extension, to Papa Jo Jones, who pointed out one major avenue through which that research might be carried out.

III. Using This Volume

The following diagram identifies the parts of each entry, which are then discussed individually:

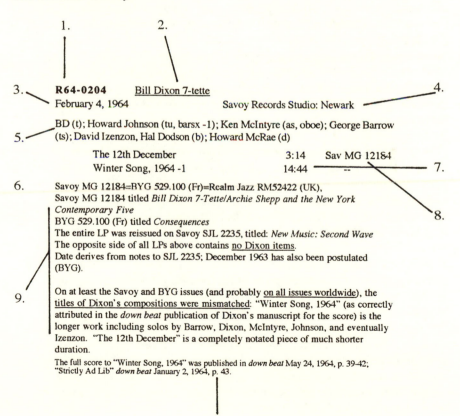

1.

2.

3. **R64-0204** Bill Dixon 7-tette

4.

February 4, 1964   Savoy Records Studio: Newark

5. BD (t); Howard Johnson (tu, barsx -1); Ken McIntyre (as, oboe); George Barrow (ts); David Izenzon, Hal Dodson (b); Howard McRae (d)

The 12th December   3:14   Sav MG 12184
Winter Song, 1964 -1   14:44   --

7.

6. Savoy MG 12184=BYG 529.100 (Fr)=Realm Jazz RM52422 (UK),
Savoy MG 12184 titled *Bill Dixon 7-Tette/Archie Shepp and the New York Contemporary Five*
BYG 529.100 (Fr) titled *Consequences*
The entire LP was reissued on Savoy SJL 2235, titled: *New Music: Second Wave*
The opposite side of all LPs above contains no Dixon items.
Date derives from notes to SJL 2235; December 1963 has also been postulated (BYG).

8.

9. On at least the Savoy and BYG issues (and probably on all issues worldwide), the titles of Dixon's compositions were mismatched: "Winter Song, 1964" (as correctly attributed in the *down beat* publication of Dixon's manuscript for the score) is the longer work including solos by Barrow, Dixon, McIntyre, Johnson, and eventually Izenzon. "The 12th December" is a completely notated piece of much shorter duration.

The full score to "Winter Song, 1964" was published in *down beat* May 24, 1964, p. 39-42; "Strictly Ad Lib" *down beat* January 2, 1964, p. 43.

10.

In the main body of the work (chapters 1-13), this layout has been adopted for each entry to separately show data regarding the name of the group; the names of its members; date and location of the performance; titles of pieces performed and where they can be found on records; additional notes about the performance; and bibliographic citations to immediate sources of the data in that item.

1. *ITEM NUMBER*: a unique code has been attached to each entry in this volume. A boldface "R" preceding the digits in that code indicates that the event was definitely recorded and the recording verifiably in someone's possession. A roman "R" shows that a recording was attempted and either was unsuccessful or perhaps no longer extant. "O" in that place is reserved for entries in Chapter 11, on Dixon's music played by others. The "U" prefix designates concerts staged under Dixon's organizational guidance in which he did not play (Chapter 12). "X" is used for the non-performing events detailed in Chapter 13.
The first two digits of the catalog number are the last two digits of the year in which the performance for that entry occurred; the two digits following the hyphen represent the month (01 through 12), and the last two the date within the month (01 through 31). Where only vague information about the date of the performance is known, the month and day have been approximated, or left null, e.g. **R68-0000** or **73-0197**.
Item numbers appear in boldface type everywhere.

2. *GROUP NAME*: as listed on records, in advertising or programs, or as can be surmised from descriptions in the absence of definite data. This name is underlined.

3. *DATE*: the exact date(s) of the event. Where a work was performed repeatedly (with the same players, etc.) in the same location over a period of time, or where several sessions were held in a sequence of days and cannot be further specified, only the beginning and ending dates will be listed; e.g., "Saturdays; July 12-31, 1975". When the actual performance dates within this span can be established, they will appear in the *PERFORMANCE NOTES*.

4. *LOCATION*: the name of the venue (where known) and city where the performance was held. Addresses are added for some more obscure or now defunct venues.

5. *PERSONNEL*: the names of all active participants in the work. Each name is followed by a parenthetical abbreviation identifying what role that player had in the performance (usually citing the instrument that person plays). Names in this field have been updated to reflect those by which the players are now professionally known or are best known, with alternate names or spellings shown in the PERFORMANCE NOTES.

Dixon is listed first (using the abbreviation "BD"), followed by the (other) leaders. Following these, the names of other participants are given in the order of the abbreviations list (see p. xvii). Unless otherwise stated, Dixon is the arranger and conductor (where applicable) for all dates under his leadership. Costume, set, and lighting designers, where their names are known, are cited in the *PERFORMANCE NOTES*.

Some "U" entries in chapter 12 show several groups on one day's program in this field; both the billing for the group (underscored) and the names of its members will appear here in that case. The placeholder "unknown" appears with an instument abbreviation where it is known that an instrument was played but not known who played it. "Others unknown" in the *PERSONNEL* indicates that names, instrumentation and number of participants are unclear. Where changes in personnel or instrumentation occur within the program (i.e., from one piece to another), arabic numerals are used in the *PERSONNEL* and *TITLE* sections to correlate pieces and the appropriate personnel.

6. *TITLE*: name(s) of the piece(s) performed. Wherever possible these are grouped in the order performed. Where the number of pieces on the program is not known (and no titles or recordings are available) this section is blank and the empty space eliminated.
Note the difference between "Untitled" and "Unknown" in the *TITLE* section: the former indicates that the composer(s) did not give a title to that work. "Unknown" is a placeholder, used where the number of pieces is known but their titles are not. Some of the author's unofficial designations using arbitrary letter names, Dixon's stage instructions, or instrumentation ("XP Rehearsal", "Play your open E" and "BD solo", for example) have been used to help differentiate one untitled work from another within the program. These titles do not appear in the index. Titles shown in italics either contain no music (such as spoken segments or solo dance pieces) or have no musical input by Bill Dixon.

In referring to the titles of musical or multi-media works in the text, some of the conventions of orthography have been waived: all titles appear in quotation marks regardless of the duration or structure of the piece. Dixon's *oeuvre* and many of the important musical works of his time do not easily conform to the customary distinctions between "Songs" and *Extended Compositions*.

In the rare instances where recording session tapes (containing complete and incomplete versions of pieces) are available, the takes have been differentiated by number where possible and an abbreviation appears to indicate whether the take was complete, incomplete, etc. as indicated in the abbreviations list.
"[inc]" following a title--from concert or studio--means that the piece was truncated on the available recording, due to technical imperfections.
"like..." preceding a title denotes a distinct musical similarity between that piece

and an issued work that Dixon has titled. The comparison might go no further than that; many pieces on programs where this term is used were constantly under development.

7. *TIMING*: duration of the piece when played back at proper speed, provided wherever possible. The appearance of an exact timing generally indicates that the tape has been scrutinized in preparing this volume. Timings for certain pieces have been roughly estimated based on Dixon's recollections or a cursory survey of the recording; these estimates are prefixed by "c." or "ca.".

8. *ISSUE*: the first commercial release of the title, shown on the same line and listed by the record label's catalog number. Any additional information about this and subsequent releases of that music is given in the beginning of the PERFORMANCE NOTES section for each entry. Unissued recordings are identified using the phrase "BD rec." (or "private tape") where Dixon or another party maintains a tape of the performance. Unless otherwise indicated, all issues given are of 12" microgroove records released in the USA.

9. *PERFORMANCE NOTES*: a description of the event. The first lines of this area are used for further details about the issued recordings, where applicable. Foreign and domestic LP or CD equivalents, whole or partial reissues, and titles of the records are cited here. Also in the PERFORMANCE NOTES may be described the details of the piece(s), the event, or how that item relates to other performances and Dixon's career as a whole, often as described in his words. Again, all quotes otherwise unattributed are of Bill Dixon. Issues surrounding the relative certainty of date, location, players, etc., will be discussed here as well.

10. *BIBLIOGRAPHIC CITATIONS*: pertaining to any part of the entry. Any public, printed sources of substantive information (however sketchy or oblique) about the performance will be cited here. Quotes in the *PERFORMANCE NOTES* tagged with simplified citations (title or author) are footnoted in full here. Record reviews are not shown: John Gray offers a comprehensive index of these in his work, *Fire Music: A Bibliography of the New Jazz 1959-1990* (Westport, Connecticut: Greenwood Press, 1991), p. 202-203. Dixon's *L'Opera Volume One* " A Collection of Letters, Writings, Musical Scores, Drawings, and Photographs (1967-1986)" (Bennington, VT: Metamorphosis Publishing, 1986) is cited here so frequently that complete bibliographic information is not shown for each reference; rather, cites appear simply as "*L'Opera*, p. 66" for example.

The group name, date, and location sections are filled for every item, using the most detailed information available. Where no personnel or titles* are known, or where no discographic or bibliographic data apply, those fields remain empty.

IV. Abbreviations

Proper Names

ASBD	Archie Shepp-Bill Dixon Quartet/Sextet
BCVT	Bennington College, Vermont
BME	Black Music Ensemble
DTW	Dance Theater Workshop, NYC
FFIE	Free Form Improvisation Ensemble (1962-65)
GWU	George Washington University
JCG	Jazz Composers' Guild (1964-65)
LENA	Lowe East side Neighborhoods Association
MfY	Mobilization for Youth, NYC
NDG	New Dance Group Studio, NYC
NRT	Non-Resident Term (BCVT) late December to early March
NYAQ	New York Art Quartet (1964-65)
NYC	New York City
TIOS	Dixon's piece "This //// Is Our Strategy" (1976)
UNJS	United Nations Jazz Society
UNS	United Nations Secretariat, NYC
UOTS	University of the Streets, NYC
UWM	University of Wisconsin at Madison
VAPA	Visual and Performing Arts building, BCVT
Apt	Apartment
Av	Avenue

Instruments

c	cornet
t	trumpet
pocket c	pocket cornet
frh	French horn
mellophone	
tb	trombone
btb	bass trombone
tu	tuba
picc	piccolo
fl	flute
afl	alto flute
bfl	bass flute
cl	clarinet
bcl	bass clarinet

oboe	
engh	English horn
bsn	bassoon
ss	soprano saxophone
as	alto saxophone
ts	tenor saxophone
barsx	baritone saxophone
vln	violin
vla	viola
cello	
g	guitar
elbg	electric (Fender) bass guitar
b	bass
p	piano
harp	
vib	vibraphone/vibraharp
marimba	
elp	electric piano
d	drums
perc	percussion
arr	arranger
cond	conductor

Take Descriptions

ct	complete take
fs	false start
inc	incomplete take
mst	master take

Record Labels

BN	Blue Note
Font	Fontana
Sav	Savoy
SN	Soul Note

Countries

(Dk)	Denmark
(F)	France
(It)	Italy
(J)	Japan
(NL)	Netherlands
(UK)	United Kingdom
(USA)	United States

V. Bill Dixon on Records: A Summary

The following is a simple list of the issued recordings that feature Bill Dixon performing, arranged in chronological order of release. The first issue of each recording is shown here, next to the entry/ies in this discography for sessions that were part the album.

Archie Shepp-Bill Dixon Quartet Savoy MG 12178   **R62-1000a/b**

Bill Dixon 7-tette/Archie Shepp and the New York Contemporary Five
Savoy MG 12184   **R64-0204**

Cecil Taylor: *Conquistador!* Blue Note 4260   **R66-1006**

Bill Dixon: *Intents and Purposes* RCA Victor LSP 3844   **R66-1010;**
R67-0117;
R67-0221

Marzette Watts Ensemble Savoy MG 12193   **R69-0999;**
U69-1009

Franz Koglmann: *Opium/For Franz* Pipe (Austria) PR 152   **R76-0806**

Bill Dixon: *In Italy Volume 1* Soul Note (It) 1008   **R80-0611a/b**

Bill Dixon: *In Italy Volume 2* Soul Note (It) 1011   **R80-0611a/b**

Bill Dixon: *Considerations 1* FORE (It) THREE   **R73-0001;**
R73-0197;
R74-0100;
R75-0607;
R76-0929

Bill Dixon: *Considerations 2* FORE (It) FIVE   **R72-0495;**
R72-0499;
R73-0098;
R74-0530b

Bill Dixon: *1982* Ferrari Gallery (It) [Unnumbered]   **R70-0428;**
R73-0197

Bill Dixon: *November 1981* Soul Note (It) 1037/38   **R81-1108;**
R81-1116

Bill Dixon: *The Collection*
Cadence Jazz Records CJR 1024/25

R70-0000;
R71-0714;
R73-0098;
R73-0099;
R73-0100;
R74-9996;
R74-9998;
R75-9995;
R75-9997;
R76-0200;
R76-0300

Bill Dixon: *Thoughts* Soul Note (It) 1111

R85-0516a/b

Bill Dixon: *Son of Sisyphus* Soul Note (It) 121 138

R88-0628

Bill Dixon: *Vade Mecum* Soul Note (It) 121208-2

R93-0802a

[Various Artists] *Verona Jazz* Nettle (It) 001

R80-0606

Tony Oxley: *The Enchanted Messenger* Soul Note(It) 121284-2

R94-1120

Bill Dixon: *Vade Mecum II* Soul Note (It) 121211-2

R93-0802b

Bill Dixon: Odyssey [private edition] —forthcoming as of 1998

all listings for *The Collection*
plus: R70-0428;
R70-0592;
R70-0599;
R70-0899;
R73-0097;
R73-0197;
R73-0202;
R74-0100;
R74-9998;
R82-0200;
R90-0321;
R92-1204

CHAPTER ONE

Beginnings 1925–1960

"The way to get me away from something is have everybody dig it--then I'm off and running. I don't trust people, and if too many people are digging it, then what you're doing is not what you think it is. That's been my experience. I may be super-sensitive about it; I've rarely been wrong."

"I am William Robert Dixon Sr.; my father was William LeRoy Dixon. My oldest son (1949-1991) was William Robert Dixon, Jr., and my second son (b. 1965) is William Robert Dixon II. I can also tell you that if I had other children, they would all be William Robert Dixon. I believe in that.

"There were five of us children, and I was the oldest. My brother Milton was two years younger than I; Mary, my halfsister, was two years younger than my brother. My halfsister Lydia was two years younger, and then my halfbrother Benny. So only Milton and myself had the same mother and father. I was never legally adopted and retained my name Dixon. My sisters and my youngest brother had the last name Williams.

"I was born on October 5, 1925, on Nantucket Island, Massachusetts. How or why my family originally settled there, I don't know. I spent the early years of my life there. My family moved to New York--to Brooklyn first and then to Harlem--in 1933 or 1934.   Interestingly enough, we lived on 134th Street (at various times at 134 West, 120 West and 123 West) between 7th and Lenox Avenues, and in the next block was the Schomburg collection was housed in a branch of the public library. Years later, I was to find out that there was an after-hours club not too far from my house--Monroe's Uptown House [169 West 133d]. Also in my block lived Al Cooper, of the Savoy Sultans. P.S. 89, on the corner of Lenox Avenue between 134 and 135, was the elementary school I attended. We also lived later at 48 East 134th Street.

"Coming to live in Harlem was like culture shock for me. On Nantucket there was a small population--white, black, and Portuguese--that lived there year round. It was a very intimate surrounding. When we moved to Harlem, I had never seen so many people in my life--let alone black people.

"My mother [Louise Wade] was a writer and both she and my step-father read voraciously: she novels and he detective stories and mysteries. We had no furniture of any consequence, just bookshelves. One could buy books very inexpensively on a section of 125th Street between Lenox and Fifth Avenues that was lined with bookstores just like (as I was to find out later when I started to travel) along the Seine River in Paris: used books for sale or trade. Books were very important. We benefited and added to that reading experience by listening to the stories acted out on radio shows: *I Love A Mystery*, *The Green Hornet*, *Inner Sanctum*; the Cecil B. De Mille productions on Lux Playhouse. I even heard Orson Welles's original production of *War of the Worlds*. And then, of course there was the music.

"I have never liked spirituals; they always made me uneasy. I think it's because my mother always sang blues and spirituals around the house, and we were poor. We were on 'Home Relief' (what they would now call welfare) for two or three years. We would do spirituals in school. Otherwise, the music in school was what we call concert or 'classical' music--I wasn't remotely interested in it.

"The Lafayette Theatre was then on 7th Avenue [2227] between 132 and 132d Streets in Harlem. Movies were shown there, there were black vaudeville shows, and all of the established black bands played there, at the Apollo Theater [253 West 125th Street], and the Harlem Opera House [209 West 125th Street]. One night, shortly after we'd moved to Harlem, my stepfather [Edward James Williams, Jr. of New Bedford, Massachusetts] took me to the Lafayette Theatre, and I saw Louis Armstrong fronting a very large band. Armstrong came out and started to play, and that immediately got my attention. Walking back home, midway from the theatre to my house holding my stepfather's hand and unable to forget the sight or sound of that golden trumpet that Armstrong had played, I distinctly remember looking up to him (he was a big man) and saying 'I want one of those'.

"As for role models, at that time whenever you saw a black man in the movies he had grease on his face, rolling his eyes, bucking and winging, and having to call white people 'Mister Charlie'. The role models for most of the people I knew were these musicians; they weren't the writers, because they didn't have that kind of visibility. They weren't the doctors or lawyers, because to be a doctor or lawyer, you had to be middle class to afford those studies. But the musicians wore suits, they were sharp, they were written about, and they were the best at what they did. We had always had Black painters and writers, but you can't tell the difference between [the work of] White painters and Black painters. You knew who had invented this music, though. Everybody did. It was acknowledged. That was what made the pull toward this music so strong: everyone realized 'I can learn to play a horn; I don't have to worry about trying to get into the New York Philharmonic, because I can play at the Apollo'.

"I was also acting in and directing plays; we used to do things at the 135th St. YMCA. They had a legitimate black theater and a symphony orchestra--sort of an elevated situation. Once a year, there was a symposium for the elementary schools, a gathering of children who spoke well and had good memories. I remember one year I won the first prize for reciting this Frederick Douglass piece in a competition against the students from my school--among them [filmmaker] Bill Greaves and [actor] Al Popewell. I was involved in drawing and painting, (not that much painting, but I drew incredibly well, from the standpoint of what people call realism) and I did a lot of dramatic parts. That was my thing; it wasn't music.

"Going to school I came into contact with a group of people from other places and from a better social and economic class, and I began to meet people my age doing music. Sonny Payne was already doing professional work on the drums. So he might play at an assembly, where I might recite something--"Rime of the Ancient Mariner", "Casey at the Bat", etc. When I went to junior high school (Frederick Douglass, P.S. 139) I sang in the boys choir. We were preparing for a concert, and then my voice broke, so that was the end of that.

"The first time I wanted to learn an instrument was a disaster. I got involved with a school music program and said I wanted a trumpet. As it happens now sometimes, kids want one instrument and the band director may have too many of that so he puts another one in your hand, and that's just the way it is. So they gave me this clarinet. I think I lasted with the clarinet less than a couple of months. I don't like the clarinet to this day. I asked for a trumpet again, and they didn't have one, so I said 'forget it'.

"Teachers of mine convinced my parents that I had "talent" in the visual arts and it wouldn't be a good thing to send me to the local high school. They wanted me to go to the High School of Music and Art--which was condsidered the best high school-- and to this day I don't know why. I was already being conditioned to think of commercial art and not fine art. I did a lot of book and magazine illustration, lettering, calligraphy. So I looked for a school that taught that and went to the High School of Commerce downtown in the 60s and I majored in Art there.

My second year in high school I met a couple of kids who could play. One comes to mind named Ascagni, who played cornet. Than I started taking Spanish, and at that time the Puerto Ricans and Cubans weren't all over New York. They were only up town between 110th and 116th--Spanish Harlem. So to practice my Spanish, I spent a lot of time around there, and I discovered Latin music. And then I had a kid in one of my classes who used to sub for his father in the band they hand at the Park Palace on 110th. That's how good he was, and he was my age.

"I did my last year in high school in New Bedford, Massachusetts, and I remember working there one summer after school, I saw a trumpet--an old King--that cost $36. I paid this man so much money every week and eventually got the horn. I didn't have enough money for a teacher; I fooled around with it and didn't do very much.

"I was drawn to music; I just liked it. However, there was no way for me to study it. We were frightfully poor and one didn't (when I was coming up) ask for something that was obviously well beyond the realm of possibility. No one told you 'Follow your dreams'."

GI Bill

Dixon enlisted in the Army and was inducted at Fort Devens near Boston. "My stepfather and I took our physicals together for the draft. Before they called him up, he had a birthday and he became too old. I enlisted so that I wouldn't be called into the Navy. I reported in June of 1944." Dixon was 18 years old. "My basic training and technical training were in Camp Breckenridge in Morganfield, Kentucky. Then we left to go overseas in February of 1945.

"When the war in Germany ended [May, 1945], I had been in Kaiserlautern and Arles, and my outfit was on its way to the Pacific theater, where the fighting was still going on. That war ended while we were still en route, and they brought us back to the States. After a leave I was stationed at Fort Francis E. Warren in Cheyenne, Wyoming to finish my term of service. By then I was trying to find a way out of the Army: I found a section of the Army regulations by which I could be classified as a surplus soldier. I had been sent to one theater of operations and couldn't be sent to another one. I therefore became a 'surplus soldier' and could be 'discharged from military service at the convenience of the government'. Day and night I was in the library preparing to file for my own discharge. About a week later I was discharged that way, in February [?] of 1946 at Fort Dix, New Jersey."

Dixon exited the Army, was married, and began to play the trumpet all in 1946, at age 20. He was married and enrolled at the (now-defunct) Hartnette Conservatory of Music in September of that year. "When I really came to terms with the trumpet--to study the instrument and do something with it--was when I came out of the service. One day I just said 'I think I want to do it'. There was never any encouragement. When I make up my mind to do something, I do it. Once I made up my mind to do music, I poured everything into it. I started studying in 1946. I didn't know if I had any musical talent--I don't know that to this day. I've had to work a lot harder than a lot of other people, but that's not the point. The irony is that I knew so many people who went on to become very good musicians, who just did it. In my initial days of study, I would have given a finger just to be able to play whole notes and half notes in a good band.

"By 1948, I was already playing jobs, so I know it can be done. I couldn't play too high, however I always had a good sound; I could hear very well and take reasonably good solos. Reading didn't come too difficult... and by 1948 or '49 I was already writing for groups in New York.

"The turning point for this music happened with Charlie Parker and Dizzy Gillespie in terms of musicians (*all* of them) finally having to be as good as the music required. There were reasons for that, too. That music was developed during, and at the end of, World War II. Veterans of that war have never had a memorial. In some ways, though, we had a better one: the GI bill, which let you study anything you wanted. A lot of musicians--working Jazz musicians--went to school under the bill to learn more. They could all play, but they had never had any harmony, theory or counterpoint. The reason there were Hartnette and Metropolitan-type conservatories was that places like Juilliard or the Manhattan School weren't equipped to handle this sort of students. You couldn't even study the saxophone at Juilliard. (I remember when Duke Ellington gave a sizable amount of money to Juilliard for something, people remarked that one-third of Ellington's orchestra was made up of instruments that weren't taught at the school.) In my opinion, that was the turning point both in terms of music study and the knowledge of how to get a piece of *music* done."

Hartnette

Dixon studied at the Hartnette Conservatory in midtown Manhattan through 1951. The school was strategically located proximate to 52d Street, the music stores, and a variety of institutions in the music.

"All of the faculty members at the Hartnette Conservatory were working musicians. I can't say with any definition that teaching was the first thing that these guys wanted to do, but they were damn good at it. The bass teacher at Hartnette was named Pat Caruso. Lee Hedden was a very advanced guitarist, who also taught arranging and composition, while Charlie Byrd taught Jazz guitar. Hedden was part of a faculty chamber group with flutist Paige Brook and the clarinet teacher with whom I studied harmony. Saxophonist Jimmy Brokenshire taught the Schillinger system at Hartnette. He had been a member of the Dorsey bands. Benny Ventura, Charlie's brother, taught saxophone there. There was a rather handsome trumpet player there-- old style: he looked and played like Bunny Berigan--named Jimmy Blake." Dixon encountered Blake at the school, but later studied with Steven Gitto.

"[Gitto] was marvelous. He had only one arm and only the three fingers on that one needed for the trumpet valves. Gitto had played with the Edwin Franco Goldman band, playing march music. I think he was from Connecticut. He and I played duets, out of the Arban book. I was also rather fanatical about the Charles Colin exercise book; then someone told me about Max Schlossberg's exercises [See **R73-1100**]. Tony Fruscella also had written some very good exercises for me. Tony would show up and do various things at Hartnette--that's how I met him--but he was rather erratic about being there. I met him through little Chick Eubanks, the hump-backed alto

player who played in the First band at Hartnett. They would get musicians and go
down to do sessions, or sometimes use the practice rooms at Hartnett." Bands not
affiliated with the educational program, including the 1948 Benny Goodman Sextet,
would often rent space in the rehearsal rooms or bandrooms of the school.
"In that building there was another music school, the Metropolitan School, which
Kenny Dorham had something to do with."

Dixon lived in Queens from 1946 to 1949. "Before I went to the Bronx I had lived on
173d Street in Jamaica, Queens, and the musical crowd I was then with all used to
play out there. I moved to 315 E 143d Street in the Bronx in 1949 and lived there
until 1958. I had a wife and child while in school, but I could still afford to study full
time because of the GI Bill, which gave me I think $105 per month. I also worked
part time doing a lot of copying for working bands, and if I sold an arrangement there
would be some kind of money coming in. I wrote arrangements for Latin bands for
five or ten dollars apiece. I used some of the GI Bill for art studies, so the money ran
out shortly before I finished at Hartnett."

"I was first spending a lot of time with this bass player in Queens, Harold Perkins.
He introduced me to Mal Waldron. Perkins had come to music late, just like me; we
started at the same time. He auditioned for one of Mercer Ellington's bands at a time
when he could only play in [open and] first position[s] on the bass, and he beat
everybody out and got into the band. He wasn't that interested in writing, but
through him I got to know Booker Foster.
"Foster was the first person I began to play with regularly--trumpet and tenor. He and
I had met at Hartnett. He lived out in Long Island [in Queens], not too far from me.
He was a very good musician. We were very close musically; we worked together in
quintets, transcribed music off records together to analyze it--a lot of Savoy records,
and all of the Dizzy Gillespie large band records in the period from about 1946 to
1950--and wrote things together for the school big bands.
"Like anyone else, I was absorbing all this stuff, and [one of the first of my charts
played by the Hartnett band] was what you call a kitchen-sink arrangement. That
first sound was so thick with stuff it almost cracked the walls. I loved it. The guys
were looking at me like 'what the...?', but my teacher, Carl Bowman, was conducting
it, so they [played it as it was written]."

"You didn't learn how to play in school; you learned the mechanics of making music,
but in order to play, you've got to *play*. In certain ways, learning how to play
creative music hurt musicians financially, because they were doing it for nothing, but
we had to. That's why the union frowned on sitting in, because the club owner was
getting music for free. You might go to a session for three hours and--with so many
people sitting in--end up playing only one tune. But invariably someone would hear
you while you were playing and like your tone, or your ideas, or they might have a
way to use your sound for something and take down your telephone number--a kind of
'networking'. Whenever you got a job, those were the people you called. That was
another benefit of the sessions: other musicians could hear what you sounded like."

"George Barrow once called me down to the Suntan Studios [operated by the distinguished Black athlete Fritz Pollard on 125th Street] and said that the guy who had *the* experimental band in New York at the time, Neal Tate, was looking for players. Tate wrote some very difficult, adventurous music. I got there late, and all of the trumpet players had shied away from the first chair part, so that was the only one available. I think he had about five or six trumpets, and of course I had to sit down in front of the hard part. I did as much as I could, but it was some tough music. I don't know how many rehearsals I went to there.

"When I first started going to Suntan Studios, the name of the game was just meeting people, networking. The union hall at that point was very racist and absolutely useless for us for getting jobs, because the contractors always called their regular people.

"There was a lot of rehearsal band activity in Harlem at the time I was at Hartnette, and we had to take every opportunity to play. On Saturdays there were all of these bands rehearsing, and we roamed the streets looking for something. Musicians who wrote always carried a piece of music with them that they wanted to hear, in case they got a chance to try it out on the rehearsal band. We always carried our instruments everywhere we went. I got jobs just for having the trumpet with me and a union card. Small group things--sitting in and learning the repertoire--were no problem, but how many opportunities were you going to have to learn how to play in a section? How many to write for more than a quintet? These bands might never work, but they would at least rehearse.

"I first heard Dave Bailey when he was the drummer in Herbie Jones's large rehearsal band--one of the best I've ever heard in my life. I never played in the band but made all of their rehearsals. You didn't go to a rehearsal just because you were going to play; you could learn just as much from watching the rehearsal and being prepared to play if the opportunity came, and I did a lot of that. They rehearsed every Thursday at the YMCA (on 135th Street in Harlem) in the Fifties before Jones, who was a magnificent writer and trumpet player, went with Duke Ellington. [Trombonist] Buster Cooper was also in that band . I knew him and his brother--a bass player-- from when they both were students at Hartnette."

315 Lenox

BD (t); Harry McDuffy (tb); Unknown (b, d, and/or p)

"There was a tenement building on Lenox Avenue--number 315, between 125th and 126th Streets--that had rehearsal space. In that building there was also an African Nationalist organization, and they staged a lot of social events. On Sundays they also had very intense listening sessions with African music. I met these people and played at functions of the organization.

"I used to hang out with a very good trombone player named Harry McDuffy, and we did a lot of playing in those circumstances at 315 Lenox. (He was a staunch nationalist who was into the political program there.) McDuffy was in every band--large or small--that I put together. Bassoonist Tommy Horsford (who doubled alto) also had something to do with those events.

"Harry and I had a quartet that played for their dinners and social events to raise money on Fridays and Saturdays at the same location. Whoever landed that particular job was the leader of the group for that night. We tried to get as many players as we could within the traditional Jazz instrumentation, playing calypsos and all of the traditional songs. They didn't care what we played as long as we played the melody. So we would play the melody (I-IV-I or I-V-I chord patterns) and then play what <u>we</u> wanted.

"I met both Gus Clark--he later became Gus Dinizulu--and Jimmy _____ there--both conga drummers, and they used to come to the Sportsmen's Club [See **53-0097**]. (They were the first people I knew who wore their hair 'natural', in what we now call an 'afro'.) Gus Clark played African drums originally; before he began the dance troupe he was also an excellent photographer in a studio on the east side where I used to go and rehearse, while they took photographs of me. They had let me know that there were these sessions on Sundays where musicians came in and played real African music and discussed it.

"I never joined any of those political parties; each wanted to tell people what to do artistically. So these people had a clear view of what the music for their platform should be. They weren't anti-Jazz, but they basically stopped with all of the developments of traditional African music. That was their stance; they didn't know what modern Jazz musicians were talking about."

"Those were some of my beginning days of learning how to play the instrument."

R51-0097   [Unknown pianist's quintet]
ca. 1951   Corona, Queens

"In the early Fifties I played with one band that I really liked in Corona, Queens. I
don't remember the leader's name (he was the piano player), but there was a very
experienced tenor saxophonist in the band named Joe Carnegie. He worked for the
subway. It was a regular quintet--tenor, trumpet, piano, bass, and drums. I used to
like to play "On the Alamo", around the time that Dizzy Gillespie recorded the piece.
I had one acetate recording of that band. The leader lived in a house in Corona and had
a nice recording studio in the basement; he recorded one of our tunes and gave us
copies."   Without a record, making private recordings that were then cut to reference
"acetates" was the only way for the band to "try out" for potential engagements,
short of actually playing in person.
"Around that time I also worked with another tenor player named J.C. Cheeseman,
who lived in the Bronx."

52-0097   The Tune Timers
ca. 1952   Guido's/Tune-Timers' Lounge: Astoria

Shad Collins (t); others unknown;

Johnny Smith (g); others unknown;

Astoria is on the northern edge of New York's borough, Queens. Dixon sat in with
the regular band here occasionally. When the establishment was known as
"Guido's", the ensemble called the Tune Timers (piano, guitar, bass, vibes,
drums--often adding Shad Collins on trumpet) was in residence. After they as a group
purchased the club, it was re-named the Tune-Timers Lounge.

53-0097   Bill Dixon Trio
ca. 1953   Bronx, NY

BD (t); Cecil Taylor (p); Sid MacKay (d)

Dixon put the group together to play a PTA meeting.
"My then-wife said she had been asked by people who knew I was a musician if I could
get a group together to play this meeting of theirs. They needed music for the thing,
and they only had enough money for three musicians. As far as I know, it wasn't a
complete concert. Without considering what might be 'appropriate', I called Taylor
and MacKay, just thinking that here was an opportunity for us to play."

"Cecil Taylor was the principal underground musician in New York at that time
who--whether people wanted to believe it it or not--was working in a way that
previously hadn't been thought of as what Jazz musicians did. People even to this
day don't understand that you might actually be into something important even if you
don't work at Birdland or any of the major clubs--those given the most exposure and
designated "important" beacuse someone has said so--that you aren't working on
your craft. A club is a club; it doesn't make any difference where it is. The critical
establishment has never really understood that when they "discover" a person, the
person didn't start at that point. Rarely have they been able to document anything or
speak to the issue of that person's viability as an artist, because they've had no
knowledge.

"I know of no major writer who knew about certain places where all of this activity
was beginning to take shape in the Fifties. That wasn't where they were focusing.
They acted as though one didn't exist if one didn't work any of the places where they
went to review groups. Common sense should have informed them that every
musician who wasn't originally "acceptable" to be employed in these places hadn't
killed himself. They were doing something, somewhere. That 'somewhere' was
where a lot of this music was being played.
"The place where I first met Cecil Taylor (in 1951) and many other musicians was up
in Harlem, called the Sportsmen's club. That was where I first heard Tina Brooks.
(Now everyone raves about Tina Brooks: I remember when he couldn't get arrested.)
The Sportsmen's club was a private social club between 144th and 145th Streets on
7th Avenue, underneath the Roosevelt Theater. It was a small place, very neat and
clean, beautiful little dance floor, bar, booths, and a bandstand. That was the place
where you took your girl when you were catting. For whatever reason, Thursday
night was the night for this music. The person who introduced me to that place was
the saxophone player Floyd Benny, with whom I was later to go to Alaska in the
Tommy Roberts band. [See **54-0009**]
"There was the 'L' bar, on Broadway, Connie's--not to be confused with Connie's
Inn, which was further down. Connie's was across from Small's (where we also
played) and used to be Henry's Sugar Bowl, an ice cream parlor when I first came to
New York. Then the Lotus Bar on 132d Street and Lenox Ave. Across the street from
that on 131st street was the Club Baron, then the 125 Club on 125th Street. Those
were the principal places uptown people doing this music found to play;...also the

Putnam Central in Brooklyn. Now, I doubt whether a major critic or writer ever set foot in any of those places. They didn't even know the village that well, really."

53-0699   Dixon Rehearsal Band
before 1954   315 Lenox Avenue, NYC

Harry McDuffy (tb); Tommy Horsford (as); Ike Bradley (p); Oliver "Buckles" Washington (d); others unknown

"Periodically I rehearsed a very large band at 315 Lenox Avenue. I would save money and call some of the best musicians in town; we paid one or two dollars an hour for the hall; the players weren't paid anything. George Barrow was a part of this, and I got some of Dizzy's trumpet players [from his big band of the earliest fifties] including Isak Abdenur [spelling uncertain]--a high note specialist--and a trumpeter who wore thick glasses and specialized in hard parts. Ike Bradley was the piano player. We rehearsed my arrangements until the money for renting the studio space ran out. There were a few of my compositions, but largely my arrangements and some of Bradley's.
"While Suntan Studios was a better facility, it was generally used by the bands working the Apollo theater, so it wasn't as accessible. I rehearsed a lot there in other people's bands, but I myself never rented any space at Suntan Studios."

Dixon recalls having had some reference lacquers of his and Ike Bradley's arrangements recorded by these bands in studio demo sessions, possibly including Bradley's co-composition with a woman called "I'm in a Mess". That piece was subsequently recorded by Dizzy Gillespie, sparking a controversy over authorship of the piece.

54-0099   <u>Tommy Roberts Band</u>

1954   Anchorage and Fairbanks, Alaska

Roberts (voice); BD (t); Floyd Benny (as)*; unknown (g); Evelyn Freeman (p, arr); Sid MacKay (d)

*sub Howard Johnson (as, p) for Benny midway through this Alaska stay.

Dixon signed on with this band for what was expected to be a tour of several weeks duration; their stay turned out to be nearly a year at the 1042 Club in Anchorage, the Elmendorf Air Force Base, and another club in Fairbanks. Dixon replaced Charlie Shavers as the trumpeter with the group; he joined as a way of creating a diversion from some of his activities in New York at the time. "On that trip I just went to work every day, and that was it. I got more money when I went to Alaska for making music than I had ever made, as we were on a weekly salary. (This was before Alaska was a state, and it was a roaring boomtown.) All of the officers' clubs were open 24 hours a day. There were a lot of Jazz musicians in the Air Force who played on their days off. There was simply a lot of music up there." The show also included an act known as the Spence Twins. Dixon finished the arrangements for them that Floyd Benny had begun.

"The group came back; we layed over in New York, and they were going on to Australia. I didn't want to go, so I quit. There was finally a dispute over money owed to the band members by Roberts: He ended up owing me a lot of money. I had to make a claim against him before the American Federation of Musicians. We (I also wrote Sid MacKay's case) couldn't appear; we had to do it all by writing. We won and the AFM required Roberts to pay."

It appears that Dixon had returned to New York by the time of Charles Mingus's December 5, 1954 concert at Carnegie Recital Hall. "I was cooling it a while when I came back from Alaska. I had been gone a year and done all that playing. When I came back it was to make my next move, to decide what I was going to do. The first option was to go to Australia with [Tommy Roberts] but I didn't get along with those people, and it was only a show band."

"While I was in Alaska, I had done a lot of corresponding with *Time* magazine. I wasn't a writer, but I liked to write (I had belonged to the Countee Cullen Creative Writers Group, led by educator Pathenia McBrown at the Schomburg Library.) *Time* wanted to train a person as a pre-editor; I answered an ad, and when I came back to New York I had an appointment. I went to the Time/Life building, and to make a long story short, I was racially discriminated against the minute they saw I was black. I have never let people get away with that. I was very uncool in those days, so I went out. I cursed everybody out, made a big scene, and stormed out of the building. I found myself walking toward the East Side and remembered that a high school friend of mine was working as a security guard at the UN. He introduced me to a woman who worked in personnel there and she asked why I didn't join [the UN]. So I thought about it, went in for an interview, and a few weeks later I was hired on a three-month contract for the General Assembly. At that time I was a very good typist, knew Oxford spelling, and could do verbatim dictation." Dixon worked at the UN from 1956 until 1962.

55-0600
After first quarter of 1955

Suite for Jazz Horns

This piece was never performed, nor was it written with a specific performance in mind. Dixon composed it after returning from Alaska.
"I did it just to write and it looked good on paper. I wanted to write something that had more formalism (for want of a better word) in it--key and tempo changes, odd meters. I don't know why; I just did it. It was very long. The instrumentation was like a brass quintet--not unlike "Mirage" [**R65-1208**]. I may have been influenced in my thinking by J.J. Johnson's 'Poem For Brass' (the record came later) but those pieces and pieces like that were being done in concert at the time . There was a lot of that kind of music in the air in New York--Robert Prince, Teo Macero... We all liked Alex North, who had done a lot of film music. Leith Stevens's score to the film *Destination Moon* may have influenced this piece, except that mine (as I recall it) was probably more linear.

"I always did a lot of writing, but not on that large a scale. I was very interested in writing for television. I would just write, and it was real composition, it was just was never going to be performed. I did some writing in Alaska, but not that much in depth. Just like everybody else, I was for the longest time saturated with the idea of the large Jazz band. In the middle Fifties, I wrote to [arranger] Bill Russo inquiring about studies with him. I liked the way he scored for brasses. While Ellington's was my favorite band, I also listened to Boyd Raeburn; for a while I didn't think anyone could write as well as George Handy. I liked Gene Roland's writing, Chico O'Farrill, Walter "Gil" Fuller, Jimmy Mundy, Neal Tate, George Russell, Raymond Scott, Claude Thornhill, Johnny Richards, Billy Strayhorn. I listened to the things those musicians did.

"This is what happens when you come to something late, being in such a desperate search for information. Sometimes, erroneously, you think that the more you know, the more you'll be able to do. That's not always the case.

"Around that time I was trying to break away from just being academic with the material. I was trying to play, but I really would have liked to have had things that I had written played by large ensembles. One of the things I didn't like about Jazz was that everything was a trio or quartet (to be practical, because the work needed to get done and might not wait for large band opportunity) or, if you were lucky, a quintet or sextet. I didn't know why creative musicians settled for that. I didn't know why it had to be that or a big band, or why 'orchestra' was a bad word."

"Center features Jazzman Dixon" *New Milford Times* [1960: date unknown]

58-0020   Jimmy Jones

NYC

BD (arr); Jimmy Jones (b); Sid MacKay (d); others unknown

Blue Haze

Doxy

"Jones was a bandleader who worked in the post office. Sid MacKay was playing in his 15- or 16- piece band. When we came back from Alaska Sid tried to get me into the band, and for whatever reason I never got in. They had a couple of good trumpet players; none was going to move. The band played dances, not concerts, doing very traditional pieces. They rehearsed twice a week at the Audubon Ballroom, and because I had to have something to do I went to all of the rehearsals.
"The guys in the band wanted something a little more contemporary, so I was asked to write some things for the band--no originals, but arrangements on some of the pieces of the day. That was not an *avant garde* situation. *down beat* had published the solo that Percy Heath plays on Miles Davis's [March, 1954 Prestige] recording of "Blue Haze". I just took that solo, wrote it out for the bass player--Jones--and made an arrangement of it. It was just a matter of putting voicings to it.

"I was also doing a lot of painting, and there were a couple of dance teams that I was writing acts for. I also used to transcribe Miles Davis solos, analyze them, and sell them to the players ... things like that. Cecil and I were doing things at that time; I brought Sid MacKay down to Cecil's place to see what he was doing in preparation for the *Looking Ahead* recording. And there was constantly the Sportsmen's Club activity--a lot of playing in sessions all over, really."

WBAI

Dixon first traveled to Europe in the Summer of 1958 on a UN assignment to service the Second Peaceful Usage of Atomic Energy Conference in Geneva, with stops in London and Paris.

"I met Don Ellis on Les Davis's Saturday afternoon program on WBAI after having just come back from the trip. Davis let me speak about my trip, etc., and then Ellis had his turn to speak and play his music.

Dixon subsequently hosted his own programs of music performance (**62-1121** et seq.) and interviews with musicians (**X63-0899**), in addition to sponsoring and/or appearing in the radio series of John Tchicai (See **R63-0395** and **O63-0627**) and Don Heckman (**65-1099**).

He moved from the Bronx to 119 Bank Street at the beginning of 1959, after coming back from Europe.

59-0000   <u>Unknown</u>
1959   United Nations: NYC

BD (t); Joe _____ (g)

      <u>No Exit</u>

This combination performed Dixon's notated and improvised music for a production of <u>No Exit</u> that gave probably two performances in the small theater in the Secretariat library.

Dixon commonly played duets with guitarists in this period--in less formal situations--private parties, etc. "Once some friends of Fausto Pollicino arranged for us to do a private party for airline stewardesses and pilots in someone's apartment--just trumpet and guitar. We played just anything we wanted, but always appropriate. This is how I was getting things solidified on the horn: you practice, you have to play."

Vita/resumé of 1964; "Center Features Jazzman Dixon" *New Milford Times* [1960: date unknown]

59-0003   <u>Outdoor session</u>

probably early 1959   Peter Moore's Apt: Commerce St., NYC

BD (t); Earl Griffith (vib); others unknown

[Greenwich Village photographer] "Peter Moore, whom I met when we both worked at
the UN, had a beautiful apartment with a garden on Commerce Street across from the
Cherry Lane Theater, where we (collectively) used to throw parties. The
photographers were notified; I would supply the musicians; [they] would take
pictures, and we played....[O]nce Cecil was supposed to come, but because they
couldn't rent a piano, he couldn't play, so I got Earl Griffith to come."
Dixon had probably just moved to the Village at this point, though he had first met
Moore while still living in the Bronx.

59-0579   Bill Dixon-Vinnie Gerard

probably 1959   Copa City, Queens

BD (t); Ollie Richardson (b); Vinnie Gerard (p); unknown (d)

add: Big Miller (voice)

"Gerard had played with Charlie Parker, whom he called 'Yard', and showed me certain
harmonic things that Bird liked. Vinnie used to come by my house [on Bank Street]
all the time. He played a lot like Dick Twardzik.
"I met Vinnie Gerard about 1959. He drank at least three pots of coffee at a sitting.
I was using a young drummer from the Bronx--a young kid I knew, who developed
into a player. Vinnie had done some playing at the Roue [see next]. Bassist Ollie
Richardson and I rehearsed a lot at my house with Gerard. We used to drive around
(Vinnie had a car) on Long Island looking for work, and came upon the club Copa
City--where we talked to the new owner. We auditioned on the spot as a duo; he gave
us a couple of weekends with the quartet. The Friday night we opened it rained
terribly; we got lost and showed up maybe two hours late. The owner was ripping
mad when we got in.
"We did our first set--reasonably good--of the Jazz standards of the day. Then the
owner said he wanted us to back the blues singer Big Miller: that wasn't part of the
deal. I was kind of stunned because *we* had gone out and auditioned and gotten the
job--and Big Miller wasn't there. So Big Miller shouts some blues while we play.
After that set, Richardson, as musicians are sometimes prone to do, sat down at the
piano and started playing 'elementary' 'Claire de Lune'. We started talking and
eventually the owner said 'You guys are all right but you've got to get another piano
player, because your piano player doesn't make my Big Miller sound good.' I said,
'Your Big Miller is lousy, man.' We did the next set--Big Miller was trying to sing
something--and the owner said, 'Let the bass player play piano, or that's it'. So that
was it.

"It was very difficult for Vinnie--he was playing well and nonetheless being insulted.
I don't know if it reflects badly on Big Miller or us, as much as it shows the cleavage
between the Blues as an art form, a feeling, and the Blues as a commercial prospect.
Big Miller did what he did, and it was unfair for the manager to say he had to be on
this bill, without having his own accompanist, or having worked out something with
our pianist. That again is an undercurrent of how the nightclub circuit works. This is
the only music I know where everyone irrespective of background, how that person
feels, or the genre is supposed at any given moment to be able to stand up and play
effectively together, merely to please onlookers, or listeners--being slick, quoting
from tunes to make people laugh. What that has to do with playing any more, I don't
know. The OLD-fashioned jam session was built primarily for musicians, and if you
weren't a hip audience, you had no business being there. I'm not saying that
musicians shouldn't be able to play together effectively, but I will say that
sometimes it does not work."

Coffeehouses

"The first thing to happen for the new music didn't happen in any club. Before the
club there was the coffeehouse. They were used because the owners there paid so little
money in overhead that they didn't give a damn who played in the place, and there
was an entire coffee house circuit. I initiated that, because I saw no use in trying to do
Sundays or Mondays at the Five Spot. It didn't make sense to me that you were going
to possibly have to wait out your whole life before you could play.

"[The coffeehouses] didn't just switch over [to having music policies]; they were sold
on the idea. No coffeehouse was doing the music other than the Playhouse on
MacDougal Street--right next to the Eugene O'Neill Theater. Sun Ra was there, and it
was the headquarters for the entertainer Tiny Tim; I played there, but I never liked the
Playhouse.

"Le Figaro used to do classical, renaissance, and medieval music on Sundays. One
Sunday I remember hearing classical music coming out of Le Figaro, and I asked
myself 'Why not this music?' I started to sell the idea, and eventually we had a
string of places where we played. And then it was a simple matter of getting all the
others to take notice and do it. It began to fall apart finally when I went to Local 802
to try to get them to set a scale for it."

A 1961 *Village Voice* "Cafe Roundup" shows that the Roue, Figaro, Showplace, Take
3 and Phase 2 were all already in operation.

Village Voice February 23, 1961.

59-9910

late 1959 forward   Cafe Roue: 115 Christopher Street, NYC

New Milford Times 1960: "Dixon was the first musician to organize the free chamber
concerts in New York's Greenwich Village. He instituted the programs several years
ago, and they rapidly became highly popular with the public."

"The Roue's music policy was a smashing success: first of all it was a huge place,
right next to the Theatre D'Lys, and they were showing The Threepenny Opera
[advertised in the June and July, 1959 *Village Voices*, it appears to have run there for
all of 1959]. For our Sunday afternoon concerts, people would leave the theatre after
the matinée, and go right into the cafe. One of the special qualities of the Roue was
that it was spacious, with large windows facing the street that let passersby see what
was going on inside. Don Heckman lived in the middle of that block, and on the
corner Les Davis.
"The owner, Sean Neiland, a theater person himself, was very easily sold. He only
had to pay for a trio--the house rhythm section--and the rest of the music he got for
free as people sat in. He sold a very bad cup of coffee for fifty cents, and made a
fortune with that. There were other, non-monetary benefits attached to this. The
musicians, all virtually unknown except to themselves, could play whatever they
wanted, with whom they wanted, how they wanted, for the length of time they
wanted, to a remarkably well-informed and enthusiastic audience. Of course, the idea
of the "set" (a standard amount of time for a group to play) was recognized and the
pieces of music called were within the framework and vernacular of the standard
material of the day: 'I'll Remember April', 'On Green Dolphin Street', 'Stablemates',
'Doxy', 'The Way You Look Tonight', works by Ellington, Porter, Gershwin, etc.
"We did Sunday matinées and Monday nights. There were always more horn players
(Pete Yellin, Rocky Boyd, Matt Notkins, Louis Brown, Art Williams, Al Neese) than
there were pianists (Paul Bley, Carla Bley, Earl Griffith--he didn't particularly like to
carry his vibes around--Valdo Williams, Vinnie Gerard, Hod O'Brien, Lefty Sims, and
the now well-established writer Frank Conroy, who, like musicians' dentist Eliot
Oxenburg, only played in the key of C) or bass players (Ollie Richardson, Wade
Davis, Ali Jackson, Ray McKinney) or drummers (Al Manion, Howie Kadison, Jual
Curtis ... I also seem to remember Omar Clay being there..., Sunny Murray, etc.) I met
Louis Brown when I started doing things at the Roue. He was playing clarinet then (I
don't like the clarinet), and I didn't even know that he played tenor.
"Everyone wanted to play and while they were waiting, musicians sometimes made up
a peer-group audience themselves. People learned from each other, took criticism
from each other, and in so doing made the Cafe Roue a special scene for the
unknown-but-serious-about-his-work 'jazz' (as we were then called) musician"

The Roue was opened to the public not later than January, 1960, although only the
visual arts presentations were reviewed in a 1960 article in the *Village Voice*. The
earliest known listing for the Roue's music program there was in the *Voice* Bulletin
Board, announcing a Monday night workshop on January 25, 1960. The next such
listing is for Saturday afternoon, February 13, from 3 to 11:00pm. Later in the year
the Jazz Workshops were listed in more detail, even including the name of the
group's leader. Other than Art Williams, Dixon does not recognize the players named

in April's Roue advertising in the *Voice*: Frank Sands, Irwin Fields, Jerry Williams, John Caviglio, Leon Jackson. His operations at the Roue were one night a week-- first Sundays, then Mondays, and eventually both--but apparently the Roue's music policy enlarged in time, as Dixon became involved in the Sunday sessions at Drid Williams's (see **6 0 - 0 2 2 1** et seq).

Some tape recordings were apparently made at the Roue, and later transferred to lacquers for Dixon to submit as samples of his work.

"Center features Jazzman Dixon" *New Milford Times* [1960: date unknown]; "Art" *Village Voice* February 24, 1960, p. 10. BD's article "Sunny Murray"--slated for Publication with the FORE records set, *In the Sign of Labyrinth*, illuminates this period.

59-9992   Lynn Oliver's rehearsal big band
probably 1959   Lynn Oliver's studio

BD (t, arr)

While working at the UN and living in the Village, Dixon learned of this situation
from the New Zealand trumpeter/arranger Ed Comer, also a copyist for Gerry
Mulligan's Concert Jazz Band.
"Oliver had a studio [250 West 89th Street] near the New Yorker Theater where all the
bands rehearsed, and he was able to have his own rehearsal band by copying the book
of every band that rehearsed there--Gerry Mulligan, Maynard Ferguson, etc. He had
real rehearsals for the people [in his band] because they were playing *real* music. He
ran it like a school, and I think people paid for it.
"I used to go to Lynn's; they always could use a trumpet player. This is how I kept
my eyes up. I used to go around, sitting in with the large bands. I would do it until I
got known, and then eventually in the last half hour I would say 'Could you play a
chart for me?'--never full pieces; I might do a chorus or something. I was checking
out voicings....my stuff. I met Sy Johnson and Rolf Ericson there."

"In the large band, probably the most important part was for the first trumpet. The
way the music is written, it's generally a melodic part--it's high, demands a lot of
strength, and good tone. All the phrasing for the trumpet section is set by the first
player. In a chord-based music, when you start to distribute the notes of the chord,
the first part is playing the melody. The second, harmony, part is going to move in a
certain way [relative to the contour of the melody]. By the time you get to the third
and fourth parts, they're moving around intervallically to meet the remaining notes
of each chord. Playing a third trumpet part actually is very good for you technically,
because it teaches you to hear those intervals. It's not as 'easy' as playing a melodic
part where you know the contours of the melody and can sing it.
"It's interesting if you want to learn something about the instrument. Everyone
would think that the two principal parts would be the first and second chairs--first, for
obvious reasons, and second, because you get to take the solos. That's not
necessarily the case."

60-0000   Bill Dixon Group
ca. 1960   Greenwich Village, NYC

BD (t); *possibly* Matt Notkins (as); Ollie Richardson (b); Al Foster (d)

There was a painter and his sister (who also painted) who were having a private party
at their loft and they hired us. I must have used [Richardson and maybe Notkins]. It
was the most fantastic loft in the Village I have ever seen. They had two groups: we
played the first part, and coming up as the second one was Billy Taylor's group.

"I was the first one to use Al Foster, and I met him when he was 15 through John
Mehegan and these Jazz Arts Society people. [See **U60-0001**.] I used him for
lecture/demonstrations at Forest House in the Bronx (when I was president of the
UNJS, I did these things all over New York) or playing private parties when I needed a
drummer". See also **X61-0397**.
related to *Village Voice* ad.

60-0004   Bill Dixon-Clebert Ford
early 1960s   Brooklyn, NY

BD (p);
Clebert Ford (reading)

"Once at a private party someone said they wanted Clebert to do a dramatic reading or
something like that. Clebert just looked at me and says: 'Play [piano] for me'. I
think he and I did a few things after that...It was beautiful, really.
"In those days, we took every opportunity to play anything. That's what everyone
did. We'd be playing and a poet or a writer was always jumping up on stage wanting
to read something, and we didn't take an attitude like 'What are you doing?'"

60-0011   Bill Dixon Quartet[?]
ca. 1960   Hudson Guild: 426 W 27th Street, NYC

BD (t); Matt Notkins (as); Ollie Richardson (b); others unknown

"I think I met someone who invited me to take part in one of these events at the
Hudson Guild--the connection may have been made through LENA" (cf. **X60-0000**).

60-0012   Bill Dixon Quartet (?)

ca. 1960   Henry Hudson Hotel: NYC

BD (t); Matt Notkins (as); unknown (b)

This was a dance staged to benefit an African organization. Dixon's recollection of its coincidence with the Congo independence movement places this activity in or before the first half of 1960. Ollie Richardson was not the bassist.

Endre Sik, *History of Black Africa Volume IV* (Budapest: Akadémia Kiadó, 1974), p. 297 et seq.

60-0202   Bill Dixon Group

probably after January, 1960   Four Steps Coffee Gallery: NYC

BD (t); *probably* Dudley Watson (b); others unknown

A rainy night; this was one night of a short engagement (probably made up of weekends and Mondays) at the short-lived club, located at 64 East 7th Street.

Dixon recalls playing very well. Belgian reed player Bobby Jaspar, living in New York at the time, came to hear this performance and appreciated it. The Four Steps was about a block away from the Jazz Gallery; it is suspected that Jaspar may have been playing there with Miles Davis.

First known mention of the Four Steps (a "new coffee gallery") in *Village Voice* February 10, 1960, p. 10.

60-0207   Jazz Ballet

before February 21, 1960   DW Studio: 17 West 24th Street, NYC

BD (t, p); Drid Williams (choreography, movement); 5-6 other dancers, and musicians unknown

Choreographer/dancer Drid Williams, the proprietor of DW studio, met Dixon through composer John Benson Brooks (see **62-0499**). Williams, probably in her thirties at the time, had advertised a Dance Anatomy Class at this location since at least the late spring of 1959. Dixon's collaborations with Williams apparently began with this piece written for and rehearsed with her. (The phenomenon and the billing were "Jazz Ballet"; that was not the name of a specific piece.) In return, he used the space to run weekly sessions at the studio (see **60-0221**). Matt Notkins, Al Manion, and Howie Kadison are likely to have taken part in the "Jazz Ballet" as well as the subsequent sessions. The piece may have been staged formally only this one time, though it was also rehearsed copiously at the DW Studio.
"When we ran out of places to do things, when the situation started to get messed up with the coffeehouse scene--the Roue, etc.--I wondered if she would rent out her studio on Sundays. She asked if I would write a piece for her, and that's how it began. Until that time I was playing a lot, but all of my writing was private, at the house."
Cited in BD vita/resumé of 1964. "Strictly Ad Lib" *down beat* April 14, 1960, p. 47; advertisement in *Village Voice* March 2, 1960: p. 10.

60-0221   informal sessions

February 21-April 24, 1960   DW Studio: 17 West 24th Street, NYC

BD (t);
the sessions are known to have included at various times: Matt Notkins (as); Al Manion (d); Howie Kadison (d), possibly Louis Brown (ts)

Village Voice advertisements uniformly read: "William R. Dixon and Ollie Richardson present NEW CONCEPTS IN CONTEMPORARY JAZZ, showcasing new works and new talent". It is likely that these events were held every week for the given period; all performances but March 20 were advertised.
These were Dixon's sessions (of music with no dance) held in exchange for his participation in **60-0207**. All episodes ran from 4:00-9:00pm on Sundays. They were open to the public ($1.00 admission).

By the time of *down beat*'s mention of the sessions, there were "future plans" of "presenting the works of George Russell and John [Benson] Brooks." Those events never happened.

Advertisements in *Village Voice* February 17-April 20, 1960, between pages 2 and 11, depending on the issue. Cited in BD vita/resumé of 1964. reported in "Strictly Ad Lib" *down beat* April 14, 1960, p. 47.

Phase 2

"I started the music policy at the Phase 2 [302 Bleecker Street, NYC], where David Gordon was the proprietor--he taught literature I think at Columbia. It was the best coffee house in New York when it opened, because it had a beautiful garden in the back, and I approached Gordon about doing music there. I went in first, then I got Cecil [Taylor] there, then came Paul Bley, and then Roswell Rudd and Steve Lacy. Later on Eric Dolphy played there with the poet Ree Dragonette."

The first known advertisement for the Phase 2 ran in May,1960, and Dixon recalls that he probably began presenting music there shortly thereafter, as reflected by the UN Jazz Society field trip to an August performance. See p. 336.

The club had come under new management by February, 1964 after which it advertised only as a supper club, and then resuscitated a musical program with other goals, eventually hosting Richie Havens and other singer-songwriters.

First advertised in *Village Voice* May 4, 1960, *p.* 7;
UNJS trip in *Village Voice* August 25, 1960, p. 12.

61-0000 Fausto Pollicino-?
ca. 1961 NYC

Pollicino, Dixon's colleague at the UN (and a fellow artist), was to script the film Red Afternoon using Dixon's music. While it seems certain that the film was never finished, it is not known whether Dixon's score was ever recorded or still exists.

61-0095 UNKNOWN FILMMAKER-Bill Dixon
ca. 1961 Unknown recording studio

BD (p)

Dixon was commissioned to create the sound track for a film about a Boston youth beginning to play the trumpet. "I think once the director came to the studio to show the rough cut. Otherwise, I would go see the film, remember things, and then go into the studio, tape something from the piano, and give it to him." It is not known whether the film was ever completed, screened, or distributed. The studio was on 10th Street between Broadway and University Place.

Dixon was approached about the project while he was still employed at the UN. The fact that he and Shepp used the same studio when in the production stages of **R62-1001** a/b generates the probable dating above.

61-0700   Bill Dixon-Don Cherry

probably 1961 ??   near Bleecker and Bank Sts: NYC

BD (t, pocket c); Don Cherry (pocket c, t)

"Don Cherry was bringing another approach to the instrument that I found very very exciting. Then I met Don. I sought him out and this one particular night I ran into him in the west village. I was rather curious about the pocket cornet. As we were talking it started raining and then I tried to play his horn and he tried to play mine. So we talked and played for maybe a couple of hours right out there in the street."

R61-0709   Bill Dixon Trio

July 9, 1961   Bitter End Cafe: 147 Bleecker St., NYC

BD (t), Dudley Watson (b), Joe DiCarlo (d)

Walkin'	9:55	private tape
Blue 'N' Boogie	5:36	--
Straight No Chaser	7:29	--
Surrey with the Fringe on Top	8:28	--
But Not For Me	8:42	--
Cherokee (inc.)	6:06	--
There Is No Greater Love	8:34	--
My Funny Valentine	4:17	--
It Never Entered My Mind	8:59	--

Dixon was musical director of the Bitter End at the time, beginning shortly after the club opened. He organized sets on weekend afternoons. "I did music there before Woody Allen came in. They were so cheap they didn't have a piano; that's why there's no piano on that Sunday afternoon date. I left the Bitter End on very bad terms." Dixon's tenure there ended before his partnership with Archie Shepp formally began, and their groups never played there. Dixon and DiCarlo met through the postings at the musicians' union (AFM) Local 802 that linked musicians with gigs.
"This is the way people were feeling about music, even the standard literature: It was like having a suit that you no longer could keep altering, cutting down the pants, letting this out ... Sooner or later the suit was going to have to be discarded. I think the most difficult thing was getting drummers to give up metric time."

Dixon was filmed in a performance at the Bitter End--not necessarily this one--by the mime teacher Carlo Mazzone. The film is believed to still exist but is not immediately accessible.

61-0799   Wilbur Ware-Don Cherry [sic]
probably second half of 1961   The Speakeasy Jazz Cafe: NYC

BD (t); Wilbur Ware (b)

The Speakeasy was located at 177 Bleecker Street. Dixon: "I used to do duets there
with Wilbur Ware, who really loved my playing. At first I went in there one night
when Don Cherry was supposed to be doing something. He wasn't there, so Wilbur
invited me to play."

The Speakeasy continued to be important as a staging ground for the new music; in
subsequent months were presented groups led by Lalo Schifrin, Don Heckman, and
Cherry with Pharoah Sanders, very shortly after the latter arrived in New York.

Around this time, Dixon gave roughly three lessons to Ornette Coleman at the dawn
of his trumpet playing, loaned him a mouthpiece, and took him to see Frank Zottola
to get his own mouthpiece.

CHAPTER TWO

Dixon-Shepp 1961–1963

61-0900   <u>Archie Shepp and Co.</u>
second half of 1961   White Whale Coffee Shop: NYC

BD (t); Don Cherry (c); Steve Lacy (ss); Archie Shepp (ts); Jimmy Corbett and
one other--Buell Neidlinger or *possibly* Henry Grimes--(b); Denis Charles (d); Ed
Blackwell (rhythm logs)

  Stablemates

"I met Archie Shepp in the winter. It was a cold night, probably 1960 or 1961. I was
with Jimmy Corbett, the bassist, on my way to the Jazz Gallery to see Miles Davis's
sextet with J.J. Johnson. Archie came walking around the corner wearing an
aviator's hat and goggles from World War l, and Jimmy introduced us.
"Later on I was playing with a trio at the Bitter End around the time of [**R61-0709**].
Archie invited me to the White Whale [84 East 10th St.] when the group [above] was
playing there.
"The night I sat in, Steve Lacy was also sitting in; we played 'Stablemates'.
I used to go around there a lot to see them, because that was one of the best groups in

the new music, and I mean that. Archie had a piece in 5/4 called 'Viva Jomo', named for Jomo Kenyatta. He and Don played beautifully together, and each one of them also played piano very well. It was a nice little club, too, run by a black man."

The White Whale was in operation by May, 1961, and presented "Archie Shepp and Co." by August 3, if not earlier. The Miles Davis group described above was apparently performing at the Jazz Gallery by the end of 1961.

Advertised in *Village Voice* August 3, 1961; Davis's group in *Metronome* August, 1961, p. 5.

61-1199   Elaine Shipman

probably fall 1961   Ligoa Duncan Galerie des Arts: NYC

BD (t); Archie Shepp (ts); Tom Perry (snare drum); Elaine Shipman (choreography, movement); unknown others (movement)

This is the first formal collaboration of Shepp and Dixon, and Dixon's first meeting with Elaine Shipman. The gallery was at 230 East 80th Street.

Elaine Shipman: "I was in a school like the Dalton School--started as part of the Dewey idea of arts in education. Don Oscar Beck started this early children's laboratory school, on 72d near Lexington. He had earlier started the WPA dance program and was also in community education of children through the arts.

"The students were ages 13 to 17. We were there all day--we didn't actually live there, but we would be at the school until maybe 8 or 9 at night. We who were choreographers would have access to all these very disciplined dancers who weren't choregraphers, and we had composers who took us seriously. Dance-music collaborations were a large part of the school.

"Beck had married a dancer who in the thirties had been connected with the Isadora Duncan school. She taught Duncan techniques to us, and he was friends with all these Duncan people who would come and give us special classes. So the Jazz thing was far from our training." Through the Duncan connection, Elaine Shipman knew of Isadora's brother, Raymond, and of his daughter, Ligoa. Shipman: "Ligoa Duncan had a gallery on 80th Street, which she made available to me to do pieces anytime.So we used to do projects in her gallery a lot--teenage kids, many younger than I was, and a couple of adult dancers. We did a piece called "Billy the Kid". Bill Dixon had come up to see some of those earlier pieces (including 'Uptown Locale' [see **62-0615b**]) done at the Ligoa Duncan Gallery. I think Ornette Coleman also came to see some of them.

"Beck knew there was a movement in New Jazz/New Music and was increasingly interested. So when he would meet someone face to face, he was ready to ask 'Why don't you come around and give a talk to the kids?' and would bring people together. We students went out to [artistic events] together, and to these jazz things that were then part of our consciousness. He was that kind of teacher: he believed that gifts were gifts. Don was attracted to any sort of intensely gifted young people around him. Don has never gotten the acknowledgement he deserved for being a brilliant educator in this idea that the arts are a wonderful vehicle for children to learn to think, solve problems, be committed, etc.

"I had a friend at school who knew [critic and radio host] A.B. Spellman and knew all of these people, so I met Archie separately from Bill. I told him I was doing this project and wanted to use some of his type of music for it, rather than what we had at the school. Charles Ives was actually my other choice, but because of the general atmosphere of creative people, it made more sense to use live and new music."

Dixon: "Archie had introduced me to Elaine. He and I had played before, so he knew how I played. We did our first work at the Ligoa Duncan gallery, which was up near Second Avenue. On the day of the concert, Shepp called Dixon because Don Cherry, who was supposed to make the gig, could not be there.

"On the night of the performance, people were coming into the theater, and Archie was still playing the piano trying to write some pieces. The place is almost filled with people and Archie's composing the music. I said to him: 'Why don't we just play instead?' so we did it that way. It was supposed to be one night, but it carried over for several weekends."

61-9997   <u>Archie Shepp-Bill Dixon</u>
probably late 1961   a Catskills resort, NY

BD (t); Archie Shepp (ts); Chick Foster (d)

On at least one occasion Shepp and Dixon were employed by a contractor who came to an appointed place in Harlem on a weekly basis to pick up musicians (whoever showed up) for gigs in the coming weekend in the Catskill mountain resorts of upstate New York. For Dixon and Shepp it was a short-lived (one night?) enterprise, truncated due to a mutual disenchantment between the musicians and the proprietors.

62-0299   Robert Williams Benefit
                     Rockland Palace, NYC

"Just after *Into the Hot* [a Gil Evans-sponsored recording of, among others, Cecil
Taylor's group including Archie Shepp, made October 10, 1961], Archie didn't even
have a copy of [the record]. We were on our way uptown to play a benefit for Robert
Williams--with the Max Roach-Abbey Lincoln group (with Mal Waldron), Archie and
I--and before we went there, we went by Gil Evans's house (I knew Evans
peripherally; Archie didn't really know him) and got a copy for Archie. By that time
we had been playing already, and we were getting ready to do our record"
(R62-1000a/b).

Robert Williams had been at the center of a group of armed black citizens of a town in
North Carolina fighting to protect their rights to integrated public facilities and to
go about their daily activities unmolested. After several confrontations with the
local authorities and repeated refusals of the federal government to recognize or assist
the movement, the violence came to a head. For their safety Williams and his family
left North Carolina covertly in mid-1961, coming directly to New York; they later
sought shelter as fugitives in Canada (late October, 1961), Cuba (1962), and
eventually China (fall, 1963). The benefit at which Dixon and Shepp performed most
likely occurred while Williams was in Cuba, where he was involved in a movement to
champion Jazz on Havana radio and (from a distance) the foundation of the
Revolutionary Action Movement to unify civil rights activities in the US.

"There were all of those social activities going on. We would have played a benefit
for anyone who allowed us to play. I didn't even know who Robert Williams was; I'd
read about him, of course, but there were some people who were really gung ho about
the thing. I had no idea that *Freedomways* and those things were interconnected. I
wanted to play and it was a good forum to play in.
"That was when I first got involved with *Freedomways*, because when you went out
into the hall they had copies of the magazine. They were soliciting people to write
for the magazine. At that time I was getting ready to apply for a Whitney
Fellowship, and I was looking for a magazine to publish a folio of my paintings.   I
went to *Freedomways*, and they were interested in my work (until they saw it) but they
asked me to do some writing." In 1967, *Freedomways* published Dixon's reviews of
the *Encyclopedia of Jazz in the Sixties* and *Four Lives in the Bebop Business* . They
refused his review of LeRoi Jones's *Blues People*: "They said it was too critical of
Jones. No one was saying what I said about the book, and they didn't want to get on
'Roi's bad side."

Robert Carl Cohen, *Black Crusader: a Biography of Robert Franklin Williams* (Secaucus, New
Jersey: Lyle Stuart Inc.: 1972). *Freedomways* Third Quarter, 1967, p. 253-257.

62-0316   Archie Shepp-Bill Dixon Sextet

March 16, 1962   Maidman Theater: 42d Street, NYC

BD (t); Archie Shepp (ts); Kiane Zawadi (tb); John Neves, Butch Warren (b); Denis Charles (d)

     Tempus Fugit

Dixon arranged and rehearsed all pieces this group played. "We played such pieces out of the (then) repertoire as 'Tempus Fugit' by Bud Powell, George Russell's 'Stratusphunk', Shepp's 'Viva Jomo'. I had gotten the coda wrong for Powell's piece and was corrected by Denis Charles."

This concert series, planned for two days, was produced by Amiri Baraka (then, and hereinafter) LeRoi Jones. Reflecting the affinity between Shepp and Jones, the billing for the ASBD group was "Archie Shep [*sic*] Sextet"

The first night, March 16, was a Friday; the next night's concert was cancelled. *Village Voice* Jazz journalist Robert Levin wrote that the engagement "did go on for one set before it was decided that a party someone knew about back in the Village might make for greater possibilities of communication." Levin was compelled to retract this depiction in a subsequent issue. Ted Curson led a group (with Pat Patrick) that played the same event. The space was also referred to as the Maidman Playhouse.

Dixon: "If you want to know something, I started writing music before I could play. Writing came very natural; for anyone writing is easier than learning an instrument. Notes can only go up or down, move laterally in patterns, etc., and no matter what you put on paper, someone's going to be able to play it. But learning an instrument is something else. I've been writing a long time, but I never showed any of my writing seriously until Archie Shepp and I got together."

Throughout their partnership, Shepp and Dixon used a number of different performers on bass and drums. J.C. Moses was perhaps their earliest 'regular' drummer, although he is virtually invisible in that role in extant documentation. He preceded the Bronx drummer Howard McRae and apparently played in the group more frequently. In addition to Edgar Bateman, Paul Cohen, Lex Humphries, and Charles, Stu Martin is known to have played at least once with the Archie Shepp-Bill Dixon groups--probably with the Sextet.

Denis Charles was professionally known as "Dennis" Charles through the first forty years of his career. In the mid-nineties he confirmed that his name had been spelled with one "n" at birth and has since reverted to that spelling. It is used exclusively in this text.

Village Voice March 15, 1962, p.10 ; Robert Levin "Facets of Order" *Village Voice* March 22, 1962; unpublished July 26, 1989 letter from BD to Chris Sheridan at *Jazz Journal International*; LeRoi Jones "New York Loft and Coffee Shop Jazz" *down beat* May 1963, p. 13/42: also in *Black Music* (New York: William Morrow & Co [Apollo ed.]: 1968), p. 96.

62-0420   Archie Shepp-Bill Dixon Quartet
April 20, 1962   82 Second Ave, NYC

BD (t, flgh); Archie Shepp (ts); others unknown

Robert Levin reported in the *Village Voice* that "Shepp...and Dixon...do play
Saturday nights at various East Village addresses (consult the ads in this paper for the
current location) but their services are generally rendered free and only the alternating
rhythm sections are paid."

Dixon: "We were hired for what worked out to maybe $5.00 per man. So Archie and I
didn't take any money; instead, we could use that money to get a good bass player and
a good drummer." The early formations of the Archie Shepp-Bill Dixon Quartet
"played for any event--too many to remember. That was how you kept a group
working. Do you know how many bills I've played on with Pete Seeger?--Women
Strike for Peace, all of those things. Those were the only people who wanted us, and
they had all of these benefit concerts."
Advertisement reads: "ON GUARD presents JAZZ WORKSHOP; Fr. Nites: Dancing,
Refreshments, Music by Archie Shepp-Bill Dixon 6. Admission $.99 from 9pm".
Dixon: " 'On Guard' was the group raising the money for our trip to Helsinki [cf.
62-0727]. They put on all of these things for that purpose."
Village Voice ad April 19, 1962 p. 8.
Robert Levin "The New Thing" *Village Voice* [quoted from above] June 14, 1962, p. 13.

62-0427   Archie Shepp-Bill Dixon Quartet
April 27, 1962   67 Second Ave, NYC

BD (t); Archie Shepp (ts); others unknown

Same advertisement as **62-0420**.

62-0498   Archie Shepp-Bill Dixon Quartet
probably late spring 1962   Town Hall, NYC

BD?? (t); Archie Shepp (ts); others unknown

Perry Robinson: "Our country would not help this [festival] because of the cold war,
so they had the American World Youth Festival contingent that got together to raise
money to send people over. Part of that was a Town Hall concert with a few groups

from this American contingent: Archie and Bill had a group, and I brought a quartet there with Henry Grimes. Cecil, who was originally supposed to go, may also have been there." Robinson recalls definitely that Shepp was at this concert; however, he has no ironclad recollection of Dixon at the Town Hall event.

Likewise, Dixon: "Perry Robinson was sitting in with Archie and myself all over New York before we went to Finland. To my knowledge I have never played in Town Hall, and it doesn't seem likely that I would have done it and not remembered it."

62-0499   John Benson Brooks

first half of 1962   Brooks's Apt.: 535 Hudson Street, NYC

BD (t); Don Heckman (as); John Benson Brooks (p); Howard Hart (snare drum)

A rehearsal session or a series of them were held at the home of Brooks; it is possible that not all of the musicians named above attended each one. Hart (perhaps better known for his poetry) routinely used a very small drum set consisting of a snare drum and possibly a cymbal.

Dixon knew of composer Brooks through his recordings and writings on the music for the *Jazz Review*. They met in the late 1950s by way of a mutual friend whom Dixon knew from the United Nations. At that time, Brooks was circulating a petition to bring back into print the 1956 RCA Victor Jazz Workshop record by George Russell's Smalltet. He introduced Dixon to Russell, to Ornette Coleman's music via the alto saxophonist's LP *Somethin' Else*, and to the periodical, *die Reihe*, dedicated to serial, electronic, and dodecaphonic music. For the next few years Dixon and Brooks shared their ideas about music and composition, and the latter had a significant impact on Dixon's outlook as a composer.

"Brooks wanted me to take Don Ellis's place when Don went out to the coast, and I had no problem with the music. I don't recall if I rehearsed that much with the whole group. I know I rehearsed with John, but by the time they got ready to do something, Ellis was back." There were no public performances in this configuration.

The group with Heckman and Ellis was rehearsing by the fall of 1960, though the former's association with Brooks putatively dates to 1959. Ellis appears to have been active in New York through much of 1961, whereas he was certainly on the road (in many directions, including the Pacific coast) by mid-1962, so it is likely that Dixon took his place at that time. Brooks was listed in the 1961 AFM directory at the Hudson street address; these events are circumscribed by Brooks's move to the East Side, and the end of Heckman's participation with Brooks, probably shortly after their June 2, 1962 performance.

Anthony J. Agostinelli, *Don Ellis: A Man For Our Time (1934-1978)* (private printing: Providence, Rhode Island, 1986), p. 2.

62-0511   Archie Shepp-Bill Dixon Quartet
May 11, 1962   82 Second Ave, NYC

BD (t); Archie Shepp (ts); others unknown

Same advertisement as **62-0420**.

62-0519   Archie Shepp-Bill Dixon Group
May 19, 1962   547 Broadway, NYC

BD (t); Archie Shepp (ts); others unknown

Advertisement similar to **62-0420**. Saturday

62-0526   <u>Archie Shepp-Bill Dixon Group</u>
May 26, 1962   27 Cooper Square, NYC

BD (t, flgh); Archie Shepp (ts); unknown (b); J.C. Moses (d)

Private tape ?

Advertisement similar to **62-0420**.
Saturday

Marzette Watts retains a recording with the above personnel from one of the group's
concerts at this location--presumably but not necessarily the May 26 event.
27 Cooper Square was the building above the Five Spot where LeRoi Jones and
Marzette Watts lived at the time of this concert. Shepp may still have been living on
6th Street (as he was when he met Dixon). Around the beginning of 1963, he too
moved into the 27 Cooper Square building.
Shepp, Watts, and Jones were (apparently then) part of a political action group
known as the Organization of Young Men. Watts met Dixon through the
Organization, though Dixon had only a tangential association with the activities and
alignment of the group. "They were trying to be as political as they could; a lot of
activities were staged at Cooper Square."

Dixon recalls the allegiances that germinated in the OYM as the root of the (1965)
philosophical opposition between the Jazz Composers Guild and Jones's Black Arts
Repertory Theater. "This is where the plan was initiated [some time later] to place
Archie out there; he was going to be the next public figure in the music." Watts
reports that Shepp was a fallback choice in this role: Albert Ayler, as it was first
agreed, would be the beneficiary of the Organization's support and publicity, but with
Ayler leaving the country for the fall of 1964, their focus shifted to Shepp. Since
Dixon and Shepp were by this time no longer coleading their group, the wave of
positive press surrounding Shepp (beginning no later than his August 10, 1964,
recording, *Four for Trane,* and including Jones's *down beat* profile of him) was
matched by a general decision to freeze Dixon out.
Dixon: "Jones and I never did get along anyway. First of all I found them artificially
political. Jones's Black Arts Repertory Theater was all built on poverty funds: how
revolutionary were you if you were taking money from the parent society and then
mumbling and grumbling? On the other hand, all of the Cellar and Guild activities
were self-supporting, and unlike the Judson poetry, dance, and rehabilitation
programs, we paid rent."

See also **U64-1004** and the text following **U65-0122**.

62-0615a   Archie Shepp-Bill Dixon Quartet
June 15-16, 1962   Le Metro: 149 Second Avenue, NYC

BD (t); Archie Shepp (ts); unknown (b); unknown (d)

62-0615b   Elaine Shipman: New Dimensions Dance Company
June 15, 1962   The Living Theatre

BD (p); Elaine Shipman (choreography, movement); unknown (movement)

Three Dimensional Harlem

Following the previous year's work with Shepp and Dixon (**61-1199**) Shipman enlisted Dixon to compose music for "Three Dimensional Harlem", a full-length ballet. Her description of this collaboration with Dixon shows some of their points of shared aesthetics, in addition to illuminating the New Yortk artistic spectrum in which they both worked.

Elaine Shipman: "Bill lived on Bank Street; Don Oscar Beck lived on Grove Street, and he and his wife used to bump into Bill and [Dixon's then-wife] Jeanne, so then Don told me about this interesting musician whom he had made friends with. Archie Shepp must have said something to Bill, and then when Beck said something to Bill, the whole thing clicked. This was the first full-fledged piece I did in my whole life." Dixon: "Well, you never would have known that because she exuded so much confidence running those rehearsals. Elaine is a remarkable person."

Shipman: "I remember walking around 125th street, and going past a record shop that always had music coming out, and people grooving to it. I was objectively fascinated with that whole thing; *it's a dance.* That is, if you stand long enough on the corner, eventually everything happens right there. Some of [what went into 'Three Dimensional Harlem'] was just that kind of method--standing, observing. It also came from Don and John Cage's view of reality, that life is just all right there in front of you. But then you have to assimilate it in an artificial way, and that was the hard thing, technically. That's what I found out from the project: once I had gotten these trained dancers to do what I wanted, none of it looked as good as it had on the street. We had to put it through a vocabulary, a system.

"Before I did 'Three Dimensional Harlem', my first inkling about all these Harlem things was a piece called "Uptown Locale". That was the pilot project for it. It was also before I had gotten Bill and Archie, and I was using music [on records] by Dave Brubeck and Miles Davis. Don was the one who said: "This is not very original. There are guys around town, a movement happening where the real thing is developing. " He was the one who pushed me to contact Bill Dixon and Archie Shepp."

Dixon: "Elaine rehearsed that a lot at Michael's Studios on 8th Avenue (between 45th and 46th Streets) Sunday mornings I used to get up and go uptown and rehearse: watch them dance and write down ideas."

Shipman: "Later I thought it was odd that a Cunningham dancer, Judith Dunn, would be working with Bill, because he didn't seem that unconnected, or that minimal. That was not his philosophy; with his music I always felt that the dance did have some interpretational relationship with the music." Dixon: "When I worked with Elaine, that's the way I did it. Mind you, I was older and knew more when I started to work with Judith Dunn."

Shipman: "When I was doing "Three Dimensional Harlem", I was involved with Bill's score, as opposed to the way I work with Meredith Monk or with John Cage. I definitely respected all of his musical realities; they had the shape of the dance. He collaborated in a rhythmic way with the movement; that is, the music is toned to what the human body can do.

"Through some connection the Living Theater was empty on Sundays. We were used to doing performances as kids that were public anyway; that's how the school worked. We did these projects, finished them, and then performed them. Beck never had any money, being an artist who was into education, rather than a Ph.D. educator like Dewey, for instance, and he was always fierce [in securing these places to stage our performances]. Don saw that I liked to do choreography, and where we could have just done these things in his studio, he would always encourage me to find an outside place--and 'don't worry about the money', he said. But because we were depending on donated spaces, favors, and connections, we often had to move from the scheduled spot for the performance to another location."

Dixon: "Archie and I were playing at Le Metro, and she scheduled her thing that night. The performance was originally slated for the East 11th Street Theater, then changed to the Phoenix Theater (334 East 74th Street), and finally (with only hours before the scheduled start) the Living Theatre was decided on. While Archie was playing one of the sets, I took a cab to the Living Theater to do the thing on piano and came back. It only got one performance." Programs for the event were printed to show the originally proposed site and personnel, with Shepp and Tom Perry (d). Additional performances slated for June (probably 16), 17, 22, 23, 24 at 3:30 and 8:30pm did not materialize.

Amsterdam News Saturday, June 16, 1962; p. 19. Details from concert program; also cited in Dixon's 1964 vita/resumé.

62-0622   Archie Shepp-Bill Dixon Quartet
June 22-23, 1962   Le Metro, 149 Second Avenue, NYC

BD (t); Archie Shepp (ts); unknown, *sub* Art Davis (b); unknown (d)

From advertisements: "Fred Martin and Lee Brody present FOLK MUSIC AND
COMEDY (Rudy Challenger and Lou Gossett & others)/ JAZZ ESCALIERE [*sic*]
Archie Shepp-Bill Dixon Quartette Every Fri., Sat. 8:30pm till ?"
Dixon: "This Lou Gossett who is now an established film star [professionally known
as Louis Gossett Jr.]--he and I had the same manager at one time."

The regular bassist for this job was Muslim, not Don Moore. "Our bass player got
sick at one point. John Coltrane was playing at the Jazz Gallery, so Archie went
around to the Gallery and got Art Davis [then playing Coltrane's two-bass
group]--this is how I met him. Davis came in on his break and did a set with us at the
Metro".
Dixon recalls only one weekend here, but at least one other was slated (**62-0629**),
and their appearance the previous weekend would support the explanation under
62-0615 more closely. Coltrane's group was at the Village Gate for the preceding
two weekends, which argues against the possibility that June 22-23 coincided with
Shipman's ballet.
Village Voice June 21, 1962, p. 8.

62-0629   Archie Shepp-Bill Dixon Quartet
June 29, 1962   "The *New*" Le Metro, 146 2d Av, NYC

BD (t); Archie Shepp (ts); unknown, sub Art Davis (b); unknown (d)

see also **62-0622**
Ad here shows the ASBD "every Friday" at 10:15pm and not on Saturdays.
Village Voice June 28, 1962, p. 7.

62-0695   Archie Shepp-Bill Dixon Quartet
mid-July or earlier, 1962   Club 65: 8th Street, NYC

BD (t, flgh); Archie Shepp (ts); others unknown

One of several performances held to raise funds for the Helsinki trip.
Club 65 was a union hall.

62-0725   <u>Archie Shepp-Bill Dixon Quartet (sic)</u>
late July 1962   Helsinki Youth Festival, Finland

BD (t, flgh); Archie Shepp (ts, *possibly* barsx); Perry Robinson (cl); Don
Moore (b); Howard McRae (d)

> Stratusphunk
> Kucheza Blues
> In A Mellotone
> Viva Jomo

"This was at the time of the US and USSR saber-rattling against each other in the cold
war; Finland was considered a 'Communist' country and this was a 'Communist'
festival. Cecil's group was supposed to go, and my group was supposed to go. As it
came down to the wire, Cecil made an ultimatum that he wanted his name to be bigger
than anyone else's name. I told Archie that if anyone's name was bigger than mine I
wasn't going anywhere. Evidently, either Cecil said he wasn't going, or they decided
to have everyone's name the same size, I don't know. Anyway, Archie and I went,
and that is why Cecil went to Scandinavia on his own afterward [November, 1962]."

The Shepp-Dixon Quartet had been originally interested in playing at the First
International Jazz Festival Festival (in Washington, D.C.) that summer which
featured groups of John Benson Brooks and George Russell. When that failed to
materialize, they seized this opportunity. Coincident with the Youth Festival, the
United States Information Agency sponsored an exhibition in Finland, of paintings
by Mark Rothko and Jackson Pollock, and both Jimmy Giuffre and Herbie Nichols
performing.

"The day before we left for Helsinki, the quartet was supposed to rehearse at my
house, but Archie never made it until that night, and the rehearsal was therefore
cancelled." Howard McRae was engaged to make the trip as the group's drummer, as
J.C. Moses was apparently committed to other jobs in that period. In order to have
more time for writing the music and copying parts, Dixon took the Swedish liner
Kungsholun from the US to Helsinki (landing in Göteborg, Sweden). The rest of the
group traveled separately, by air. "I took the ferry from Stockholm to Helsinki.
When I arrived there were numerous photographers on hand, and I was interviewed on
the dock. One thing that people <u>did</u> notice about that trip was that I was the only
musician with a front page picture in the Finnish press.
"I met up with Archie and when we had our first rehearsal; Perry [Robinson] was there,
and we invited him to join the group. Perry had gone over with another group on a
cruise ship, but they were stranded when they got to Europe. It wasn't that Perry was
asked in the USA to join the group. He ended up there at the Festival with no group,
and we asked him in. Perry and Archie might conceivably have discussed him joining
the group before that, but I hadn't known about it.

"[Russian poet Yevgeny Aleksandrovich] Yevtushenko had arrived at the festival that
afternoon--I recognized him because his picture had just been on the cover of *TIME*.
He came in while we we were rehearsing, and he asked after Allen Ginsberg or LeRoi

Jones; he was speaking Spanish. Perry spoke fluent Spanish and explained that they weren't there, but we informed him that we were going to do this concert that night.

"Our concert was held in a large, beautiful theater. We used to play under blue lights, and we were always concerned about trying to find the place on stage where the sound was best; being bunched up didn't work all of the time. It wasn't theatrical, although it looked theatrical. When our time to go on came, the reed players had still not appeared. Howard McRae, Don Moore and I waited until the last minute. We waited as long as we could, and then we started without them. Perry and Archie came in ten or fifteen minutes late. I was told later that this too looked very theatrical, but really they just came out on stage when they got there. People thought it was planned. As providence would have it, the group played very, very well. We would segue from one piece into another--no stopping.
"The concert was a smashing success, and people just jumped up on the stage. Then all of the sudden it got quiet, because Yevtushenko was coming down the center aisle with a group of 4 or 5 other Russians, all carrying these cases that later turned out to be Russian vodka. They got up on the stage and began to pass the vodka out. Then Yevtushenko grabbed me around the shoulders and made a toast: 'To Jazz musicians: the poets of the world.' That was the event that night.

"We also played one afternoon on a bill with [guitarist] Jacques Brel. On another occasion we played a huge session in another huge hall with a lot of musicians. Then we went to Turku, Finland and played in this fantastic hall with a 10-foot Steinway, and when we came out to play, the entire stage was covered with roses. That theater had no microphones; the seats were acoustically situated so they weren't necessary. People began to come to our rehearsals in a gym there, and the kids would dance outside. Finally they asked, 'Why don't you just play outside?' So the little kids were dancing to this 'revolutionary', 'avant garde' music and having a great time. On the trip we stayed in huge dormitories, and I practiced in a patch of old-growth woods nearby."

Shepp brought a baritone saxophone on the trip to Europe; Dixon's scoring for some of the group's repertoire called for Shepp to play it, and for Dixon's fluegelhorn. John Tchicai met Shepp and Dixon on this tour and (later) attended some of the group's New York performances. Dixon: "I didn't hear Tchicai play in Sweden, but he was very enterprising and showed up at every one of our concerts and even the rehearsals."

Orkester Journalen November, 1962; *Kansan Uutiset* (daily) July 29, 1962.

62-0799   Bill Dixon Group

late July/early August, 1962   various clubs (?) in Stockholm

BD (t); Perry Robinson (cl); Albert Ayler (ts); Don Moore (b); Howard McRae (d)

"After the Youth Festival we split up: Archie traveled on to the Soviet Union; I went back to Stockholm, where Perry, Don Moore, McRae and I worked."

A later playing engagement for the group in Czechoslovakia was conceived, but did not come through.

While in Stockholm Perry Robinson introduced Dixon to Albert Ayler. Dixon: "We found a few jobs there, and met Ayler, who played with the group. We shared a thing one night with some members of the Count Basie band at a session in the Gröna Lunds, a park in Stockholm. Clarinetist Putte Wickman led a band including Idrees Sulieman that also played there. That was really the first time I heard Albert play, but he didn't always play with us. He was working on his first record and wanted me to do the music, but I didn't know at that time how I felt about Albert's music. He was one of the nicest people you'd ever meet, but he was literally in a panic about getting this record of standards done." Basie's full band also played (and was recorded) in the Gröna Lunds that summer; their stay in Stockholm from August 8 to 12 provides a useful target for the activities Dixon describes. Ayler finally made his records of standards--without Dixon's input--October 25, 1962.

Robinson recalls having played in a club in the Old Town in Stockholm. Dixon also played copiously with Lars (Lasse [?]) Werner and other Swedish musicians that summer. Based on his experiences abroad, Dixon proposed to Bill Coss of *down beat* a European trip during which he could keep a journal for publication. The magazine rejected his proposal but subsequently published a similar journal by Don Ellis.

Dixon returned from Europe that summer, and quit working at the UN on August 31, 1962. "For me to just stop everything and concentrate on music, it took a long time. [That trip] was enough to make me want to take the chance and see if I could do it." The latter part of this trip also marks the beginning of a period of embouchure troubles (see **63-0606** et seq.).

Don Ellis's "Warsaw Diary" was published in *down beat* January 3, 1963.

62-0800   <u>Archie Shepp [sic]-Bill Dixon Quartet</u>
probably August, 1962   Carnegie Institute, NYC

BD (t, flgh); Houston Person (ts); Don Moore (b); Howard McRae (d)

The Shepp-Dixon group had been engaged to play a benefit at the Carnegie Institute (possibly for the brother of Kenyan Labour Minister Tom Mboya) but Shepp was late in returning to the States from the summer's activities, so Houston Person deputized for his part in the group.

R62-0900   <u>Informal session</u>
Probably late 1962   John Benson Brooks's apartment

BD (t); Don Heckman (as); Archie Shepp (ts); John Benson Brooks (p)

    Fine and Dandy

"Once I took Archie down to Brooks's and we played. In trying to make up our minds about what to play, John took out a deck of cards. He did a chance operation with the cards and we ended up playing 'Fine and Dandy'.

62-0997 <u>Archie Shepp-Bill Dixon</u>
possibly late 1962   Mobilization for Youth , NYC

BD (t, flgh); Archie Shepp (ts); unknown (b); Howard McRae (d)

During the time that he and Dixon worked together, Shepp went to work in some
capacity for the federally-funded Mobilization for Youth anti-poverty program in the
Lower East Side. Some formation of the Shepp-Dixon group performed at at least one
of the organization's functions. The program was launched in mid-1962, and Shepp
likely would haven taken part during its strongest period, after he and Dixon returned
from Helsinki.
Dixon: "Their program was pretty good insofar as they <u>did</u> have people doing things.
Archie was teaching music there; they had ensembles, some segment of which he was
in charge of. I would go to some of the ensemble things, and when Archie got the
job, the whole band went down there and played--Howard McRae and the rest. It was
the usual thing: you played music for these kids and tried to initiate a discourse. The
name of the game was keeping them off the streets."
Mobilization for Youth aimed at improving connections with the lowest income
bracket, primarily through channeling political power in housing, politics, and
general welfare. Its sizeable subvention came from a Presidential allocation of 1962
for a pilot program of the war-on-poverty. By late 1963, the MfY was facing charges
(leading to official investigations) of mismanagement relating to the incongruity of
using federal funds for what were perceived as socialist aims. According to the
Village Voice, the investigations and suspicion were fueled in part by the charge that
some MfY staffers were Communist party sympathizers, had ties to Cuba, or had
attended the Helsinki World Youth Festival. Shepp had done the latter, of course, and
conceivably, by the vector of the Robert Williams fund-raising activites (see
62-0299), could also have been linked to supporting the Cuban government.
"Archie lost his job there because of the political thing; he was very much in the
limelight. Don't forget, Archie had already written his play, <u>The Communist</u>."
It is unclear exactly how deep Shepp's involvement with the MfY went, but the entire
incident demonstrates the public gravity of a Communist reputation such as shadowed
him and Dixon following their high-profile performance in Helsinki. Dixon aroused
enough suspicion as an *avant garde* musician, a vocal opponent of unfair
discrimination, and an enlightened, internationalist thinker to be black-listed and
denied work for a large part of his early career. His association with the 1962 World
Youth Festival and the eventual formation of the Jazz Composers' Guild added
'Communist activities' to the list of accusations.
Susan Brownmiller "Mobilization--One Year Later" *Village Voice* October 28, 1965, p. 13.

R62-1000a   Archie Shepp-Bill Dixon Quartet
probably mid-October, 1962   Unknown studios: NYC

BD (t, flgh-1); Archie Shepp (ts); Don Moore (b); Paul Cohen (d)

63-114 Trio	8:59	Sav MG 12178
63-115 Quartet	9:24	--
63-116 Somewhere -1	6:00	--

MG 12178 =BYG 529 101 (Fr)=Supraphon [unknown number] (Cz); see below
MG 12178 titled *Archie Shepp Bill Dixon Quartet*
BYG 529 101 titled *Peace*

The Savoy record was also released in Czechoslovakia on the Supraphon label
through a contact that Shepp and Dixon had made during their 1962 stay in
Scandinavia. There were some difficulties transacting payment out of
Czechoslovakia, but the the deal was apparently completed, and copies of the
Supraphon record are known to exist.

This was the first record by either Dixon or Shepp as a leader and the only one to
document any of the 1961-3 groups that they coled. "Paul Cohen was studying with
George Russell, and he was in law school at NYU [Cohen apparently also had attended
the Lenox School of Jazz in 1959]. The night we were doing the recording, we had
booked the studio and something went wrong: we needed a drummer right away. I
went to George, because I had heard Paul rehearsing with George's group. He hadn't
played with us before that."

Dixon wrote "Trio" and "Quartet". He had been a composer for most of his
professional career as a musician, but not until 1960 did he feel comfortable playing
his own compositions in public. By 1963, he was playing no pieces *except* his own.
"The Quartet played the standard, common literature, and then Archie's 'Viva Jomo',
but never any pieces of mine. 'Trio' and 'Quartet' were written when we really started
bearing down to get a record. I wrote them after we came back from Europe. Then
they were worked on and worked on, and they became the first pieces of mine that we
played in public. After that it was easy, and finally there was nothing in our book
except originals."
"Trio" may in fact have been finished earlier, so that it could be played in Helsinki.
Both pieces became part of the group's regular repertoire. In 1963 Dixon arranged
'Trio' for the New York Contemporary Five (see **R63-0817**), and it was also played
in 1964 by other Bill Dixon groups.
"Somewhere" was a Shepp favorite--on record and on stage.

The record was produced by Dixon and Shepp; they submitted the edited master tape to
Savoy in sequence and ready for mastering, and therefore master numbers probably do
not relate to order of recording. The agreement with Savoy allowed for a ten-year
lease--for the sum of $1.00.
Preparations for this recording and **R62-1000b** may have been done at the site of
61-0095; one or both of the two recording dates were probably also made at that

studio. Some part of this recording was undertaken at a studio in midtown, probably in the block bounded by 7th and 8th Avenues; 54th and 55th Streets. Art Chryst was the recording engineer.

Dixon also planned the layout for the LP jacket. "I fought like the devil for that design, so that it would just have the photograph on the cover, and you had to turn it over to see the text."

"When I first started to do music, I did it because I wanted to know something about music. It was an endeavor that had to do with me, and me alone. In the initial years I never had the confidence that I would record. It wasn't like today [1992] where if you play for three weeks you can make a recording. At that time even people who were considered giants of the music were sort of limping along, not getting much work. In addition, a recording had more significance than it has today. It gave you entrée to performance in a club; you <u>had</u> to have a record.

"By the time [making a record] began to surface as a possibility and a necessity if I was going to make the next logical step, I had no background and no support system. No one had ever even told me that anyone would be interested in my work. Black people never found enough things in my music or in my painting for me to be legitimately black for them; white people knew I wasn't white. Where was the confidence going to come from to convince a record company to invest money in what I did? That was never in the vanguard of my thoughts. When I became ready to record, I had a singular purpose: I was going to do what I wanted to, and no one was going to make me do what I didn't want to do. I never had the problem--in the few offers I had from record companies--of someone having the audacity to tell me who I was going to use, what pieces to play, or how long they were going to be... It never occurred to any of those people I dealt with, because I didn't carry myself that way."

R62-1000b   Archie Shepp-Bill Dixon Quartet
October, 1962   possibly same as **R62-1000a**

BD (t or flgh); Archie Shepp (ts); Reggie Workman (b); Howard McRae (d)

   115 Peace   9:35   Sav MG 12178

This piece may come from the same date as **62-1001a** .
Bruyninckx's attachment of the piece "Avalon" to (one of) the session(s) for MG
12178 is erroneous. The group neither played nor recorded such a piece at any time.
However, it may be a mis-listing of Dixon's piece "Afternoon", which was then
coming into the ASBD repertoire.

"We were doing a new kind of music, and these musicians wanted to play.
As for the players, Reggie Workman is a master bassist and knew exactly what to do.
The reason he gets the solo is because he's Reggie. He had an established reputation,
and in certain ways I was glad that he thought that much of the music that he would
want to play it."

Walter Bruyninckx *Sixty Years of Recorded Jazz* Mechelen, Belgium: Bruyninckx, 1977.

62-1121   Archie Shepp-Bill Dixon Quartet
before November 21, 1962   WBAI Studios: NYC

BD (t and/or flgh); Archie Shepp (ts); others unknown

WBAI had a day-long fundraiser entitled "A Live Day of Broadcasting" which was to
include no pre-recorded programming. That day marked the first appearance of the
Quartet on WBAI Radio.
This "Live Day of Broadcasting" and subsequent ones of the same nature were hailed
internationally and effectively initiated the current era of public radio, in which
on-air fundraising provides stations' primary sustenance.

Info from WBAI program guide.

62-1206   Archie Shepp-Bill Dixon Quartet
December 6-9, 1962   Cafe Avital: 20 St Marks Place, NYC

BD (t and/or flgh); Archie Shepp (ts); Jimmie Stevenson, Jr. (b); Lex
Humphries (d)

A *Village Voice*-like advertisement billed the engagement as Tuesday through
Saturday, 9:00pm-2:00am; Sunday afternoon: 5:00-9:00pm. Month, dates, and year
are not given there.
Robert Levin's article, however, cites "Thursdays through Sundays"; it is not clear
whether the Quartet's series had already begun by the December 6 publication date of
his article. Other similar performances are referred to in *down beat*, reviewing
R63-0119.

George Russell was in the audience at one of these December performances and
departed rather obviously in the middle of the second piece, reflecting his dislike of
the proceedings. His piece "Stratusphunk" was in the group's repertoire. Dixon: "At
that time: we were still only playing two original pieces of mine: 'Trio' and
'Quartet'. We played Archie's piece 'Viva Jomo' and 'In a Mellow Tone'; we didn't
play 'Somewhere' that much. 'Peace' was the only Coleman tune."

"McLean, Shepp, Dixon" by Robert Levin in *Village Voice* December 6, 1962, p. 10; "Strictly
Ad Lib" *down beat* January 17, 1963, p. 10.
Judson concert reviewed in *down beat* March 14, 1963, p. 36.

62-1213a   Archie Shepp-Bill Dixon Quartet
December 13, 1962   WBAI Studios: NYC

BD (t, flgh); Archie Shepp (ts and/or barsx); Don Moore (b); Howard McRae (d)

> *see below*

With this broadcast Shepp and Dixon initiated a series of six one-hour episodes on alternate Thursday evenings at 9:30pm, called *Jazz in the Studio*. At the time Dick Elman was in the administration WBAI .

Included in one or more of the WBAI broadcasts were Dixon's compositions "Enigma", "Trio", "Quartet", "Afternoon", "Metamorphosis, and/or "Metamorphosis [II]". The other pieces played included George Russell's "Stratusphunk", Randy Weston's "Kucheza Blues", Ellington's "In a Mellow Tone", Cecil Taylor's "Cell Walk for Celeste", a Herbie Nichols composition--possibly "Terpsichore" (Dixon: "I was introduced to Nichols's pieces by Archie, through Roswell Rudd. I can remember going down to Roswell's studio when he lived around Wall street [his residence at 190A Duane Street?] and dealing with those Herbie Nichols pieces")--and Gershwin's "The Man I Love": "I played it on fluegelhorn, playing the first 16 bars *a cappella*, with the band coming in on the bridge." A typical program in this series included the musicians coming to the studio, turning the lights out, and playing nearly uninterrupted for an hour.

Dixon does not specifically recall having played at the Avital (**62-1213b**) and done this radio performance all in one night, but the coffee house show probably started late enough for them both to have occurred sequentially on the same night. The remainder of the broadcasts are listed as **62-1227, 63-0110, 63-0124, 63-0207, 63-0221**.
Listed in WBAI program guide

62-1213b   Archie Shepp-Bill Dixon Quartet
December 13-16, 1962   Cafe Avital: 20 St Marks Place, NYC

BD (t and/or flgh); Archie Shepp (ts); Jimmie Stevenson, Jr. (b); Lex Humphries (d)

Extrapolated from Levin's article cited in **62-1206**
Village Voice-like advertisement.

62-1220   Archie Shepp-Bill Dixon Quartet
December 20, 1962   Harout's: 14 Waverly Place, NYC

BD (t, flgh); Archie Shepp (ts); *probably* Don Moore (b); Paul Cohen (d)

Levin: "The Archie Shepp-Bill Dixon Quartet, no longer at the Cafe Avital, opens
tonight (Thursday) at Harout's on Waverly Place."

Harout's [pronounced with second syllable emphasized and rhyming with 'boot']
earlier in the year had advertised being closed on Sundays; Dixon and Shepp's
engagements may therefore have been extended weekends Thursday through Saturday.
The club in the coming years was an important venue for some of the groundbreaking
groups in the new music, including (frequently from May, 1962 forward) the Steve
Lacy-Roswell Rudd Quartet, and the debut of the New York Contemporary Five (see
R63-0799). Though the club was presenting Jazz again in mid-1965, its heyday
had ended by March of 1964, by which time the music policy had reverted to "Native
Music" in conjunction with its "Armenian Cuisine".

Robert Levin "Freddie Redd" *Village Voice* December 20, 1962;
new music policy in *Village Voice* ad March 12, 1964.

62-1227   Archie Shepp-Bill Dixon Quartet
December 27, 1962   WBAI Studios: NYC

BD (t, flgh); Archie Shepp (ts and/or barsx); Don Moore (b); Howard McRae (d)

Jazz in the Studio: second of 6 radio broadcasts; See also **62-1213**.
Listed in WBAI program guide.

63-0000   Bill Dixon Group [ASBD?]
probably first half of 1963 or earlier   Midtown International Center

cited in vita/resumé 1964

63-0110   Archie Shepp-Bill Dixon Quartet
January 10, 1963   WBAI Studios, NYC

BD (t, flgh); Archie Shepp (ts and/or barsx); Don Moore (b); Howard McRae (d)

Jazz in the Studio: third of 6 radio broadcasts; See also **62-1213**.
Listed in WBAI program guide.

R63-0119   Archie Shepp-Bill Dixon Quartet (with guests)
January 19, 1963   Judson Hall: 165 West 57th St, NYC

BD (t); Archie Shepp (ts); Don Moore (b); Lex Humphries (d)

In the second half of the program add: Roswell Rudd (tb); *probably* sub Denis
Charles (d) for Humphries.

> Quartet
> Blues Tune
> Scattershot
> Spheroid
> Trio
> Second Movement for Elaine Shipman's
> Lonely Lovers
> Ballad for Les   *excerpt*   1:14
> Metamorphosis
> Motif

Saturday, apparently 8:30 pm. Dixon composed all of the pieces, except Don
Heckman's "Scattershot", one by Shepp ("Second Movement for Elaine Shipman's
Ballet", "a piece that Archie was still working on, but we first had done it at the Ligoa
Duncan Gallery." [cf. **61-1199**]). *Trio* was not new, but the others were all written
for this concert. Dixon: "That was a very thoroughly rehearsed performance; I played
my butt off."
The concert program misnames Lex as "Len" Humphries. Humphries appeared at a
handful of other Shepp-Dixon events; Denis Charles played only with larger
formations of the group and never with just the Quartet. Rudd and Charles were
added/substituted by design: Dixon had rehearsed certain of the pieces with them in
the group, so they played that part of the concert. Heckman had rehearsed the group
in his piece, which was also written specifically for this concert.

Norman Seaman produced the concert. Dixon: "It would never occur to ten musicians
to each put up $100.00 and rent a place; no, you had to get a producer. That's how
Norman Seaman had the Carnegie Recital Hall, Town Hall, and Judson Hall. He would
take his money to run the ads, and print the brochure, and you had to pay the players
in your group. Seaman was known for that. I met him up at Camp Unity, a left-wing
camp in upstate New York. If I'm not mistaken, Perry Robinson got me involved
with Seaman. It wasn't really my cup of tea to relax and lie around in the sun, but I
went up there a couple of times. I went up and took my horn anyway, and there was a
group there playing something and asked me to sit in. Norman Seaman heard that and
introduced himself, and we started talking about the Judson Hall concert. That's the
only one of his concerts I worked."

In his liner essay for the second New York Art Quartet record (*Mohawk* Fontana 681
009 ZL), John Tchicai recalls this concert as his first meeting with Roswell Rudd and

therefore a touchstone for the 1964 formation of the New York Art Quartet. Tchicai also cites Denis Charles on drums.

George Hoefer "Caught In the Act: Bill Dixon-Archie Shepp" *down beat* March 14, 1963, p. 36; also reported in *CODA*; details from concert program.

63-0124   Archie Shepp-Bill Dixon Quartet
January 24, 1963   WBAI Studios: NYC

BD (t); Archie Shepp (ts and/or barsx); Don Moore (b); Howard McRae (d)

"Jazz in the Studio": fourth of 6 radio broadcasts; See also **62-1213**.

Dixon's compositions "Lonely Lovers", "Motif", and "Spheroid", premiered at the **R63-1119** Judson Hall concert were part of these later radio shows.

Listed in WBAI program guide.

R63-0207   Archie Shepp-Bill Dixon Quartet
February 7, 1963   WBAI Studios: NYC

BD (t); John Tchicai (as); Archie Shepp (ts and/or barsx); *probably* Don Moore
(b); *probably* J.C. Moses (d)

Metamorphosis	*excerpt*	1:04
Introspection	*excerpt*	2:26

Fifth episode of "Jazz in the Studio" live programs; see also **62-1213**.

"Metamorphosis" and "Introspection" were recorded at WBAI with an
instrumentation parallel to that above. It is not certain that they come from this
session, nor was an expanded instrumentation of the Shepp-Dixon Quartet announced
for any of the first five "Jazz in the Studio" events. However, it is likely that Tchicai
joined the group only after the Judson Hall concert (**R63-0119**), and certain that the
sixth episode of the WBAI series was given over completely to "Scandinavian
Sketches", which factors point to this broadcast as the most likely source of the
recording. The two very short excerpts appear on Dixon's Compilation tape A.
" 'Metamorphosis' started in 1962; the first version was done with Archie and me.
There's a tape of that. I think there were some sextet arrangements of it; I have some
of the manuscript. I used to write those things for Tchicai because he could play
those wide intervals; he wasn't a scalar player. When Archie and I had the group
together, I didn't write out parts. Everyone had the score, so it was easier to read; you
didn't have to count out anything. 'Metamorphosis' was one of the first pieces I did
that way."

This "Metamorphosis" shares only one common segment with the RCA Victor
recording of the piece: the long line theme of **R66-1010**'s section **C** was used in
this 1963 version as the A component in an AABA chorus construction.

[Alto saxophonist] "Sonny Simmons--shortly after coming to New York with with
Prince Lasha--heard a performance of the piece, probably before an audience, or
possibly one of the broadcasts. He came over to my house and we discussed it. I gave
him a lead sheet." Simmons later recorded a piece called "Metamorphosis" (for his
August 30, 1966 ESP-Disk record, *Staying On the Watch*) which contains a heavily
altered reduction of Dixon's "Metamorphosis" as its theme. That recording credits
Simmons as the composer.

Listed in WBAI program guide

R63-0221   Archie Shepp-Bill Dixon Augmented Quartet
February 21, 1963   WBAI Studios: NYC

BD (t); Archie Shepp (ts); Roswell Rudd (tb); Perry Robinson (cl); John Tchicai (as); Guy Hampton (ts); Lowell Slocum (barsx); Gary Newman, Jimmie Stevenson, Jr. (b); J.C. Moses (d)

Scandinavian Sketches		c60:00	
parts I-II	*excerpt*	1:12	BD rec
part III	*excerpt*	3:12	--
part IV		10:47	--
part V		18:40	--

Culminates "Jazz in the Studio"; see **62-1213a**.

The work was played for a full hour on the broadcast. Extant portions on tape include the last 30:00 and two very small segments of other themes from the first half of the piece. Those two composed excerpts appear on Dixon's compilation tape A, where the second half of the broadcast (two written sections and the solos that follow each) survives uninterrupted on a different tape. With the solo piano segment as part I of the composition--not performed at WBAI--the two excerpts would have to represent at least parts II and III, and the other tape at least parts IV and V.
Jorgen Frigård's article in *Politiken* reports that J.C. Moses should be credited as the vocalist, shouting "Freedom, Freedom".

An excerpt of the solo piano portion of this piece was included in Dixon's Compilation Tape B, introduced as follows: "['Scandinavian Sketches'] was done for the Radio Station in Stockholm when I made a tour there in 1962. Part one...is scored for piano." The piano section was not performed at WBAI, but Dixon played it at least once at the Cellar (He plays the piano part; see **R64-0830**).
Dixon's Account of Career shows a Stockholm performance from 1963, which is otherwise untraceable and of which Dixon has no knowledge; it may be in error.

Bill Wood (later professionally known as Vishnu Wood) was originally scheduled to be the other bassist, along with Stevenson. The information above has been altered to match the tape box personnel, with Newman instead. Likewise, Howard Johnson was slated to play baritone saxophone; he does not recall having made this performance, supporting the listing above. Hampton was an old friend of Sid McKay, and Dixon met him through that connection. Bassist Gary Newman played frequently with the emerging Archie Shepp-Bill Dixon Sextet.

Relative to this performance: "Those were the beginning stages in the music--we don't need to do that any more. Simply because you're excited and carrying on doesn't mean that much music is going down. You can hear where certain things are blocked out because there's <u>too much</u> enthusiasm (and then the musicians' singing along with the thing is distracting). But that's the way an artform evolves. It has to develop through these stages. Space wasn't something that anyone handled well in those days. These guys weren't thinking about the development of a new language; that all came from hindsight and analysis. They wanted to play and were not interested in playing tunes anymore.

"It's like being in a candy store in terms of the language, as if all of the sudden they don't need to speak only in the present tense--and then they go ape [shifting tenses unnecessarily]. The difference between what people think is this thing they call playing 'freely' and the reality of it is that the rules are more rigid. Playing chord changes is relatively easy compared to facing all of this limitless expanse of possibilities: What do you do?

"Common sense has to prevail: you find out what works and develop it. What doesn't work you have to immediately abandon or stay with it--like Coltrane did--to make it work.

Politiken (probably Copenhagen) "10 March 63" The article seems to have been filed on March 1 by Jorgen Frigård (a Danish correspondent posted in the U.S.). BD's translated copy of the article, however, registers Sunday, March 10 as the date of that issue; ad in *Village Voice* February 21, 1963, p. 7; also listed in WBAI program guide.

63-0420   ~~Archie Shepp Bill Dixon Sextet (?)~~
~~probably April, 1963~~   Stage 73: 321 East 73d Street, NYC

"We were close to the theater district in midtown, Manhattan, so when the theaters let out at night, people could come to these concerts where we might play from midnight until 5 or 6:00 in the morning. We played long; we didn't play sets. You needed another kind of place for that, and the places that made sense were the lofts near the theater district and the coffee houses next to the theaters. The owner would pay for a trio--piano, bass and drums--and then you had up to maybe forty other musicians who were going to play.

"Archie and I were trying to hold performances after the show. We had negotiated with Stage 73 for maybe a month about doing this thing, and at the last moment, we got bumped just when we were ready to go, because all of the sudden they put Liza Minelli out at the very beginning of her career." Based on Dixon's description, this must have been Minnelli's first recognized theater role, in Best Foot Forward which ran at the off-broadway Stage 73 from April 2 until October 13, 1963.

R63-0495   John Tchicai

spring, 1963   Apt. of John Benson Brooks: NYC

BD (t); John Tchicai (as); Jimmie Stevenson, Jr. (b); Sunny Murray (d)

For Helved, -1 ct	10:13	BD rec
For Helved, -2 fs	1:30	
For Helved, -3 ct	10:22	

Tchicai recorded this tape as an audition demo (submitted to program director Eric Salzman at WBAI) when he sought a radio performance or series under his own name. WBAI asked him for documentation of his work, and Tchicai set up the session to make such a tape. He enlisted Stevenson, Murray, and trumpeter Don Cherry to make the date. Dixon arranged the piece (and was the liaison with Brooks, who had good recording equipment), so he was on hand. When Cherry failed to appear, Dixon subbed on trumpet. Peggy Brooks's operation that day cut short the time for this recording. Brooks was living on the east side by this time, at 99 Lexington Avenue, the same location as R**62-0900**.

Tchicai's participation in **R63-0221** preceded and probably prompted his own petitions for a WBAI radio appearance. He eventually did at least two programs for WBAI (Thursdays June 27 and July 11, 1963, 8:15-9:15pm) and Dixon may also have appeared as a guest "toward the end of that series". The demo recording must then be later than **R63-0221** and earlier than the radio programs.

Tchicai broadcasts advertised in *Village Voice:* June 20, 1963, p. 20 and July 11, 1963, p. 10.

63-0515   Archie Shepp-Bill Dixon Quintet

May 15-18, 1963   Astor Place Playhouse: NYC

BD (t); Archie Shepp (ts); *probably* Don Moore and one other (b); *probably* Howard McRae (d)

434 Lafayette Street
Nightly concerts were scheduled for 8:40pm on May 15, 16, 17 (Wednesday-Friday), and two shows (9:00, 11:00pm) on Saturday May 18. Dixon recalls that only two nights may have happened. The event was one segment of a month-long series. $2.00 admission. Advertisement reads: "Muriel Morse Presents Jazz Concerts by..."

Candidates for the second bass here include Jimmie Stevenson and Gary Peacock.

ad from *Village Voice.*

63-0524   <u>Chameleon Dance Group</u>
May 24, 1963   Judson Hall: 165 West 57th St, NYC

BD (t and/or flgh); John Tchicai (as); Archie Shepp (ts); *possibly* Don Moore
and/or Alex Lane (b); *possibly* Charles Moffett, Sr. (d)

Barbara Bull, Sally Cohen, Dina Dahbany, Mimi Garrard, Mary McKay,
Elizabeth ("Betsy") Rasumny (movement)

          Rufus

Definitely a Friday sextet performance
The Chameleon group included the six dancers above and three assistants: Ann
Carlton, Meikel Guy, Wanda Pruska. $2.50 admission. 8:30 pm. See also **63-0606**

"Archie's 'Rufus' was a piece of material that he used and changed; it went through a
lot of permutations. I think the first complete version I heard was [here], because the
instrumentation was good. It was more of a saxophone piece, especially the way
Tchicai and Shepp played together, the sinuousness of the two saxophones."

John Tchicai had met up with the Shepp-Dixon combination in Scandinavia during
their 1962 trip there (**62-0725**). Coming to New York in the beginning of the
following year, Tchicai was asked to join the group, and by the spring of 1963
became a regular member of the ASBD Sextet.

"When Tchicai joined the group we added another bass player, so it became a sextet. I
wanted another bass player in there; I honestly can't tell you why I wanted to use two.
It may have been that the bassists we used all became free at the same time--who were
you going to choose? I don't think it was purely for artistic reasons. But with the
three-horn front line, it was too much for one bass player and a drummer. The two
basses gave a real balance. Alex Lane played like Scott LaFaro, but with a fuller
sound--if you could have both at the same time--and he could 'dance' more."

Details from concert program and announcement in *Village Voice* May 16 , 1963, p. 11.

63-0595   Archie Shepp-Bill Dixon Quintet
ca. May 1963   Five Spot, NYC

BD (t); John Tchicai (as); Archie Shepp (ts); Gary Peacock and *probably* Jimmie
Stevenson, Jr. (b); *probably* Charles Moffett, Sr. (d)

> Metamorphosis

A host of bassists filled the second chair in the new Shepp-Dixon Sextet, including
Bill Wood (now known as Vishnu Wood), Gary Newman, and probably Lewis
Worrell. Peacock may also have made other performances in the same timeframe.

Dixon played this event with "a frightening toothache".
"[Radio host] Les Davis had the Saturday Afternoon Jazz program at WBAI. Then he
started producing some Sunday afternoon concerts at the New Five Spot [St. Marks
Place. Contrary to Les Davis's recollection, *Village Voice* listings from the time
confirm that these sessions had begun by January 30, 1963 (2:30pm)]. The
Quartet/Sextet was getting ready to come to a close, and the New York Contemporary
Five was getting together. This was the one time we worked there." Dixon's account
matches Martin Williams' *down beat* report that "Peacock recently played a weekend
at the Five Spot with ...Shepp and...Dixon," pinpointing this as the same
engagement.
Davis citation: *Village Voice* January 24, 1963, p. 30; Martin Williams: "Gary Peacock and the
Beauties of Intuition" *down beat* June 6, 1963, p. 16.

63-0596   Archie Shepp-Bill Dixon Sextet
late spring 1963   Steve Kopovick's studio: 39th St., NYC

BD (t); Archie Shepp (ts); John Tchicai (as); Gary Newman and *probably*
Jimmie Stevenson, Jr. (b); unknown (d)

Kopovick, Irwin Goldstein, and Caesar _____ had a studio where "the sextet
functioned a lot. They took pictures and we played. We set up performances in their
lofts near the theater district where people could come by after the theaters let out; we
could play until five or six o'clock in the morning. Paul Chambers also used to come
in there."
Kopovick's Studio was on 39th between 5th and 6th--in the rapidly disappearing
hat-district.

63-0597   <u>Archie Shepp-Bill Dixon Sextet</u>
late spring 1963   a Clinton Street loft: NYC

BD (t); Archie Shepp (ts); John Tchicai (as); 2 unknown (b); Charles Moffett, Sr. (d)

LeRoi Jones reported in a *down beat* article that Dixon and Shepp were part of a lower east side underground loft bill that featured vocalist Earl Coleman and the Don Cherry/Billy Higgins/Henry Grimes combination.
Dixon: "There used to be a lot of concerts on Clinton Street. Cecil lived on Clinton Street at the time; he and I and a number of people used to go down there to play. Mobilization for Youth was down there; Edith Schomburg (who hosted talks at her home) was down there. In other words, because of the proximity of these places both to each other and to where a lot of dancers and musicians lived, there was a lot of activity there. Jones [cited below] is talking about a singular event, and there was a stream of similar musical activities going on."

Two other less definite situations illustrate the strange bedfellows created by Dixon and Shepp's working associations.
"There was a leftist group that Archie and I played for on the Lower East Side--occasionally on the weekend or weeknights. They would just have affairs for their members, get-togethers. They weren't dancing; they were talking the whole time we played. "

"Once we played for a Republican Club social event on 72d Street. We played there because someone had heard us play and hired us. Archie kept coming over and saying to me that a man was bugging him about playing 'My Melancholy Baby' or 'I Wish I Could Shimmy Like My Sister Kate'--real square stuff. I finally had to invite the guy to get off the stage. Of course, in those days we played our regular book."

LeRoi Jones "New York Loft and Coffee Shop Jazz" *down beat* May 9, 1963, p. 13 and 42; reprinted in Black Music (New York: William Morrow & Co [Apollo ed.]: 1968), p. 96.

63-0606   <u>Archie Shepp-Bill Dixon Quintet</u>
June 6, 1963   St. Marks-in-the-Bowerie Church: NYC

BD (t and/or flgh); Archie Shepp (ts); *probably* John Tchicai (as); others
unknown

Part of a series of events at the Church sponsored by the LENA (Lower Eastside
Neighborhoods Association: 119 Suffolk Street) that included films (by Jim Henson
and Shirley Clarke); dance (Chameleon group, see also **63-0524**); poetry; chamber
music; theatre; and "Jazz" in a program curated by Freddie Redd (including the groups
of J.R. Monterose, Randy Weston, Bobby Timmons, Dizzy Reece) on June 5; and
then The Shepp-Dixon Quintet, Jackie McLean, Jeremy Steig, Steve Lacy, Don Ellis,
and others scheduled for Thursday, June 6, 1963.
Village Voice Jazz reporter Rob Reisner reviewed what he identified as the second
night's performance, citing that Redd, Weston, and Monterose performed on <u>that</u>
bill, alongside Lacy, Booker Ervin, and "many newcomers". Shepp and Dixon are
presumed to have been counted in the last category; however, "a curfew left a large
knot of musicians who were anxious to play". Dixon was present for this event, but
<u>the group may not have actually performed</u>.
The same article announced that (presumably because of the overwhelming turnout)
free Wednesday night programs of Jazz would run throughout July, starting on the
10th; weekly concerts were held there in August as well). Yet a later article describes
the continuation of these St. Mark's Church events now under the sponsorship of the
periodical *Umbra* as the "Freedom North" arts festival ("saluting the Freedom
Movement and showcasing the works of Negro painters, sculptors, photographers,
poets, and musicians") with no further mention of LENA. On July 24 and 31, Jazz
events including Archie Shepp and Freddie Redd were to take place; it is not clear--but
quite possible--that the Shepp-Dixon group performed there. Dixon: "When we had
the Sextet we may have done <u>something</u> for *Umbra.*"

Details from program schedule; *Village Voice* May 30, 1963, p. 24; Rob Reisner "LENA and the
Jazzman"*Village Voice* July 4, 1963, p. 9-10; "Negro Arts Festival at St. Mark's"*Village Voice*
July 25, 1963, p. 15.

63-0624   <u>Archie Shepp Bill Dixon Sextet</u>
probably June 24, 1963   Living Theater, NYC

BD (t); Archie Shepp (ts); *probably* John Tchicai (as); 2 unknown (b); unknown (d)

"One of the last times that Archie and I played together, the Living Theater had a benefit for LeRoi Jones (when it was on 14th Street, near 6th Avenue), and Archie and I put the Sextet together. Don Cherry also played there with a group. It may have been sponsored by the *Evergreen Review.*"
According to an announcement of this benefit in the *Voice*, "[b]oth Jones and his wife are both recovering from hepatitis. Among the performers will be Jazz pianist Cecil Taylor, singer Anita Ellis, poet Frank O'Hara", etc.
Dixon: "That was one of the best performances that the group ever did. It was <u>electrifying</u>."

Nevertheless, By mid-1963, the embouchure change that Dixon had been undergoing since the Helsinki trip (**62-0725**) began to consume his playing altogether. "I had the problem and ignored it--in fact, I created my own embouchure problem. I was playing very well, except that I had difficulty when I tried to do certain things that I didn't normally do anymore. I wanted *everything* that I played to come to me easily: I don't know if that's realistic; it still doesn't happen today.
"I talked with a musician who advised me that I wasn't getting enough lip into the cup of the mouthpiece. So I tried that and--sure enough--it *seemed* to be better. It took a few days once I started to do it, but one day the first sound I got out of the horn was a C above high C. I said, 'Oh, wow--and this is all I had to do?' But after a few days of doing that I couldn't go <u>below</u> high C. Within the space of, say, ten days, I tried to get back to where I was before. I was halfway able to get back there, but one day I got up and couldn't play a damn thing. After going this way and then that way it threw the whole thing out. So that's what brought the problem on.
"I called Don Ellis and some other trumpet players, and then I called [trumpeter and teacher] Charles Colin, and all he said was, 'Put the horn underneath the bed and I'll see you Saturday.' He gave me these marvelous exercises, but it was going to take time."
For most of the rest of 1963 Dixon was not actively playing at all and concentrated instead on writing and arranging. In that period he also hosted a regular series of radio interviews with musicians and composers (see **X63-0899**).
Meanwhile, Shepp and Tchicai had begun to collaborate on their own; Tchicai laid plans for what became the main activity of their group the New York Contemporary Five, a residence in Copenhagen in September-November, 1963.
"Benefit for LeRoi Jones" *Village Voice* June 20, 1963, p. 5.

R63-0799   New York Contemporary Five
summer, 1963 STUDIO   NYC

BD (arr); Don Cherry (c); John Tchicai (as); Archie Shepp (ts); Don Moore (b);
J.C. Moses (d)

-2 omit Cherry

Rufus	Font 681 013ZL	
Trio	--	--
Sound Barrier *aka* Cisum	--	--
Rufus -2	Font 681 014ZL	
Wo Wo *aka* Hoppin' -2	--	--
For Helved -2	--	--

Fontana 681 013ZL, titled *Consequences*, reissued with the same title as 881 013 ZY
(Europe), SFON 7077 (Japan), 195J-25 (Japan), and [CD] PHCE 1001

Fontana 681 014ZL, titled *Rufus*, reissued with the same title as 881 014 ZY
(Europe), SFON 707? (Japan), 195J-26 (Japan), and [CD] PHCE 100?

Dixon wrote the book for and rehearsed the New York Contemporary Five in
preparation for the group's engagement at the Jazzhus Montmartre in Copenhagen;
see also **R63-0903** and **R63-1012**. Those preparations also included a
concert--apparently the group's debut--in New York August 17 at Harout's. In
addition to composing "Trio" and "Afternoon", he arranged many of the pieces in
their original repertoire on a commission from John Tchicai. Dixon conducted the
weekly rehearsals, often held at Tchicai's apartment [probably 150 East 46th Street].
"In those days John wrote these very sparse but rather attractive lines that lent
themselves to doing certain things--placing a cluster here, or inverting the melody
for a counterline. He would write these things and give them to me; I would then
arrange them, set the harmonies, and so forth. These pieces would have been the
material that he used [in the radio broadcasts cited in **R63-0395**]".

Most of the quintet recording session released on Fontana is believed to have been
made in New York on or around August 23, 1963, just prior to the group's departure.
That date was cited in text accompanying the *Rufus*, LP, which seems to have been
undertaken as a pilot for *Consequences*, or in Cherry's absence. The two records have
different sound characteristics, suggesting different sessions, rather than the first and
second halves of one date.
On the *Rufus* LP, "Wo Wo"--elsewhere explained as a nickname for Danish critic
Jorgen Frigård--was titled "Hoppin' ", and despite having only two horns uses the
relevant parts of Dixon's arrangement. The same is true for Shepp's piece "Rufus".
However, "The Funeral" as recorded at the same session omits Dixon's ensemble
introduction. The chart for "Sound Barrier/Cisum" is sometimes credited to Dixon
and sometimes to Don Cherry, its composer. Dixon identifies this as his
arrangement.

1968 Account of Career; Bill Dixon "Dixon Digs at Jones" *down beat* January 2, 1964, p. 6-7;
Harout's concert advertised in *Village Voice* August 15, 1963, p. 10.

R63-0903   New York Contemporary Five
fall, 1963 LIVE   Copenhagen

BD (arr); Don Cherry (c); John Tchicai (as); Archie Shepp (ts); Don Moore (b); J.C. Moses (d)

Afternoon		not recorded
Cisum *aka* Sound Barrier	11:10	Sonet LP 36
O.C.	6:40	-- --
The Funeral	5:05	-- --
Mik	7:30	-- --
Consequences	8:40	Sonet LP 51
Wo Wo	5:55	-- --
Trio	15:35	-- --
Ezz-thetic		uniss

Sonet LP 36 (Dk) was reissued as Polydor (UK) 623 235, Storyville (Dk) SLP 1010, and Delmark 409 (USA), titled *Archie Shepp In Europe, vol. 1*
Sonet LP 51 (Dk) was reissued as Polydor (UK) 623 267 and Storyville 1009

The NYC5 performed at Copenhagen's Jazzhus Montmartre from September 3 to November 15, 1963, making several radio braodcasts in the same timeframe. The group was recorded live at the Montmartre on November 15, 1963 at the close of its run there. All pieces above are from that recording.

In a 1968 *Jazz Monthly* interview, Tchicai reported that the proportion of Dixon's compositions and arrangements in the group's book declined throughout their stay in Scandinavia, which begins to explain their representation among the pieces on the Sonet recordings.

While it is not known to have been recorded, Dixon's composition "Afternoon" was certainly played on the trip.
Anthony Barnett "John Tchicai of Three Continents" *Jazz Monthly* October, 1968, p. 2-6.

R63-1012   New York Contemporary Five
October 12, 1963 et seq. FILM   Copenhagen

BD (arr); Don Cherry (c); John Tchicai (as); Archie Shepp (ts); Don Moore (b);
J.C. Moses (d)

Trio [film take]		soundtrack
Trio [rejected]		unissued
Consequences	7:40	Font 681 013ZL

Fontana 681 013ZL, titled *Consequences*, reissued with the same title as 881 013 ZY
(Europe), SFON 7077 (Japan), 195J-25 (Japan), and [CD] PHCE 1001

The "Trio" take from <u>Future One</u> was apparently the first of two versions from a
Copenhagen studio recording of October 12, 1963. Unbeknownst to Dixon and most
of the group's members, this piece was sold for use in the film directed by Nils Holt,
which also features visual footage of the group performing. The other take was
rejected.

The New York Contemporary Five made a final recording for Savoy (on the opposite
side of Dixon's **R64-0204**, nominally under Shepp's leadership) in early 1964, and
may have made its last public appearance at the Wildcat (224 West 29th Street, New
York) starting February 6, 1964. Mike Hames and Roy Wilbraham's *Don Cherry on
Disc and Tape* offers the most complete documentation of the group's known
recordings.

"Strictly Ad Lib" *down beat* January 16, 1964, p. 10; Wildcat advertised in *Village Voice*
February 4, 1964, p. 16; Mike Hames and Roy Wilbraham *Don Cherry On Disc and Tape* (UK:
printed privately by the authors, February 1980), p. 6-7.

R64-0204   Bill Dixon 7-tette
February 4, 1964   Savoy Records Studio: Newark

BD (t); Howard Johnson (tu, barsx -1); Ken McIntyre (as, oboe); George Barrow
(ts); David Izenzon, Hal Dodson (b); Howard McRae (d)

The 12th December		3:14	Sav MG 12184
Winter Song, 1964 -1		14:44	--

Savoy MG 12184=BYG 529.100 (Fr)=Realm Jazz RM52422 (UK),
Savoy MG 12184 titled *Bill Dixon 7-Tette/Archie Shepp and the New York
Contemporary Five*
BYG 529.100 (Fr) titled *Consequences*
The entire LP was reissued on Savoy SJL 2235, titled: *New Music: Second Wave*
The opposite side of all LPs above contains no Dixon items.
Date derives from notes to SJL 2235; December 1963 has also been postulated.

On at least the Savoy and BYG issues (and probably on all issues worldwide), the
titles of Dixon's compositions were mismatched: "Winter Song, 1964" (as correctly
attributed in the *down beat* publication of Dixon's manuscript for the score) is the
longer work including solos by Barrow, Dixon, McIntyre, Johnson, and eventually
Izenzon. "The 12th December" is a completely notated piece of much shorter
duration.

This is Dixon's first real play after his embouchure troubles. "The first record had
come out, and Savoy was pressing us to do a second one. That's the only reason it
was done then. Archie and I had the contract to do a second record [together]; it was
supposed to be a quartet or a sextet." In the interim, though, Shepp began giving
signals (including press profiles in which he spoke exclusively about other projects)
of beginning to withdraw from the partnership with Dixon. "Archie and I split up the
group, and I was stalling for as much time as I could get [to rebuild my embouchure]
before making the recording.
"Finally I thought I was ready. We'd rehearsed a lot, but going into the studio I could
not do any second takes. There were false starts, but no complete ones. We had a
couple of problems getting started and I could feel my strength going. Ultimately I
had to call upon everything I knew to get through that. If you'll notice my sound
wasn't quite as secure as it might have been."

down beat reported before the recording date that Dixon was preparing the music for
two Savoy records. Though the company had such designs, there were never any
formal plans to hold another session after this one. Dixon later redirected Savoy's
eagerness for more music, taking the opportunity to record some of his students'
work (see **U67-0300** et seq.).

"After that record date, when I started freelancing, I needed things to do to make
money. I can transcribe, so I began to transcribe Savoy's gospel music to create lead
sheets so they could register the copyright for new recordings."
The full score to "Winter Song, 1964" was published in *down beat* May 24, 1964, p. 39-42;
"Strictly Ad Lib" *down beat* January 2, 1964, p. 43.

CHAPTER THREE

The Guild 1964–1965

64-0295   <u>Cecil Taylor Unit and guests</u>
Winter, 1964   Take 3 Coffee House: NYC

BD (t); *possibly* Roswell Rudd (tb); Jimmy Lyons (as); Albert Ayler (ts); Carla Bley, Paul Bley, Cecil Taylor (p); Gary Peacock (b); Sunny Murray (d)

The Take 3 was at 149 Bleecker St.
"I remember one night, we [the musicians above, and others] were all sitting in and I think we split ten dollars; we each got something like 75 cents. The place became a headquarters for the new music: we were playing off the door's proceeds from selling this vile cup of coffee, so naturally the owner didn't tell us what to play."

Cecil Taylor played copiously at the Take 3 before and after his fall, 1962 trip to Europe. The presence of Ayler in New York, however, limits the date of this event to after late 1963. Assuming that the group was Taylor's, its regular members would have been Lyons and Murray, with Ayler a frequent sitter-in. The presence of Peacock and Paul Bley apparently prefigures the Peacock-led trio that worked at the Take 3 for a month starting in the third week of January, 1964. The Billy Higgins-Don Cherry Quartet's early March appearance at the club to unveil their "bright new musical revue" *You're Not Listening* probably postdates the period that Dixon describes.

When Charles Lloyd was selected as the newest "discovery" of George Avakian at Columbia Records, Lloyd approached Dixon about writing the music for his first record. Dixon: "At that time, I had to decide whether I wanted to do something like that: it would have given me a little bit of money, but wasn't going to help me. In the end I had to tell him that I wasn't going to do it.

"That was around the same time that George Russell asked me to join his group." Russell said that he didn't work enough to keep a group constantly employed but wanted Dixon, Don Cherry, Thad Jones, and Al Kiger each to have a copy of his book and be on call for jobs. "The day before he asked me, I had said to myself, 'I've got to decide whether I can wait for calls from these cats and just keep playing or [make a commitment to do just my own music]' Then the next day George called me and I had already made up my mind. I had to agonize about the decision, but once I made it, I never went back."

Peacock in *Village Voice* January 16, 1964, p. 8; Higgins-Cherry ad in *Village Voice* March 5, 1964, p. 14.

64-0500   Bill Dixon

ca. May, 1964   NYC

unknown musicians

down beat reported that Dixon had been commissioned to write the soundtrack for a film about the NYC garment industry, also citing that "a string quartet and a Jazz Combo are to play it".
The film never came fully into fruition; it may have been shot but was never edited, and the music may or may not have been recorded. It is also unclear whether Dixon planned to play in the piece.

"Strictly Ad Lib" *down beat* May 7, 1964, p. 42.

The Cellar
Spring, 1964   Cellar Cafe: 251 West 91st Street, NYC

After the time of embouchure troubles had passed by early 1964, Dixon became
involved in playing and programming events at the Cellar Cafe. A fuller picture of
his associations with the artistic operations of the venue is presented in
U64-0414 et seq.
John Gilmore, Pat Patrick, Marshall Allen, Barre Phillips, Lewis Worrell, David
Izenzon*, Cameron Brown, the poet Hart Leroy Bibbs, Calvin Newborn[e] (g), and
Midge Pike (b) are known to have worked in Dixon's performances at the club. Some
other Dixon groups of that period (not necessarily at the Cellar) used Brian Trentham
(tb) and Steve Swallow (b).

*David Izenzon's ancestors spelled their family name thus. By the first United
States-born generation in his family, the name had been anglicized to "Izenson", but
early in the bassist's professional career he chose to revert to the original spelling,
which is used exclusively in this volume.

Many of Dixon's Cellar Cafe performances were recorded, though none of the full
recordings of them are currently at hand, if they still exist at all. Later in the Sixties
he prepared a tape of excerpts from recent works to submit as a portfolio, and that
tape survives, providing small glimpses of the Cellar events of 1964.
"All of the pieces on [Compilation Tape B, i.e. **U64-0395**, **R64-0816**,
R64-0830, **R64-1003**, and **R64-1228**] were rehearsed while I was living on
103d Street. [One reason for compiling it was that] at that time I was very much
interested in having an opportunity to write for television. I had to have something
to show, and this tape was what I later on sent independently to several agencies.
The only nibble that I got was from one person who told me that I could write
incidental music for radio shows: they would give you an instrumentation, you would
write the music, they'd record it, and you'd be paid. You never got credit for the
music. I decided I didn't want to go that route.
"I used to see a lot of things on television I wouldn't have minded writing--I wasn't
interested in playing for television, nor even remotely interested in writing jingles.
I wanted to write for instrumentations beyond piano, bass and drums, to make some
money, and to do it in a place where I could feel comfortable."

64-0628   Bill Dixon Quartet

June 28, 1964   Cellar Cafe: 251 West 91st Street, NYC

Bill Dixon (t and/or flgh); others (likely saxophone, b, and d) unknown

In order to avoid using Dixon's name, this 4:00pm concert was billed as "The Jazz
Quartet". For the first few months of his association with the Cellar, Dixon was
involved in a transitional moment in his personal life and preferred not to be
identified in the advertising, even for his own performances. "One day I abruptly
moved up to 103d Street. So for a while I had the apartment uptown and the one on
Bank Street simultaneously.
"Having no money, I went to Savoy and got an advance on the transcription work I
was doing there. For the first few weeks after that, I couldn't do anything except try
to pay Savoy back the money, so I was working night and day, 12 to 16 hours at a
stretch. I lived off tea and raisin cake my first month. By the time I met [Cellar
operator] Peter Sabino I couldn't use my name."
Sabino therefore concocted nondescript billings for Dixon's first few appearances at
the club as a leader. "I eventually decided it was time for me to do a concert and he
listed it that way; I never would have referred to myself that way. [He was presented
under the headings "Great Jazz Trumpeter" and "The Jazz Quartet in Concert" in
addition to the August 2 billing] It was amazing: I got as many people to come to my
concerts when they didn't know who I was, as when I was using my name. That was
what impressed Peter Sabino, and we started talking about getting a liquor license and
doing the October Revolution. By **R64-0816** this gave way to advertising that
made no secret of Dixon's identity.
Advertised in *Village Voice* June 25, 1964, p. 12.

64-0775   Peter Sabino

mid-1964   Cellar Cafe: 251 West 91st Street, NYC

BD (t); others unknown

Peter Sabino (director); Steve Press, John Schmerling (reading)

    War in 5 Part Harmony

Sabino selected the texts, settings, set, and arrangement of parts for this closely
scripted multi-media work. It entailed the above voices reading excerpts collected
from *The War Years* (a compendium of diaries and letters written home by American
soldiers in World War II), Sabino's writing, and the poetry of Siegfried _____, all
alternating or coincident with Dixon's music, pre-recorded war sound effects, use of
gun-props by other participants, and the screening of John Huston's once-outlawed
wartime documentaries, The Battle of San Pietro and probably Let There Be Light.

The guitarist Calvin Newborn[e] may have taken part in this event.
Isidor F. Stone *The War Years 1939-1945* (New York: Little Brown, 1988).

64-0799   Bill Dixon
July, 1964   Cellar Cafe: 251 West 91st Street, NYC

BD (t, flgh); *probably* Giuseppi Logan (as); others unknown

        The Lavender Ladies

The only known reference to this performance comes from Dixon's spoken
introduction to the excerpt of "The Lavender Ladies" on his Compilation Tape B,
where he describes the piece as "an extended dance suite in three parts. It was first
performed at the Cellar Club in July of 1964." However, Dixon believes in retrospect
that there was never a dance component to the work.

64-0802   Bill Dixon Quartet
August 2, 1964   Cellar Cafe: 251 West 91st Street, NYC

Bill Dixon (t and/or flgh); others (likely saxophone, b, and d) unknown

For the same reasons given in in **64-0628**, this event was billed without using
Dixon's name. Instead, the advertising read: A JAZZ CONCERT that few will ever get
a chance to hear again, with an IMPORTANT JAZZ TRUMPETER at..."
4:00pm

Advertised in *Village Voice* July 30 , 1964, p. 14.

R64-0816   <u>Bill Dixon Quintet</u>

August 16, 1964   Cellar Cafe: 251 West 91st Street, NYC

BD (t); *probably* Giuseppi Logan (as); unknown (ts), (b), (d)

Advise and Consent		BD rec
part one *excerpt*	2:00	

The excerpt of part one appears on Dixon's Compilation tape B. This was Dixon's first Cellar performance for which his own name was used.

"At the time, Giuseppi Logan was 'studying' with me, meaning: he wanted to know certain things, and I needed an alto saxophone player, so he played all of my concerts, and occasionally I would let him have some of his things played in the group. He had a great deal of difficulty with getting people to play his music. I think at the time I was the only trumpet player who could play his music, and I loved playing it.
"No one sounded in an ensemble like Giuseppi. He held his head back all the way, explaining once, 'This way my throat is completely open,' so he could have more air coming through his windpipe. He used to pride himself on playing up to the fourth octave on alto. The things that made him different as an improviser were the way he placed his notes, that sound he got, and then what the others in his group played behind him. His pieces were very attractive for those reasons. Giuseppi had his own points of view about music, which is what this music is supposed to be about. We got along."

"While I lived on 103d Street I had a garden apartment where we rehearsed out in the open air. I would finish something at these rehearsals and then go down to the Cellar and play it, because it was just a few blocks away. (This is before I had complete access to rehearse in the Cellar, but I could rehearse any time I wanted in my house).
"I was using alto (Logan) and tenor saxophone (probably Bob Ralston or Joe Farrell), sometimes trombone (It must have been Gary Porter), and myself on trumpet. We rehearsed music specifically for performances, either at the Cellar [or for such things as the theater production described below]. I never wanted to do something and then go hunt for a player. The thinking instead was: *Who do I have ? Will this be able to be done?* I remember one piece--done once or twice up at the Cellar--for four or five horns; I can't think of the name. Otherwise, to get that many parts, I would use the bowed bass. In fact if you talk with Reggie Johnson, he would let you know that I practically taught him how to bow. I used the bass as a baritone voice, not just walking time. I didn't do the traditional unison horns with the rhythm section separate. After a while I always had a mass of sound, even the way the drums were used--to have them accenting or filling in <u>parts</u>.

"There was a theater director whose wife was an old radio actress living in a nearby building. They heard us rehearsing one day through the air shaft between the buildings and went knocking on doors to find out who in the hell was playing that music. I think they said they had looked for two days. The husband was a Kafka person; he was doing a Kafka piece, and this sound was what they wanted for a production." After introductions, it was proposed that Dixon score the music for that

upcoming Equity Actors production, which may have led to Dixon writing "Spectra".
"[The piece they heard] would not have been "Spectra", but it must have had a sound
like that. 'All the King's Women' [O64-0395] had the same kind of sound, which
allowed a lot of latitude.
"We had three or four rehearsals for this Equity Actors' thing, but I don't think we
ever did a performance. I don't know why it was never done. I was very suspicious of
theater people, but they were legitimate."
Advertised in *Village Voice* August 13 , 1964, p. 10.

R64-0830   Bill Dixon Group
August 30, 1964   Cellar Cafe: 251 West 91st Street, NYC

Bill Dixon (t and/or flgh, p); others (likely at least saxophone, b, and d)
unknown

   Scandinavian Sketches   *excerpt*   2:30   BD rec

The "Scandinavian Sketches" recording might logically have come from **64-0802**,
R64-0816, or this August 30 event. The excerpt appears on Dixon's Compilation
Tape B.
"Part one of 'Scandinavian Sketches' was scored for unaccompanied piano, and part
two for the ensemble. This tape of the solo piano part was made at the Cellar. The
whole piece was never performed; the largest part of it was done at WBAI
(**63-0221**), and part of it here. That was it. I don't know why I never finished it
really, but these two parts comprised the entire piece."
One possible reason was that "eventually the instrumentation became too unwieldy; I
would have never been able to pay for a group as big as the WBAI 'expanded Quartet'"

"At the Cellar, I would perform anything that I was working on. 'Scandinavian
Sketches' had been commissioned for Swedish Radio. When George Russell wrote
commissions, he would write for the Radio Orchestra, and that's what everybody else
did. I wasn't writing for the Swedish Radio Orchestra, but for any instrumentation. I
later found out that the person I had been dealing with actually didn't have the power
to commission works. I was paid, but this was a minor official. So they never really
even got a copy of it. Somehow people in Sweden knew about the piece, but parts
were never turned in to them.
"During that time, Swedish Radio had an office on 6th Avenue in the 40s. I had a
connection there and used to periodically go up and do [spoken] broadcasts for them
on what I was doing in music. It was a very small operation. This was all because of
that one trip I had made in 1962; Bertil Sundin [whom Dixon met on that visit] may
have had something to do with that. When I finished a piece of music I would go up
there and discuss it."
Advertised in *Village Voice* August 2 , 1964, p. 110.

64-0990   <u>Barbara Holland-Bill Dixon-Peter Lurie</u>
mid-1964   Cellar Cafe: 251 West 91st Street, NYC

BD (t); Peter Lurie (p);
Barbara Holland (reading)

The music to this "multimedia assault piece" was played live; Holland read an epic
poem that she had written.
Dixon had met Lurie at the Cellar, where they played duets informally.

R64-1003   *October Revolution in Jazz*: Bill Dixon Sextet
October 3, 1964   Cellar Cafe: 251 West 91st Street, NYC

BD (t and/or flgh); Giuseppi Logan (as, and other winds); Bob Ralston (ts); Gary
Porter (tb); Reggie Johnson (b); Rashied Ali (d)

-2: BD (flgh); Reggie Johnson (b)

Spectra		*excerpt*	1:36	BD rec
Trio	part one	*excerpt*	1:48	--
Trio	part two -2	*excerpt*	1:21	--
Song for Children				
Serendipity				

The well-known *October Revolution in Jazz* concert series was curated by Bill Dixon.
A complete schedule of appearances at the four nights appears as **U64-1001**
through **U64-1004**. Dixon's Sextet was scheduled to go on at 11:00pm.

The excerpts of "Spectra" and "Trio" were included in Dixon's Compilation Tape B.
"Spectra" was reported in *The Villager*, perhaps indicating that it was to be performed
on **R64-1003**. The article cites the piece as the commissioned soundtrack to a
Swedish film that would play in the U.S. in 1965. Dixon in 1996 has no recollection
of the film or the commission, but supports the notion that it could have been played
at the October Revolution. His spoken introduction to the piece from Compilation
Tape B clarifies: "Spectra...was used for the music to Kafka's The Trial in a version
which was done in one of the coffeehouses in Greenwich Village three years ago [with
the above instrumentation]. It was also performed at the Cellar Club on 91st Street in
October of 1964". See also **R65-0526**.

The two takes of "Trio" are likewise not cited directly to the *October Revolution*, but
to the same location, month, and year. "I don't remember what I played in my set at
the October Revolution; 'Trio' could very well have been one of the pieces. It was
done a myriad of ways even into the Cellar years--that [uptempo version in the
excerpt of part one] is one of the more radical ways." Assuming that the very subdued
part two excerpt comes from the same concert, this would truly be an extreme reading
of the piece.

"Song for Children" was cited in draft correspondence with Alan Bates of Fontana
Records.

The only evidence for "Serendipity" having come from this concert is in Dixon's
1968 Account of Career.

The Villager September 24, 1964.

64-1030   Bill Dixon Sextette
October 30-31, 1964   61 4th Avenue: NYC

BD (t and/or flgh); Giuseppi Logan (as); Bob Ralston (ts); Reggie Johnson (b);
Rashied Ali (d)

Part of the "Pre-Halloween Jazz Party" put on by the newly formed Jazz Composers
Guild; see **U 64-1030** for additional groups performing and the pages preceding that
entry for a discussion of the foundations of the Guild. The venue was the loft home of
vibraphonist Ollie Shearer.

According to *down beat*, Dixon was to have led "a 10 piece group" in a program of
pieces by Cecil Taylor, Morton Feldman, and Charles Wittenberg in performances at
Columbia, Brown, and Rutgers Universities in the late fall of 1964; these concerts
never took place.

ad in *Village Voice* October 29, 1964. "Strictly Ad Lib" *down beat* December 16, 1964, p. 42
University concerts listed in "Strictly Ad Lib" *down beat* October 8, 1964; *The Villager* September
24, 1964; *BMI The Many Worlds of Music* November 1964.

64-1107   Bill Dixon 7-tette
November 7, 1964   Cellar Cafe: 251 West 91st Street, NYC

BD (t); Gary Porter (tb); Robin Kenyatta or Giuseppi Logan (as); Bob Ralston
(ts); others unknown

>   Metamorphosis [I]   c.30:00
>   The Lavender Ladies

Robin Kenyatta supposedly performed in the first "The Lavender Ladies" (**64-0799**)
but he is thought not to have entered Dixon's group until **R64-1228**, q.v.

The possible bassist(s) on this 8:00-11:00pm engagement include Reggie Johnson,
Barre Phillips, Lewis Worrell, David Izenzon, and Cameron Brown. The drummer may
have been Rashied Ali, Charles Moffett, Sr., or another musician.
Dixon's later accounts-of-career cite this as a Contemporary Center performance, but
are presumed instead to indicate this November 7 Cellar performance. Although the
Cellar program was in its waning days and the Guild using several alternative venues,
it is not likely that there were any JCG events at the Contemporary Center in 1964.
Archie Shepp's group was also scheduled to perform the same weekend. See text
following **U64-1231**.

"Strictly Ad Lib" *down beat* December 16, 1964, p. 42; *Village Voice* November 5, 1964, p. 12.

R64-1228   *Four Days in December*: Bill Dixon Quintet
December 28, 1964   Judson Hall: 165 West 57th St, NYC

BD (t and/or flgh); Robin Kenyatta (as); Bob Ralston (ts); Reggie Johnson (b);
Rashied Ali (d)

Serendipity		20:42	BD rec
Song for Children		19:26	--
Lavender Ladies	*excerpt*	:54	--

A 4:52 "Serendipity" excerpt also appeared on Dixon's Compilation Tape B, where
he introduced the sample as "short selections of parts A&B". Indeed, there are two
different composed themes that seem to flow with no edits.

Dixon's and Cecil Taylor's groups played on the opening night of the *Four Days in
December* concert series, December 28-31, 1964. The series schedule was solidified
by mid-November and advertised then in the *Village Voice*, in addition to the
citations below. The remainder of the performances are shown in **U64-1228**
through **U64-1231**.
Giuseppi Logan, the regular altoist in Dixon's group at that time had injured his arm
or hand and could not play--hence Kenyatta's appearance, his first with Dixon.
Dixon was introduced to Kenyatta (then playing uptown with Pucho and his Latin
Soul Brothers) through Louis Brown. Kenyatta became such an effective part of the
group as Logan was recovering that the latter never rejoined Dixon's outfits.

Hugo DeCraen and Eddy Janssens postulated in their *Marion Brown Discography* that
Brown played with Dixon's group in this series. Brown played with Archie Shepp's
group on December 30 in the festival, and conceivably also **U64-1108**, but was
n o t in Dixon's group at this or any time.

Dixon hired Jerry Newman to record his set. As there had been no other provision
made for documenting the series, Newman was engaged on the spot to record the
remaining performances of the festival.

Dixon apparently launched a brief and fruitless negotiation with Alan Bates (then
representing Polydor and Fontana Records) for an "80 minutes of music=2 LPs"
release of the above three pieces. The proposal fell through due to Dixon's
dissatisfaction with Fontana's (lack of) terms and the way the company undertook
other releases of music by Guild artists (Carla Bley, Shepp, the Jazz Composer's
Orchestra, Paul Bley, the New York Art Quartet, etc.).

On the day before the *Four Days In December* began [Sunday, 2:00pm], Dixon had
been the master of ceremonies at a Village Gate benefit for the periodical

Freedomways, at which Len Chandler, Max Roach, and Abbey Lincoln and John Coltrane appeared. Dixon did not perform.

Bob Zelman "Harmonic Highlights" from *Columbia Daily Spectator*, early 1965; Ad in *Village Voice* December 10, 1964, p. 22 and December 17, 1964, p. 16; *New York Times* December 29, 1964, p. 21; *down beat* February 11, 1965 p. 37-8; *Nation* February 8, 1965, p.149-50; *New Yorker* February 27, 1964; Hugo DeCraen and Eddy Janssens: *Marion Brown Discography* (Brussels: New Think Publications, 1985), p. 1; *Freedomways* benefit ad in *Village Voice* December 17, 1964, p. 22; John S. Wilson "Avant Garde Series Offers Cecil Taylor and Dixon Quintet" *New York Times* December 29, 1964, p. 21.

64-9090   Bill Dixon-Cecil Taylor-Ornette Coleman
Late 1964   11th Street, NYC

BD (t); Cecil Taylor (p); Ornette Coleman (vln)

As described in *L'Opera*, this was an impromptu performance during Coleman's "retirement" from playing in public, and around the time that he was approached by Dixon and Taylor about endorsing the philosophy and activities of the Jazz Composers' Guild. The three met and played briefly in a triplex apartment on West 11th Street that had been loaned to Coleman. Bud Powell's presence to witness this event limits the date to after August, 1964, when he returned to the United States, and Coleman's January, 1965 re-emergence limits it at the other end.
Coleman refused to assist the Guild and referred obliquely to the organization's entreaties in interviews of the time: "I have nothing against being useful in a group--political or whatever--but if they were looking for the same thing I am, there wouldn't have to be a group."

Dixon: "What the Guild wanted from John Coltrane was different: I wanted Trane and his group not to go to work. I was calling a strike of every club in New York that had any music called 'Jazz' played in it, and I wanted to do it for a weekend. I wanted to let club owners know that if these cats weren't playing in their places, then they were just bars. After [his support didn't come through] the idea was abandoned. It wouldn't have worked unless there was a figure like John Coltrane to go along with it. They didn't want *avant garde* players in the places anyway."
See also **U64-1014**.

L'Opera p. 76; Coleman interviewed by Dan Morgenstern "Ornette Coleman from the Heart" *down beat* April 8, 1965, p. 18.

R65-0295   Bill Dixon-Alan Silva Trio
probably early 1965   NYC

BD (t and or flgh); Alan Silva (b); Bob Fuhlrod (d)

Unknown #1	8:14	BD rec
Unknown #2	4:14	--
Unknown #3	4:26	--

Fuhlrod played with a red light bulb inside his bass drum.
This live recording comes from an intimate setting, probably a coffee house and
definitely in New York City.

"Alan wanted to study, and under the guise of a teaching situation we began to do
these duets. We worked on a weekly basis for a time--no publicity--in small coffee
houses and possibly art galleries in the Village. We played on a small scale, in front
of maybe 30 or 40 people. It was under the underground.

"When Alan and I first started to play together, he could never play the same way
twice. I would say 'Could you play that again?' 'I don't think so, man'. The tape
recorder for us was the key; [what was recorded] was the composition."

65-0319   Bill Dixon Septet

March 19-20, 1965   Contemporary Center: 180 7th Av NYC

BD (t); Gary Porter (tb); *probably* Robin Kenyatta (as); Bob Ralston (ts); others unknown

From the eleventh weekend that the Guild presented music in 1965. 9:00pm Personnel for this group is assumed similar to that of **64-1107** (and therefore to have evolved from the situation described in **64-0816**). The repertoire may also relate to those sources.

"To show you the kind of attention we attracted, I remember when Miles Davis's Quintet was playing downstairs at the Vanguard, Herbie Hancock, Tony Williams, and Wayne Shorter were upstairs at our concert, and Miles had to send for them when his set started." Davis's performance may have coincided with this Guild concert or another earlier in the winter.

"I was having less and less to do with the Guild, but it hadn't folded yet. Like anything else, once you see that you can't do anything about a certain situation, you can't stand around and lament that. I had more interest in the thing than they did. Now, you could say I had more vision, or I was more stubborn, or there weren't as many people interested in my work so I had more to invest in this organization--you could look at it any way you want. After a while I had to cut it loose. I was very sick--physically--during those days; I was clearly the only one suffering from the whole thing. But in all of the time I was going through that stuff, I never missed a day of practice. Otherwise I could have sat up there and been a politico... I wasn't about to stop playing, because I had been doing that long before the Guild. But I had to decide what I could do."

This was probably Dixon's last performance in NYC before leaving for a respite in Chicago as the Guild began to collapse. "Chicago was having its worst cold spell in 100 years; I took the train." He spent most of a month in Chicago to clear his head, with no contacts and no agenda. He returned to his Bank Street address after the trip. See also the Guild discussion following **U64-1004**.

Village Voice March 18, 1965, p. 24.

R65-0409   <u>Jazz Composers Guild Orchestra</u>
April 9-11, 1965   Contemporary Center: 180 7th Av NYC

BD (cond, arr); Mike Mantler (t); Roswell Rudd (tb); Perry Robinson (cl); Steve
Lacy (ss); Ed Curran, Robin Kenyatta, Jimmy Lyons (as); Ken McIntyre (as,
bcl); Bob Carducci (ts); Fred Pirtle (barsx); Kent Carter, Steve Swallow (b);
Barry Altschul (d)

The Lonely People *rehearsal*   44:47   BD rec

This Friday-through-Sunday (10:00pm) series presented works-in-progress by Dixon
and other Guild composers. The first two days' "workshop performances" (i.e., open
rehearsals) led up to a concert on Sunday. Dixon's rehearsal recording comes from
Saturday night, on which Bley read through her piece first, and Dixon next,
concluding near 2:00am Sunday.
The personnel listed matches that of the rehearsal recording except that
Kenyatta--definitely present at the Sunday performance--was apparently absent for
the Saturday rehearsal. Personnel cited in *down beat*, however, applies to a general
schema for the JCG orchestra and the other pieces in the series. See also
U65-0409. Dixon played only to demonstrate to Mantler during the workshop
element.

This was almost certainly Dixon's last involvement with the Jazz Composers' Guild.
"The remaining members of the Guild invited me to do this: I think everyone knew
that it was going to be my last stand with them. I had sketched out some of the
orchestra ideas, and one of my goals was to be able to get a tape of the music. The
instrumentation was a marvelous one."
"The Lonely People" was not fully realized at the Saturday rehearsal, but recorded
evidence supports the placement of this score as a natural developmental step
between Dixon's earliest recorded orchestral projects (**R63-0221** and **R64-0204**)
and the more fully evolved "Metamorphosis 1962-66" (**R66-1010**).

The activites of the Bley/Mantler orchestra continued even after the breakup of the
Guild, under the names "Jazz Composer's Orchestra" and later "Jazz Composers
Orchestra Association". In 1971, Dixon conducted an open workshop for the latter
incarnation (**R71-0329**). See **U64-1229** for an explanation of the Jazz
Composers Guild Orchestra and **U64-1231** about the Guild's activities at the
Contemporary Center.
"Strictly Ad Lib" *down beat* May 20, 1965, p.11; *BMI Many Worlds of Music* July, 1965; The
Jazz Composer's Orchestra [uncredited article] *Jazz Monthly* July 1968, p. 7.
One line from Dixon's score for this piece is printed in *L'Opera* p. 18.
Peter Sabino photographed the Sunday performance.

R65-0526   Bill Dixon Ensemble
May 26, 1965   Theatre East: 211 E 60th Street, NYC

BD (flgh, t); Bennie Maupin (ts, bcl); Alan Silva (b); Roger Blank (d)
another musician and a trombone are visible in the film.

Barbara Holland (reading an epic poem)
Actors included Arnold Johnson, Crystal Field, Jack Aaron, and a well-known
actress visiting from Mexico, Jana _____

      The Trial *excerpt*   Wealth of A
      No Exit *excerpt*   Nation
      Blood Wedding? *excerpt*
      UNKNOWN

The multi-media work *Images* used a scene excerpted from each of the above theater
works, with actors reading the parts, and film projections.
Film footage of this performance was included in William Greaves's film, *Wealth of
a Nation*, **R65-0695**. "Bill Greaves had originally come to the Cellar and wanted to
film there but couldn't, so he filmed at Theatre East, a children's theater. It was small
and intimate--a beautiful little theater. I rented the place myself.
"We must have rehearsed a month--I think at Edith Stephen's studio--for this one
night. The original group was Silva, Rashied Ali, and maybe Ken McIntyre. When I
finished the last planned rehearsal the night before the performance, I wanted one
more. The rest of the guys said they weren't going to make another one before the
performance; I didn't say a word. When they left I got on the phone, got a new band,
and rehearsed it the day of the concert for 12 hours. So I had two bands show up; the
old band was not allowed in."

The performance entailed a mating of many media and levels of activity. Dixon's is
the prominent name in the advertising; the ensemble was featured in segments
between works by Lorca, Sartre, Kafka, and Barbara Holland. Lawrence Sacharow (see
R65-0816) directed the actors. Holland had also written an epic poem that was to
be recited. Including this and **59-0000**, Dixon has set music for at least 3 No Exits.
" 'Spectra' may have been used in the version [of The Trial] done at *Images*. I don't
see myself having written something else. That was a long work." See also
R64-1003.
John Murray, subsequently with WOR radio, co-produced the *Images* event. Dixon
had met Murray at the White Whale Coffee Shop.

Advertisement in *Village Voice* May 13, 1965, p. 26. *Villager* September 24,1964; "Strictly Ad
Lib" in *down beat* July 1, 1965, p. 15 refers to this concert in the past tense.

R65-0695   Bill Dixon Ensemble
late Spring, 1965   unknown studio: NYC

BD (flgh, p, celeste, possibly also t); unknown [see below] (tb); *probably* John Gilmore (bcl); Marshall Allen (as, oboe); Alan Silva (b); Roger Blank (d, tympani)

Wealth of a Nation   20:44   16mm film

Dixon's boyhood classmate (now filmmaker) William Greaves commissioned him to write the soundtrack to his film Wealth of a Nation, originally titled The Dissenters, made for the United States Information Agency. The work was circulated to embassies worldwide, translated into dozens of languages, and given international awards. However, it was considered a propaganda film for export only and could not be screened in the US. Greaves's film deals with "the importance of freedom of individual expression in human society."

Unable to project film in the recording studio, Dixon measured the music segments with a stopwatch and metronome.
Marshall Allen's line for oboe near the end of the film is completely notated.
The trombonist may have been Mark Weinstein, Brian Trentham, Gary Porter, or a member of the Sun Ra Arkestra, but was none of the following: Ali Hassan, Ted Nance, Garnett Brown, Jonas Gwangwa, Kiane Zawadi [formerly Bernard McKinney], Bernard Pettaway. Hugo DeCraen and Eddy Janssens's *Marion Brown Discography* notwithstanding, Brown appears in none of the film, nor of its audio track.
In addition to providing the studio soundtrack, Dixon was also featured in the film as one of Greaves's examples of self-determination and individuality. That profile entailed sync-sound footage from the *Images* concert (**R64-0526**); Dixon's music for the film's incidental score was performed separately. Greaves's final version of the film used only a fraction of the total amount of music recorded at the soundtrack sessions (or, for that matter, the concert) and few of the passages of music are left unobstructed by narration or the other sound layers.

As is the case with the many other films he made for the USIA, Greaves is certain that the audiovisual outtakes from Wealth of A Nation were turned over to the Agency. He believes by 1997 that they have since been destroyed.

BMI Many Worlds of Music, May, 1965 and "Strictly Ad Lib" *down beat* June 3, 1965, p. 9 (both announcing the commission); Hugo DeCraen, Eddy Janssens *Marion Brown Discography* Brussels: New Think, 1985, p. 27.

R**65-0695**   Herb Golzmane-Bill Dixon
mid 1965 or earlier   New York City

BD (flgh)

New York Collage   16mm film

This was the soundtrack to an 8 minute film by Herb Golzmane (his name is correctly spelled thus), who had been Dixon's upstairs neighbor on Bank Street.

Some of Golzmane's films were screened in New York at Movie Subscription, 244 Horatio Street on July 30, 1965. It is not known whether New York Collage was among them. No print of the film has been located. Dixon probably scored for another of his films, and it is likely that Alan Silva appears on that soundtrack.

Golzmane's film was miscited in Keith Thompson's "Bill Dixon: Too Long In the Background" *Pieces of Jazz* (1970) 106-108. Golzmane directed this film and not direct Future One. That film was made in Denmark by Nils Holt. See **R63-1012**.

R**65-0797**   Maxine Haleff-Edith Stephen-Bill Dixon
mid-1965   NYC

BD (t or flgh); Alan Silva (b)

Forbidden Playground   9:35

Maxine Haleff's film was built around images of Edith Stephen dancing and a separate soundtrack of music. Dixon: "Maxine actually filmed it in the playground (on the monkeybars) at Hunter College, where she worked. I was there the day she filmed it. But Alan and I played the music indoors. There's a thing where the breaking of glass is on the soundtrack. I think that was something Edith wanted."
Dixon definitely recalls recording music that was intended to be the soundtrack for Forbidden Playground, but apparently it was not used. Instead, Haleff incorporated a piece of music by Sun Ra's Arkestra as the audio track. To further confuse the issue, Stephen choreographed a work for her dance company (performed April 22, 1967 at the State University of New York) titled "Forbidden Playground" that used the music of Morton Feldman.
Dixon: "Our recording of the score was done on 14th Street, between 5th and 6th Avenues, probably a place Edith had access to. The day we were going to do the recording, we met Tony Fruscella, who had a friend with him. Fruscella had just come back from Mexico; they had just gotten into the city at Penn Station, and had taken the subway downtown from there."

Dixon had met Stephen while working at the UN.
Dance World 1967 by John Willis (New York: Crown Publishers Inc., 1967) p. 95.

65-0816   The Summer Players
August 16-17, 1965   St. Thomas the Apostle Church: NYC

Student Orchestra: personnel unknown

> The Exception and the Rule
> The Doctor In Spite of Himself
> House of Butterflies
> The Tortoise and the Drum

The Summer Players were sponsored by the "Administrative Committee of the Group Theater Arts City-Wide Co-ordinating Committee, organized around representatives of 115 churches from all the boroughs". In the wake of the Harlem riots of 1964, this program was put in place to give young actors and musicians a constructive artistic outlet, while also producing free, accessible presentations that would draw other youths away from the streets.

That series of summer programs also encompassed daytime outdoor performances by day of The Tortoise and the Drum (?) by student actors and the same student orchestra, co-ordinated by Michael Schwartz. For the entire summer, the company staged these four pieces, two directed by Sacharow and two by Schwartz.
Lawrence Sacharow, the artistic director for **65-0526**, directed Brecht's play, The Exception and the Rule (adapted by Eric Bentley) and Dixon composed music for the songs in Brecht's play. The group and situation described here toured the city for roughly 2 months in the summer of 1965. Rehearsals were held at Riverside Church for performances at playgrounds and churches in Harlem--St. Mark's Church uptown, for instance--Brooklyn, and the Bronx. Those listed above and at **65-0819** are the only dates and locations known for certain.

From Dixon's "Account of Career":
[I] worked as a composer at Riverside Church for a pilot program of theatre, sponsored by the Office of Economic Opportunity, the Neighborhood Youth Corps,the New York Mission Society, and about 100 Harlem Churches. My duties consisted of composing the music for four plays--two adult dramas and two children's plays: Brecht's The Exception and the Rule, Moliere's The Doctor In Spite of Himself, an African phantasy, and Ruth Krauss's House of Butterflies. I hired an orchestra of young people, between the ages of 16 and 21, largely recruited from depressed areas of the city, who were paid $1.50 per hour for a six-hour day, five days a week.
I trained them in the elements of musicianship--sight reading, sight singing, rhythmic dictation, harmony, theory, arranging, counterpoint, composition conducting, and transposition. I also gave classes in musicological studies (the origin of the clefs, the use of the bar line, history of western notation, etc.). In addition, I trained this orchestra (which consisted largely of flutes, clarinets, brasses--trumpets, trombones, and a tuba--and alto and tenor saxophones and percussion) in the performance of the music for the productions, which were subsequently performed in various neighborhoods. I also instructed a group of singers in performing the vocal parts for the Brecht piece.

This staging is not to be confused with another version of The Exception and the Rule that ran nearly concurrently (at least May 27-September 30) at the Village Mews, 141 West 13th Street. That Isaiah Sheffer production was also based on by Bentley's adaptation; however, its score was by Stefan Wolpe and used trumpeter Charles Sullivan.

RCA Victor was interested to record Dixon's score for the Summer Players' production on its Red Seal series, not realizing that the William R. Dixon credited with the music for The Exception and the Rule was the same person as the "Jazz" musician Bill Dixon. Apparently because of publishing complications involved in making a recording of the Brecht piece, that project was put on hold. Dixon was subsequently invited to do *Intents and Purposes*. (cf **R66-1010** et seq.).

Dixon's son William II was about to be born (in September, 1965) so his activites on site at the performances were gradually curtailed as the Summer went along. "I finally trained one of the boys in that orchestra to conduct the pieces without me."

An undated program from the Brecht production exists, and an undated newspaper article (possibly *New York Times*), titled "Plays will be given in Harlem Churches." also *Village Voice* August 12, 1965, p. 24.

65-0819   The Summer Players
August 19-20, 1965   Mt. Morris Park Musical Grove: NYC

student orchestra: personnel unknown

        The Exception and the Rule

See **65-0816**.

65-1099   Don Heckman ?? Group
after September 18, 1965   WBAI Studio, NYC

BD (t, flgh); Don Heckman (as); unknown (bcl??); *possibly* Joel Freedman (cello); unknown (b); unknown (d, perc)

        Nouveau Ne

The premiere of this piece was a live broadcast for WBAI. Heckman, like Bill Dixon, had a broadcast history as musician/host with the radio station. Heckman's Saturday night series comprising interviews and performances in old and new styles may have continued long enough to have been the platform for the premiere of Dixon's composition. There is a slim chance that a recording survives.

65-1108   Nova Brass Quintet
November 8, 1965   Hudson Park Library (10 7th Avenue)

Eugene Citronbaum, Gerard Weiner (t); Paul Rosenblum (frh); Mark Weinstein (tb); Fred Hollis (tu)

Mirage for Brass Quintet

This was the first public performance of "Mirage" (also known as "Mirage (for Brass Quintet)"), commissioned for this instrumentation by Gerard Weiner. It was one part of a program of brass music, with other works by Anonymous, Purcell, Lully, Adson, Pezel, Nagel, Higgins, Weiner. Rehearsals for the concert were held at the apartment of Dick Higgins, well known for his relationship to the Fluxus movement. See also **R65-1208**.

65-1116   Aldo Tambellini
November 16, 1965   Astor Place Playhouse: NYC

Aldo and Elsa Tambellini (painting); BD (flgh and/or t); Alan Silva (b); Ron
Hahne ("spiral machine"); Benn Morea (sound effects)

Calvin C. Hernton (reading)

>   Black Zero

This 8:00pm performance was part of the Filmmaker's Cinematheque's New Cinema
Festival I, November 10-18, for which the Astor site (434 Lafayette Street) was
rented, rather than using the organization's headquarters building.
Painter Tambellini staged this multi-media piece. He and his wife worked together
on visual creations, mostly (at least in this period) with "Black" as their organizing
principle and primary color, as evidenced by "Blackout", "Black Plus X", "Black Is",
"Black #2" (which also used Hernton reading), etc.
Dixon: "The Filmmaker's Cinematheque used to have thirty-day performance series
[during which a different event was presented each night], and this was the event for
one of those nights. Aldo Tambellini painted only in black, and he was working on a
series called 'Black Zero' with a man making machine noises.
"Alan Silva and I were playing duets at that time. Tambellini invited me to play in
his piece, so I made a couple of rehearsals to see what they were doing. He wanted me
to play to this painting. He had a huge, specially-prepared screen that reflected light
in a certain way and an old-fashioned slide projector--the kind that used a removable
glass slide. When he put a painted slide in and it projected on the wall, because of the
heat of the lamp on the slide, it caused the colors to melt and bleed; it looked as
though the wall were coming alive.
"Meanwhile Tambellini had this weather balloon being pumped up, and making a
bass sound, a steady cantus firmus that gradually began to rise in pitch. That was
going on, and Alan Silva and I played to that painting. It could sound contrived, but
it wasn't. Everyone believed in it. See also **65-1215.**

"In preparing the piece, Aldo and I almost came to blows over something very
simple: he wanted us to play right there in the audience. I was still very
proscenium-stage-oriented and didn't want to be seen. I told him so and we had a big
falling out. I walked out the night before the performance. Ultimately I performed it
just the way he wanted it, and it worked. It was a smashing performance."

Dixon's care of his son, William II was incorporated into a not-lessened schedule of
activities: as a one-month-old, William II attended the rehearsals for "Black Zero"
(and many of Dixon's other musical functions in the Village) in a bassinet on loan
from Ellingtonian trombonist Quentin "Butter" Jackson.
L'Opera p. 128; advertised in *Village Voice* November 11, 1965, p. 12 and 22.

CHAPTER FOUR

Dixon-Dunn 1966–1968

"About a week after the [6 5 - 1 1 1 6] concert, [dancer/choreographer] Judith Dunn called me. She had been struck by that performance, and asked if I would work with her. That's how we started to work together." Judith Dunn had worked with Tambellini previous to either of their collaborations with Dixon. "Judith Dunn knew a lot of musicians, but she was absolutely isolated from this music. (She knew Cecil Taylor from his performances at the Judson Church, when he had done some work with the late dancer Freddie Herko. She had never done any music with Cecil, but he had been on the crew of something and was involved there.) When she heard my work with Aldo Tambellini in 'Black Zero', she told me that was the sound she wanted to use."

Judith Dunn's professional reputation as a dancer was established in the Merce Cunningham Company of 1958-63, and her teaching credentials even earlier with an appontment at Brandeis. While married to the influential composer and educator Robert Ellis Dunn, she also became well-known as a founding member of the Judson

Dance Workshop--*the* avant garde dance movement in New York at the time (1962). Both Judith Dunn's Cunningham-rooted choreography and her much-touted physical grace and prowess as a dancer in others' works were important to the early Judson program.

Dixon: "When I met Judith Dunn, the work came first, then I started to play for her classes, and then we began teaching the composition courses collaboratively.

"I had worked with all kinds of dancers: I used to go to the studio of the 'primitive' dancer Ned Williams's Studio in the Fifties--just to watch. I would also go to watch rehearsals at Michaels's Studios. In those times, as a Jazz musician, there was always a dancer coming to you with a nightclub act or interpretive dances... I did a lot of work like that. When we were learning to play, we had to play for dances and were drawn into it whether we wanted to be or not.
"The person from whom I learned the most in terms of the aesthetic of dance, and the feeling tone and intimacy of the artform, was the New York dancer/choreographer named Nancy Meehan [Candido]. She was a principal dancer with Erick Hawkins; I never worked with her then because she was dancing with his company and didn't have her own. She had lived next door to me, and we spent hours talking about dance and music and painting. Drid Williams and I also used to talk a lot about dance.
If you're taking this music as an art, you try to link it to all of the things that any artform has. The first involvement I had with creating works that combined the two--music and dance--was with Judith Dunn."

Erica Abeel "The New New Dance; Modern Dance Is No Longer the New Dance" *Dance Scope* Fall, 1965, p. 25-26.
Regarding the Judson Dance program, *Ballet Review* Volume 1, #6 is essential.

R65-1208   "Brass Quintet and Duo"
December 8,1965   McMillan Theatre, Columbia Unversity,

BD (flgh); Charles Sullivan, Eugene Citronbaum (t); Barbara Elliot (frh); Mark Weinstein (tb); Lawrence Fishkin (tu); Alan Silva (b)

Mirage, for Brass Quintet and Duo   14:13   BD rec

Dixon and Silva are both heard in an interlude late in the piece.
Other pieces in the concert composed by Bernard Frum, Andres Lewin-Richter, Ran Blake (three premieres), Anton Webern, and Walter Carlos.
Ran Blake organized this concert, one in a series of which the next was to be January 7, 1966. Whether all were curated by Ran Blake is not known.
The piece was rehearsed at Dixon's studio, 119 Bank Street.
See also **R65-1108**.
Details from concert program.

65-1215 <u>Aldo Tambellini</u>
December 15-6, 1965   Bridge Theater: 4 St Marks Pl., NYC

BD (flgh and/or t); Aldo and Elsa Tambellini (painting); Alan Silva (b); Ron
Hahne ("spiral machine"); Benn Morea (sound effects)

> Black Zero

See also **65-1116**.
Advertising for this happening showed:
"ALDO TAMBELLINI's Flashing Lumagrams (hand-painted projections), RON
HAHNE's Spiral Machine, BENN MOREA's clamorous sound machine, the strident
jazz of BILL DIXON and ALAN SILVA on horn and bass, the hard poetry of CALVIN C
HERNTON, flashing light and gas-masked heads form a continuous experience in
SOUND   LIGHT   MOTION."

"Black Zero" was also performed the next month at The Bridge without Dixon.
Tambellini continued to stage his sound/image happenings, including a series
starting January 7, 1966 that used the music of "Dizzy Reece and Co." The piece was
staged many times in New York and Canada over the next several years, often with
music by cellist Calo Scott and not again including Dixon.

Advertised in *Village Voice* December 9, 1965, p. 20 and 22; other Tambellini events in
Village Voice January 6, 1966, p. 24 and April 7, 1966, p. 31.

66-0219   Bill Dixon-Judith Dunn*
February 19-March 27, 1966   Dance Theater Workshop, NYC

BD (t); Judith Dunn (choreography, movement); Alan Silva (b)

    Groundspeed

Dance Theater Workshop [hereinafter "DTW"] located at 215 West 20th Street, NYC
Actual dates of these "Saturdays at Nine" concerts were February 19 and 26, and March
5, 12, 19, and 26.
"Groundspeed", the first collaborative piece by Dixon and Dunn exists in at least
three different scored versions, where the first was titled "Ground Speed: for
fluegelhorn and bass", and the second "Groundspeed [A Trio] for dancer, doublebass,
and fluegelhorn. Composed by Bill Dixon (1966)." Whichever was used here, this
performance, during the DTW's Third Studio Series, was the premiere of the piece.
See also **66-0899**.

"When I first rehearsed with Judy she had worked on part of 'Groundspeed' already. I
looked at it, and very traditionally I wrote down some things I wanted to work on.
Then I decided I wanted to use Alan on it.
"She and I were the first ones to bring live music to the DTW; before that they all
were using pre-recorded music. Judy was known in all of her work for using live
music.
"The costume instruction was this: we were to dress like we were going out to dinner
at a reasonably nice place. Judy wore a white dress with light pink stockings on, and
high heels. At that time, I wore a tweed jacket, a British yellow tattersall vest, and
jodhpur boots or suede shoes. I remember discussing with Alan that he should have a
jacket and tie on." Some photographs of rehearsals for this performance may exist.

Once they were working together, both Dixon and Judith Dunn made an ironclad
committment to their partnership. For the next six years Dixon organized no
performances in New York of music without dance and collaborated with no other
choreographers/dancers in New York or Bennington. Dunn, who in the founding
days of Judson had appeared in others' pieces as often as in her own, ceased to create
dances with other music than Dixon's or to perform in other choreographers' works.
The Dixon-Dunn combination was presented in the late days of the Judson project and
elsewhere alongside Dunn's former Judson and even Cunningham colleagues.
Dixon: "When Judy and I began to work together, I saw the way the dance world
treated our collaboration and the way the music world treated it, and we were socially
involved, too. It was a very racist attitude: she was isolated, and I always thought it
was both because of her associations with this music and specifically with a Black
man."

* The "Bill Dixon-Judith Dunn Company of Musicians and Dancers", as their group
eventually came to be known, was also called the "Judith Dunn-Bill Dixon
Company...". For performances in dance programs, Dunn's name came first, and for

concert programs of primarily music, Dixon was named first. This volume has adapted that policy to show Dixon's name first for all of these collaborations.

"Theater Workshop Bill Presents New Talent" *New York Times* February 21, 1966. "Theater Workshop Series Is Interesting if Uncommunicative" *New York Times* March 21, 1966, p. 36; *L'Opera* p. 128; advertised in *Village Voice* February 17, 1966, p. 27; Bill Dixon "To Whom It May Concern" *CODA* October/November 1967, p. 8.

R66-0315   Bill Dixon-Judith Dunn-Alan Silva

March, 1966   Richmond Professional Institute, VA

live: BD (t and/or flgh,); Judith Dunn (movement); Alan Silva (b)
on pre-recorded tape: BD (t, perc); Alan Silva (b)

Motorcycle (on tape): trumpet + perc		7:52	BD rec
trumpet + bass		12:06	--

Groundspeed

Astronomy Hill [no music]

Dunn, Dixon, and Silva traveled to Richmond for a week of rehearsals and performance of the above works. Dixon prepared a tape of "Motorcycle" for their stay: two duos (trumpet/drums and trumpet/bass) were taped on Dixon's recorder, then re-recorded to a quartet using equipment at the home of John Herbert McDowell into the final version of the pre-recorded tape. In this premiere musical performance of "Motorcycle" with original music, Dixon and Silva improvised against the quartet tape for a total of six instrumental layers. Dunn's footfalls are clearly audible in both layers of the recording, suggesting that they were taped with her movement for scale. After a whole day of technical rehearsals, the performance at Richmond "came off like a dream."

The first incarnation of Judith Dunn's "Motorcycle" predated her collaborations with Bill Dixon. It was performed December 6 and 7, 1963 at the Judson Dance Workshop with music (from a radio) by Robert Dunn and danced by nine dancers from the Judson program. With that version by default as "Motorcycle I", Dixon refers to the collaborative performed versions of 1966 as "Motorcycle II". See also **R66-0718**.

"Groundspeed" featured just the trio live.

Dunn's 1963 piece "Astronomy Hill" included no music, but Dunn does speak during the piece.

Details of the 1963 "Motorcycle" from: "Judson: A Dance Chronology" in *Ballet Review* vol. 1, no. 6 (1967), p. 60; Advertisement for the earlier "Motorcycle" in *Village Voice* December 5, 1963, p. 12; and review in Jill Johnston "Motorcycle" Village Voice December 19, 1963. Ruth Emerson "Remembering Bob Dunn" *Movement Research Performance Journal* #14 Spring 1997, p. 9; Don McDonagh *The Complete Guide to Modern Dance* (Garden City, NY: Doubleday & Company, 1976) p. 368.

66-0330   <u>Bill Dixon-Judith Dunn-Alan Silva</u>
March 30-31, 1966   The Bridge Theater: NYC

BD (t); Judith Dunn (choreography, movement); Alan Silva (b)

Groundspeed

These two 8:00pm concerts of dance works comprised Aldo Tambellini's Dance Light Carnival. In addition to Dixon and Dunn, the festival included Mime Garrard, Rachel Fibich, Mary McKay, Jackie Cassen, and Carol Ritter.

Dixon and Silva were slated to take part in an April 2 benefit concert at the Five Spot Cafe. Sunny Murray's 18-month old son, Wayne, was killed in a household accident in New York (March, 1966), and the concert was organized on Murray's behalf. As the event ran long, <u>Dixon and Silva did not play</u>, but the day's musical events cast some light on their activities at the time: Earlier the same day Alan Silva had auditioned for Jimmy Giuffre's group, and pianist Dave Herman, Dixon's student, apparently cut a demo recording using Silva on bass.

Dixon brought Judith Dunn to the benefit concert, and also the Cunningham dancer Carolyn Brown, who was married to composer Earle Brown.

Advertised in *Village Voice* March 24, 1966, p. 30.

R66-0405   Bill Dixon-Judith Dunn-Alan Silva
April 5, 1966   Studio 55: WNET Studios, NYC

BD (flgh); Judith Dunn (choreography, movement); Alan Silva (b)

    Groundspeed   WNET b'cast/rec

This Channel 13 television appearance entailed a paid rehearsal (10:30-11:30am)
and taping (12:00noon-1:00pm). Recorded for *The Wednesday Review*, It aired on
that program from 9:00-10:00pm on April 13, and was re-run on the following Friday
between 7:30 and 8:30pm.

The Channel 13 holdings have probably been subsumed into the NET
collections-at-large of the Library of Congress Recorded Sound Division or (less
likely) the Museum of Television & Radio in NYC.

Critic/pianist Bill Mathieu visited New York probably in the late spring and played
with Dixon and Silva. In a letter postmarked June 6, 1966, he referred to that
meeting in the past tense. Around that time Dixon and Mathieu (then writing for
down beat) were to initiate a correspondence on topics in the new music to be printed
in the magazine. Primarily due to philosophical differences, that exchange of letters
was discontinued shortly, and none were ever printed though some survive today.

66-0501   Sunny Murray and his Quartet
May 1, 1966   The Cellar: 20 Shipman Street, Newark

BD (t); Sunny Murray (d); Perry Robinson (cl); Noah Howard (as);
Alan Silva (b)

Rehearsals for this event were held at Murray's Manhattan apartment; a photograph
from the rehearsals is printed in *L'Opera*, seventh in the folio that follows p. 64.

Dixon: "Sunny had wanted to study with me at the time, but I wasn't interested. Cecil
said Sunny had arranged for this gig and had some music, and asked if I would go over
and help him out. So I said to Sunny that I would do it on one condition. I had a piece
of music I was working on: could I do that on the program? So we did about three
pieces of his music and then we did mine."

Norman Howard's group including Pharoah Sanders played in a group opposite
Murray's at this event.

Advertised in *Village Voice* April 28, 1966, p. 24.

R66-0515   [unknown singers]
first half of 1966   NYC

BD (arr); *possibly* Robin Kenyatta (fl); Tom Moore (cello); unknown (g); Warren Chiasson (vib); *possibly* Bob Pozar (d); 4 unknown (voice)

I Remember (?) -1	c. 3:30	BD acetate rec
I Remember (?) -2	c. 3:30	-- --

"One night I came home from a rehearsal and a man and a woman were sitting up in my house. They seemed to be legitimate and made some promises...
These people ran a vocal outfit. They had a stable of singers for whom they wanted to start a company; they had a ton of money and wanted a library. They would groom and promote these singers to appear in small clubs. My task was to write a lead sheet so that if they went into a place that had two horns, piano, bass, and drums, they could drop these arrangements of standards on them with no rehearsal.

"At that time I was desperate for money. I wrote maybe half a dozen things for them in a couple of months, and the day I was supposed to sign a 2- or 3-year contract, at the last minute, it became too complicated, and I decided I didn't have time to do this. I met them all at the same time I met Mark Sadan and worked on **R66-0897**. I was working with Judy, and she even came to a couple of the sessions.

"Before that I had done some arrangements for a male singer, Tory Winter, who lived in my building. He sang around the Catskills--a very nice guy, not an especially good singer, but he had a good voice, like Johnny Hartman. I coached him for a while, and I think I had written a whole book for him. He recommended me to these people. I also had written some lead sheets for Yolande Bavan, about the time she was about to join Lambert Hendricks & Ross group as Annie Ross was leaving. These were just arrangements of tunes for them."

66-0599   <u>Bill Dixon-Judith Dunn</u>

probably spring, 1966   Radcliffe College: Cambridge, MA

BD (t, flgh); Judith Dunn (choreography, movement)

Dixon and Dunn led a one- or two-day lecture/demonstration on their work, most likely performing some of the pieces cited in the preceding entries.

"Judith Dunn gave one of the most remarkable forms of what we call the lecture-demonstration. Siamesed with the performance, she could come out and speak to people in a very unpretentious fashion--not educating people, or making them appreciate the thing, but letting them see her there as a *live* program note.
"I too have always felt that there is a point, after you've forced people to be that attentive during a concert, when you can take a breath, and there's time to say something. We are a verbal society; while words cannot adequately convey the intention or even explain how the piece has been put together, there is a way to frame some things that can illuminate. I've become very comfortable with that, and it's become almost a part of the performance."

R66-0673   Bill Dixon Sextet

late June 1966   Judith Dunn's loft: 1024 6th Av., NYC

BD (t and/or flgh); Judith Dunn (choreography, movement); Makanda Ken
McIntyre (as, bcl); Louis Brown (ts); Bob Cunningham (b); Tom Price (d)

Pomegranate: Parts I and II   37:00   BD rec

A rehearsal for Dixon's 1966 *Newport Jazz Festival* appearance. Some background
information about Dixon's appearance at Newport follows **U65-0416**.

For the Newport appearance, Dixon had originally conceived a quartet piece to use
Alan Silva. Silva made some of the rehearsals for the piece but began to work more
steadily with Cecil Taylor after recording on Taylor's *Unit Structures* LP (May 19,
1966).
Dixon: "We had worked quite a while on a piece to take to Newport, but Alan had a
difficult situation: he was married, had a day job, was rehearsing with me, playing all
night with Cecil Taylor, and trying to do some things with Sun Ra. Cecil had a very
good group with Henry Grimes. I used to talk with Cecil and say 'You could really use
another bass in the Unit. What about Alan? Besides he'd make a good foil for
Henry.' Alan could play with Cecil at his house, but Cecil wasn't ready to use him
publicly. Eventually Cecil thought about it, invited him in, and Alan then said to me
he had to make a choice."
Silva opted out to work with Cecil Taylor. Sunny Murray, whom Dixon then
approached to replace him, declined, and the quartet music was never performed.
Dixon organized the above group and music from scratch. "Had Alan and I continued
working together, I never would have done *Intents and Purposes*" (**R66-1010** et
seq.).
Newport handbills and advertising went to press before Dixon organized his revised
Sextet. The program showed Silva, Sunny Murray, and Sam Rivers in the group.

A group of photographs (some of which have been published) show Dixon, Dunn and
Silva rehearsing for the first Newport piece at Deborah Hay's studio on Great Jones
Street. The photographs further confirm that these rehearsals were recorded, although
the tapes are now believed to have been lost in storage. Perhaps in the same
instances, Dixon was audio-recorded by Daniel Berger and Alain Corneau on a
February-May, 1966 visit they made from France with the intent to lay groundwork
for a documentary film on the new music. They used still photographs of Dixon,
Dunn, and Silva in a 12-minute pilot film whose whereabouts are now unclear.

Judith Dunn's loft at 1024 6th Avenue, formerly the studio of dancer-choreographer
Paul Taylor, was the site of innumerable sessions, rehearsals, and recordings from the
period of Dixon's collaboration with her. (She apparently acquired it sometime in
the first half of 1966.) There Dunn conducted her own "Classes in Dance"--first
advertised in June, and with Dixon playing mainly trumpet--and eventually
improvisation workshops, though some students recalled that she shared with other
former Cunningham dancers the problems of trying to attract students to her classes
while the Merce Cunningham program was still active as a teaching institution.

Dunn still taught at the Cunningham studio into the mid-Sixties, with Dixon again playing for her technique classes.

Dixon: "When I first met Judy her schedule entailed teaching in Washington and at Sarah Lawrence College, so she was always traveling back and forth on the shuttle. Once we started to work, her activities became more centered in New York. The object for both of us was to avoid so much teaching that we couldn't get any work done. There had to be a balance." See also **66-0909**.

Dunn's classes advertised in *Village Voice* June 2, 1966.
Photographs of Dixon, Dunn, and Silva rehearsing the first Newport piece at Deborah Hay's studio appeared in Bill Dixon "Collaboration 1965-1972; Judith Dunn-dancer/choreographer, Bill Dixon-musician/composer" *Contact Quarterly* Spring/Summer 1985, p. 7-12.

R66-0702   Bill Dixon-Judith Dunn Group
July 2, 1966   Freebody Park: Newport, Rhode Island

BD (t, flgh); Judith Dunn (movement); Louis Brown (ts); Makanda Ken McIntyre (as, bcl); Bob Cunningham (b); Tom Price (d)

        Pomegranate: Parts I and II   VOA rec

As was customary and ideal for Dixon's groups, the musicians played in the round on stage. "There were only six of us, but we took up the whole stage. I like playing in the round, no matter how large the group. My instructions are always very simple: From where you are, you should be able to hear everyone, and if you can hear everyone's part, you are at exactly the right volume. When you play in the round, the music comes in to the players. Playing in the traditional configuration (facing the audience) the music is going away from the musicians, and they can't hear it."

Dixon was photographed (in color) at this performance; at least one of the images published in the Japanese periodical *Swing Journal* shows Dixon playing the English Besson fluegelhorn that he used until its theft in early 1967. See also **R76-0628**.

General overview/photo essay of the Newport perfs--possibly from *CODA*. John S. Wilson: "In the Afternoon Four Small Groups..." *New York Times* ; Leonard Feather "Newport 66" *Jazz Magazine* # 133 (August 1966).

R66-0711   Bill Dixon-Judith Dunn
July 11, 1966   Judson Memorial Church, NYC

BD (t, flgh); Judith Dunn (movement);
-1: *add* Louis Brown (ts); Mark Weinstein (tb); Bob Cunningham (b); Howie
Kadison (d)

Dew Horse	7:50	BD rec
Pomegranate Parts I and II -1	32:15	--

First of three weekly Dixon-Dunn concerts in the Monday evening presentations of
the Judson Dance Theater; the others were **R66-0718** and **R66-0725**--all billed as
Concert of Music and Dance.
Drummer Kadison met and played with Dixon earlier in the Sixties on loft jobs and
sessions at the Cafes Roue and Wha?

"Pomegranate Parts I and II" consists of two themes played sequentially as a
continuous work [see also **R66-0673** and **R66-0702**].
Ruth Noble designed Dunn's ("tank suit") costume for the piece.

Judith Dunn composed "Dew Horse" without music in 1963, before she met Dixon.
She had attempted to organize a version with music by her then-husband, Robert
Dunn, but the project was aborted. Working with Dixon she found a way to stage the
piece along the lines of what she had envisioned. Dixon refers to their collaborative
version of the piece as "Version II", reserving the earlier designation to the 1963
layout.
For "Dew Horse", Dunn would appear from the wings of the stage to dance a solo,
recede, and then Dixon took the stage to play a solo. He disappeared, and the cycle
was repeated several times, but with Dixon coming out from a different part of the
backstage area each time, or playing in a different quadrant of the stage. By the third
or fourth rotation, they remained in view together and performed as a duo. The work
lasted roughly 25 minutes.
Its title has been represented in official sources as both one word and two words. The
piece is also discussed in *L'Opera*; spelling here has been adjusted per this heading.
"Dew Horse" on the audio tape recording is not representative of the actual duration of
the performance, as the movement segments with no music were edited out. Further
explanations of the genesis and meaning of 'Dew Horse' are available in *L'Opera*.

"Costumes were very very simple in our work. The premium was on the outfit that
allowed her to be most comfortable and show the lines necessary to the piece. It
wasn't casual: each piece always had both a regimen and a look. The costumes were
different from one piece to another and consistent from performance to performance."
Dunn changed costumes for each of the pieces on these programs.

A 1966 Judson performance of "Dew Horse" was photographed by Linda Moser.

L'Opera p. 53-5; Jacqueline Maskey "Judith Dunn and Bill Dixon, Judson Memorial
Church, New York, July 11, 18, 25, 1966" *Dance Magazine* September, 1966, p. 30-31; the
three Judson concerts were advertised in *Village Voice* July 7, 1966, p. 17 and subsequent
issues, and in a one-page flyer.

R66-0718   Bill Dixon-Judith Dunn
July 18, 1966   Judson Memorial Church, NYC

BD (t, flgh); Judith Dunn (choreography, movement); Ric Colbeck, Marc Levin
(t); Mark Weinstein (tb); Joel Freedman (cello)

-1: Dixon, Dunn, and Freedman only

Motorcycle (Part I and Part II)	16:40	BD rec
Nouveau Ne	11:00	--
Groundspeed -1	12:25	--

The musical portion of "Motorcycle", performed with brass instruments placed some
distance apart in the balconies, revolves around the fugue of a tone row that Dixon
composed:
The subject is played once as written, backward the next time, then in halves,....
there are further repetitions. At the critical crescendo point, Freedman enters in a
cello solo. "I haven't heard a cellist yet--white or black--that played the way Joel
Freedman played. He was remarkable." Other discographical citations
notwithstanding, this is the correct spelling of Freedman's name.
Dunn's costume for "Motorcycle" had her wearing a tank top.

Judith Dunn named "Motorcycle" in an earlier version before she began to work with
Dixon (see **R66-0315**), and not relative to the motorcycle outside the church on
West 4th Street that is audible on this recording.

Dixon met Colbeck when the latter approached him about studying the instrument--at
that time Colbeck had a Constellation 38B cornet, the same make and model as
Dixon's trumpet.

As **R66-0711** plus: *Dance Magazine* November, 1967, p. 48-51and 66-7;
CODA October/November, 1967, p. 2-10;

R66-0725   Bill Dixon-Judith Dunn
July 25, 1966   Judson Memorial Church, NYC

-1: BD (t, flgh); Judith Dunn (movement, choreography)
-2: BD (t, flgh, tambourine); Marc Levin (mellophone, perc); Mark Weinstein
(tb); Joel Freedman (cello); Paul Breslin (b); Howie Kadison (d);
Chuck Atkins (conga)
-3: Judith Dunn (choreography, movement, voice)

Dew Horse -1	8:45	BD rec
Metamorphosis [inc] -2	12:45	--
Astronomy Hill		

Judith Dunn mentions in the notes to RCA LSP 3844 three realizations of
"Metamorphosis" during her time with Dixon:
a) an "unrecorded version in which brass predominates"
b) **R66-0725**
c) **R66-1010**, the definitive recording of the work
R63-0207 shows some details of the early history of "Metamorphosis". An earlier
version of the piece was played in 1962-63. It evolved through several years in a
non-linear fashion; for instance, it was never performed with Alan Silva.

Though some structural landmarks of the familiar **R66-1010** "Metamorphosis" are
recognizable, the instrumental parts for this Judson performance differ substantially.
The main theme of section letter **C** is obvious after a solo segment by Weinstein
(therefore, similar to letter **A** of the final version). Kadison also has a solo moment
(**D₁**) in the final section before this performance is truncated. On the whole, this
developmental "Metamorphosis" seems to allow less-prescribed playing on the part
of Levin, Weinstein, and Freedman, where the RCA Victor version uses those
instruments in closely plotted supporting figures.

Dunn's solo "Astronomy Hill" used no sound other than her speaking voice.

Around this time, Dixon gave two trumpet lessons to Donald Ayler. "He was without
a doubt the loudest trumpet player I had ever heard, with a range of about an octave,
and absolutely no flexibility, but it worked <u>perfectly</u> with Albert. A lot of trumpet
players used to hear how I could get a very quiet sound and have all of that movement
quality. They would ask, 'How do you do that?' And I would say 'I <u>work</u> on it. You
don't seem to understand, I work hours at a time on this stuff, and I have worked at
playing quietly.' After a while I said to Don, 'Don't worry about it...' "
As **R66-0711**.

R66-0897   Bill Dixon

late summer 1966   New York City

BD (*probably* t and/or flgh); Louis Brown (ts); Unknown (b); Unknown (d)

      The Good Life at Grossinger's   16mm film

Dixon composed the soundtrack for this 20-minute film directed by Ken Smallman and Mark Sadan. Sadan, once passing on the street in front of Dixon's building, had heard him practicing and subsequently invited him to create the music for his film. Dixon subsequently met Ken Smallman, who was then living on 9th street.

Sadan and Smallman created the film as a promotional device for the Ellenville, New York resort, Grossinger's. Inquiries in the mid-Nineties reveal that the still-active resort still possesses--and may screen--a promotional film of this vintage that is possibly The Good Life at Grossinger's, though this has not been verified.
cited in Dixon's 1968 Account of Career

66-0899   Bill Dixon-Judith Dunn

August, 1966   Public school cafeteria, NYC

BD (t); Mark Weinstein (tb); Judith Dunn (choreography, movement, perc)

      Groundspeed

This performance was cited in Dixon's Account of Career. The public elementary school was on Avenue B between 4th and 6th Streets. Dixon and Dunn performed for the students.
"We did 'Groundspeed' a lot because it only required three people."
This performance is singular for the presence of the trombonist playing the part that had usually been played by Alan Silva (b) or Joel Freedman (cello). Another Dixon orchestration of "Groundspeed" for guitar in that role was also probably performed at least once.

This event was held on the site of the current P.S. 64/196 complex.

66-0909   Bill Dixon-Judith Dunn
September 9, 1966   Central Park, NYC

BD (flgh); Judith Dunn (choreography, movement); Marc Levin (pocket t);
Robin Kenyatta (as); Bob Pozar (perc)

    Groundspeed

From the Fourth Annual Avant-Garde Festival, curated by Charlotte Moorman. The
fearless avant garde-ist and cello player Moorman masterminded these multi-media
events, gathering representatives of vanguard and experimental movements in dance,
theatre, happenings, music, literature, the visual arts, etc. The previous year's
festival occurred at Judson Hall, and the following (1967) on the Staten Island Ferry
(Dixon and Dunn were to have taken part in the latter; see **67-0802**). The 1966
Central Park chapter was held on the mall and ran for 18 hours, commencing at
6:00am. A photograph of the Dixon-Dunn group in action was set in the *Village
Voice*'s photo collage review of the event.
This festival is not to be confused with a later Moorman event in Central Park
(possibly 1968), which found the Sun Ra Arkestra and other musical groups
performing from flatbed trucks that coursed through the park.

Percussionist Robert Frank Pozar is referred to hereinafter as "Bob" though he was
also professionally known by his full name and parts thereof, and as "Cleve Pozar".
Dixon met him through Ed Curran [then Dixon's student], who at one time was a
custodian at St. Marks Church and held rehearsals there of his groups with Pozar.
Pozar had first appeared in New York under auspicious circumstances as leader of the
1963 Notre Dame Collegiate Jazz Festival-winning trio that played the Village
Vanguard in mid-June of 1963.

Dixon described having worked often with as/ts/bcl combinations that included
Kenyatta and/or Byard Lancaster. The summer of 1966 is the likeliest juncture when
their paths would have crossed in Dixon's groups, largely, it seems, in unidentified
performances. Both also doubled on flute, and Lancaster on bass clarinet.
Kenyatta recalled in a 1968 article that he had enjoyed a three year association with
Bill Dixon, which began with the preparations for **R64-1228** and continued at least
until the **R66-1010** date on which both he and Lancaster appeared.
Lancaster first met Bill Dixon at an informational meeting leading up to the October
Revolution, but probably began playing with the group somewhat later. Kenyatta
and Lancaster were eventually offered their first leader sessions by the Atlantic
subsidiary, Vortex, the release of which records circa 1967 loosely marks the end of
their respective tenures with Dixon.

In September, 1966, Dixon and Dunn began to teach together at the New Dance Group Studio, apparently the first ongoing teaching activity they undertook together outside of Dunn's loft.

Dixon: "Alvin Ailey taught there, as had a lot of people at one time or another. The Studio [254 West 47th Street] was opened in the Thirties, begun by a very socially minded group believeing that people who held jobs in the day should be able to learn how to dance. They started classes at night for people who worked. A whole lot of activity came out of that place."

Judith Dunn had conducted classes at the studio for some time, including "Sources for Dance Activity", in which "specialists in various areas of dance" offered "two hour lecture demonstrations." That weekly class from the Summer of 1965 preceded her collaborations with Dixon, but he later played for her technique classes, probably starting with the fall term of 1966 that opened on September 26. Dunn taught that class on Wednesdays (11:00am-12:30pm) and "Experimental Composition" with Dixon as a special weekly course.

Dixon: "Judy taught at the New Dance Group for income. First she had a house accompanist to play for class, and then we decided it made more sense for me to do it, since we were collaborating. When I started doing her technique class, I wasn't that proficient on the piano, so I did the class on trumpet--that made a big stir. No one was doing that, and people first came around out of curiosity. It was very difficult using the trumpet that way--stopping and going, etc. I was functioning in a creative way within a commercial enterprise, and I really don't have the temperament for that; I had been through that before and wanted to do something else. Eventually I realized that there must be a reason why everyone who plays for dance class either plays drums or piano: everything you played had to imply the rhythm. Deciding that I should probably become more proficient on the piano ayway, I began to lean toward that for the classes. Then later we moved into composition."

See also text at the beginning of Chapter Five.

Dixon's Account of Career; *Village Voice* August 25, 1966, p. 66, and September 15, 1966, p. 15.
New Dance Group information in "Dance Classes" *Village Voice* June 24, 1965, p. 23 and
Village Voice September 15, 1966, p. 19, and November 3, 1966, p. 22.
Michael Cuscuna "The New Voice of Robin Kenyatta" *Jazz & Pop* August 1968, p. 44-46.

R66-0926   Bill Dixon Orchestra
September 26, 1966   Judith Dunn's loft, NYC

BD (t *and probably* flgh); Jack Jeffers (btb); Byard Lancaster (bcl); George Marge (engh); Robin Kenyatta (as); Kathi Norris (cello); Jimmy Garrison, Steve Tintweiss (b); Bob Pozar (d)

Marc Levin (perc) is missing at the beginning of the rehearsal.

    Metamorphosis   BD rec

This is the first documented rehearsal for Dixon's RCA Victor recording, originally contracted for a quartet.

"I was thinking musically, that's all.
"Everyone [in the Jazz Composers' Guild] had been to see about getting a record on RCA Victor. I didn't go. I didn't feel I stood a chance, and I wasn't chasing around after record companies. Victor turned everybody else down. But because someone there had been struck by a performance of Brecht's The Exception and the Rule (**65-0816** et seq.) that I had done, and because there was only one setting on record of that play's score, they became interested in that as a Red Seal recording. RCA Red Seal eventually found out that "Bill" was the same person as "William R." Dixon. I was invited to visit a recording session, to see the studio and talk; Alan and I went because we were working together. I was very noncomittal. I asked them, 'Why don't you see what I *do* first? Right now I'm working on this piece for Newport...'--which at that time I still thought would be a quartet piece, so subsequently I was offered a chance to make a quartet record.
"After I performed at Newport [**R66-0702**], Brad McCuen [the RCA Victor producer] jumped up on stage with a contract in his hand, and so did John Hammond [of Columbia Records]. I was preliminarily committed to RCA, and when I got back to New York I signed with McCuen to do a quartet piece, even though he had seen the sextet piece at the Festival. He still had in mind what he had mentioned before, a quartet. I never did think of a quartet piece, and instead started working on 'Metamorphosis 1962-66'". That work was performed less than a month after the Newport concert.

"I had these people; I knew what everyone sounded like and what I wanted the piece to sound like. I had wanted a harp but I didn't know anyone who played that instrument. I was trying to compensate for that by using Levin playing additional percussion parts vis-à-vis Pozar's playing. I didn't mean a harp in the way that it usually functions, but insofar as sound can be displaced over a large area. With all of the layers moving, it would have made a lot of sense. I used the cello like a tenor saxophone, but I didn't want the breathing quality of the tenor."

"The piece wasn't done by committee; I wrote it." The September 26 rehearsal is a section-by-section reading of the parts of the piece. Relative to the structure outlined in **R66-1010**, the rehearsals of individual sections ran as follows:

A 2:12
B 2:04
C 1:09
D$_1$+I$_1$+I$_2$ 3:20
E [brief]

A 2:35
B 2:31 with no solo part
B 1:24 BD plays solo

There is strong evidence from instructions and questions between the movements that this is the musicians' first look at their parts. One of the players enters the rehearsal studio while the music is in progress--possibly Tintweiss, who arrived late to the first rehearsal and was therefore not invited to the second. Bassist Sirone (then known as Norris Jones) was also supposed to take part in the record but, unable to attend the rehearsals, he too was replaced.

Of the musicians selected for the "Metamorphosis" date, Pozar and Levin were Dixon's students at the time, and Lancaster and Kenyatta frequent participants in Dixon-Dunn projects. "At that time I was interested in Byard more for his bass clarinet than his alto." Lancaster had introduced Dixon to Kathi Norris. The late George Marge was a respected studio player of all members of the single- and double-reed instrumentaria. (In addition, he had been well-known to Dixon as a regular member of Rod Levitt's recording Orchestra of the period). Tintweiss was originally slated to make the record, as was Jack Jeffers. After Jeffers was out of the project, "Jimmy Cheatham basically had to get through a part, and he did so very well."

R66-0929   Bill Dixon Orchestra
September 29, 1966   Judith Dunn's Loft, NYC

BD (t, flgh); Jack Jeffers (btb); *probably* Byard Lancaster (bcl); George Marge (engh); Robin Kenyatta (as); Kathi Norris (cello); Jimmy Garrison, Reggie Workman (b); Bob Pozar (d); Marc Levin (perc)

    Metamorphosis   BD rec

This rehearsal began with an unbroken reading of the work as it then stood (ca. 12:00). Relative to the outline of the **R66-1010** version, these sections made up the September 29 reading:
A 2:18
B 2:44
C 1:00
$D_1+I_1+I_2$ 5:22
E 0:41

There were undoubtedly other preparations of 'Metamorphosis': an October 9 rehearsal (the day before the record date) was recorded, though it appears no longer to exist on tape. By that time the personnel had also been distilled to a near-final state; all the players from the RCA recording were present except Workman.

R66-1006   Cecil Taylor Unit

October 6, 1966   Van Gelder Recording Studio

BD (t); Cecil Taylor (p); Jimmy Lyons (as); Henry Grimes, Alan Silva (b);
Andrew Cyrille (d)

Conquistador!-1		unissued
1781 Conquistador!-2	17:51	BN BLP 4260
1782 With (Exit)-10	19:17	BN BLP 4260
With (Exit)-?	17:10	BNCDP
		784260 2

Blue Note BN BLP 4260=BST84260=B1-8 4260, and CDP 7 46535 2, all titled
Conquistador! The master take of each of the two titles appears on these issues.
Blue Note CDP 784260 2, also titled *Conquistador!*, reissues the two LP takes as well
as the alternative "With (Exit)".
Van Gelder's Studio is in Englewood Cliffs, NJ

Dixon recalls that there were several other superior and lesser takes for each of the
pieces. In fact the recording process involved several readjustments to the studio
layout. Eventually it was decided that the project might be better served by recording
in mono, but then the mono takes (which Dixon considered better) were thought
unissuable as not hi-fi.

When first approached to do this date, Dixon suggested that the record include the
regular trumpeter in Taylor's group, Michael Mantler, instead of himself. Taylor,
however, felt that Dixon's presence was essential.
The Unit traveled to Europe within two weeks of this recording; Taylor had arranged
to bring exactly the group that made the record. Dixon "didn't go because they were
breaking the group in at [the Jazz bar] Slug's in the Far East. In fact, Cecil and I had a
falling out about that. I told him 'You know I can't work a nightclub; *you're* not
supposed to do that either'." The group therefore made the trip without Dixon and
(for the second time in five years) without its regular bassist--Grimes--who
apparently had other recording commitments during that time.

Michael Cuscuna and Michel Ruppli *The Blue Note Labels* (New York: Greenwood Press, 1988),
p. 184.

R66-1010   Bill Dixon Orchestra
October 10, 1966   RCA Studio B, NYC

BD (t, flgh); Jimmy Cheatham (btb); George Marge (engh); Robin Kenyatta
(as); Byard Lancaster (as, bcl); Kathi Norris (cello); Jimmy Garrison, Reggie
Workman (b); Bob Pozar (d); Marc Levin (perc)

Metamorphosis 1962-66   13:20   RCA LSP 3844

LSP 3844 (stereo)=LPM 3844 (mono) later released as (J) 60221 and (F) FXL1 7331

"I finished writing 'Metamorphosis' and knew it was what I wanted to record, even
though I didn't literally have a contract for that large a group. When I walked into the
recording session with all of those people, no one said a word. I said I wanted to
record in the round, and McCuen asked me, 'Are you interested in a musical record or a
stereo record?' So we made a musical record in the round." Ultimately Dixon even set
the ensemble recording balance from the engineering booth. "My part--the very
high line over all of the written parts--wasn't supposed to be 'virtuoso-trumpet-
player-over-the-ensemble'. Traditionally, they would have raised the level of that
part. The engineers couldn't understand why I would want to play all of that stuff and
it not be heard. I wanted it to have a wispy quality, but where you could still hear it."

"Brad McCuen introduced Stanley Dance: 'We've brought him here because we want
Stanley to write the liner essay.' I asked him, 'Have you ever written anything about
me? No. I want Judith Dunn to do it.' That was my first meeting with Stanley Dance.
So I burned all bridges that first goddamn day."

The work was recorded in segments that were spliced together. The following
schematic shows where the musical (letter-named) sections of the piece begin; it may
not indicate where all tape edits were made.

1. 0:00-2:54   **A**--BD (flgh) solo
2. 2:55-3:52   *bass interlude (both)
3. 3:53-6:26   **B**--Kenyatta (as) solo
4. 6:29-7:49   **C**--long line theme
5. 7:50-8:50 D_1--Pozar solo
6. 8:51-10:37 I_1--on cue during D_1, winds largely in unison; BD solo [all
                        played twice]
7. 10:38-11:10   *alto saxophone (Kenyatta) over D_1 density
8. 11:10-12:44 I_2 --on cue, add cyclical ensemble figure in half notes; BD ad libitum
9. 12:44-13:26   **E**--coda

The asterisked segments had not appeared by the time of the September 26 and 29
rehearsals. Excerpts from the score used for this recording are printed in *L'Opera*, p.
98-99.

"That was <u>exactly</u> where I was at the time. The recorded 'Metamorphosis' is for me
the definitive version of that piece.
"You see, the difference between this music and formal concert music had to do with

both what the so-called composer wanted and how it could be done. In the European concert tradition, musicians were trained to read a part under the conductor's direction, and it wasn't authentic if it didn't follow those directions. Their basic symbol was that academic calligraphy: notes on the page, rhythmic subdivisions, key signatures, bar lines. In the entire history of <u>this</u> music that wasn't the way it was principally done; in fact, a lot of musicians began to think that reading the music took away from the creativity of it.

"We view the orchestra through the conductor, to the degree that while people could criticize Miles Davis for turning his back on the audience as being rude--thinking that he shouldn't be giving his attention to his musicians--that's what the conductor is *supposed* to do. If a conductor ever turned around and looked at you in the audience, you would consider that showboating, i.e., he's not paying enough attention to that orchestra.

"But *Intents and Purposes* was all written. The notation on that is really something; time signatures go by just like you would bat your eye. Up to that time, I was a very dictatorial writer. That's the way I thought about music--I didn't trust the players. I didn't want them doing what *they* did. (If you want to do what you do, then go get your own band together.) After the record, I never did music like that again. I found out that there was another way to get it done. I began to find a way to deal with communicating with the players: I could imply. I could use hand signals--not to be theatrical. You don't have to be jumping up and down and whipping the players this way. Time-signatures don't exist in your hearing, they exist on paper. So if a person wants to sit down and transcribe something, he can go to musical glory heaven dealing with all of these time changes: it's there if you want to hunt for it."

At this and the subsequent RCA Victor sessions, Dixon recorded a spoken voice track that was to have been issued with the music discussing and explaining the genesis of these pieces, his own music, and the state of affairs in creative music. That tape is presumably held unused in the RCA (now BMG) music library. A silent motion picture of Dixon recording this spoken track--and likely part of the recording session as well--was made by Judith Dunn. Producer Brad McCuen recalls that the spoken track was pressed into a promotional interview disc for radio airplay. No copies are known to date, but a likely repository for one might be with McCuen's donation of musical paraphernalia to Middle Tennessee State University.

RCA Victor finally balked at releasing the work on the Red Seal banner. Adding insult to injury, the LP was subtitled "The *Jazz* Artistry of Bill Dixon", contrary to the composer's wishes. Despite these frictions, *Intents and Purposes* was hailed by the musical community and the press alongside Ellington's *Far East Suite*, which was recorded for RCA Victor later that year with the same producer.

Dixon made the *Intents and Purposes* recordings using the English Besson fluegelhorn and the Conn Constellation 38B trumpet. See also **R76-0628**.
Score excerpts in *L'Opera* , p. 98-99.

R66-1073   Bill Dixon-Judith Dunn

mid-October 1966   Judson Arts Workshop: W 3d St,NYC

BD (flgh); Judith Dunn (choreography, movement); Marc Levin (cornet); Ed
Curran, Byard Lancaster (as, bcl); Kathi Norris (cello); Bob Pozar (d)

The Judson Arts Workshop was begun by Art Levin and Reverend Howard Moody of
the Judson Church. Created as a response to the growing debate and concern over the
drug culture of the west village, the progam's mission was to provide a constructive
outlet for teenagers in the area of MacDougal Street. It occupied a storefront space on
West Third Street, between Sullivan & Thompson, virtually donated by New York
University. Judson-connected artists from four disciplines--dance, music, mixed
media and theater--each led sessions on a regular schedule at the space, with each
convening once during the week and once on weekends. "It was a huge
storefront--people would look in the window and just walk in. There were also
dancers who came by and danced."
The *Village Voice* profile below mentions the performance as "four weekends
ago"--covering a Friday, Saturday, and Sunday component--therefore possibly
October 22-24 or an adjacent weekend. That writer suggested that the program would
exist for only a few weeks without further funding. However the drama division of the
JAW was still active and advertising as late as December, 1966.

Several tapes from this situation have survived, revealing an ensemble of
(near-absolute) beginners on clarinet, alto and tenor saxophones and conga drums, in
addition to the players named above. On one, they attempt a a rudimentary reading of
Miles Davis's "Seven Steps to Heaven" in waltz time. Dixon: "That wasn't like an
ensemble; I just let those people do whatever they wanted, stopping them every now
and then. They were enthralled because they were grooving [despite their lack of
instrumental skills]. In their zeal for wanting to play the solos, those players didn't
care how they got through the line. It just kept them off the streets..."

Dixon's compositions "Voices" and "Metamorphosis" for the RCA Victor recordings
(**R66-1010** and **R67-0117**) and "Solos" were also rehearsed here on an occasion
different from the one described in the article, although the open-door policy of the
JAW project was respected at least in part. "When I finished rehearsing my group I
would stop and all of these other people could just join in.
"I wrote some ensemble parts when I had a lot of people, or I would just verbally tell
people what to do. When I was rehearsing 'Voices', I included anyone who came in--I
just assigned another part. Sometimes good musicians would come by--I know Sunny
Murray did--and then I would design a situation to include their talents." Murray's
visit on November 11 was recorded, and Randy Brecker's on November 28; other
tapes are from October 18 and 31.

Those or other photographs of Dixon and Dunn in this setting were taken by LeRoy
W. Henderson.

Stephanie Harrington "Choreographing a Rumble in Avant-Garde Storefront" *Village Voice*
November 17, 1966, p. 14-15; Jack Anderson"Judith Dunn and the Endless Quest" *Dance
Magazine* November, 1967, p. 48-51 and 66.

R66-1102   Bill Dixon-Judith Dunn

November 2, 1966   North Lounge: Hunter College, NYC

BD (t); Judith Dunn (choreography, movement); Marc Levin (pocket c); Byard
Lancaster (bcl); Kathi Norris (cello); Bob Pozar (d, perc)

-1: add Dunn (vcl)
-2: add Dixon (flgh); Levin (mellophone); Lancaster plays as, fl and no bcl
-3: Dixon, Dunn, and Norris only

Voices -1 [inc]	9:23	BD rec
Solos -2 [inc]	8:30	--
Unknown		
Metamorphosis		
Groundspeed -3		

Dixon refers in *CODA* to a three-piece program, but other sources show all of the
pieces named above.

"Voices" was premiered at this concert.   Pozar preferred using a written drum part for
the piece, as he did here and on the recording date, **R67-0117**. Rehearsal tapes
exist of Pozar, Norris, and Levin working out the synchronization of their parts,
centered on the drum figure that occurs at 8:45 in the recorded version. Dixon's "List
of Compositions and Performances" shows both "Voices" and "Solos" as 20-minute
works.

The "Unknown" selection was also a Dixon-Dunn collaboration.

"Metamorphosis"--as usual--had no dance component.

Though listed in *down beat* as a quartet appearance, this concert was in fact played by
the sextet. Some sources also incorrectly show the date as November 23, apparently
the date of another group's performance at the same site.

Dixon's written part for Pozar in "Solos" as printed in *L'Opera* reveals some of the
strategy of his manuscript design: "The drummer looks at this and he knows exactly
what everyone is doing; it's a small score. His part verbatim is on the staff, and
above the staff is a reduction of the corresponding melodic configurations. So he
knows exactly how what he's doing relates rhythmically. It's not about counting but
listening and looking."

Bill Dixon "To Whom It May Concern" *CODA* October/November, 1967 p. 3; "Jazz-Dance
at Hunter" *Village Voice* October 27, 1966, p. 24; "Strictly Ad Lib" *down beat* November 17,
1966. Further data from Dunn's liner note for LSP 3844.
Drum part from the score of "Solos" is printed in *L'Opera*, p. 100.

R67-0117   Bill Dixon Orchestra
January 17, 1967   RCA Studios, NYC

BD (t, flgh); George Marge (afl); Byard Lancaster (bcl); Kathi Norris (cello);
Jimmy Garrison (b); Bob Pozar (d)

> Voices   12:08   RCA LSP 3844

LSP 3844 (stereo)=LPM 3844 (mono) later released as (J) 60221 and (F) FXL1 7331

Dixon: "Like a lot of guys I used to use various nonstandard time-signatures. I had
written one part in six-four, and Jimmy Garrison managed to play it in four-four. He
ignored the markings and made it work. He is one of the few guys who could pull that
off." This is the same section discussed briefly in **R66-1102**.

"I liked the sound I got on the RCA Victor record (and the most representative piece
of that is in 'Voices'), but I couldn't keep it. It was already beginning to change in
[**R66-1006**]. I was just working on other things."
One written line from this recording is printed in *L'Opera* at p. 162-63.

R67-0125   Gene Friedman-Judith Dunn-Bill Dixon
January 25, 1967   unknown recording studio, NYC

BD (cello)

> Index 1964-66   3:50   16mm film

"I played the cello actively for about four or five years. Eventually, once I got to
where I was spending all of this time with the trumpet solos, there was no more room
for the cello; I didn't have time for it.
"The day I was supposed to do this music for Gene Friedman's film, I was also getting
ready to go out to Ohio State [University, see next entry] for a brief residency, and I
went over to Savoy Records to take care of some business. (I used to transcribe their
gospel music.)
Dixon had been staying with Marc Levin and was moving into the 224 East 7th street
apartment that actor Roger Robinson was vacating. "When I came home someone
had broken into my house, and I was supposed to do this film score. They had taken
my horns, but not the cello.
"What I did was very interesting: I played the cello and overdubbed it four times, as a
string quartet, except that in each of the overdubs, I changed the tuning. I only used
the established cello tuning once."
The visual portion of Friedman's four-minute film employs an analogous
manipulation of images of Judith Dunn dancing: the images are superimposed and
double exposed; some move forward and others in reverse.
notes to RCA LSP 3844

67-0127   Bill Dixon-Judith Dunn

January 27-28, 1967   Pomerene Hall: Ohio State University

BD (t, flgh, cond); Judith Dunn (movement, choreography), unknown (tb); James Payton (oboe); unknown (b)

> Groundspeed
>
> Dew Horse
>
> (Improvised) Piece for Helen Alkire

Dunn was an artist in residence for three weeks at the Columbus campus of Ohio State University, teaching daily classes in "Cunninham dance technique" and "experimental methods of composition". Dixon made the trip as a "guest visiting artist" in residence for three days during that period, giving two public performances. One *Lantern* article below points to performances at 2:15pm, while other sources confirm a more probable 8:15 concert time on both days.

The bassist was a member of the Columbus Symphony Orchestra; he played a written part probably from the score to "Groundspeed". All other participants were student musicians or student dancers.

Helen Alkire directed the dance program at Ohio State and it may be she to whom Dunn's letter (s) in *Dance Perspectives* were written.

Judith Dunn "A Letter to Helen" *Dance Perspectives* number 38 (Summer 1969), p.44-7; *Columbus Dispatch* Friday January 6, 1967; *The Lantern* January 9, 1967; *The Lantern* January 20, 1967; Bill Dixon "To Whom It May Concern" *CODA* October/November, 1967, p. 8; *Jazz & Pop* November, 1967, p. 52; details from concert program.

67-0210   Bill Dixon-Judith Dunn

February 10, 1967   NYU School of Education: NYC

BD (t, flgh); Judith Dunn (choreography, dance)

> Dew Horse

Dixon and Dunn performed in the facility at 35 W 4th Street. "It was a small theater, and I came out to the edge of the stage--an old wooden stage. I remember that distinctly."

The "Modern Dance Club" of New York University's School of Education was presenting events at the same venue into May, 1967; presumably the same group Dixon and Dunn's appearance.

Cited in Dixon's Account of Career; *Village Voice* February 9, 1967, p. 40; *Village Voice* May 4, 1967, last page.

67-0211   Bill Dixon-Judith Dunn
February 11-March 11, 1967   Dance Theater Workshop, NYC

BD (t, flgh); Judith Dunn (choreography, movement, film, *possibly* voice);
Byard Lancaster (fl, bcl); Kathi Norris (cello); Bob Pozar (d, perc)

-1: Dixon, Dunn and Norris only

> Nightfall Pieces
> Dew Horse*
> Groundspeed-1

Judith Dunn's 8mm film was screened as part of the performance.

The Seventh Studio Series ran February 11-March 12, 1967, covering Saturday and
Sunday performances. Dixon-Dunn performed "Nightfall Pieces" on the "Saturdays at
Nine" program only; therefore on February 11, 18, 25, and March 4, 11. *down beat*
suggests that this month-long series occupied parts of March and April: perhaps
there were later performances. The series's other works were by choreographers Rod
Rodgers, Jack Moore, Cliff Keuter, Kathy Posin, Jeff Duncan, Nancy Lewis, David
Krohn, Tina Croll, John Wilson, and Art Bauman.

"When Judy and I started to work on something, the conversation would be very, very
simple. We had to know the size of the space, how much time we had to do this
thing, and what the budget was, because that determined how many people we could
use. Those factors would be applied to whatever we were working on to shape the
piece. Anything else was open season. So our work didn't have the conventional
orientation of a dance work."

Dunn named the "Nightfall Pieces", which premiered here and was revisited often in
the ensuing 19 months. "There were some sections of one of the 'Nightfall Pieces'
where she drew some large pictures of herself and then proceeded to dance those
pictures. The point was to free up the imagination as much as you could within the
limits of the resources available. There's always some catalyst that will give you an
idea to do something. We didn't have to hunt for anything at all because the constant
activity of work provided a flow of ideas. When she became interested in using super
8mm films, she used to like to take pictures of various things, and they would be
projected at certain times in the pieces. It wasn't a gimmick; that was the way we
worked: whatever each one wanted to do became a part of the thing, with no
restrictions. Now, she and I were both intelligent. I wasn't going to do something
that clashed or knocked her thing out, and I also wasn't going to do anything that
underplayed it necessarily. The question was: How could you make two things
become a third thing?
"The 'Nightfall Pieces' for the recording [**R67-0221**] were <u>only</u> for the recording,
and they weren't lifted from the dance piece. The recorded ones were never played in
public [by the composers; see **O78-1130**]. They were auditory pieces, but she gave
them the same name. That was one of a couple of pieces we could do on very short
notice. Don't forget, she was learning how to improvise at that time. All of these

other things that people see, like 'Dew Horse', were notated; she had her own notation. But it was a very adaptable piece."

Dancer/choreographer Jack Moore had co-founded the Dance Theater Workshop. He, and occasionally Dunn and Dixon, also taught courses there. Moore was on the dance faculty at Bennington College before either one was there--based in NYC but teaching in BCVT.

Dixon's attribution in *L'Opera* of a February, 1967 "Groundspeed" appears to refer instead to the premiere from a year earlier. The piece was performed in a retrospective series in 1967 (**67-0519**) but there is no further trace of a February event there.

Walter Terry "Workshop Launches A New Dance Series" *World Journal Tribune* February 13, 1967; Clive Barnes "Dance: Productive Theater Workshop" *New York Times* February 13, 1967, p. 41. *L'Opera*, p.128; *Village Voice* February 9, 1967, p. 20; "Strictly Ad Lib" *down beat* April 20, 1967, p. 46; also cited in Dixon's Composition List and DTW files; *Dance World 1967* by John Willis (New York: Crown Publishers Inc., 1967) p. 95.

R67-0215   Bill Dixon

1967   Judith Dunn's loft: NYC

BD (t)

      Solo   15:20   BD rec

While neither a performance nor a published recording, this is one of the first representations of Dixon's unaccompanied trumpet music (apparently not part of a dance collaboration) that he ever made public, using it in radio broadcasts of the late Sixties.

R67-0221   <u>Bill Dixon (orchestra)</u>
probably February 21, 1967   RCA Studio B: NYC

BD (t); George Marge (afl)

-1: add Dixon (overdubbed flgh)

Nightfall Pieces I -1	3:47	RCA LSP 3844
NIghtfall Pieces II	2:25	--	--

LSP 3844 (stereo)=LPM 3844 (mono) later released as (J) 60221and (F) FXL1 7331

Judith Dunn cites in her liner note for RCA LSP 3844 that the two "Nightfall Pieces"
here relate as components of the 20-minute work of the same name commissioned by
the DTW (see **67-0211**). In an April, 1967 letter printed in *Dance Perspectives*,
Dunn mentioned that she and Dixon were "on the outskirts of a second Nightfall
piece", probably referring to a sequel to the complete DTW version and not to the
versions I & II on LP.

In the spring term 1967, Dixon and Dunn taught a special course called
"Experimental Composition" at the New Dance Group Studio (see **66-0909**),
apparently beginning in February. They were part of a 22-member faculty for
"Modern, Indian, Jazz, Haitian, and Ballet" instruction.
Dancer/educator Thais Barry, one of seven students in that class at the NDG, reported
extensively on Dunn and Dixon's teaching methods as part of a paper for a fieldwork
course in her master's degree program at Columbia University Teachers College:

The class met for a total of fifteen sessions, with each one hour and thirty minutes
in length. Ms. Dunn and Mr. Dixon taught the class together, working as an equal
team. Their major aim was to get the students to become self-directive in their
choreography.
Dunn and Dixon wanted each student to become his own critic, to evaluate his
own work in terms of his own individual aims, goals, and expectations. They
refused to assume the role of critic, although on a few occasions they did so. In
essence, they approached the student as a mature person and as a mature
choreographer. At first,this approach was somewhat unsettling, as one is
trained to expect the teacher's evaluations.

Throughout the sessions, the class was given various movement problems...
intended to present the students with new ways of looking at and
experiencing time, space, movement dynamics, and relationships to other
dancers. In an exercise called "The 50s", the class was asked to perform fifty
gestures of our own choosing, using our own timing and spacing, to be completed
at the end of thirty seconds. The students were given a signal to begin, and the
thirty seconds were clocked off on a stopwatch. We were given several variations
on this exercise, for example 40 movements in ten seconds, or 30 movements in
thirty seconds. The purpose of the exercise was to explore a new relationship

between movement and time [in contrast to] the usual relationship of movement performed in relation to a beat with a prescribed tempo.
During one session the group was asked to travel across the floor as the teachers counted to 20 [with] the following stipulations: (1) we could move freely within the space, meaning that we could go back to a place we had been but were not to arrive at the opposite side of the room until the count of 20; (2) at some time during the 20 counts we had to all meet at a designated space on the floor. This was an exercise designed to develop an awareness of space in relation to time and sensitivity to surroundings and other dancers. Once we practiced moving in a slow-motion manner, trying to find the subtle dynamic changes of this movement quality. Another problem was to experiment with making various movements in relation to [Dixon's] high, low, and medium pitched sounds....

A major portion of the class time was spent in presenting and working on assignments. The first, ...due on the second class session, was to compose a piece five minutes long. We were instructed not to use music. There were no further limitations. Success meant doing something that lasted exactly five minutes....
At the end of the second session,... I was asked to take the parts of my piece (upon investigation I discovered it could be broken down into five main parts), arrange them by chance, and have the piece again take five minutes.
For the second assignment, we were given a choice between either a two-minute or three-minute piece. Following this, we had to compose a three-minute set piece [i.e., choreographed, using all of the students] piece and a three-minute partially set piece. The partially set piece was to be primarily improvisational.

A large percentage of the sessions were exploratory discussions, usually spontaneous and unplanned. For example, during one session Mr. Dixon mentioned that he couldn't understand why so many dancers were willing to create only half a piece. To him, a dancer who choreographs a dance and uses someone else's music is creating a piece which is only half his own.

The last two sessions dealt with sound; our assignments were to make audio tapes.... Several dance films were shown and we experimented with altering the accompaniment. The purpose for doing this was to see how one's reactions to the movement were altered as a result of hearing different accompaniments.

See also **68-0125**.

Dance Perspectives number 38 (Summer 1969) p.44-47; Walter Bruyninckx *Sixty Years of Recorded Jazz*
Thais Barry Ed.D. Untitled paper for "Field Work in Physical Education" p. 1-8.

67-0408   Bill Dixon-Judith Dunn
April 8-9, 1967   New Dance Group Studio: NYC

Bill Dixon (t, flgh); Judith Dunn (choreography, movement)

    Dew Horse

Dixon and Dunn were co-billed on this 8:00pm concert with another faculty member at the NDG Studio, Hadassah, a specialist in Indian dance. The Dixon-Dunn pieces probably were drawn from Dunn's choreographed works--some or all of the following: "Dew Horse", "Groundspeed", "Nightfall Pieces"--with no new works unveiled.

Dixon later referred to a "Dew Horse" as part of the program of a May, 1967 NDG performance; that citation is assumed instead to describe this concert.

Dixon and Dunn formed a class in dance composition to meet at Dunn's 1024 6th Ave loft twice a week (Saturdays at 11:30 and Thursdays at 6:00) starting April 13, this time advertised with "Musicians/Dancers with Bill Dixon".

Dixon: "We may have done that for one or two terms, because it was very difficult with scheduling all of these things, going back and forth, and still managing to do our own work. But the Saturdays worked out so that we could have a regular meeting--with all of the musicians. Even if they had some other kind of work, they would certainly be free on Saturday mornings. A lot of musicians would come who really weren't 'in the group'. The dancers were all studying with Judy and wanted an opportunity to deal with composition and dance in a larger context with music; they paid to take the class.

"In those days I would come in and always have written material for the musicians. The written things formed a library so that when I used different players, I had certain things for set instrumentations. At that time there weren't many opportunities for people to play written things of this nature, and they wanted to do that. It allowed me to have one more activity that wasn't just a rehearsal. We would read through the part and then start dealing with interpretation: How could we make it come alive? I was never that concerned with what people call sight-reading, *per se*. Judy also notated at that time, and was only starting to leave that behind. I would rehearse the musicians in one corner while Judy was working something out with the dancers in another corner; after an hour we would put it together, see how it would work, and mark off solos."

Village Voice January 19, 1967, p. 20; *Village Voice* April 6, 1967, p. 8 and 48; 1968 Account of career.

67-0519   Bill Dixon-Judith Dunn

Weekends: May 19-28, 1967   Dance Theater Workshop, NYC

Bill Dixon (t); Judith Dunn (choreography, movement)

      Groundspeed

May 19, 20, 21; 26, 27, and 28 were the actual dates on which the Dixon-Dunn pieces were performed--Friday and Saturday nights (9:00pm) and Sunday afternoons (5:00pm) with a special performance added on May 25. *down beat*, however, suggests that the month-long series occupied parts of April and May: perhaps there were earlier performances.
These 1967 performances were part of a "Spring Retrospective Series".

The entire program of 8 dance pieces by various artists may have been performed each night of the series.
Details from series program; *Village Voice* May 11, 1967, p. 20; *Dance World 1967* by John Willis (New York: Crown Publishers Inc., 1967) p. 95.

67-0799   Bill Dixon-Judith Dunn

July, 1967   Goucher College: Towson, Maryland

BD (t and/or flgh, cello); Judith Dunn (choreography, movement, film, *possibly* voice)

      Nightfall Pieces III

Title as cited in Dixon's Account of Career, from which also:
"...part of Goucher College lecture/performance sponsored by the Summer Institute of the History of Performing Arts in America. A work for musician-dancer-tape-film-spoken word." "The Goucher Lecture" is shown in McDonagh (below) as a discrete work of choreography, suggesting that an original work separate from "Nightfall Pieces" emerged.
Dixon and Dunn arrived at the college the day after H. Rap Brown's insurrection in Cambridge, Maryland.

"Strictly Ad Lib" *down beat* November 19, 1967, p. 14; Don McDonagh *The Complete Guide to Modern Dance* (Garden City, NY: Doubleday & Company, 1976) p. 368; details from concert program.

67-0809   Bill Dixon-Judith Dunn
Wednesdays: August 9-30, 1967   Dance Theater Workshop: NYC

BD (t, flgh); Judith Dunn (choreography, movement, voice)

Nightfall Pieces III

Actual dates for these concerts were August 9, 16, 23, and 30.
This may have been the edition of "Nightfall Piece" that Dunn referred to being "on the outskirts of" in her April letters to Helen Alkire (see **R67-0221**). The series billing as "New Works by..." would then still have been applicable to the latest chapter in a continuing series of developments for that work. Dixon recalls one DTW version of the piece with Dunn's 8mm film, and one without that had a different instrumentation, supporting the conclusion that the second one belongs here. Other choreographers in the concerts were Frances Alenikoff, James Cunningham, Elizabeth Keen, Jack Moore, and Gus Solomons, Jr.

Dixon and Dunn taught choreography at the DTW in the fall term, October 2-December 9, and advanced and beginning dance classes at the New Dance Group Studio (Wednesday 7:00-8:00pm) starting September 25. Their activities together heretofore had comprised teaching, touring, and performance opportunities including themselves and sometimes members of Dixon's musical ensembles. By the late summer of 1967 they were laying the foundations for a larger group--primarily adding other dancers--that would maintain a consistent membership, a prototype for the Bill Dixon-Judith Dunn [or *vice versa*] Company of Musicians and Dancers. The Graham-school dancer Barbara Ensley (acquainted with Dunn from studying with her briefly at Cunningham's studio ca. 1966) attended one of Dunn's classes and was invited to a subsequent improvisation workshop held across several consecutive days, and eventually to rehearse one of the pieces that Dunn was working on.

That piece was to be performed at Charlotte Moorman's Fifth Annual Avant Garde Festival, a 24-hour marathon gathering on the Staten Island Ferry. *down beat* erroneously reported that the Dixon-Dunn group had participated in that event; they in fact did <u>not</u> take part, though the festival happened as planned. As Dixon states, "I would remember playing on the ferry." Ensley recalls that this was to be the first performance she would make with the Dixon-Dunn group, but their appearance was called off, owing to Dunn's concern that the late autumn weather on a ferryboat would not be conducive to a healthful dance performance.
Thus the first of their collaborations designed for the larger group of dancers was the "Workprint" that premiered at the DTW (**R67-1105**).

"Strictly Ad Lib" *down beat* November 16, 1967, p. 14; Advertised in *Village Voice* July 27, 1967, p. 12 et seq.; *Village Voice* August 10, 1967, p. 11; *Dance World 1968* by John Willis (New York: Crown Publishers Inc., 1967), p. 97; Don McDonagh "Audience Invited to a Cough-along with Dance Piece" *New York Times* August 10, 1967.
DTW classes in *Village Voice* September 14, 1967, p. 23

R67-1105   Bill Dixon-Judith Dunn Group
November 5-December 10, 1967   Dance Theater Workshop: NYC

BD (t, flgh); Wesley Whittaker (tb); Byard Lancaster (bcl); Robin Kenyatta (as);
Kathi Norris (cello); Richard Youngstein (b); Karlhanns Berger (vib); Bob Pozar
(marimba and percussion); James Cunningham, Tina Croll, Barbara Ensley,
Dorothy Krooks-Friedman, Judith Dunn (movement)

-1 choreographed by Judith Dunn
-2 choreographed by Jeff Duncan; Dwayne Hoggard, Toni Lacativa, Deborah
Jowitt and Jeff Duncan *replace* Dunn, Ensley, and Krooks-Friedman

> Workprint -1   32:50   BD rec
> View: Part I -2

DTW's Tenth Studio Series featured performances of two programs--one every
Saturday at 9:00pm, and "Workprint" and "View" in the program that ran Sundays at
5:00pm. Actual dates of the Dixon-Dunn performances were then November 5, 12,
19, 26, and December 3 and 10. This concert series has sometimes been miscited to
November, 1968, but all hard evidence points to it having happened here and only
once.

Croll, Cunningham, Lacativa, and Ensley had all taken part in one or another of
Dunn's classes or workshops in previous months. Vibraphonist Warren Chiasson
made some rehearsals for these events in place of Berger and probably at least one
concert at the DTW.

Dixon's tape contains "excerpts" from a November concert--presumably one
continuous segment.
This is another piece for which Dixon recalls writing a marimba part for Bob Pozar at
his request. (Pozar also had read his solo part for "Voices" and "Solos" from
R66-1102, as in *L'Opera*, p. 100.)

Dunn and Dorothy Krooks-Friedman performed "blind duets" in "Workprint".
Dixon: "They had blindfolds over their eyes, and had to affect the duets without
actually touching each other. They just sensed one another. The music is done in
such a way to drown out their abillity to hear each other's presence. It has more to do
with feeling the air move; feeling the *presence*. That part of the work developed from
an exercise that she created, as far as I know." They apparently wore blindfolds for
the entire piece.

Details from DTW concert program, handbills, and *Village Voice* November 2, 1967, p. 22;
Dance World 1968 by John Willis (New York: Crown Publishers Inc., 1967), p. 98.

R68-0000 University of the Streets
much of 1968 University of the Streets, NYC

BD (t); Clifford Thornton (c); Leo Jones, Jacques Coursil (t); Richard Dunbar (frh); Sam Burtis, Wesley Whittaker (tb); John Buckingham (tu); Dave Chamberlain (flute, ss); Marzette Watts (bcl); Sonny Simmons (eng h); Monty Waters (B natural ss); Leopanar Witlarge (as); Sam Rivers (ss, ts); Arthur Doyle (ts); Sammy Clark (barsx); Warren Chiasson (vib); Susan Elrauch (mezzo-soprano voice)

Large Orchestra Piece 1	29:00	BD rec
V + VI rehearsal Reel	17:50*	--
"XP"	18:00	--
"XY"	17:20	--

See also **68-0715**.
Titles in quotation marks are given for identification only. Others are written on original tape boxes.

"There was a group of young Puerto Rican men called the Real Great Society; I had seen them on television earlier in the Sixties. Realization descended on them that fighting in the streets and killing each other were counterproductive, so they got together, designed programs for community education, and secured some corporate financial backing. They used to talk to students at Harvard, etc. about their plans for social reform. Various people gave them money, but more importantly they were able to attract a number of college students who could teach on different subjects at their headquarters [East 7th Street at Avenue A]--wallpapering, design, acting--things that normally would be inaccessible to Lower East siders, and everything was free.

"At one point, a representative of that group came to ask if I would teach a class for this program. My schedule was kind of tight, but Sunday mornings were free. I insisted on being paid for one reason: if a thing is to have value, then people have to pay for it. Once those classes began, no one from the community came, but the classes were very very popular and drew musicians from as far away as Westchester County. It was a successful class but wasn't ostensibly serving the purpose.
"While I was teaching the class, there would always be a lot of musicians out in Tompkins Square park playing in public--beating drums, drinking wine... I approached the program's management and made a deal with them to teach not only these Sunday music appreciation classes but also courses in elementary musicianship to these people in Tompkins Square, to entice them to come in. In exchange for me teaching them, they would rehearse a piece of my music. That was approved and I even got enough money to hire a few other people to teach the classes. So I showed these musicians how to instruct the classes (starting with the basics--harmony, rhythm, theory, etc.). That way I had several assistants because I couldn't be there all of the time." Giuseppi Logan and Arthur Doyle were at various times employed to teach classes or rehearse sections of the orchestra.
"Because the Real Great Society people were calling this the 'University of the Streets', I proposed that the music wing should be called the Free Conservatory. It

was based on the principle that we would go beyond teaching classes to form an orchestra, because for composers in this music there was no availibility of that size group. I made the proposal; it was well received, and I was able to get enough money to pay everyone who participated. I got some strong musicians--professional players who were in the union, and I paid them union scale. I began to rehearse these ideas, and the enterprise spread like wildfire. Before long I had a lot of people, but eventually some of my contemporaries began to approach me about hiring other musicians: every time I turned around someone wanted a job, and that wasn't the business I was in.

"Eventually there developed some philosophical differences between the Real Great Society and myself. Some members of the group insisted that my music and my approach to music were not relevant to the community, so they hired someone else--Kenny Dorham, Jackie McLean, Andrew Hill, and then others. Admittedly I was a little put off when the people who had invited me to do this thing began to be aesthetically concerned about the kind of music I did. I wasn't going to be teaching dance music; I wasn't sought out to do those things.
"The overall concept was a very reasonable one--to have a place where musicians could rehearse, teach, and, for those who wanted to develop and experiment, take part in this large orchestra. Anyone who wanted to take those classes could do so. I really was concerned about the social situation of musicians who wanted to learn more and couldn't afford to go to school. At least in school you had entrée to a school band or something; these guys in the street didn't have that. My attempt to do something about that was evidently severely misunderstood. No one else did that there after I left--understandably, because it was a lot of work."

Dixon was involved in the UOTS for around a year, perhaps beginning in late 1967 and continuing into the fall of 1968. The Free Conservatory Orchestra never performed in public. The music above comes from rehearsals, with personnel as listed present on the day(s) of recording. At least "XP" and "XY"--and possibly all of these pieces--were recorded in the first quarter of 1968.
The personnel given is skeletally representative of the collective personnel for the Orchestra's existence. Participants in the orchestra not documented above included: Marc Levin (cornet, mellophone); Frank Dalessio, Cliff Satlow, Raoul _____ (t); Steve Carter, Jimmy Cheatham (tb); Larry Fishkin (tuba); Robert Palmer (cl); Marsha Heller (engh, oboe); Barney Rostainge (ss); Sonny Fortune, Giuseppi Logan, Jimmy Vass, Mark Whitecage (reeds); Travis Jenkins, Duane Larrabee, Terry Pippos, Dewey Redman, Pharoah Sanders (ts); Raymond Marshall (bcl); Steve Witkin (cello); Ron Carter, Mario Pavone, Gene Perla, Reggie Workman (b), Bobby Few (p); Roy Haynes (d); Peter Wharton (electric tambourine); and, according to an August 10, 1968 budget/personnel list, Don Heckman (as, cl); Art Lewis (perc); Earl Cross (t); Leslie Waldron, Dave Burrell (p); Wajeeb (b); Tom Moore (cello).
"Dewey Redman came in to a rehearsal when the piece I was doing was completely notated. (For whatever reason, that's the way I used to do things then.) He introduced himself to me and asked to play in the orchestra. I said that I didn't care--if he *could*. He sat down in the section and he *couldn't*, but he got to the essence of the music without utilizing the part that he had sat down in front of, and he changed the entire thing. That's how good a musician he was. He didn't do what was there, but he put

something superior in its place. So those things are possible. Sometimes even people who know absolutely nothing can come up to the task, because they don't have a thing to get rid of; they don't have to fight through what they think they know."

"I wanted these masses of indiscernible sound going on, with a multiplicity of rhythms. I came up with a system to signal when I wanted parts to begin. No one played straight down from A to B to C. I moved them around using hand signals: everyone knew what two fingers etc. meant, and in the middle of a section I could signal a player to break off immediately and do something else. All the players had to do was watch their parts and watch me; eventually some liberties were allowed with the solos.

"I wanted a mezzo-soprano. It was the first time I worked with a single voice working in opposition to a large ensemble like that. (I called Roswell Rudd, knowing that he had used someone in one of his pieces, and he recommended Susan Elrauch.) She had some notated parts, for the areas I wanted her to be in, and gradually I let her just *do*. I would have loved to have used a large string section, but it just wasn't available. Marc Levin's mellophone was as close as I could come to a french horn until Richard Dunbar started coming to the rehearsals."

Relative to the score segment on *L'Opera* p. 101: "The idea was to let everyone give his own idea of what 20 seconds was. Since everyone's idea wasn't the same, you got that sort of mix that could never be arrived at through notation or counting." An incidental notation in the margins of the vibes part on p. 103 indicates that some of the realizations at the UOTS drew on Dixon's lines composed for "Voices" and "Papers".

The original tape of one of the above segments was lost in the hands of record company representatives while under consideration for the Deutsche Grammophon avant garde series of LPs.

Written music for the vibes' Part V appears in *L'Opera* p. 58, the B-flat saxophones at p. 175, the english horn's Part VI on p. 16, and full score sections on p. 164-65 An oboe part for the first section is in *L'Opera* at p. 102, and the vibes part at p. 103; Don Heckman "Jazz Rock" Stereo Review November, 1974, p. 74-78.

R68-0125   <u>Bill Dixon-Judith Dunn Company of Musicians and Dancers</u>
January 25, 1968   Canterbury House:Ann Arbor, Michigan

BD and 2 others (t); Judith Dunn (choreography, movement); unknown (cello);
unknown (b); unknown (voice)

Untitled 1	c. 8:00	BD rec
Untitled 2	c.10:00	--
Nightfall Piece(s)		

Bill Dixon and Judith Dunn traveled to Ann Arbor at the special invitation of a
composer/faculty member there--possibly related to or similar to the ONCE Festivals
from the Sixties.
Their trip is thought to have included a large orchestra piece (perhaps then Dixon's
main impetus to make the trip), composed for a student orchestra and omitting Dunn.
All musicians taking part were local to Ann Arbor.

Two separate pieces on tape apparently differ in instrumentation: one includes cello,
the other bass. The "Nightfall Piece" may in fact be one of the two recorded segments
whose times are given.; however, he tape seems to come from an informal workshop
situation.

68-0224   <u>Bill Dixon-Judith Dunn Company of Musicians and Dancers</u>
February 24-March 30, 1968   Dance Theater Workshop

BD (cello, t); Jacques Coursil (t); Howard Johnson (tu); Travis Jenkins (ts)
Judith Dunn, Barbara Ensley, Jack Moore (movement)

      Papers

Dixon-Dunn performances were held every Saturday at 9:00pm; therefore, February
24; March 2, 9, 16, 23, and 30

"One night while Judy and I were working I said to her, 'I would like to do a work
where I do everything' --except the movement, of course. I did the music. I designed
the costumes. I did the make-up. Each one of the dancers had to wear something that
emitted sound, so I made these huge necklaces of balsa wood. I laminated each piece,
and each had its own sound. This was time-consuming.
"For the decor--I'm a paper-airplane fanatic. I haven't made any in years, but I used to
make incredible paper airplanes that didn't fly, but they looked good. I made close to
200 paper airplanes out of newspaper--wouldn't fly if you put a motor in them. We
hung all of these paper airplanes from the ceiling at various levels, so that the light
shaped through them.

"I'll never do it again; I almost went crazy, but that was the piece. I got that out of my system. I wanted to do a piece that was completely everything I did." Apparently the work concluded with the members of the company eating oranges out of a bowl.

L'Opera shows a score segment relating in instrumentation and intervals to some of "Papers", though it appears to indicate that these ideas were transplanted to Dixon's teaching at Bennington. "This was an exercise that worked its way into a piece. Those pitches have to be used, but the rhythms could vary. I did this a lot to allow beginners to do something. Even if you told them to play it in unison, they read it down just they way you wanted, because they were unable to play it exactly in unison."

Thais Barry, who took Dunn and Dixon's "Experimental Composition" class at the New Dance Group (see **R67-0221**) in her master's degree field research, later became the director of the M.A. program in dance education at Columbia University Teachers College and hired them as adjunct instructors to teach two courses there. By July of 1967, Dixon and Dunn had given a guest lecture at Teachers College and subsequently taught the modern section of a technique class ("Modern Dance and Ballet Technique") and a class in experimental composition. Each class met once a week for fifteen weeks during the academic year, and daily for three consecutive weeks in the summer. (Though Teachers College had held an important place in the history of modern dance education since the mid-Twenties, dance classes were still administered by the department of Physical Education. The Dance program, which Thais Barry conceived and implemented--with course course work specifically designed for dance as opposed to dancers taking courses in physical education--was only beginning to emerge as a degree-granting body when Dixon and Dunn taught there in 1968.) Their teaching endeavors were supported by the New York State Council for the Arts.
Dixon: "We were still doing the course when we came to Bennington, and when we did 'Relay' [**R70-0428**], we brought the tapes of it down to the classes at Columbia."
"The classes were very simple: we taught dance composition together, from the musical standpoint, the choreographic standpoint, and how we worked. Students who had musical problems could also come to me, and I played for Judy's technique class. When the students were getting ready to strike at Columbia [late April,1968], she and I had nothing but graduate students. We had the choice to hold classes or not, and I said, 'If they're having a meeting, these students should go to that meeting; I'm not teaching a class today, and I'm not going to the meeting.' " See also **68-0599**.

Bill Dixon's work was programmed on the *Just Jazz with Ed Beach* program of New York radio station WRVR on Wednesday, April 3, 1968. It is known that he played (at least) music from the Judson Hall concerts of July, 1966 and some then-current rehearsals from the UOTS from lacquer copies.

L'Opera p. 128; *New York Times* March 3, 1968, p. D16; *Dance World 1968* by John Willis (New York: Crown Publishers Inc., 1967), p. 99.
Part of the score to 'Papers" is printed in *L'Opera*, p. 9 and the related exercise at p. 102.

68-0599   Bill Dixon-Judith Dunn
probably spring term, 1968   Riverside Church: NYC

BD (t, flgh); Judith Dunn (movement)

As part of the dance faculty of Teachers College, Dixon and Dunn were asked to take part in the annual student showcase, probably held across 2 or 3 nights, during which they would have performed once. Teachers College had no suitable performance space on its campus, and therefore used the auditorium at nearby Riverside Church.

Like some other Dixon-Dunn collaborations, this performance was photographed by Charlotte Victoria.

R68-0617   Modern Dance Workshop (Judith Dunn-Bill Dixon)
June 17-July 5, 1968   George Washington University, D.C.

Bill Dixon (overdubbed t, perc); Judith Dunn (choreography); various dancers (movement)

1:09	BD rec
3:35	--
0:57	--
1:53	--
1:57	--
15:40	--
2:21	--
1:58	--
2:15	--
1:04	--

Dunn and Dixon were artists in residence in this instructional program. Dixon created a tape in New York of trumpet and pecussion lines (apparently using a large bass drum) that could be played back continuously during the dancers' recital. The pieces variously employed overdubbing, feedback, and controlled distortion. This complete reel ends with Dixon's un-overdubbed 1:47 solo and a multi-instrumental recording of trumpet, piano, and percussion (9:09).
Some tapes of this music have been variously labeled "Roberta's Piece" and "Three Short Pieces"

Dixon recalls that at the time of this teaching engagement he was writing a piece using several double-basses for the UOTS orchestra.
ad in *Dance Magazine* May, 1968, p. 70.

68-0715   <u>University of the Streets Orchestra</u>
Summer, 1968   130 East 7th Street, NYC

similar to **R68-0000**

"While in Washington, D.C. at George Washington University, I took the shuttle
back once a week to rehearse the [UOTS] orchestra and did a lot of writing for it. The
piece came to me very easily and I really composed much of it on the airplane. I
wasn't thinking about making one, two, or three pieces; it just became a long piece
of music with various places for solos."

One of Dixon's notebooks shows an instrumentation scheme for "an evening length
work. Leo Jones, contractor" to be rehearsed in the summer of 1968. Forty
instruments are listed: 6 (t), 3 (tb), (btb), 3 (frh), 3 (tu), (afl), 2 (eng h-doubling),
(ss), 2 (as), (bcl), 2 (ts-doubling), (barsx), 4 (cello), 4 (b), 2 (vib), 2 (p), 2 (perc),
(voice). The same ledger projected six weeks of rehearsals--three times a week for 3
hours apiece and with each player/copyist/etc. paid $7.50 per hour for the rehearsals.
These initial cost projections may begin to show why the event was finally not
carried out.
This entire description probably relates to Dixon and Dunn's plans for a dance
component for the work. One rehearsal was held at the Merce Cunningham Dance
Studio (34th Street and 3d Avenue)--with the music played back from tape, rather than
a live run-through.
Dixon: "Judy had choreographed a comparable piece, but the two were never
performed together. The music was done at the University of the Streets (several of
her dancers came and heard the music while it was taking shape), and the dance
portion at the Merce Cunningham Studio (I went to see that developing). Then I went
to BMI and tried to get them to fund the whole thing. This would have been a real
magnum opus; we were talikng about a 2- or 3-evening length work. That was when
the UOTS activities began to take shape as an event; prior to that I was just writing
and rehearsing these people, teaching them the parts." In their enthusiasm to see the
project realized, the dancers offered to take part for no pay. That notion may have
been slightly less appealing to the musicians, who were already being paid for their
rehearsals. Dixon and Dunn did not entertain the idea of a performance without
paying the players.

At one point the advertising agency Kenyon and Eckhardt became interested in
helping to support the activities of the parent Real Great Society program, and Dixon
commissioned local filmmaker Nancy Kendall to create a documentary of the
rehearsal footage that he could use to apply for a grant from the company. Her
(silent) film was completed and submitted; Kenyon and Eckhardt then sent
representatives to evaluate Dixon's program, and eventually Dixon was invited to
meet with the company's president. The grant proposal was ultimately rejected on
the ground that the Free Conservatory program, thanks to Dixon's initiative in
acquiring a budget, equipment, and staff, was not needy enough. The film survives,
though.

Howard Shanet was approached about Dixon doing a reorchestrated version of the UOTS piece for the Columbia University Orchestra, funded by BMI. "I needed a large orchestra and wouldn't have been able to put together a group of that size." The plan fell through.

Dixon was contacted by Sam Adler, the opera director at Channel 13 about doing a part of the television series they were projecting. After cursorily hearing the music and meeting Dixon in person, Adler dismissed the idea.
Dixon: "Being a Black man in America can put incredible blinders on your vision. If I'm turned down for something, I don't know really whether it's because of the quality of my work or because I'm Black. That's been the history."

Dixon left the UOTS in late 1968. "Returning from Bennington once, I found the door locked, and that was the end of it."

68-0815   Bill Dixon rehearsal group
1968   NYC

Richard Dunbar (frh); Wesley Whittaker (tb); Marzette Watts (ts); Ann [Watts?] (cello)

This small phalanx of the University of the Streets Free Conservatory Orchestra engaged in specialized studies in a rehearsal group that met at Dixon's 7th Street Apartment and played his written music.

Though there were different pieces read every week, some of the materials this group encountered may relate to the sketches shown at *L'Opera*, p. 17.

R68-0700   Bill Dixon
ca. 1968   NYC

BD (t)

[all untitled]	21:00	BD rec
	2:55	--
	2:31	--
	1:15	--
	1:24	--
	1:31	--
	1:12	--
	1:00	--

CHAPTER FIVE

Bennington/Madison
1969–1972

In September of 1968, Dixon and Judith Dunn both joined the faculty at Bennington College [hereinafter "BCVT"]. The Bennington, Vermont institution had been founded in the mid-Thirties as a liberal arts school for women and in its first three decades supported a high level of scholarship in avant garde movements in many disciplines, perhaps known most luminously as a citadel of modern dance education and practice. By the late Sixties, the Dance faculty included Jack Moore and Martha and Jo Wittman.

Dixon: "Modern dance is the only artform for which the college level is considered professional. It was born in the College, and in the absence of money, the work could not be sustained outside of that environment. Until the mid-Seventies, very few musicians of any substance had gone to college--that wasn't where the activity was carried out--whereas <u>all</u> dancers go to college.

"My appointment at Bennington was in Dance but I was teaching an ensemble class in music. I was never an artist in residence; I started out in a tenure track position. In the beginning I was part-time in Dance, which meant that I had to be on the campus two days a week. For that I had all the responsibilities of a full-time faculty member (counseling, committees, etc.).

"My obligations were these: I played for Judith Dunn's technique class, and she and I taught collaboratively choreography--that is, Dance Composition--and improvisation." All dance students were required to take a composition and a technique class each term. From the very beginning of their time at the college, Dixon played (usually piano) for Dunn's technique class and piano or trumpet for the improvisation class they taught together, "Improvisation for Musicians and Dancers". There is evidence from class recordings that Dixon used an ensemble of musicians to accompany some meetings of Dunn's Tech III class in (apparently) the spring of 1969.

"I had a class called something like "Contemporary Studies in Performance Practice", for which I had an ensemble. There was no recognized Black Music teaching wing, and the Music Department had stated emphatically that there was no color to music, so I don't know where students got their credit for the class I taught. I taught the piano--not keyboard harmony, but technique--and I taught instrumental practices irrespective of the instrument. Any trumpet students would also take a trumpet tutorial with me. The first were Mei Mei Sanford and David Carrier. Over the [26] years I didn't have more than a dozen people to study the instrument seriously, because I didn't teach songs--I taught the *instrument*. So most of the trumpet students through the years came from outside (Jim Tifft; Stephen Haynes, who started before he was a student here; Lester Finley, who was studying at Empire College; Devon Leonard, also never a student here; Alex Huberty; Mark Sutton and Rebecca Ducette from Williams College, who took my tutorials in the very end.)"

One class Judy and I taught ["The Collaborative Process"] was very simple: we dealt with improvisation, in both music and dance. We wanted a large block of time, and for the class to meet once a week. [Bennington faculty member] Lou Calabro had been a Jazz drummer before he became a "composer" and it seemed only fitting that we should ask him to participate. So we all three would teach the class together. Calabro only came a couple of times before he and I had a disagreement. I was trying to do the music that these students could handle. My feeling in those days was that if I could get them to hear, then I could get them to move in certain ways, so ear training played a large role--holding tones, moving from one tone to another etc.--to create a rubric through which people could function, having gone through it. Lou came into one class and found it depressing, saying that there was 'no variety', and stalked out." Dixon's concluding analysis of this teaching attempt is reprinted in *L'Opera*.

"One of the first things we started with was solos: musician take a solo/dancer take a solo. Those are the things that are easiest and most accessible to do, and students could work their way up as we gave correction.

"There were four constituencies in the class: musicians, dancers, choreographers, and composers, all in the same room. The latter two could watch the proceedings and write down what they were going to do and organize it for others. Someone would do something, the others would analyze it. One says 'She should have done thus-and-such', so we said: 'OK, at the point where you feel she should have done something else, you go do what she should have done.' Rather than it just being very drily theoretical or critical, everyone who had something to say had to put into action what s/he was critiquing. *That* was how they learned.

"Everybody had to do something, no matter how poorly. They couldn't continue all term being poor at it, and they couldn't just be critical. In fact, no one was allowed to say what they "liked"; that is not constructive criticism. If it was a dancer and a musician, for instance, the critique might include: 'We could tell when you were just playing the things you know, because we hear it. We can also tell when you played what you thought would help; those things will not work.' Or 'The piece ended three minutes ago; why did you continue?' There was a lot of strong critiquing that required a lot of time.

"We would give an assignment like this to a dancer (the class meets once weekly for three hours): make five movements every day that you can do from any point in the room, and that you know by heart. The student would say: 'What's your definition of a movement?' 'We'll let you make your own definition of what a movement is; learn 35 of them.' That meant by the next time the class met, there were 35 movements that person had learned. We were talking about building vocabulary."

L'Opera p. 13-4.

68-0999

BCVT

BD (p)

Dixon was at Bennington two days a week during this time. He remained a New York resident until returning from Wisconsin in 1972.

"I started playing for dance classes as soon as I came to Bennington and continued after I came back from Madison. When I first came to the college, I wasn't especially interested in being just an accompanist, so I would only play for Judy's classes. Right away, I disagreed with the way dance classes were conducted. The dancers had to spend the first half hour as a warmup, and I wondered, 'Why don't they just come into the room warmed up?'
"The dancers were very unknowledgeable musically: they would take a piece of Webern, take a piece of George Russell, a little Schubert here at the beginning... I was shocked. 'Don't you people know what you are doing?' I stopped that immediately when I came to Bennington. Even the term, 'music for dance' was offensive; music is for music.

"I had a great time, but I had to bring them around to my way of thinking. 'NO, I don't play blues. NO, I don't do gospel. I don't do Chopin. I don't read fast enough to sit up there like an accompanist and go through something'. I hit that room playing piano, and about a half hour after I started playing I looked up, and about fifty people were crowded into the room wondering what was going on. Judy had to say 'Now, this is Bill Dixon. He is not an accompanist, he's a musician-composer.'
"I didn't play for dance class like anybody you've ever heard, because being an accompanist wasn't my orientation. I used to tell them when I was playing for dance class: 'I don't feel like playing the same thing over and over again. Why should I, as long as that rhythm is intact?' My time was impeccable, and the sound was just [whatever I wanted].
"Later when I had acquired more tact and skill on the piano, I started playing for other people. Jack Moore asked me if I would play for him. He was remarkable because whatever you did, that was what he wanted and used. Jack had a gift: if it was something he didn't want, he had a way of turning the time around, so you would be compelled to change what you were doing because you knew he didn't like it.

"Every musician should play the piano as a foundational instrument: you can look at it and see the juxtaposition and distance of notes, unlike the trumpet and saxophone, where you snatch the notes out of the air without being able to see the relationship. When I was studying I didn't have the time to be learning two instruments, and the trumpet was my principal. About 1958 I started with the piano. One summer I just rented a piano and stayed at it 12 hours a day until I could do something.

"Ten years later, one of the things that was very useful was playing for these dance classes. So that I could learn the piano more, I just transposed everything I learned to play into every key. That was great for me. I started out with a very small vocabulary, but I could do it all over the piano. I used it like an exercise. I had to make it interesting for me: I could work on chords, I could work on melodies... That was how I developed my proficiency on the piano. I couldn't sit down and practice the piano eight hours a day, because I was battling the trumpet. I PLAYED the piano, and then when I needed to know more, I would work on certain things. Then I started teaching keyboard harmony once people had heard me play. I created that course with a clear notion of what beginners needed to know. I stripped away all the stuff you didn't need to know right away, and left the essentials.

"I wrote dozens of contemporary piano songs--not pop, but Ellington- or Strayhorn-styled songs that grew out of playing the piano in that context of dance classes. When I became very attached to Hugo Wolf, I wrote some songs like I imagined he would have written. I really liked the form of the song--some of Berg's songs, for instance--but there was no place for me to go doing that. So I just wrote them and used them where I could. Generally, if students asked me I would use those pieces for them. So I had two outlets: playing for class, and doing some things for performances. Finally I became disenchanted again with playing the piano the way they wanted [in dance classes]. There are too many people who 'play' the piano; I wanted to make music on it. See also **78-0099**.

68-1020   Bill Dixon-Judith Dunn
October 20-November 9, 1968   Riverside Church, NYC

BD, Frank Dalessio (t, flgh); Judith Dunn (choreography, movement, film, possibly voice)

Nightfall Pieces III

Actual dates of these DTW-sponsored performances are given in advertising as October 20 and 26, and November 2 and 9 (the "Nov 8" shown in a *Village Voice* announcement of the concerts is believed erroneous). Dixon's performance lists show this as a 45-minute "complete performance of all sections, reorchestrated score; fall series presented by Dance Theater Workshop."

For the series three programs were spaced across the four weekends, including many of the notable DTW choreographers of the moment.

1985 Composition list; reviewed in Nancy Goldner "Dance Theater Workshop at Theater of the Riverside Church, NY; weekends Oct. 18-November 10, 1968" *Dance News* December, 1968, p. 12; Anna Kisselgoff "Dunas's 'Express' Arrives" *New York Times* October 21, 1968; advertised in *Village Voice* October 10, 1968, p. 35; John Willis *Dance World 1969* (New York: Crown Publishers, Inc., 1970) p. 103.

68-1029   <u>Bill Dixon-Judith Dunn Company of Musicians and Dancers</u>
October 29, 1968   New School for Social Research, NYC

BD, Frank Dalessio, Jacques Coursil (t); Judith Dunn (choreography,
movement, film, possibly voice)

-1: *possibly* add Steve Witkin (cello)

       Nightfall Pieces (reorch) -1
       File Box Piece

This is the same reorchestration of "Nightfall Pieces" that was part of **R68-1020**.
For reasons that are not clear "File Box Piece" was listed in Dixon's 1982
Composition list as "File Box Piece II"

Dixon and Dunn were presented in the fourth of five weekly showcase concerts at the
New School, in cooperation with Choreographers Theatre. The series, *Inside
Modern Dance II*, coupled live performances on each program with relevant films.
Laura Foreman curated the series.
"Judith Dunn did not improvise when I met her. She notated her work. 'Motorcycle',
'Astronomy Hill'--those were heavily notated. 'Groundspeed' was completely
notated. As far as I know, the first piece she performed where she did any
improvisation was "Pomegranate" (**R66-0702**). I used to ask her: 'What is the
fascination with learning how to do something? You create something, and then no
matter how many times you do that, you do it exactly the same way--even facing the
same way?' What dancers do is to make up something and learn it, so then if they
have a memory lapse, the whole thing is blown. For me, that was too slow. You'd
see dancers stop because they had forgotten what came next.
"The name ["File Box Piece"] was very utilitarian. Judy had certain directions about
movements and combinations of movements--what she was going to do, how many
people to use, and that kind of thing--written on file cards, and she kept them in this
box. It was almost like a chance routine.
"The funny thing about chance was--I never saw those people <u>taking</u> a chance. Now,
Jazz players take a chance. I always disagreed with the philosophy of chance
operations; I understand a bit more about it now, but it just doesn't work for me,
because whatever [the chance offered you], you had to have the ability--intellectually,
physically, and creatively--to carry the thing out. A lot of them would let the
instructions do everything, so they never really <u>created</u> anything. When Judy and I
worked with the music, I never used any of that, and eventually she stopped relying
on it.
"I used to ask Judy in practice: 'Why do you give yourself a barre? You're not going
to do any of that. Why use it in practice if that's not what you're going to perform
with?' To me it seems so simple because I don't believe you can do everything. You
can be what you are *doing*. Whatever it is you're working on, that's what you are at
that moment--which doesn't mean you can't have a lot of moments.

"She began to see what the possibilities were, and by the time we started working
together at Bennington, she was already into it. At Columbia [see **68-0302**], the
subject was not improvisation, but composition. Unfortunately, most people make

them separate. I think they are the same, just with different time frames. Everything is composed of something, whether you know it is composed of these things or not. Nothing just appears. And even if it does appear, it's made up of elements. With pre-ordaining something you have this luxurious amount of time to sit down, formulate, erase, change, etc. When you just do something, you're doing exactly the same thing, except that you don't have the ability to change anything. Once it's done, that's it, and if you examine it, it has a form--beginning, middle, end, etc. I had to come up with a definition early on. I said what made it composition was the assembling of elements that are accessible to everyone into a new order. Improvisation was exactly the same thing, except that its realization was so immediate that you couldn't go back and change anything. That made it easier to teach those two things together. That teaching is done a disservice by ["teachers"] being overtly intellectual about one thing, which they think is composition, and very slummingly vulgar about what they think improvisation is."

Trumpeter Coursil has described his work in Dixon's ensembles in the *Actuel* article below.
Dixon's work in New York with three trumpets appears to have bridged into the next year as well: a rehearsal tape is known from ca. May, 1969, including Leo Jones, Marc Levin, flutist Dave Chamberlain, and two others.

1985 perf list ; Advertised in *Village Voice* October 3, 1968, p. 27; John Willis *Dance World 1969* (New York: Crown Publishers, Inc., 1970) p. 105.
Jacques Coursil "Répétition chez Bill Dixon"*Actuel* No. 3 (January-February), 1969, item #11.

R68-1128 Bill Dixon-Judith Dunn Company of Musicians and Dancers
November 28, 1968   Commons Theater, BCVT

BD (t); Judith Dunn (choreography, movement, voice); Frank Dalessio, Jacques Coursil (t); Steve Witkin (cello)

Nightfall Pieces (reorch)   33:30   BD rec

This is the same reorchestration of "Nightfall Pieces" that was part of **R68-1020**. It also represented one of the first public 'performances' of Dixon and Dunn in the BCVT community, both introducing the other faculty and students to their presentations and galvanizing a group of their dance students who would become increasingly involved in their activities together.

"I did this concert at Bennington--one of the 'Nightfall Pieces'--using the other trumpet players. The Music Department freaked out over it--seeing me play something from written music.
"Later, as I was going toward my second year, the President of the College called me in to tell me that the Department had done something unprecedented: they had voted

unanimously that they wanted me to become part of their full-time faculty. I didn't want to be "full-time" because I had work that I was doing elsewhere, but he explained that if I were there one more day a week [for a total of three] it would count as 'full-time'--and my salary would double.

"To give you an idea of what money was in those days, Bennington was known for having the highest tuition for a liberal arts college in the country, yet the faculty salaries were the lowest. But there was a tradeoff: I could not have taught in a place like this if it weren't for having the winters and summers off. In addition, I was never told what or how to teach.
"I could do anything I wanted, Judy and I were working together, it was a way for us to do more work and have access to people--and there was the income... I decided to take the job for a year and save my money in order that it would give me enough to go to Europe. That's why I came to Bennington. I didn't have the courage to go to Europe like Alan Silva and so many other musicians were doing in 1969--not having anything, not living too well, and trying to do things that they weren't doing over here. It went nowhere for them. That's why I never went at that time. I wanted to wait until I had enough money to maintain my lifestyle (take my books, get a decent place to live, etc.).

"So once I committed myself to teaching, I resolved that this [BCVT] was where I would do my work. I made it work for me. If I had not had all of the people who wanted to work with me--who knew my work or whom I had taught in New York or other places--I never could have begun to do any work here. There were no people in Bennington who could do anything. So in exchange for these people from outside being able to do work with me, I was able to use them in these ensemble situations. With all of its shortcomings, being at Bennington was fine for me.

"By the time I began to consider going to Wisconsin [summer, 1971] I had gotten tired of fighting these people. There was no money, there was no space--it was always something. In addition, Bennington was as racist as any northern institution was, in that subtle, intangible way. Every year they used to vote on the budget I was going to get. It seemed that I was always in a meeting trying to explain why they should give me what I needed to teach their students. I caught on to that right away. When I got here, I was first hired out of funds designated for what they called 'Black Culture'. That meant that they were paying me, as a black faculty member, out of the money that they should have been spending to have people come up and lecture."

At the time Dixon came to Bennington, the Music faculty included Henry Brant, Lou Calabro, Viola Farber, Vivian Fine, and Gunnar Schonbeck. "Immediately when I started to work with the Music Department it didn't work out. They were a performing division; they never really were a teaching division. We had different definitions of teaching. They were into learning-by-doing and had these untrained students writing pieces that no one there could play. So they had to hire outside musicians to come in and play those compositions. They gave a lot of concerts, and right away got this fetish for having me as a trumpet that they could add into their concerts. I was asked to play in concerts of music that I was not interested in--I even bought another instrument since most of that literature is for the C trumpet. I did this a few times; I had done it in conservatory, but that wasn't why I had gone into music, to sit down and play a piece of music where you have to count out forty bars with someone conducting and you come in... Eventually I had to tell these people that that was not my thing. Anyway, little by little I fell out with the music department."

Bennington Banner November 27, 1968.

R69-0999   Marzette Watts
probably fall, 1969   Savoy Records Studio, Newark

BD (p); Marzette Watts (ts); Juney Booth (b); J. C. Moses (d)

-2 omit Dixon

Play It Straight	3:45	Sav MG 12193
F.L.O.A.R.S.S. -2	4:57	--
Joudpoo -2	4:04	--

Savoy MG 12193 titled *Marzette Watts Ensemble*. Produced by Bill Dixon.
"Play It Straight" was reissued on Savoy SJL 2235, *New Music: Second Wave*

This was probably the first of definitely two dates that went into Watts's Dixon-produced record. [The other date is documented in **U69-1009**; they were probably recorded within two months of each other.]

Personnel on both dates is substantially revised, according to the recollections of Dixon, Watts and Steve Tintweiss, from that erroneously given on SJL 2235.

Dixon recalls appearing on piano *in lieu* of the scheduled pianist, who failed to arrive. Watts's compositions "F.L.O.A.R.S.S." and "Joudpoo" were apparently recorded at the above session, but both without Dixon. According to the LP jacket, as few as three pieces may have come from the other date.

R69-1095   Improvisation Class [Judith Dunn-Bill Dixon]
probably fall, 1969   BCVT

BD (t); others unknown

> Improvisation class   c.60:00   BD rec:
> audio and video

Probably a class-setting shot for documentation rather than a performance.

Dixon and Dunn also created exercises for refining the students' understanding of their methods and aesthetics, as distinct from the more traditional approaches that predominated in modern dance pedagogy. Some assignments from Dunn's lesson plans in their first year at Bennington stipulated, for instance, that all movements be performed as fast and as slowly as possible. Others entailed creating sequences that elapsed in exactly 15, 30, 60, or 120 seconds, or stopping a given floor exercise intuitively after so much time had expired.
Following are some examples of class assignments from Dunn's notebooks for her classes in 1968 or 69:

Assignment: Intermediate Composition (due 10/23):
Make six graphs: a graph consists of 12 drawings, paintings, or photographs arranged in space in any fashion you choose. Each graph must be realized as a dance phrase--the spatial arrangement of the 12 = the pattern [path?] in which you move. Each of the 6 graphs must be performed without reference to papers, etc. Each must be performed as fast as possible,
> *as slow as possible,*
> *and medium.*

Assignment: Beginning Composition:
Make 5 movement units of varying lengths: take a pair of dice or a pack of playing cards (use 1-10, Jack, Queen).
1. Draw a body. Divide it into 12 parts in any fashion you wish and number the parts 1-12.
2. Throw the dice or choose a card once: the number that results indicates how many parts of the body will be used in [that?] one movement unit.
3. Throw or choose now to determine which parts will be used. If the result =7, there will be 7 choices made.
4. Make a movement unit out of the parts chosen; 2 of the 5 must move through space.

R69-1099   <u>Ulysses Dove-Bill Dixon</u>
fall 1969   BCVT

BD (t, flgh); Maryanne Finckel (b)

      Piece for Ulysses Dove   BD rec

While Bennington College remained a women-only institution until 1969, there were provisions made for some advanced male students of the arts to be attached to the departments as "fellows". Ulysses Dove had such a role in the Dance Department (as did Andé Peck concurrently, and Peter Stevens slightly later). He apparently started at Bennington the same semester Dixon and Dunn began their appointments, and while there was better known to his fellow students as a dancer than choreographer.

Dove choreographed a work to be presented at Dartmouth (separate from the BCVT Dance Department's 1970 tour through New England) and approached Dixon to create music for it. That music was played back from tape at performances of the work. "When he graduated [1970], Dove went into the Merce Cunningham company, then Alvin Ailey's company, and then began to choreograph for every major company in the world."
Finckel, a Bennington student long before, was a pianist/doublebassist and teaching assistant at the time of this recording.

The final version used for Dove's piece may be an edited form of what is on the existing tape.

R69-1210   Concert of Improvisation I&II [Judith Dunn-Bill Dixon]
December 10, 1969   Carriage Barn: BCVT

BD (p, t, flgh); Arthur Doyle (fl, ts); Sam Rivers (fl, ss, ts); Scotty Holt (b);
Andrew Cyrille (d); Susan Myers, Paula Sepinuck, Megan Bierman, Erika Bro,
Cheryl Niederman, Peter Stevens, and *possibly* Connie Allentuck, Karen
Lierley, Mary Kinal, Cathy Weiss, Leslie Berg (movement)

51:11   BD rec:
audio and video

Dixon and Dunn eventually formalized their teaching efforts in improvisation with
the classes Improvisation I (spring, 1969) and Improvisation II (fall, 1969) that may
have continued in the spring of 1970. Dunn seems not to have danced in this event.
Dixon: "I wrote some rather complex music that, with the solos, they played very
well. Nothing was rehearsed. The dancers may have worked on *things*, because
dancers are prone to work on *things*. They were students, but we didn't have student
musicians of that caliber on campus." This concert was a point of culmination of one
or both of those classes, probably including their combined membership. "That was
the final test: you put the two people in the room and let them do something. It was
music, dance, and performance." Though connected to the class, this was billed as a
public concert and not just a large-scale class exercise. It was also the only work
cited by some of Dunn's retrospective materials in summation of the major works of
that year.

Dixon had met Doyle in the UOTS Orchestra, through which Doyle first met Sam
Rivers. This Bennington appearance was Doyle's first in a small ensemble with
Dixon. Holt was a replacement for Sirone, who had been scheduled to make the date.

R69-1211   Concert of Improvisation I&II [Judith Dunn-Bill Dixon]
December 11, 1969   Carriage Barn: BCVT

BD (p, t, flgh); Arthur Doyle (fl, ts); Sam Rivers (fl, ss, ts); Scotty Holt (b);
Andrew Cyrille (d); Susan Myers, Paula Sepinuck, Megan Bierman, Erika Bro,
Cheryl Niederman, Peter Stevens, and *possibly* Connie Allentuck, Karen
Lierley, Mary Kinal, Cathy Weiss, Leslie Berg (movement)

[inc]   1:35:59   BD rec:
audio and video

See **R69-1210**.

R70-0000   Bill Dixon

"1970-1"   probably Dunn's loft; definitely NYC

BD (t)

Mosaic	:36	CJR 1025
Albert Ayler	:53	--
Unknown 1	brief	uniss; BD rec
Unknown 2	3:32	--
Unknown 3	5:06	--
Albert Ayler alternate tk	1:10	--
Unknown 2 tk-2	3:36	--
Unknown 4	2:25	--
Unknown 5	2:42	--

CJR 1025 is the second record of a two-LP boxed set on Cadence Jazz Records, CJR 1024/5, titled *The Collection*.
The two issued pieces may not come from the same episode, but they were unquestionably recorded in the same acoustical environment and time period.

Dixon began working on this series of pieces the summer he spent in Washington [see **R68-0617**].

Stephen Horenstein entered the Bennington sphere of Bill Dixon in March, 1970. Bostonian by birth, he was a trained saxophonist, performing mainly on alto from age 7. When Horenstein later wanted to branch out into playing flute, he began to study with Marcel Moyse in Brattleboro, Vermont, and while staying in Bennington briefly he was introduced to Bill Dixon and his music by happenstance. Horenstein gradually became committed to Dixon's methods and music, primarily a duo "apprenticeship" with Dixon in which he played mainly tenor saxophone and piano (his flute studies were shortly discontinued as Horenstein "moved in" to the Bennington program.). A certain portion of his work with Dixon was also evolved in the tenor-piano duets they played in Dunn's dance classes, and Horenstein played for others' dance classes as well.
Though never formally enrolled as a student at Bennington, Horenstein became a stalwart member of the ensembles and teaching staff of the Black Music program in his ten years at BCVT.
His first performance on the campus was the premiere of the Dunn-Dixon work, "Relay" (See next).

The sketches at *L'Opera* p. 59-60 (for trumpet and tenor in unison) are representative of some of the music that Dixon wrote for Horenstein and himself.

R70-0422   Bill Dixon-Judith Dunn Company of Musicians and Dancers
April 22, 1970   Carriage Barn: BCVT

BD ("amplified trumpet"); Judith Dunn (choreography, movement) *with*:

-1: Christopher Bishop (elbg); Penny Larrison, Paula Sepinuck (movement)
-2: Ann Carrier (afl); David Carrier (t, flgh); Steve Horenstein (bcl); Barbara
Ensley, Martha Wittman, Jack Moore, Pamela Tate, Jo Wittman, Peter Stevens
(movement)

> Groundspeed -1   video rec
> Relay -2   prob video rec

This concert and the following were billed as "Two Evenings of Music and Dance"
The erstwhile trio piece "Groundspeed" (usually Dixon, Dunn, and one other
musician) was rearranged by Judith Dunn for three dancers.
"Relay" was doubtless given its premiere performance on this occasion: it was also
staged the next night, and on **R70-0428**, although Dixon recalls only one
performance of the *complete* work as described at **R70-0428**. He remembers Chris
Bishop performing in the piece, and while Bishop is verifiably on **R70-0428**, he is
not listed for the program from this concert. Bishop, a rock bassist "with a very
attractive sound on the Fender bass guitar", was the first person Dixon met at
Bennington.
Details from concert program.

R70-0423   Bill Dixon-Judith Dunn Company of Musicians and Dancers
April 23, 1970   Carriage Barn: BCVT

BD (t, flgh); Judith Dunn (choreography, movement)

-1 *add*: David Carrier (t, flgh); Ann Carrier (afl); Stephen Horenstein (bcl);
Barbara Ensley, Martha Wittman, Jack Moore, Pamela Tate, Jo Wittman, Peter
Stevens (movement)

> Dew Horse   video rec
> Relay -1   prob video rec

This performance of "Dew Horse" was the videotaped version that Dunn used to
communicate the dance to Cheryl Lilienstein for the **R82-0415** re-creation, q.v.
L'Opera p. 53-55.

R70-0428   Bill Dixon-Judith Dunn Company of Musicians and Dancers
April 28, 1970   Carriage Barn: BCVT

On overdubbed tape: BD (t, p); Chris Bishop (elbg)
Live: Bill Dixon (flgh, cond); Judith Dunn (choreography, movement); David
Carrier (t); Ann Carrier (afl); Stephen Horenstein (bcl); Chris Bishop (elbg);
Jack Moore [also voice], Martha & Jo Wittman, Pamela Tate [also voice]*,
Barbara Ensley, Peter Stevens (movement);

Vocalizations of all dancers are audible.

Relay: Dance #1 (t/t)	9:55	Ferrari 1982
Relay: Dance #2 (t/p)	1:47	BD rec
Relay: Dance #3 --	2:18	--
Relay: Dance #4 --	2:44	--
Relay: Dance #5 --	3:33	Ferrari 1982
Relay :Dance #6 --	4:31	BD rec
Relay: Dance #7 --	7:16	Ferrari 1982
Relay: Dance #8 --	5:54	BD rec
Relay: Dance #9 (t) and (elbg)	3:19	BD rec
TOTAL PERFORMANCE DURATION	46:09	

*1982 Composition list notes "child": this is Pamela Tate

Edizioni Ferrari 1982 is an untitled LP issued in very limited quantities by the Ferrari
Gallery (see below).

"Relay" was a dance-music collaboration partly written during the winter term
1969-70. It was the first fully-formed Dixon-Dunn piece to be conceived, rehearsed,
and performed entirely at Bennington.

Jack Moore, dancing in a gorilla costume made by Poppy Lagos, simulates Tarzan's
vocalizations. Other costumes were designed by Ruth Nobel--extrapolated from her
design for "Pomegranate" (**R66-0711**): all of the dancers wore the same style in
different colors.

Bill Dixon's multitracked trumpet and piano parts (and duet with Chris Bishop) were
pre-recorded for the concert. The tape was played back into the performance space,
and further music was created live by the ensemble. "I did that because I didn't have
that many musicians. I didn't use tape to be cute, but because I wanted that many
layers. All the pre-recorded tapes are of me playing, with one exception. Also, Steve
Horenstein at some point plays a segment I wrote for him [cf. **R70-1100**]." The
overdubbing idea coincided with Dixon's proposed experiments in multi-track
recording at a NYC studio with an engineer from Vanguard Records, which might (as
might "Relay") have included even more trumpet tracks, had they come to fruition.

The sum of these layers of music survives only on an video-cum-audio recording of the performance (total time is longer than the duration of the multitrack trumpet tape, as there are sections during which that tape is not playing).

The tape of Dixon's multitracked solos was preserved separately, and some were issued on his 1982 Edizioni Ferrari record. The opposite side of that LP also used recordings of Dixon's unaccompanied trumpet solos [**R73-0197**]. Disc labels on many (if not all) copies of the LPs were reversed. The Ferrari Gallery issued the record in conjunction with an exhibit of Dixon's visual artworks that is referred to in *L'Opera* .

L'Opera, p. 79.

70-0515   Bill Dixon-Judith Dunn

May or early June, 1970   Commons Theater, BCVT

BD (t); Judith Dunn (choreography, movement); *possibly* Stephen Horenstein (ts); Christopher Bishop (elbg); Megan Bierman, Cheryl Niederman (movement)

    At Midnight   c30:00

The piece had been rehearsed in the school term, leading up to this presentation. Dixon, Horenstein, and Bishop were audio-recorded on May 30, 1970 on a tape labeled Tech III. While it not likely that Dunn's technique class would have been involved in the making of "At Midnight", it is plausible that Dixon recorded the musical component on that day in a trial run for the subsequent (?) performance of the piece.

 Cheryl Lilienstein (née Niederman) recalls that the piece was highly regarded by the performers--perhaps strengthening Dunn's conviction to ask Bierman and Niederman (her students at Bennington for two years already) to become part of the nascent Company of Musicians and Dancers. See also **R70-1215**.

R70-0592   Bill Dixon

May, 1970   BCVT

BD (p)

Chiasmus	7:17	BD rec
Shards	1:50	--
Pasquinade	6:00	--

Part of the handful of Dixon's solo piano pieces not from concert performances (see **R74-1206**). Dixon also began writing a piece for three pianos in this period, which was neither completed nor performed.

R70-0593   Bill Dixon-Stephen Horenstein
May, 1970   BCVT

BD (p); Stephen Horenstein (ts)

      Octobersong   BD rec

Possibly from two different days or sessions of recording: left and right channels reverse mid-way through the tape, suggesting that microphone placements were switched, or the system disassembled entirely.
This is an informal studio session--likely in Dixon's studio in Jennings--comprising many fragments and re-started readings of the piece, none complete.

Dixon's "Octobersong", composed for Marzette Watts's **U69-1009** recording, enjoyed a myriad of performances, including **R70-1215**, and its incorporation into the late orchestral work, "Letters: Round Up the Usual Suspects", **R90-1205**.

"Those duets with Steve and various drummers were always done for one very selfish reason: I had to play, and this let me do it. I would find someone to do duets with. You couldn't do duets with beginning students, because there was very little they could do. So how do you teach a person to play when there aren't enough of his peers to play with?
"In fact this was the way I chose to teach drummers, because you can teach more to a drummer playing a linear instrument than with piano. For me, doing those things was always teaching myself something, while teaching them, and being able to play. I became very good at that. When you hear me in a duet, you don't miss the piano, or the bass. That is, it is a good, or successful, duet." Dixon's subsequent duets with drummers Henry Letcher, Ehran Elisha, and Matthew Weston; bassists Xtopher Faris and Jeremy Harlos; guitarists Tony Ackerman and Matt Henderson; keyboardists Leslie Winston and Tony Widoff; and reed player Paul Austerlitz were some of the primary examples of this activity throughout his tenure at Bennington.
A score to "Octobersong" (for flute) published in *L'Opera* p.176. It is not clear for whom the flute part was created.

R70-0599   Bill Dixon
ca. 1970   BCVT

BD (t)

      Pedal   BD rec
      Hush   4:50   --

R70-0609 Ensemble

June 9, 1970 BCVT

BD (occasional t); Ann Carrier (fl); Erika Bro (cl); Stephen Horenstein (ts); Carl? Freedman (vln); Martha Siegall (cello); Janet Spangler (p); Chris Bishop (elbg) 2 unknown (d);

BD rec

Typically for his first years at Bennington, Dixon had few steady players to rely on, and almost no regular body of musicians that could be called an ensemble. Known to have participated in Dixon's fall, 1970 ensemble class (Elements of Composition and Contemporary Improvisation for the Musician) were Ann Carrier and Eric Dash (fl); Doug Roberts (fl, bcl); Henry Carnes (g); Chris Bishop (elbg); Darrell Nichols (perc); and Stephen Redmond (unk).

"In an ensemble, this one reads well, but can't play; this one can play, but can't read... So you've got to create a situation where everyone can do something. "My feelings about teaching then were also different. Now I know what bad teaching is, and what no teaching is, and I don't believe it's the primary responsibility of the teacher to encourage or motivate. I believe the teacher's got to be so in charge of that material that when the students see it done, they want to do it. That is the motivation.

"And they want to hear you play. It's not useful to remain aloof and do nothing. I don't believe in that form of teaching anymore. At some point you've got to do--not as a demonstration--you've got to do something. There were two reasons I played so much with the people I taught: first, I needed to play; and second, if I hadn't there would have been no playing. I did it enough to the point where they could get over their inhibitions about playing with me, and then they started to do something. I did that right from the very beginning. I wasn't going to give up who I was, no matter whom I was "teaching'--theoretically or otherwise. I started seeing things that way then. I stopped it in the Eighties, because students were coming through with a different kind of attitude--wanting to have me prove something to them.

"When I first started to teach at Bennington and had all of these beginners who didn't know anything, I asked myself: 'Why would I sit down and explain a major scale or blues progression to these people?' That's not the way any of us start. You don't begin to speak by someone giving you a few words of vocabulary; you start by imitation, and then someone gives you correction. So I said 'Here's the instrument. Make a sound: what can you do?'

"It's really quite egotistical to think that you can *teach* anyone anything. What most of us do is find the best examples of the art or craft, and show them to these students, so that they see what the possibilities are. The gifted and committed students then extrapolate from that. So it's a constant examination of the best examples, practicing your craft, and then trying to do something. "In recent years, we've been telling people to 'be original', but you can't be *taught* to be original. You either are original or you are not. 'Oh, it's done this way?'; 'Oh, no one does that...?' And maybe the thing that you're thinking no one does is the new shaft of light. Can you pull it off?"

R70-0610   Bill Dixon-Steve Horenstein
June 10, 1970   BCVT

BD (p, t); Stephen Horenstein (ts, p)

Untitled tk-1	7:43	BD rec
Untitled tk-2	6:37	--

The work consists of two segments:
A) BD (p); SH (ts)
--then a caesura while they switch roles
B) BD (t); SH (p)
The piano ostinato and the phrases that initiate each's horn solos are the same for both segments.

Dixon's presence at Bennington in the summer of 1970 is further supported by (yet unexplored) tapes from August 2.

R70-0899   Bill Dixon
1970   BCVT

BD (t)

Postcard	6:09	BD rec
Fortunata	8:13	--

The Core

Judith Dunn sketched in her class notes (probably from her second term at Bennington) a still-congealing idea of how the Dixon-Dunn principles of art and education might be employed at Bennington:

> *Penny [Larrison, now Campbell] and I began to speak about a special curriculum;*
> *also about the problem of talented students who want to leave ...[illegible]*
> *The(s/r)e are students whose interests are multi--in arts or making things.*
> *"I have been thinking of a program in which a senior (or older) classman would*
> *have their entire work supervised by JD/BD for a year's period. These would not*
> *nec[cessarily] have to be dance but could be lit--music--dance*
> *....*
> *The program would be by the group which would consist of JD/BD and students. It*
> *would include technical courses; i.e., drawing, instrumental (?) done at _____ in*
> *curriculum.*
> *All 'Compositions' and a special discussion beyond (?) would be conducted by us--*
> *....would meet at least twice a week with us--and once by themselves. Individual*
> *and group projects but _____ and interdisciplinary would evolve.*
> *....*
> *The discussion would be another class meeting with us once and without (or with*
> *invited guests) once*
> *Occasionally panels or per _____ shows (?) etc would be given to the community.*
> *A report would be issued by the group about findings and values.*
> *....*
> *The group would be limited to 10 persons for the first year. The work with the*
> *present system would be considered 3/4 interdivisional--admission by*
> *consultation with dean of students/JD/BD. Open to 2- 3- 4th year students.*

The plan was never completely put into practice, but there were in the Dixon-Dunn tenure some useful changes made to the structure of the dance curriculum, reflecting a more contemporary outlook on composition and improvisation.
Barbara Ensley: "Judy and Bill organized the whole idea of the core curriculum. That completely changed the Dance Department. The thing that made modern dance different from ballet was the idea of the dancer as not only the performer but the creator. With that in mind, composition became a major part of what the dance student did at Bennington, not just taking technique classes and becoming a better technician. And that composition, along with classes in technique (the core curriculum), was at the center of each dancer's program."
Penny Campbell: "One of the ideas of the core curriculum was to focus on the composition/experimentation/showing-of-work process and put it into a course, rather than having everything [composition and technique] discrete. There was a core course in which dancers of different experiences worked together. In the old days the students would do one concert every semester, and one faculty person would choreograph for each concert. The faculty would choose which dancers' pieces were showcased and even which dancers would be in the piece; they would also re-touch the choreography, to the point that some people might say it was no longer student

work. Judy and Bill's move away from that was important. Now many concerts were allowed to happen, at different times of day, and all work was encouraged. Faculty gave feedback, but the students were encouraged to take the initiative to let their work be seen, suggesting politically that the faculty doesn't know everything. That was a big change."

R70-1100   Karen Lierley-Bill Dixon
November, 1970   BCVT

On tape: Stephen Horenstein (ts); BD's ensemble class (acoustic instruments and sonic permutations);
Live: Horenstein (ts); Karen Lierley (choreography, movement); Connie Allentuck, Kathy Bernson, Kevin O'Neill (movement); Jane Plimpton (slide projection)

    Anemone   24:20   BD rec

Lierley choreographed the work as a sophmore.

Dixon organized all of the music including:
1) a long line written for Horenstein to play as a solo--read straight, backwards, inverted, fragmented--as a live layer against two pre-recorded channels of his own playing, for a total of three saxophone parts. The only known tape relating to this performance was probably that pre-recorded tape--Horenstein multitracked playing long, feedback-esque tones similar in shape to parts of Dixon's overdubbed trumpet solos in **R68-0617**, and continuing the explorations of "Relay" (**R70-0428**).
2) a tape of the ensemble (and/or dancers) recorded making a number of sounds--wadding and tearing of paper in unison, for instance--some of which were played back at half or double speed and enhanced with reverberation in the concert.

"Anemone" was only performed once in this configuration; Dixon gave the original manuscript to Horenstein in appreciation of his prowess in the performance, and he may have played it as a solo feature thereafter. See also **74-1206**. It was the first piece of music that Dixon wrote for Horenstein.

Details from concert program; score to Horenstein's part printed in Beau Friedlander "Thus Spoke Dixon" *cRUDE* Summer, 1996, p. 4-5.

70-1199   Bill Dixon-Judith Dunn Company of Musicians and Dancers
late 1970   BCVT

BD (t); John Hagen, Stephen Horenstein (ts); others unknown

For at least one session at BCVT, Dixon had planned to use Arthur Doyle and Stephen Horenstein. Due to a disagreement, Dixon chose to replace Doyle with Richard Clay (in New York) and eventually John Hagen (in Bennington), who had by that time established his presence on the campus through joining Dixon, Horenstein, and Chris Bishop in playing for Dunn's classes.

R70-1203   Ensemble Class
December 3, 1970   BCVT

BD (t); Tony Ackerman (g); Kim Wheeler and *probably* Doug Houston (voice); Doug Roberts (fl, bcl)

                                        7:15   BD rec

R70-1215   Bill Dixon Ensemble
December 15, 1970   Jennings Hall: BCVT

BD, Arthur Brooks, Rick Conedera (t); Ann Carrier (fl); Doug Roberts (fl, bcl);
John Hagen, Stephen Horenstein (ts); Chris Bishop (elbg); unknown (d)

Octobersong/Conversation/Winter's Tales   32:30   BD rec

The known recording of these pieces was apparently realized in the relatively close
quarters of Dixon's Jennings Hall studio. The work is also listed as part of the series
Studio Workshop Performances at Bennington, a prototype of the end-of-term
showcases of the Black Music Division. The date given above has been attached to
both, suggesting that they are one and the same.
This is a continuous performance, and the three pieces are not clearly separated as
A-B-C.
"Conversation" and "Winter's Tales" may have been Dixon's orchestrations of
compositions by other members of the group.
One component of this music became "Summer Song", which was used in the later
"Summerdance" series [cf. **R71-0714**].

"When I used to come to Bennington [while still living in New York], I would devote
three hours each week in the ensemble class to creating a piece of music; I gave
myself that amount of time. Each of these pieces had been done thay way on its own
night, and this was the sum of all of them at that time. Those were all beginning
ensembles.

"If you listen very closely, you can tell that I gave some people lines that they can
play whenever they want to. I've let them play them at their own speed; they've
learned these. Very little of what they're playing is material they've come up with.
They were done in my studio where I just had the electric piano at that time.

"I had been at Bennington since 1968, and then by 1970 there were more competent
people coming into the program. That was the year that [trumpeter] Arthur Brooks
and Steve Horenstein became involved--exactly at the same time. Sydney Smart I met
at the same time, because he came up with Arthur. So Smart is probably the
drummer."

Likewise, Conedera and Hagen arrived at Bennington from Chicago simultaneously,
with the intent of auditing Dixon's classes and ensembles. Like Horenstein, they
were not formally students at the College but walk-ons in the fall of 1970 (Hagen
enrolled, however, starting in the spring of 1971). All others notwithstanding, this
is the correct spelling of Conedera's name.

Some members of this unit rehearsed for performances in New York and Vermont (?) of several works, usually with two drummers (Cook and Jackson) and two tenor saxophonists, in the following combinations, chronologically:
-Sam Rivers and Arthur Doyle [see **R69-1210** and **R69-1211**]
-Arthur Doyle and Horenstein: this group rehearsed and worked in NY
-Richard Clay and Steve Horenstein: also in NY
-John Hagen and Steve Horenstein: in Bennington only

Dixon and Dunn spent the winter 1971 Non-Resident Term [hereinafter "NRT"] in New York, formalizing what would become the most regular personnel for the Bill Dixon-Judith Dunn Company of Musicians and Dancers. Hagen, unable to go to New York for the NRT of rehearsals, went back to Chicago and was replaced for the NYC performances by Richard Clay. Both became more frequent elements of the group as Dixon decided in favor of the younger, less-experienced (non-professional) players, finding them more available and more committed to his music than Rivers and Doyle, who at that time were making their own way in New York. See also **70-1199**.

At the same time, Dunn's choice to include her students in the Company's activities had a similar impact on the dancers' orientation. Barbara Ensley, who had functioned in the group before this change in personnel, recalls the transition:
"Judy was trying to decide whether or not to use the dancers who were her students from Bennington. She said to me, 'Barbara, they're so much younger than we are, but they're really, really good...'. Penny was on her way to Japan [leaving Bennington in June; in Japan by August] when Cheryl and Erika and Megan Bierman started dancing with us. Once Judy invited in the students from Bennington--and they were still students--they were part of the company. All five of us did everything that we did." Bennington dance students Erika Bro and Penny Larrison were already in the program prior to Dunn's appointment but quickly became attached to her methods. Dixon: "The [geographical] focus shifted, and that was one of the reasons that we tried to get Barbara Ensley a teaching position here. The school had an incredible number of gifted dancers--people who had already trained in ballet, and they could do things. They had a different kind of vitality, if you want to consider the admixture."

Some other performances with these participants were undoubtedly part of the *Improvisation Nights of Musicians and Dancers* held in early 1971 that may have been videotaped.

R71-0302   Bill Dixon-Judith Dunn Company of Musicians and Dancers
March 2-3, 1971   gymnasium of St. Peter's Church, NYC

BD (t); Judith Dunn (choreography, movement); Scott Guyon (t); John
Buckingham (tu); Stephen Horenstein, Richard Clay (ts); Laurence Cook (d);
Megan Bierman, Erika Bro, Barbara Ensley, Cheryl Niederman (movement)

Day One   57:00   BD rec

Design by Richard Kerry.
Guyon was a student at Hampshire College.

Cheryl Lilienstein: " 'Day One' had--I believe--five phrases that were known in
advance. They were done in unison, but you [the dancer] couldn't do them unless
someone were to join you. They could be begun by anyone at any time. [Dunn's later
piece] 'Day Two' was a similar but entirely improvised piece. It did not have those
unisons in it."
"Day One" derived from the many New York rehearsals held in the winter at the
Hudson Arts Union (for the musicians, apparently) and Dunn's loft (the dancers), as
the term of classes at Bennington had not yet begun. Several other tapes from
February 4, 9, 10, 21, 25, and 26, 1971 (presumably of "Day One" from this
environment) survive.
One other concert tape of the piece also exists; it may be the other of these two days
or one of the Westbeth performances, **71-0417** or **71-0424**.

R71-0329   Jazz Composers' Orchestra Association
March 29, 1971   Public Theater, NYC

Bill Dixon (cond); Eugene Citronbaum, Lloyd Michaels, Enrico Rava, Charles
Sullivan (t); Sam Burtis, Roswell Rudd (tb); John Buckingham, Toby Hanks,
Bill Stanley (tu); Richard Clay, Stephen Horenstein, Lee Konitz, Pat Patrick,
Dewey Redman (ts); Karlhanns Berger, Warren Chiasson (vibes); Beaver Harris,
Laurence Cook (d)

>   Untitled Orchestra Piece   28:30   BD rec

Dixon was invited to lead a *Workshop of the JCOA*--one of several held at weekly
intervals in the spring of 1971. There were no rehearsals prior to day of
performance. "I went in, gave them the music, and then realized they wouldn't be
able to do the thing in the next 25 years. They were there for a gig. So I made a
simple announcement: 'We're going to have an open rehearsal' "; the concert was
therefore presented as a work-in-progress.

This work has strong connections to the music of "Day One" (**R71-0302**); the
instrumentation is an expanded version of that for the Dixon-Dunn collaboration,
with tuba and tenor saxophone lines common to both pieces.
The tenor saxophone parts related to the tenor line that Dixon had written for
Horenstein in "Anemone" (**R70-1100**), a sketch also under development in the
saxophone parts to performances throughout the winter. "Steve sat down next to all
of these 'heavy' New York players--Konitz, Redman, Patrick--and they asked him
'Are you sightreading that?!?' Steve then realized that there were certain things he
knew that they didn't know no matter how good they were. The lesson is: whatever
you work on is where you become the strongest."
A photograph from the workshop is shown in *L'Opera*.
Details from concert program; *L'Opera* p. 63.

71-0417   Bill Dixon-Judith Dunn Company of Musicians and Dancers
April 17, 1971   Merce Cunningham Stud.: Westbeth,NY

BD (t); Judith Dunn (choreography); John Buckingham (tu); Stephen Horenstein
(ts); Laurence Cook (d); Megan Bierman, Erika Bro, Barbara Ensley, Cheryl
Lilienstein (movement)

     Day One   c60:00

This performance and the next were part of a Dance Theater Workshop Series at the
Cunningham Studio--possibly the first at the new Westbeth facility. "Day One" was
presented at both concerts. They are believed to have been documented in film,
possibly by Richard Kerry.

Choreographer Art Bauman also presented an improvisational work in this series.
"Faculty Notes" in *Quadrille*, volume 5 # 3, 1971 p. 50; choreography described in Wendy Perron
"Improvisation Part 2: Acquaintanceship" *Soho Weekly News* January 13, 1979, p. 26.

71-0424   Bill Dixon-Judith Dunn Company of Musicians and Dancers
April 24, 1971   Merce Cunningham Stud.:Westbeth, NY

BD, Enrico Rava (t); Judith Dunn (choreography); John Buckingham (tu);
Stephen Horenstein, Richard Clay (ts); Laurence Cook, David Jackson (d);
Megan Bierman, Erika Bro, Barbara Ensley, Cheryl Lilienstein (movement)

     Day One   c60:00

Again from the the Dance Theater Workshop Series at the Cunningham Studio. This
event was photographed by V. Fladon.
"Faculty Notes" in *Quadrille*, volume 5 # 3, 1971 p. 50.

71-0448   Bill Dixon-Barbara Ensley
probably ca. 1971   Carriage Barn: BCVT

BD (t); Barbara Ensley (movement)

Barbara Ensley: "There was an event organized around the solo as a form--solo
dancer, solo musician. It was decided that since Judy and Bill did things together all
of the time, this would be one time when they wouldn't. I don't remember who played
for Judy, but Bill played for me. It seemed to me that Bill's music was very different
that time from what I had heard before; it was very melodic.... I did an improvised
solo.
"That whole concert was held sometime after 'Relay'. Some students may have been
involved, and probably the people who were teaching there at the time." This
concert may have happened as late as December 1972.

71-0508   Bill Dixon-Judith Dunn Company of Musicians and Dancers
May 8, 1971   Commons Theater, BCVT

BD, Eugene Citronbaum, Enrico Rava (t); Judith Dunn (choreography,
movement); John Buckingham (tu); Stephen Horenstein, Richard Clay (ts);
Laurence Cook, David Jackson (d); Megan Bierman, Erika Bro, Barbara Ensley,
Cheryl Niederman (movement)

          probably Day One   c60:00

Design by Richard W. Kerry
presented in a Dance Department program that also included works by Linda Tarnay
and Jack Moore.

"We had already stopped using the proscenium stage. From the very beginning at
Bennington, we reversed the process: instead of doing things on the stage, we did
them on the floor and put the audience on the stage to look down and see us. We did
that for years; in fact, it finally became what everyone did there. Why do you always
need a curtain, why are you bowing? For certain things it works wonders, but not for
everything."
"For the work we were doing, everything was important and it began the minute
people saw us. The interesting thing about the proscenium stage is that if you have
all of that--the curtain, dressing rooms, and all--that's fine, but if someone sees you
walking around heading backstage before the concert, it somehow spoils the
illusion."
Details from concert program.

R71-0714   Bill Dixon-Judith Dunn Group
July 14-August 6, 1971   Carriage Barn: BCVT

BD, Eugene Citronbaum, Scott Guyon, Enrico Rava (t); Stephen Horenstein
(bcl); Laurence Cook, David Moss (d); Megan Bierman, Erika Bro, Judith Dunn,
Barbara Ensley, Cheryl Lilienstein [nee Neiderman] (movement)

          Summerdance Part 1   8:14   CJR 1024
          Summerdance   >22:30   BD rec

CJR 1024 is the first record of a two-LP boxed set on Cadence Jazz Records, CJR
1024/5, titled *The Collection.*
Building on the close network of musicians and dancers that the Dixon-Dunn
company had created in the foregoing months, they laid plans to reserve part of the
summer for an exploratory collaboration. Dixon: "We had gotten a grant; there were
about six dancers and six musicians. Everyone was compatible, and it was a beautiful
summer. We had this schedule to start working about 11:00 in the morning and take a
break; then Judy would watch videos of the dancers, while I listened to playbacks of

the music tapes. We took dinner, and then worked some more.

"The piece ran for about an hour, and it was fully notated. As far as I was concerned, it was a series of solos, except that the musicians were told what to do. I literally taught those musicians how to play the piece. I would play things first so they could learn them, and that became part of the [layout] of the thing.

"I would play the figure first, then Enrico, then Eugene, and by that time everyone started to blend in, in staggered entrances."

The score to "Summerdance" also prefigured Dixon's three-trumpet exercises and pieces explored in Madison with Jim Tifft and John O'Brien (**R73-1100**, for instance). Part of "Summerdance" called for the trumpets playing a "unison" line but with deliberately altered tuning, some pulling out an others pushing in the trumpet's tuning slide.

"I wanted the sound to disappear on the last line, so I had the players turn around. That's not a mechanical fade; it's really an acoustical fade. That worked like a charm in the Carriage Barn."

"Summerdance" had one public performance (on August 6) and a series of daily developmental readings throughout this period, as outlined in *L'Opera*.

The segment on CJR 1024 is a small part of one day's session.

"We had the leisure of working all summer. At the end of each day, we could see what people were able to do, and what they couldn't do. Periodically I would play back things for both Judy and the dancers. The musicians, however, heard the playback results every day. This allowed them on a day-to-day basis to hear the piece in evolution, as a whole, and to scrutinize their own playing more carefully. Every other day or so, we, dancers and musicians, would all work together--not from the standpoint of synchronization (because the concept of the work had nothing to do with the dancers 'following' the music or vice versa) but to air all the elements and place them--movement, choreography (finally the dance) and musical ensembles and solos (finally the composition) together. In other words, the musicians saw and 'felt' how the dancers looked, and they 'heard' how we sounded.

"It was a beautiful summer, idyllic."

From the *Vermont Vanguard Press* : " 'Summerdance' was Dunn's last choreographed work. Her interest turned toward improvisation, and after that summer she formed an improvisational group called The Dance Company. Unlike the ensemble through which she created 'Summerdance', The Dance Company was a collective." See also **R70-1215** and **R72-1206** relative to this transition.

Known audio recordings of "Summerdance" come from July 14, 15, 16, 17 (two reels), 18 (three reels), 20 (three reels), 21, 24 and 29; and August 2, 3, and 4. There are at least eight other undated reels. Numerous videotapes of the daily sessions also exist. The "very long line" that is central to the piece was being codified at least by July 18. The piece had been further segmented by the July 21 recording.

L'Opera p. 50-52; *Vermont Vanguard Press* May 29-June 5, 1981, p. 17; part of the score is in *L'Opera* at p. 126.

Madison

"I went to [The University of Wisconsin at Madison] because I got sick of the bullshit at Bennington. I was already in a contract, so I asked if I could take an advance sabbatical, which they said would be impossible. One day the phone rang, and I was being asked to come to Madison. They promised me the world, and they had everything. (First I was suspicious. I asked Cecil [Taylor, there for 1970-71 as an artist in residence], 'If it's so great, then why are you leaving?' He had gotten a better offer from Antioch College.)

"I still hadn't made up my mind whether I wanted to go out there, because one can get tired of always breaking in somewhere--getting used to a new group of people every 6 or 8 months. Sometimes it's better to stay where you are, do what you do, and steel yourself against all of the nonsense. The last day of school before the summer [1971] I already had my classes registered for the next term (I had a very large lecture class by this time). I looked out at that group of people and heard myself tell them that I would not be teaching there for the next year. I made up my mind the last day of school. So the administration went berserk: now suddenly I was the most important man in higher education. I told them that I would arrange the replacements for my classes."

Bassist Jimmy Garrison and trombonist Jimmy Cheatham were those replacements, in the fall, 1971 and spring, 1972, respectively.

As a visiting professor in Music, Dixon's primary activity at Madison was the foundation of a Black Music Ensemble, whose forty-musician membership was selected from over 100 applicants in tryouts that he personally conducted. Throughout his two terms at UWM [fall 1971 through spring 1972], the ensemble met every day, except Sunday, allowing Dixon an unprecedented laboratory situation in which to germinate and execute his orchestral ideas. There were no performances of the ensemble in Dixon's first term there; rather, ensemble meetings tended toward experimental pieces such as an October 1 exercise of sustaining a slowly-evolving, broad cluster of sound unbroken for roughly forty minutes.

"The advantage of being at Wisconsin was having this ensemble. In the beginning it wasn't really that comfortable; there were a lot of things to get out of the way. But when the ensemble finally began to work for me, anything I could conceive I could hear done. I'm a night person, so I might wake up at 3:00am, write something, then walk in with it to the ensemble meeting that day, and they would play it. It gave me an idea of how Duke Ellington must have felt, being able to have this mass of people realize the larger ideas that way."

"Because I was a visiting professor in music at Madison, the chairman of the department requested that I rehearse in the day at least once a week, so that the entire school could see what I was doing. My first priority was to get these people to play what we had there, so I had to put the least interference, the thinnest obstacle between me and the players. If I had something written in numbered sections, I could set up all kinds of situations not by writing them down but by creating them, [assigning a segment to specific players or sections of the group, or indicating a movement or a segment by hand signals.]

"One of the strangest things that happened to me was when the department of

psychology approached me (Why were the psychology people coming to these things?) and one day I got an invitation to have a discussion with them about what they called 'non-verbal communication'. I think that was the first time I heard that expression. I had to tell them I didn't have time to go over there, but they could come and observe, so I was filmed extensively by the psychology department on how I conducted an ensemble."
We also did a lecture-demonstration with the whole ensemble at the University of Wisconsin at Barraboo" (see **R72-0503**).

Dixon also taught two classes for music professor Orville Chutney: one class on Ellington, Webern, and Schoenberg, and the other was a live rehearsal of the ensemble.
Beyond the ensemble membership shown in the next entries, an itinerant violinist and an alto saxophonist named Charles Davis spent some tim ein the Madison BME in the fall, 1971.

"Back in the early Fifties, we all thought--erroneously--that this music should be taken away from all of the distractions in the commercial venues, and placed in a college curriculum. I really believed that. Now [1994] I think that has made it too easy for people, and a lot of them haven't been able to follow through in their studies. That has caused so much of the retrenchment back to earlier areas of the music's performance and literature, because that next generation, which should have continued working toward the next extension of this music, has found itself doubtful and turned around. So now everyone who generally has their work presented or critically acclaimed is doing essentially the same thing. You can't tell me that all of these people feel exactly the same way about music."

R71-1203   Black Music Ensemble
December 3, 1971   UWM

BD (cond); Pat Lagg, John O'Brien, Jim Tifft, Jeff Borchardt (t); M. Tim
Verbich (tb); Les Edwards (fl); Virgil Jackson (bcl); Tom Lachmund, Lee Rust
(as); Stephen Horenstein (ts); John Hagen (ts, ss, contralto cl); Jay Ash,
DeSayles Gray (barsx); John Illingworth (cello); Joel Parker, Basil Georges (g);
unknown (elbg); Jeff Hoyer, Eric Schoenbaum (p); Jackson Krall, David Moss
(d); Mara Herskovits (wood block, voice); Chris Billias, Mark Hennen (auxiliary
percussion)

> Anatomy of a Piece   48:29   BD rec

One of the few named ensemble pieces during Dixon's year at Madison, "Anatomy of
A Piece" might be seen as a middle stage of development between the ensemble
exercises with which Dixon began the term and the finished state of **R72-0305**.
Later pieces during the year had working titles such as "Piece # 2" and "Piece # 3",
one or both of which may still have preceded the Mills Hall concert.

R72-0214   Black Music Ensemble
February 14, 1972   Thomas Jefferson School: Madison, WI

BD (t); John Hagen, Stephen Horenstein (ts); Jay Ash (barsx); David Moss (d);
possibly others

> Lecture/Demonstration   c60:00   BD rec

In the days after this performance, Dixon presented to the Music Department in
Madison a formal proposal for a Black Music Institute. It was generated in response
to a genuine solicitation by the department of Dixon's thought on how the
department might be improved. The text of Dixon's proposal (printed in *L'Opera*)
offers some insight into his early thinking on the topic and relates immediately to
his subsequent activities at Bennington as well. See also p. 182
"Thoughts" from *L'Opera* p. 26-31.

R72-0225   Black Music Ensemble
February 25, 1972   WHA-TV Studio: Madison, WI

BD (cond); Pat Lagg, John O'Brien, Jim Tifft, Jeff Borchardt (t); Jeff Hoyer, M.
Tim Verbich (tb); Les Edwards (fl); Virgil Jackson (bcl); Tom Lachmund, Lee
Rust (as); Stephen Horenstein (ts); John Hagen (ts, ss, contralto cl); Jay Ash,
DeSayles Gray (barsx); John Illingworth (cello); Joel Parker, Basil Georges (g);
Kent Taylor (elbg); Bill Conway (b); Eric Schoenbaum (p); David Moss (d);
Mara Herskovits (wood block, voice); Chris Billias, Mark Hennen (auxiliary
percussion); Charyn A. Simpson, Debby Holmes, Jackie Banks (movement)

    Untitled   59:03   WHA b'cast/ rec

"The TV program came about when Nina Simone--slated to do the broadcast--couldn't
get there; her plane was caught in a storm."

Dixon's broadcast on the campus television station WHA-TV was conducted as an
open rehearsal. The time shown (inclusive of all restarts, fragments, etc.) is for the
entire broadcast, which, for television purposes, was titled "Getting it Together".

72-0305   <u>Bill Dixon: Black Music Ensemble</u>
March 5, 1972   Mills Hall, Univ. Wisconsin @ Madison

ensemble personnel similar to **R72-0225**, adding probably John Cole (tu) and
omitting the vocalists and dancers

      Untitled   1:11:44   BD rec

"The concert was packed to the rafters, first of all, because I had done two radio
programs [one on the University station, and an all-night call-in interview program
in Winnebago, Wisconsin], and the television program (**R72-0225**).
"It was so heavy with drama that it really became burdensome. I was very sick that
night, but decided to start the piece in the manner that I'd witnessed when attending
some of Stokowski's Saturday morning rehearsals of the American Symphony
Orchestra in Carnegie Hall in the early Sixties. As he entered the hall and the
musicians became aware of his entrance, their conversations subsided, and the hall
gradually became silent. So instead of walking out front, I walked in the back
entrance where the audience was and started to come down the stairs. As the people
began to see me, the sound of their talking cut out. By the time I got down to the
stage it was utterly silent, and at that point I started David Moss doing this very quiet
figure--a cymbal roll with mallets--and then began my lecture. From there, it was
very mathematical in that, after I had said so many words, the members of the
ensemble started coming in one by one--*singing* the lines that they were going to
play.

"Steve Horenstein later did something similar at Pat Lagg's concert [**R72-0513**],
by playing Serge Chaloff's recording of 'Thanks for the Memory'. We had discussed
that: How can you get away from this business of everyone having to sit quietly, and
get in their last cough before the concert, etc.? That was a thing that I continued at
Bennington, where very few of our concerts started with the lights going down. The
concert starts when the performers are seen." See also **71-0508** and **R74-1206**.

The Mills Hall concert piece also entailed the ensemble's reading of a quote of
Charlie Parker from the interview excerpted in Nat Shapiro and Nat Hentoff's *Hear
Me Talkin to Ya*:
    I don't know how I made it through those years. I became bitter, hard, cold. I was
    always on a panic--couldn't buy clothes or a good place to live. Finally, on the
    coast, I didn't have any place to stay, until somebody put me up in a converted
    garage. The mental strain was getting worse all the time. What made it worst of
    all was that nobody understood our kind of music out on the Coast. I can't begin
    to tell you how I yearned for New York. Finally, I broke down.

Dixon: "Why Charlie Parker? That is such a tragic line. I don't know of any poet or
writer who could have come up with something that powerful."
The vocalization of this line was used in Dixon's ensemble class exercises during
1971-72 Madison. "I had to come up with something to make people understand the
concept of the phrase as a unit, so when they played they didn't use more air than
what they had to say required. We had gone through solos and breathing exercises,
and one very dangerous exercise where everyone would stand around in a circle and

each person turns to the next one and shouts continuously; then I had them do that with the horns. Some of these things worked; some didn't.

"One night, I had to get them to articulate freely but have a [syntactical] basis from which to do it. Mumbo-jumbo wasn't going to work, because there was no phrase structure to it. So I wrote the whole Charlie Parker quote on the board and bracketed it off so that after every fifth word one person read, someone else would enter."

That exercise did exactly what I wanted, but I knew I wanted to do more with it, and I only finished with the idea years later when I did "Letters: Round Up the Usual Suspects" [**R90-1005** et seq.]."

The Parker quote communicates its semantic content more strongly in Dixon's reading for "Pages", but the ensemble reading of it (exactly as described above) was also musically incorporated into "Bird's Word" (**R75-1205**) and "This//// Is Our Strategy" (**R76-0522**). In those pieces, the ensemble members would begin reading the passage aloud--unsynchronized, with each at his or her own pace--at Dixon's cue. He conducted crescendi and decrescendi, culminating in the sound of the consonants alone, the popping and hissing of lips breaking the air.

Part of John Hagen's role in the Mills Hall concert was to play a section from John Coltrane's "Welcome" on soprano saxophone in the ensemble passages. He also plays a soprano solo.

Hagen was part of the Madison ensemble through the fall term 1971 and into part of the spring of 1972; this is close to the end of his time there.

L'Opera p. 167 and 178 (which are identical) show some of the materials involved in this performance and the continuing development called "Anatomy of a Piece".

R72-0495   Black Music Ensemble
spring, 1972   UWM

      Orchestra Piece   11:50   FORE FIVE

FORE FIVE (It) titled *Considerations Two*.
"I conducted that piece without speaking a word."

R72-0499   small ensemble

late spring, 1972   Pres House, UWM

BD, Jim Tifft (t); Jeff Hoyer (tb); Stephen Horenstein (ts); Jay Ash (barsx);
Chris Billias (perc)

          Sequences   12:55   FORE FIVE

FORE FIVE (It) titled *Considerations Two.*

"I told the ensemble I didn't want to have to deal with someone saying to me,
'Couldn't we do such-and-such?'   My response was always 'You go do it yourself.'
So one of the first things that they did--Horenstein, Ash, Tifft, John O'Brien, Hoyer,
Billias, David Moss, and John Cole: all young turks--was form a small ensemble
within my ensemble, their own New Music group, doing concerts every Sunday in a
place on campus called Pres House. There were some other things they wanted to do;
they mainly played their own music."

Horenstein recalls that the group met 3 times a week in Pres House. Each convening
entailed a group improvisation for one hour, then an hour listening to the playback
of that day's tape recording, and one more hour discussing the music. Then they
packed up and left. That pattern held from when the group was first formed in the fall
of 1971 until the middle part of the second term, when they began to schedule weekly
concerts (though the substance of the earliest ones was identical to their private
sessions). Toward the end of the term, the concerts showcased more of the members'
compositions. Dixon's appearance here to lead the group in his own composition
was one exception to that policy, probably occurring as the last Pres House event of
the term.

Cellist John Illingworth, flutist Les Edwards, and Henry Letcher may have been less
frequent guests to the Pres House sessions.

The score printed in *L'Opera* p. 62 shows Dixon's use of one of the themes from "Sequences" in a
work two years later.

R72-0503   Black Music Ensemble
May 3, 1972   University of Wisconsin at Barraboo

Ensemble as on **R72-0305** or very similar.

> Sequences[?]

At Barraboo, the Black Music Ensemble definitively realized what amounts to the
other completely, new full-orchestra work of Dixon's time at Madison (after the
"Anatomy of a Piece"/Mills Hall performance). The work related closely to
"Sequences": that performance at the Pres house (see previous) was effectively a
scaled-down instrumentation--using the key players from the full group--performing
many of the same musical structures of the Barraboo piece. That very successful
performance at a rural satellite of the University of Wisconsin was likely the only
public reading of the work. It was followed by a question and answer period with
some members of the audience.

R72-0520   Concert of Student Compositions
May 20, 1972   Morphy Recital Hall: Madison, WI

BD (p); Pat Lagg (t); Jay Ash (barsx); Stephen Horenstein (ts); John Illingworth
(cello)

> Piece for Pat Lagg   6:50   BD rec

Premiered a week earlier (**O72-0513**), Dixon's piece was here performed again, in a
concert that also included compositions by Jeff Hoyer, Stephen Horenstein, and Les
Edwards.

This recording was slated for issue in the Italian 4-LP box set *In the Sign of
Labyrinth*, as FORE 80. See **R73-1100**.
At the end of Dixon's year at UWM, he returned to BCVT with Horenstein and a host
of the stalwart UWM ensemble members who wanted to continue their studies,
effectively transplanting the Black Music Ensemble.

Details from concert program.

R72-0900   Bill Dixon
September, 1972   BCVT

BD (t)

Unknown	2:00	BD rec
	2:24	--
	1:42	--
	frag.	--
	2:44	--
[inc.]	0:30	--
	0:32	--
	1:07	--

R72-1009   Bill Dixon-Mara Purl
October 9, 1972   BCVT

BD (t); Mara Purl (koto and/or shakuhachi)

Unknown	BD rec
Unknown	--
Unknown	--

These pieces may have come from a duo tutorial with Purl.

R72-1021   Bill Dixon-Judith Dunn Company of Musicians and Dancers
October 21-22, 1972   Commons Theater, BCVT

BD, John O'Brien, Jim Tifft (t); Judith Dunn (choreography, movement); Jeff
Hoyer (tb); Stephen Horenstein (ts, bcl); Jay Ash (barsx); Mara Purl (voice,
koto); Erika Bro, Barbara Ensley, Robert Kovich, Penny Larrison, Cheryl
Niederman (movement)

          1972 [Day Three]   BD rec

Saturday and Sunday concerts at 8:30pm

The general schema of the piece performed here seems to be ABCBA. A tape from the
October 21 event is known.

Larrison returned from Japan, rejoining the (late summer) Bennington preparations
for this piece. Dixon may not have literally returned to Bennington by this time, but
his return to the work was anticipated, though changes in Dunn's philosophy and/or
working practice during Dixon's time away in Madison were tangible to the members
of the company. See next.
Set design by Richard W. Kerry
Details from concert program.

R72-1206   Bill Dixon-Judith Dunn Company of Musicians and Dancers
December 6-10, 1972   Riverside Church, NYC

BD, Jim Tifft, John O'Brien (t); Jeff Hoyer (tb); Stephen Horenstein (ts, bcl);
Jay Ash (barsx); Mara Purl (voice, koto); Judith Dunn (choreography,
movement); Erika Bro, Penny Larrison, Barbara Ensley, Robert Kovich, Cheryl
Niederman (movement)

            1972-73 [Day Three]   55:00   BD rec

A short excerpt containing the koto solo may be issued in the Mara Purl (cassette?)
collection called "Koto Kapacity" as Milford-Haven Music MMK-200.

This was the last public performance of the continuous history of Dixon-Dunn
collaborations (1966-72). While Dixon taught in Madison, Judith Dunn had spent
the year in Bennington and New York evolving first "Day Two" with herself, Megan
Bierman, Bro, Kovich, and Niederman, and then a new approach that included no
music as such.

Dixon: "When I came back from Wisconsin, we did that last season [fall, 1972], but
Judy was gradually moving toward stripping everything down, stripping all the
formal elements out of her work. She didn't believe in costumes anymore, so they
performed in street clothes. My view was, people have seen you all day long walking
around in those clothes, and then you come in here and call this special? It's not
special.' I asked her: 'How could you just come in off the street and do something?
You look ordinary.' "
Cheryl Lilienstein [née Niederman] describes that interim's work, starting in 1973:
"As dancers we never did have an intentional relationship either to Bill's music or to
Peter Lackowski's talking: whether the viewers saw or heard a relationship was up to
them. If anything Peter's talking seemed less emotional than Bill's music. His
voice was an instrument in the room that created a rhythm and tonality. There was no
attempt to have the dancing have anything to do with what Peter was saying. In that
way the aesthetics of the performances were directly related to the work that Bill and
Judy had developed together, in which the independent creation but simultaneous
performance of music and dance generated a large and exciting artistic event." Dunn
later formalized these dances with Lackowski under the name "Life Dances" in 1973
and 1974, without Dixon.

Dixon recalls that in the pieces Dunn did shortly after the completion of "Day Two",
"she would incorporate her films, her husband (reading whatever he happened to be
reading), his dog... She was becoming freer and freer, less theatrical; that's what she
wanted. Judith Dunn had a gift: she could use anyone in anything. She took it to the
max. I'm positive that she would have found ways to organize what she was doing
into theater pieces, instead of everyone running around in jeans and thinking they're
into something.
"I think there are limits: the most liberated person in any art would be the one who
knows nothing at all. But from the moment that person finds out something, (s)he
becomes more disciplined because finally we bounce back to the things that we
know, that can be repeated. But this 'free' person who never learns anything can't

do anything. What's so interesting about that?"
From Anderson, below: "When the dancers felt they had sufficiently explored the improvisational possibilities of a sequence, they simply called 'Okay,' and proceeded to another."

Dixon: "Judy said she could finally start to do some of the things that she knew I wouldn't have cared for. We agreed that this would be the last thing we did together."

One performance was held each day for most of a week (8:30pm Wednesday through Saturday and 2:30pm on Sunday), all based on the same musical outline. Recordings are known for Wednesday through Saturday (December 6-9). The work was called "1972-73", but also referred to (particularly Dunn's contribution) as "Day Three", continuing the series that included "Day One", and "Day Two". See **R71-0302**. One assistant in these concerts was Karen Bowman, known by her maiden name as Karen Lierley (see **R70-1100**).
Kovich had rehearsed "Day Two" with Dunn in New York in the winter of 1972, and he remained in the company to make both the Bennington and New York performances of "1972 (-73)" before leaving for the Merce Cunningham Company.

Dunn kept the company together for several subsequent years of performance and teaching engagements, designed along an artistic principle of open input among the dancers and, according to some of the participants, steps toward a co-operative or communal living/working situation. Penny Campbell [née Larrison]: "In the process of producing the work at Riverside Church, a lot of the organizing fell to Judy, and she was sick of it--box office, publicity, deposits. She was tired of being the head of things. That's why when the dancers continued to work in the next phase with Judy, it was explicit that Judy didn't want to be the guru or the artistic leader. Now I can really understand how she wanted to be working with peers and not with students." Dixon continued to play for her classes at Bennington until she left the active faculty, due to a terminal cancer, in 1977. See **R81-0516**.

Dixon: "I also didn't want to be collaborating anymore. I had found that out in Madison, working with those musicians six days a week--plus the dancers weren't that hip out there. Besides trying to do the music, I was having to try to force a reltionship with these dancers. I was ready at that point to move back to doing music without dance, because I wasn't interested in what she was doing anymore."

Susan Bennet MacGregor's *CODA* article seems to correctly refer to this series as Dixon's last public performance outside of Bennington until the Autumn Festival 1976, **R76-0928** et seq.

Details from concert program; reviewed in Ellen Stodolsky "Judith Dunn and Bill Dixon: Theater of the Riverside Church, December 4[*sic*]-10, 1972 *Dance Magazine* February, 1973, p. 33 ; Jack Anderson "New York Newsletter" *Dancing Times* (London) February, 1973, p. 249; Don McDonagh "Dunn/Dixon GroupPerforms 1972-73, Hour-long Dance" *New York Times* December 6, 1972 p. 35; Robert Pierce "Dancing out of the Huddle" *Village Voice* December 14, 1972; Don McDonagh *The Complete Guide to Modern Dance* (Garden City, NY: Doubleday & Company, 1976) p. 368; Susan B. MacGregor *CODA* Jan-Feb, 1977, p. 33-34.

Solos

"In Madison I was working on these ensemble pieces in which my energies were going toward creating works for the larger group, so there was a missing link. I had to do these solo trumpet pieces for myself to counterbalance that. The traditional way would have been for me to write a bunch of large ensemble backgrounds that I could have then stood in front of and blown my brains out, but that wouldn't have been as musically fulfilling or as honest.

"I originally started doing solos because when I first came to Bennington there was no one for me to play with. I did them out of necessity and I made the solo a performing vehicle, a totality so that no one was felt 'missing'. Later on, I would rehearse the ensemble all day and into the evening, have dinner, and then go to work on the solo pieces." Most of Dixon's published solos for trumpet come from when he had 24-hour access to his studio, immediately opposite his living quarters in Jennings Hall on the Bennington campus.

"For so many of the solos, I had a tape recorder set up in my studio. When I turned the lights on I just reached over and turned the tape recorder on, so that I never had to *get ready* to record. There's a funny thing about taping yourself: even if you've been doing it the longest time, there's just something artificial about saying 'Now I'm going to record'. I wasted a lot of tape just because I had the thing going all the time, but I never had to make a decision to turn the machine on. While the solo pieces were done *in the studio*, it was more like a sketchbook than a studio recording. 'Here's an idea, let me work this out...'

"Almost everything I did with what you might call studio solos came out of this context. My use of the studio was just a little bit different from what I would think other people's use was. It made no difference whether I was in there by myself, or there were two or three people, or I was giving a tutorial, this was a real situation. If it worked, it worked well, and if it didn't work, I knew it and knew how to correct it. Nothing was frivolous.

"With the trumpet you have to find as much time as possible to work on your things from the standpoint of being real. Practice is not enough. I never practice scales hour after hour--I used to do that. In other words, for the limited amount of time I'm allowed to play, it has to be real. That was real playing, but I was also teaching myself things, and these pieces were coming out of it.

"What makes the playing more compelling, real, or challenging has to do with how truthfully you can do it--either by yourself or in front of people. If you can't do the same thing when you're by yourself that you can do before an audience, it means you need those people for the putting together of your work. For a lot of musicians the excitement of failing in front of people is a positive thing, but suppose you don't always have that group of people ready for you to fail or succeed, and you need them to do this thing. What are you going to do? Wait until you get them?

"For me, it didn't work that way. I had to make it so that whether I played in front of people or by myself I could do exactly what I thought I was trying to do. I don't have to say, 'Wait until we get to the concert'; the concert for me is all the time.

"Sometimes, if a thing is not happening, I'll stop and I'll work on that. I prefer not to, because if it hasn't been what I wanted, the more important question is: How do I

take it from wherever it is? I think the best players in this music have always done that. If you over- or under-reach a note--because there are no 'wrong' notes--that's the one you have. *What do you do with it?*
"So when people think of recording they always conjure up professional studios, engineers, perfection of this and that... I never think of that. It's too academic. The recording for me acts as notation. It is much more accurate in terms of someone being able to hear what you did, without having to imagine. They actually <u>hear</u> it.

"Some of the solo ideas I liked and made them into other pieces. I was working on long drawn out orchestra pieces for the ensemble, and these [solos] were mainly short and compressed. I would have the orchestra members perform them as solos and add piano, or make an orchestration."

After returning from Madison, Dixon also underwent the second of three significant embouchure changes in his career to date. Unlike the first (see **63-0624**), which left his chops incapaciated for some time, and the latest (1986-1991: see **R86-1116**), this one was relatively easy and "worked like it was supposed to", as is tangible in this fruitful period (1973-76) of playing trumpet solos.

Many of the following entries stem from that period, but few were clearly dated. They are therefore grouped together for ease of comprehension.

R73-0001   <u>Bill Dixon</u>
1973   BCVT

BD (t)

        Solo   6:32   FORE THREE
FORE THREE titled *Considerations One.*

R73-0093   <u>Bill Dixon</u>
1973-74   BCVT

BD (t)

        Unknown   BD rec
This solo probably belongs to the same series as "Long Alone Song".

R73-0094   Bill Dixon

ca. 1973   Jennings Hall, BCVT

Bill Dixon (t)

Unknown	c3:26	BD rec
Unknown	3:17	--
Unknown	2:57	--
Untitled Blues	2:17	--
incomplete	2:35	--
exercises (?)	3:33	--

An informal recording interrupted by frequent tape shut-offs and microphone adjustment between pieces. A regular pulse (from a clock or a metronome?) is heard elsewhere in the room, later a regular sound similar to maracas. Another musician enters the room at the beginning of the third piece; scraps of discussions are heard surrounding it and the 12-bar blues demonstration that follows.

R73-0097   Bill Dixon

1973-74   Jennings Hall, BCVT

BD (t)

Unknown	35:40	BD rec
The Somnambulist	4:30	--

R73-0098   Bill Dixon
1973-74   BCVT

BD (t)

Webern Work/Study	1:09	CJR 1024
Webern	0:14	FORE FIVE

FORE FIVE (It) titled *Considerations 2.*

CJR 1024 is the first record of a two-LP boxed set on Cadence Jazz Records, CJR 1024/5, titled *The Collection.*

There is no convincing evidence that these were recorded at the same time; they are listed together for streamlined understanding.
"Webern" was realized many times in this period and afterward, including **R73-0599**, a third issued recording on Soul Note (**R81-1108**) and two later performances in Italy (R**81-0799** and **82-1021**).

R73-0099   Bill Dixon
1973-74   BCVT

BD (t)

The Long Line	5:35	CJR 1025

CJR 1025 is the second record of a two-LP boxed set on Cadence Jazz Records, CJR 1024/5, titled *The Collection.*

R73-0100   Bill Dixon
January 1973   BCVT

BD (t); William Dixon II (voice, whistling)

I See Your Fancy Footwork #1	7:52	CJR 1024
I See Your Fancy Footwork #2	5:15	--
I See Your Fancy Footwork #3	2:45	--
I See Your Fancy Footwork #4	–	BD rec
I See Your Fancy Footwork #5	–	--

CJR 1024 is the first record of a two-LP boxed set on Cadence Jazz Records, CJR 1024/5, titled *The Collection.*
The following exchange between Dixon and his son William was issued between "I See Your Fancy Footwork" #2 and #3:
WDII: "Dad, can I go get my trumpet and play the things I know?"
   BD: "No, 'cause you've played too much today; you've got to save your chops."
WDII: "Drat!"
William Dixon II played trumpet for about a year, beginning after Dixon returned from Madison, which definitely circumscribes the "I See Your Fancy Footwork" recordings, placing them no later than fall, 1973. At least one tape box relating to these pieces was dated as above; the title (William II's) appears there in Dixon's handwriting.
William would have been in New York with his mother through the school year: he spent the winter and summer vacations [and alternate weeks] with Dixon, increasing the likelihood that these pieces are from a January wintersession. The pieces relate to and probably precede the more intentional trumpet/voice recording of Dixon and his son, segments of which are on *In the Sign of Labyrinth* (**R73-0255**).
"The pieces with William were very simple: I was working on something, and my son came into the room. I wasn't about to stop... I was too locked into what I was doing. He started to do certain things which could not be ignored, and I have always been very able to use almost any [sound element] that becomes available. In hindsight, people may find it hard to believe that that's how it was arrived at, but that's it. There was in these pieces no conscious attempt to effect a duet.
In my experience, most of the things that happen are not planned to the *n*th degree anyway. What you do is to prepare yourself by training, intuition, technical ability, and imagination to be able to receive these things in whatever shape or form they present themselves.
"My feeling was--and I continue to think it's correct--you only learn how to play by playing. Practice of the instrument is totally separate. In my opinion if you can forget what you practiced, you're better off as a player. Because you're facing what you really face. It's like, if you say "good morning" to someone in a foreign language, you expect them to answer based on what your textbook says is an appropriate response, so you're not really listening to them if they say something else. Music is the same way, in that practicing the standard figures doesn't inform the actual *playing.*"

R73-0197   Bill Dixon
prob. ca. January 1973   Jennings Hall: BCVT

BD (t)

Changes	2:54	BD rec
Dominoes	2:52	--
Shrike	:55	FORE THREE
Solo # 6	11:26	Ed. Ferrari 1982
Solo # 7	4:10	–
Shrike	2:40	BD rec
Pyramide	4:00	–
Solo # 8	6:20	Ed Ferrari 1982
End of Silence	1:00	BD rec

FORE THREE (It) titled *Considerations One*

Edizioni Ferrari 1982 (It) is an untitled LP issued in very limited quantities by the Ferrari Gallery (see below). The record was produced in conjunction with an exhibition of Dixon's visual artworks that is referred to in *L'Opera*. The opposite side of that LP also used recordings of Dixon's "Relay" [**R70-0428**]. Disc labels on many (if not all) copies of the LPs were reversed.
This is one of several known tapes of studies relating to "Shrike" and "I See Your Fancy Footwork", most apparently dating to January 1973 and/or the surrounding NRT. See also **R73-0599**.
The liner notes to CJR 1024/5 describe the process of honing "Shrike" to this version.
Solo #6 was retitled "Umbra e Luce for Sid Mackay" in 1998.
L'Opera, p. 79.

R73-0201   Bill Dixon
ca. 1973-74   BCVT

BD (t)

[all untitled]	c. 3:55	BD rec
	8:24	--
	c.12:35	--
	1:03	--

R73-0202   <u>Bill Dixon</u>
probably winter 1973   BCVT

BD (t)

For Wallace Thurman	4:54	BD rec
Pensieroso	1:01	--
Masai	1:01	--
Sttretta	1:38	--
Chalk Circle/Blue	2:39	--
Shadowland	6:22	--
Spaces	1:34	--
The Cloisters	2:04	--
Chromma	1:34	--
Sepia Sketch/For Ernie Critchlow	3:55	--
More Than Something	1:33	--
Manuscripts for Fathers and Sons	4:32	--
Poemm per I Delicati	1:44	--
Circle/Chalk/Red	5:27	--

The foregoing pieces, all titled for issue in 1998, were recorded in this order, probably on a single day.

R73-0255   <u>Bill Dixon-William R. Dixon II</u>
1973   BCVT

BD (t); William Dixon II (voice)

Mirros		FORE Unissued
(i)	2:08	
(ii)	9:25	
(iii)	3:55	

Proposed for issue on *In the Sign of Labyrinth*; see **R73-1100**.

CHAPTER SIX

Black Music Ensemble 1973–1974

"I had to be here [BCVT] because of my son William. Jeanne and I had separated, and I wasn't going to let the same kind of distance interfere that had with my other two kids. I came back from Madison because of William. So knowing that, I decided that I had to make the place work for me. I let my work be my primary focus.

"When I decided I was going to stay at Bennington, rather than take the permanent position offered to me at Madison, I really wanted to stay in Madison. For me it would have been better: they had the resources; it was larger; the entire place couldn't be threatened by one black person. I liked the town and I got better-qualified students to do the music. In Bennington there were so many little personal things that I had to be involved in, whether I wanted to or not.

"I didn't want every time I get ready to do something to have to go through a bunch of people and have them 'OK' it, or vote on the budget, or to always be asking 'Is there any money'. So I made a proposal.

"The Bennington Music Division had said that there was no such thing as Black Music, so I had no basis to say that I wanted the music to be taught here unless I could prove it. They didn't want to include it on any level. 1. They didn't think it existed as an aesthetic. 2. They couldn't do it. 3. In the past they had evinced no interest in it. So the first thing I did was to research everything that had ever been taught at the school--just for information. I found out about the Jazz weekend they had done in 1964 and a couple of things that Lou Calabro had tried to do with improvisation. "Then I was able to frame my thesis: 'You're saying Black Music doesn't exist because that's not within your purview'. Then I made a proposal that I be allowed to head a Black Music Institute--an independent entity, separate from all of the existing divisions--for which I would answer to the President. After that proposal, everyone became outraged along the lines of 'Who does he think he is? Why can't he just be in a department like everybody else?' That was turned down flatly when I first brought it up in 1973, a little while after I came back from Madison. So I went back to the drawing board and made a request to do this thing for a year--with the curriculum, budget, and everything all figured out. I was willing to make this 'audition' for a year, and if I passed I wanted to request being made the eighth department of the college.

"What happened next is really a book in itself. I was attacked in every way imaginable. The Music Department fought it as viciously as they could, but when they realized it was being considered they had to back off.
"Once the Black Music Division was formed, of course, the fight went on exactly as before, but after I had what I needed to make me stay at Bennington, I could forget about everybody else. It was never comfortable, but they couldn't get to me any more because I had a certain autonomy in the Division. I was the chairman. I had my own (tiny) budget. I've never had the ghetto mentality; my attitude was, if they don't collect garbage on my block, I'm not going to throw garbage out into my street. We were a superior teaching division with the resources we had, and taught <u>exactly</u> the same number of students with my one-and-a-half faculty members as the Music Division taught with twelve faculty members. I used to tell all of my students, 'You can't be like those people; you can't miss classes or get there late. We have to be better than they are.' We reached a point where I could actually turn down students from entering my division if I didn't think they were qualified."

Dixon describes three tenets of music education central to the outlook of his Black Music program:
1. "It's not music unless it's played." Therefore the curriculum was built around instrumental practice primarily, augmented by relevant amounts of music theory history, writing, etc.
2. "You can't wait around to be invited to Carnegie Hall. *This is your Carnegie Hall.*" All episodes of music--whether advertised, with famous musicians, before an audience, senior concerts, or not--were approached with the same intensity and dedication, on the understanding that the importance of the music to the musicians (i.e., the students) and not to the audience determined how meaningful or "successful" the concert was.
3. All teaching activities had to start from the beginning--not teaching down to the students, but assuming that everyone knew nothing, taking nothing for granted.

"In the ensemble they were forced to work on memory. As much as anything else the key was having them remember what making a certain sound felt like, so that, for example, you didn't have to have someone play your pitch in order for you to hear it. They were locked into that pitch. You see, learning chords is relatively simple. Learning sound is difficult. When you know a chord you know the pivotal places to go; sound is <u>all</u> pivotal. So if you can play from sound, then all you've got to do is strip things away, and you have the chord.

"The music was very complex, but I had to reduce the performance part so that they could do it. That is, everyone can memorize something. Remember that when they did "Letters" [**R73-0519**] there was no music in front of them--none. I didn't have them memorize it in sequence; I had them memorize what [the music for] roman numeral one was and be able to play it, then I might decide to change the sequence. What I found out then, I think Duke Ellington had found out earlier. I've heard and read about members of Ellington's band saying that he might come in and start with letter 'E', which allowed a continually contemporary point of view, and necessitated dealing with what you had. The room is not always the same every time you play in it, for whatever reason. A, B, C, D, and E over here is bland over there, so you change it. Plus, you have to have some spice for the players to keep them on edge, excited, and willing to do what you want them to do. Complacency is your enemy.

"We played in the round; I was in the center. I might decide that I wanted one group to play letter 'E', and another group to play their part of letter 'A'. But I didn't want the players to decide when a thing comes in arbitrarily. I might be taking a solo, and Steve [Horenstein] could decide to orchestrate something underneath it. Arthur [Brooks] has also been able to do it. But it is not music by committee for me. I could have the trumpet players make a figure rise organically out of the music by signalling to them: 'I want A, and I want it this way', so that they would do open A and alternately-fingered G, and that's where you get that almost Arabic cry. I liked that sound. Arthur Brooks, Tifft, Les Finley, Devon Leonard, [and later] even Stephen Haynes knew what I wanted. I could play the ensemble as I would do a solo. I wanted them to do as much as they could do they way I thought they could do it, the way I wanted it done, without anything interfering.
"So they could have this independence, but be a collective. They worked very hard, and they took criticism well.

"Eventually it changed. The ensemble members of the [Eighties and Nineties] wouldn't have survived the arduous rehearsals [of the "Letters" period]. The caliber of the students changed when the school started letting in anyone who could pay the bills. Having money is not synonymous with either having desire or ability. I had too many students who started their music studies with me disbelieving that you could learn enough in four years to become competent to do something. My experience had taught me otherwise.
"There were always students in the room in the early years of the ensembles. You'd walk into the room to find people already sitting there waiting to listen. It was an event; people brought sandwiches. Nothing had ever happened at Bennington like that, and it wasn't happening at any other place like that. The students could see their friends in the ensemble and say, 'Gee whiz, if you work hard you can do things like *this*?'

R73-0517   Black Music Festival
May 17, 1973   Commons Theater: BCVT

BD (p)

BD rec

The formal title of this series as shown in the concert programs was "Four Fairly Late
Evenings of Sequences and Events in Black Music". Other sources show "Four Early
and Late..." The series was dedicated to Duke Ellington, Charlie Parker, John
Coltrane, and Mary McLeod Bethune.
It was the first concerted effort of Dixon's students at Bennington to stage an all-out
showcase: every ensemble member took part in this three-day around-the-clock
event, the first *Black Music Festival* at Bennington.
Funds for the event were raised by students from Dixon's class (Elements of
Composition and Contemporary Improvisation for the Musician), who also provided
logistical support. Raymond Ross and David Chertok attended, exhibiting from their
photography and film collections, respectively. 40 dancers took part.
The festival was a touchstone and model for the activities of the Black Music
Division which was formalized in the following year.

One component of the first day's music presentation at the *Black Music Festival* was
this concert of unaccompanied performances, in which many of the ensemble
members took part. According to one report, it fitted into the entire day's scheme as
follows:

  Sequence I (May 17): Event ONE--open rehearsal and recording session;
    Event TWO--solos by instrumentalists and dancers

whereas the actual concert program showed a refinement of the above:
    Sequence I: Event i. "Sextet" by Jeff Hoyer
               Event ii. Solos by Dancers
                      Solos by Instrumentalists

Jeff Hoyer confirms that his work was probably performed as a demonstration of how
a recording session might be done, perfecting the segments of the work individually
and then editing them together into a new sequence. Hoyer also took part in his
solos segment (literally duets: one musician playing with one dancer) where his
portion was interrupted by a dog coming forward from the audience to take part. See
also **71-0448**.

"College Will Host Four-Day 'Sequences in Black Music' *Bennington Banner* May 14, 1973; "Bill
Dixon Directs 'Sequences and Events in Black Music' " *Quadrille Newsletter* Vol. 7 No. 3/4
(1973); "New Black Music Curriculum" *Quadrille*: Fall, 1973; details from concert program;
Christian Science Monitor.

R73-0518   Black Music Festival
May 18, 1973   Commons Theater: BCVT

BD, Arthur Brooks, Enrico Rava, Jim Tifft (t); Jeff Hoyer (tb); John Hagen (ss, ts); Stephen Horenstein (ts); Henry Carnes (g); Marcello Melis (b); Laurence Cook, Milford Graves, Henry Letcher, David Moss (d)

　　　　　Event # 3   1:30:10   BD rec

The Event #3 piece begins with Dixon's statement: "We're going to play for about two hours."
Also a part of this day's scheduled performances was Sequence II (May 18): Event ONE--"Gimel" by Stephen Horenstein. The printed program of events identified:
i. "Gimel"
ii. "Black Films" presented by Ernie Smith
iii. tba
same as **R73-0517**.

R73-0519   Black Music Festival
May 19, 1973   Commons Theater: BCVT

BD ("amplified B-flat trumpet"); Jim Tifft, John O'Brien (t); Jeff Hoyer (tb); Laura Dubetsky, Charles Morgan (fl); Susan Feiner (afl); Bill Bauman, Don Kaplan (as); Stephen Horenstein (ts, bcl); John Hagen (ts, ss); Jay Ash (barsx); Baird Hersey (g); Leslie Winston (p); David Moss, David Copeland (perc); Mara Purl, Madora Waldman, Chris Compton, Laurel Sprigg (voice)
Margaret Holloway (reading)

　　　　　Letters to Myself and Others   BD rec

From the third of four days of the first *Black Music Festival*. This was the premiere performance for the work.

The full title of this work was "Letters to Myself from Others and to Others". In concert programs and Dixon's voice it is often shortened to "Letters to Myself and Others" or simply "Letters".
Dixon: "The first version of 'Letters' went on for maybe three hours--including Margaret Holloway actually reading about 40 letters [with no musical accompaniment]. Then there were the other components: a pre-recorded tape of duets [William Dixon II singing with Dixon on trumpet--see **R73-0100** and **R73-0255**] that I had with William, some pre-recorded solos, and the very large ensemble. It was a very involved thing. That work was explored in various ways maybe a half-a-dozen times." These follow *passim* until **R74-0530a**.

Ensemble meetings for the weeks leading up to the Festival were also recorded, including tapes known for Thursdays May 3 and 10, at least one tape from an unspecified Wednesday, and a poorly recorded "Large Ensemble Piece" for trumpets, tenor saxophones, tuba and percussion. None of these reflect the layout of "Letters", though they may relate to it as sketches for some of the ensemble episodes. See also **R74-0199**.

"Letters" was plotted as Sequence III, Event ONE in the *Black Music Festival* schedule [later segments of this day's Sequence--apparently event #2 or #3--were to be the Boston Art Ensemble including Arthur Brooks and Sydney Smart, and a Milford Graves percussion concert] where the following (concluding) day was to include:

Sequence IV, Event ONE: an open rehearsal and recording session, and
   Event TWO: a panel discussion (on the topic "Composition,
     Improvisation, Collaboration" and summation.

according to some advance schedules.

In a June 21, 1983 letter to Judith Dunn, Dixon referred to discussions from April 1973 at which the concept of for a Black Music Institute was shaped. The *Black Music Festival*s acted as Dixon's "audition" toward that goal in the eyes of the Bennington College administration. The Black Music Division--the first new division in the college's history--was formed shortly thereafter, and Bill Dixon wrote its entire curriculum.

With the inception of the Division and its curriculum, three new faculty members were added: Milford Graves, George Barrow, and Stephen Horenstein, who was made a teaching associate at that time. Jay Ash, Henry Letcher, and Syd Smart were made fellows within the Division.

"New Black Music Curriculum" *Quadrille* Fall 1973, p. 55.

R73-0599   Bill Dixon

late May, 1973   *probably* Commons Theater: BCVT

BD (t)

       Webern/I See Your Fancy Footwork   2:37   BD rec

The exact provenance of this recording is uncertain. However, Dixon apparently
played solo trumpet (amplified, creating reverberation through a Revox tape recorder)
on one occasion in or adjacent to the *First Black Music Festival* (see previous
entries). It also follows that such a concert might have succeeded the extensive solo
explorations Dixon undertook in the first months of 1973. If not from the first, then
this recording may come from the *Second Annual Black Music Festival*, i.e.
R74-0526.
This untitled selection which contains elements of both pieces provides the best
evidence of a thematic connection between the bagatelle "Webern" and Dixon's more
extended exploration from the same period, "I See Your Fancy Footwork".

R73-0602   Margaret Holloway-Bill Dixon

June 2-4, 1973   Barn Studio Theater: BCVT

BD (p, el p); Stephen Horenstein (ts)

Actors: Eileen Bresnahan, Philemona Williamson, Donna Simms, Holloway,
Terri Huggins, Leslie Lowe
Margaret Holloway (director)

       Recipe   BD rec
                                                      (June 2&4)

Recipe was the first of Holloway's theater productions for which Dixon organized the
music. It was also the first play she wrote and directed. In a profile in *Quadrille*,
Holloway described the piece as a "one-character play based on improvisations",
incorporating "material accessible to me as a black woman from the South."
Holloway later entered the M.F.A. program at Yale, returning to BCVT (1976) after
one year to direct a command performance of Recipe. Dixon scored for her later
efforts, Facials [**R77-0423**], A Season in Hell [**R77-1119**], and Penthesilea
[**R79-0699**].

The musical score to "Recipe" interpolated the classic blues, "See See Rider".

Details from concert program; Alex Brown "Margaret Holloway: Playwright, Director, and
Actor" *Quadrille* Volume 11, Number 4, [ca. Summer, 1977], p. 5-9.

R73-0606   <u>Bill Dixon-John Hagen</u>
early June, 1973   *probably* Commons Theater, BCVT

BD (p); John Hagen (ts)

     Untitled   private tape

This improvised duet was part of Hagen's senior concert (one of several) probably held the night before his graduation exercises.

Hagen's was one of the first documented senior recitals under Dixon's administration of the program. By that time it was not a recognized "program", nor yet a degree-granting element of Bennington, but some of the same goals and methods that Dixon explicated in a note regarding Henry Letcher's recital (in *L'Opera*) also applied to these first concerts.

see "Senior Concert" in *L'Opera*, p. 25.

R73-1100   Trumpet Tutorial
November, 1973   BCVT

BD, John O'Brien, Jim Tifft (t);

-1: Add Tony Ackerman (g)

Trident	2:59	FORE Unissued
Triumvirate	2:51	--
Trilogy -1	8:48	--

Dixon selected, sequenced and annotated a 4-LP collection of his 1971-73 recordings that was proposed for issue by the Italian FORE record label as FORE 80 [The individual LPs were numbered 80/NINE through 80/TWELVE]. Though a finished prototype with test pressings was created, the collection, titled *In the Sign of Labyrinth*, remains unissued through 1997.

Ackerman was never a Bennington student; he made the trip from Harvard to the College for tutorials with Dixon, probably beginning before the year in Madison. This recording was made at one of those sessions or grew out out of them.

"Trident" for Max Schlossberg was based on one of that trumpeter's studies in his book of trumpet exercises. "Triumvirate" was subtitled "Statement".

"I did one piece for trumpets where I had some tune as sharp as they could relative to A440, and others as flat as they could, and I wrote a very long line for all of them to play in 'unison'. I worked on piece like that quite a while, and when I had found out as much about that as I wanted, I did the same thing having some of the trumpets in A and others in B-flat. Then we would negotiate various kinds of mutes in playing the same line, or I would have them play the same line a half tone apart. Don't forget, we've run up against the limit of what can be done with tertian harmony, or harmony in fourths, or even harmony in seconds, so there was room for this sort of experimentation. If it doesn't work, you just don't have to do it anymore." See also **R73-1101** and **O73-0000** for related items. Dixon and the other two trumpets also undertook some of these exercises with a shakuhachi player--possibly Mara Purl-- as well.

Some of these procedures were also at work in Dixon's February 1973 voicing exercise represented in *L'Opera*. "I gave the pulse, and the numbers written below the staff showed how many beats for each section. [The shaded area] was a general range of pitches, from which the definite pitches possible are shown at the end of the staff. It's a real subtlety. If the instruments were too thick in texture, then the exercise wouldn't work, because the band of pitches was so narrow.
"Don't forget, when you're working on something, it doesn't always just spring from the loins. Sometimes you have to create an artificial structure just to generate ideas."
L'Opera, p. 169-70.

R73-1101   <u>Bill Dixon-Jim Tifft-Tony Ackerman</u>
1973   BCVT

BD, Jim Tifft (t); Tony Ackerman (g)

    Trident III   6:37   FORE Uniss

Proposed for issue on *In The Sign of Labyrinth*; see **R73-1100**.
see also **O73-0000**

73-1105   Black Music Ensemble/Ensemble IV
early November, 1973   Great Meadow Facility: Comstock, NY

BD, Arthur Brooks, Jim Tifft (t); Susan Feiner (fl); *possibly* Don Kaplan,
Dominick Messenger (as); Doug Cumming, John Hagen, Stephen Horenstein;
Steve Simon (ts); Jay Ash (barsx); Glynis Lomon (cello); John Squires (elbg);
Leslie Winston (p); Henry Letcher, Sydney Smart (d)

"After the uprising at Attica [State Penitentiary], 500 of the inmates there were
transferred to the Great Meadow Facility in Comstock, New York. A Bennington
photography instructor who taught there, Roe Rappaport, came to see me, saying
that a lot of the inmates asked if I could come up there because they knew my music.
One day--what was called Black Solidarity Day--I got a call: someone who was
supposed to go up there had cancelled and they asked me if I could come, so I did.
"I taught there for a year--first going once a month, then once a week. They gave me
an upright piano, a blackboard, and a stool to sit there and do a master class on
anything the inmates wanted to know in music. I have never had students who were
that good--intense--on any level. As one guy said, they had nothing *but* time to work
on those things."

Stephen Horenstein performed solo on stage at least once at Comstock--possibly on
Black Solidarity Day; Dixon may have played then as well. Horenstein also made
many of the trips to Comstock to assist in the teaching. As an example of the
topics, he recalled one group of inmates who were very keen to have a transcription
of the ensemble parts to Marvin Gaye's hit "What's Goin' On?".

Dixon had discussed bringing the ensemble to the prison, and to investigate that
possibility the warden of the prison visited Bennington to see some performances.
The Comstock ensemble concert apparently took place at the end of the fall term
1973. A recording from November 2 is more likely a BCVT rehearsal for the prison
performance than the actual tape from Comstock.

"I took my entire ensemble and told the inmates I was going to do a lecture-demonstration. 1300 guys came into that room; it was one of the most remarkable
experiences I have ever had." Dixon also lectured about the history of the music.

Though in the period when "Letters..." was being performed often, the Comstock
ensemble piece was probably more reflective of whatever materials were then in
progress at the class meetings than any specific work.

R73-1200   Bill Dixon/Stephen Horenstein
probably late fall, 1973   Carriage Barn, BCVT

-1: BD (reading on tape)
-2: BD (p); Stephen Horenstein (p, ts); Jim Tifft, *possibly* John O'Brien, (t);
Susan Feiner (afl); John Hagen (bassoon, ts, ss); Tom Guralnick, Dominick
Messenger (reeds); Doug Cumming (ts); Jay Ash (barsx); David Moss (d); David
Copeland (hand drums); Mara Purl, Madora Waldman, Cristina Compton,
possibly Laurel Sprigg and one unknown (voice)

> Sonny's Blues -1   BC Dance video
> Unknown -2   --

Sonny's Blues was James Baldwin's short story--probably Dixon's first use of it in a
Bennington program. It serves to separate the elements of the schedule--Dixon read
the text onto a tape that was played back in the hall, diverting attention from the
shifting of chairs, music, and players from the previous large layout.

Horenstein's piece ("Unknown") included at least one ensemble segment and the
playing of recorded music of Charlie Parker prior to the piano duet with Dixon. When
that duet is over, Dixon departs the performance area, and the ensemble resumes.

The entire day's course of events can be reconstructed as follows:
i. playing of Charlie Parker recordings of "Laura" (with strings) and others.
ii. Baird Hersey's (?) ensemble piece
iii. Sonny's Blues
iv. Horenstein's ensemble piece including the piano duet
v. Horenstein reading segments of George Jackson's writings from the book
Soledad Brother. There is some possibility that this recording captured part of the
concert referred to as Six Pieces, in which pieces by Horenstein, Hoyer, John Hagen,
and David Moss (and Dixon?) were apparently performed.

John O'Brien's putative presence here may limit the range of dates for the concert:
after returning with Dixon from Madison, O'Brien remained in Bennington for a year
or less before moving back to the Midwest.

73-1209   Holly Schiffer-Bill Dixon
December 9, 1973   Commons Theater: BCVT

Holly Schiffer (choreography); Bill Dixon, Arthur Brooks, Jim Tifft (t); Ellen Ferber, Claire LeMessurier, Susan Rethorst (movement)

   Ode to Kato

Dixon composed the music for Schiffer's dance work, presented in "An Evening of Dance" alongside works by Art Berger and Ellen Ferber.

Details from concert program.

R74-0100   Bill Dixon
probably January 1974   BCVT

BD (t)

Odyssey/Interruptus	5:57	BD rec
Murmurs	6:47	--
Long Alone Song	6:38	FORE THREE
Graffiti sui Soffiti	1:53	BD rec

FORE THREE (It) titled *Considerations One*
The first three pieces comprise the suite "Three Songs for Winter" for solo trumpet.
Titles were given to the first two and "Graffiti sui Soffiti" in 1998.

The suite was recorded in Dixon's studio, but at least one piece would have been
performed in public as well; possibly all three were. Contrary to the date shown on
FORE THREE, the pieces most likely coincided with the Black Music Ensemble's
January-March 1974 winter sessions at the Congregational Church of North
Bennington. "With some of those--not all--I transcribed my solo, and took it in to
the ensemble as an exercise. It consisted of very drawn-out whole, half, and quarter
notes--not a lot of pyrotechnics. I gave it to two trumpeters--Jim Tifft, and Art
Brooks--but they couldn't play it from the written music with any degree of
authenticity. I played it once, and then they could play it, making my point that the
notes by themselves mean very very little, even with dynamics markings, etc. Music
is not played solely by the eye. The hearing factor is more important.
"A couple of pieces were done like that: originally in the studio, then taken out to the
ensemble."

"I always thought Miles Davis made the most beautiful sound; it always had an effect
upon me. He, Tony Fruscella, Armando Ghitalla, Fats Navarro, Freddie Webster, and
Clark Terry all literally found it impossible to make a bad or unattractive sound. If
you listen closely to some of those things like "Long Alone Song", you might say
that it sounds like Miles Davis's sound, using an air attack from the back of the
throat. I haven't used my tongue to attack the notes in many years. What I worked
on was stopping the air in the throat. And when tone by itself wasn't going to do it
for me, I began to explore quarter tones and multiphonics.
"I thought I was doing what [artists] are supposed to do: I moved on. I put the other
stuff behind me. Each of us has our own limitation, where we can't go any further,
even if we try. But some of us don't think we've ever reached that point.
"After a number of years of doing my things, I got to a place where I wanted to be:
knowing that I wasn't going to be called in to play on *The Tonight Show*, I didn't
need to keep playing that way in addition. I don't have to worry about whether it's a
four-bar phrase, or a two-bar phrase, whether the sound is consonant or dissonant,
whether it seems like it's all in the same key.... I don't hear like that anymore. I
stopped practicing everything and just worked on the things I needed to practice--a
little bit of time with scales, never any chords--I wasn't playing them any more--and
probably more than anything else, the intervals. *Everything* is a melody to me. I
went all out for what I wanted. What I do well, I have created myself."

R74-0199   Bill Dixon Ensemble
early 1974   BCVT

BD (t, p); Arthur Brooks (t, flgh); Jim Tifft (t); Jeff Hoyer (tb); Susan Feiner
(afl); Don Kaplan, Jemeel Moondoc (as); John Hagen, *possibly* John Love,
Stephen Horenstein (ts); Jay Ash (barsx); Glynis Lomon (cello); Mark Hennen,
Leslie Winston (p); Henry Letcher, David Moss (d)

Letters	55:30	BD rec
Letters	1:22:30	BD rec
Letters	1:18:42	BD rec

"Letters" was performed and re-worked for roughly a year between its Black Music
Festival premiere (**R73-0519**) and **R74-0530a**. The structure and textures of the
piece were also under study during an intensive orchestra workshop held in the winter
session at BCVT--at the Congregational Church of North Bennington on School
Street. Some recordings come from that situation, and most evolved from it. Hennen
and Moondoc traveled from New York to make the sessions in the fall, winter, and
spring.
Notations on a rehearsal tape from February 1 reflect that the work had congealed
enough to be seen as a "new piece" but was not referred to yet as "Letters".

The "Letters" documentation provides one of the first comprehensive studies of the
development of a Dixon orchestra work. Most complete readings included some or
all of the following elements in a different sequence each time and with widely
varying durations for each section:
--Dixon (t) duet with Henry Letcher
--two distinct unison ostinati introduced by the piano and played by all winds (one in
   4, the other 7/8; one of them is Letter C)
--Jeff Hoyer duet with Henry Letcher
One streamlined version of the layout of "Letters..." is printed in *L'Opera* at p. 123.

--John Hagen unaccompanied , then adding drums and horns
--Jemeel Moondoc duet with Henry Letcher
--Susan Feiner with cello and piano (Letter A)
--Jay Ash duet with piano
--six to ten unique, non-repetitive ensemble figures used as transitions (Letters E and
   F are two of these)
--Tifft and Brooks muted duet
--an A-minor section for piano with Tifft or Brooks muted trumpet solo
--staccato/sforzando one-note punctuations for all players cued by Dixon through
   some sections and between others (referred to as "the coda figure")

The last complete version listed above is from a series of recordings made in the end
of April and beginning of May, 1974, apparently in preparation for the Windham
College performance. Those several days of rehearsals included additions to and
realignments of the structure of the piece, refinement of some transitions between
sections, and at least four (often quite different) run-throughs of the long sections of
the work. Dixon's statement to Moondoc in one of the rehearsals is indicative of the
fluidity of structure: "Depending on how strong you are--you will tell me by what you
play what I'm going to [conduct; i.e., what segment comes next and how it enters]
and when. It'll be up to you. I will never know until you start to play how I'm going
to use the rest of these people. Sometimes you'll be playing with Henry [Letcher];
sometimes with Mark [Hennen]; sometimes with Henry and Mark; sometimes by
yourself; and sometimes you'll have to deal with that coda figure."

very brief mention in notes to Cadence CJR 1024/5;
one exercise from this period is shown in *L'Opera* at p. 107.

R74-0509   Bill Dixon Ensemble
May 9, 1974   Windham College: Putney, Vermont

BD, Arthur Brooks, Jim Tifft (t); Jeff Hoyer (tb); Susan Feiner (afl); Don
Kaplan, Jemeel Moondoc (as); John Hagen, Stephen Horenstein (ts); Jay Ash
(barsx); Glynis Lomon (cello); Mark Hennen (p); Henry Letcher, David Moss (d)

     Letters to Myself from Others & to Others   BD rec

The concert, held in the Fine Arts Auditorium on campus, was attended by much of the
general student body at the now defunct Windham College. Despite a poor or
uncomprehending reception Dixon recalls this as the pinnacle performance of a piece
that was great already.
Another, smaller work may have been added to the program for this concert--its
nature unknown.

Mark Hennen's part here was notated, as for most of the "Letters" performances.

New York critic and writer Clayton Riley was a Hadley Fellow in Black Music in the
spring, 1974 term (April 29-May 3), culminating in his May 18 lecture on The Black
Aesthetic. Riley also supported Dixon's lecture the following summer (**X74-0799**)
by having him appear as an interview guest on his talk show on WBAI-fm in New
York.

74-0526   Bill Dixon
May 26, 1974   The Carriage Barn: BCVT

BD (t: acoustic and amplified)

     Untitled

Bennington's new Black Music Division was formally recognized during the *Second
Annual Black Music Festival*, also referred to as *Six Days in May*. Dixon's solo
performance here was part of the first or second night of the festival, which also
comprised **O74-0528** and **R74-0530a** and **-b**.

Another solo tape labeled "New Piece" was recorded after April 8. It may be the same
work performed here or have some relation to **R74-9996** or **R74-9998**, or to
none of the above.

R74-0530a   Bill Dixon Ensemble
May 30 or 31, 1974   BCVT

BD, Arthur Brooks, Jim Tifft (t); Jeff Hoyer (tb); Susan Feiner (afl); Stephen
Horenstein (ts); Don Kaplan, Jemeel Moondoc (as); Jay Ash (barsx); Glynis
Lomon (cello); Mark Hennen (p); David Moss, Henry Letcher (d, perc)

Letters to Myself Pt.1	18:25	FORE Uniss	
Letters to Myself Pt.2	12:07	---	---

Both parts of this recording were to have been included on the 4LP FORE release *In
the Sign of Labyrinth* that was never issued on LP; see **R73-1100**.
It is probable that the performances selected for issue there was from the May 30
concert, but information is not conclusive. In any event, the to-be-issued parts 1 and
2 cumulatively entail only a fraction of the structural segments enumerated in
R74-0199.
Titles above are as printed in the FORE set; the full title is certainly "Letters to
Myself from Others & to Others"
Deatils from concert program

R74-0530b   Bill Dixon-Henry Letcher
May 30, 1974   BCVT

BD (t); Henry Letcher (d)

Duo # One	13:35	FORE FIVE
Duo # Two	2:14	unissued; BD rec
Duo # Three [inc]	4:42	unissued; BD rec

FORE FIVBE (It) titled *Considerations Two*

Musical activities for this day included the ensemble performance (**R74-0530a**) and
a brass workshop in which Arthur Brooks, Jim Tifft and others took part. Dixon: "I
ended up doing most of the workshop by demonstrating some of the things possible
on the trumpet. I rarely do that, because I'm not necessarily a good clinician,
anyway. The [workshop] actually ended with this [series of duos]."

R74-0595   Bill Dixon

spring, 1974   BCVT

BD (p)

Movementum	7:40	FORE Unissued
Triplex	2:40	--	--

Both proposed for issue on *In the Sign of Labyrinth*; see **R73-1100**.
"Movementum" was a live recording such as were often be included in concerts of the division, not unlike the "Vamp till Ready" pieces described in **R74-1206**. These pieces may have come from a series of spring performances.

1982 Composition list; notes to ...*Labyrinth*.

74-0612   Margaret Holloway-Bill Dixon

June 12-14, 1974   Barn Studio Theater: BCVT

BD (p); Stephen Horenstein (ts, p*); John Hagen (ts*)

　　　Recipe

This second run of Recipe, was termed "senior project in drama", presumably making reference to Holloway's graduation from Bennington that Spring. **R73-0602** was the first run.

*For the first two nights, Dixon played piano with Horenstein on tenor saxophone. When Dixon went to Milwaukee to deliver a lecture on third night (see **X74-0614**), he taught the piano part to Horenstein, who played it with John Hagen on tenor saxophone.

Among the cast were Sydney Smart, Philemona Williamson, Sarah Felder, Holloway, Terri Huggins, Leslie Lowe.

According to *Quadrille*'s Holloway profile, Recipe "holds the distinction of being Bennington's only command performance. It was restaged two years later for the dedication of the Arts Center when Margaret had decided to return to Bennington." Dixon did not take part in the "command" performance of the work, nor in any of the formal opening ceremonies for the VAPA Building. See also **R76-0522**.

Hagen, having graduated in 1973 and remained on campus since then as part of the ensemble, finally left the College to settle in New York in the aftermath of these performances.

Details from concert program; Alex Brown "Margaret Holloway: Playwright, Director, and Actor" *Quadrille* Volume 11, Number 4, [ca. Summer, 1977], p. 5-9.

R74-1017   Ensemble IV
October 17, 1974   BCVT

probable personnel: BD (p, t); Sue Feiner (afl); George Menousek (as); Stephen Horenstein, John Love (ts); Jay Ash (barsx); Larry Jacobs (g); Leslie Winston (p); David Moss (d, perc); *possibly* John Clink (conga)

Untitled   BD rec

There is a composition at root here, as given a c.20:00 reading toward the beginning of this recording. Then follow solos (many unaccompanied) by the players.

R74-1017 was the first documented session to assemble the elements of a piece played publicly in early November (see **R74-1101** and **R74-1107**). It was finally presented as an untitled work-in-progress but evolved in the same manner as the better-known "Letters..." before it and the 1975 and 76 orchestra works, "Bird's Word" and "This//// Is Our Strategy". That is, musical materials used in the piece were developed from day-to-day ensemble exercises, solos, and notated sections. Also like those other works, the various sections of this untitled piece were rearranged throughout the time that it incubated.

Dixon addresses some of the concerns of that term's work in *L'Opera*.

Arthur Brooks and Jeff Hoyer were teaching assistants. Though he appeared in the course guides as part of the Black Music faculty in this term and the following, George Barrow was on leave that entire year; he had effectively discontinued his active association with the Division by the spring of 1974.
L'Opera p. 3.

R74-1101   Ensemble IV
November 1, 1974   BCVT

probable personnel: BD (p, t); Susan Feiner (afl); George Menousek (as);
Stephen Horenstein, John Love (ts); Jay Ash (barsx); Larry Jacobs (g); Leslie
Winston (p); David Moss (perc); *possibly* John Clink (cga);

add John Squires or Buddy Booker (elbg)

                              c40:00   BD rec

The rehearsal includes at least one (fairly complete?) reading of the piece and Dixon
accompanying the individual soloists and ensemble.
cf. **R74-1107**. Bassist Garvell Booker was known as "Buddy Booker" during his
tenure at Bennington, by which name he is mentioned hereinafter.

Dixon: "I don't believe in the Socratic method of teaching. (Someone says: 'What's
a C^7 chord?' and you say: 'What do you think it is?' If the person had been thinking
in the first place, he wouldn't have asked you.) So I probably do overkill in terms of
presenting information. I've found that it works. You have to codify in order to have
a platform from which (if you get into trouble) you can say 'I'm supposed to be doing
this.'
"In hindsight, I may have been a little forceful about what I disallowed in the
ensemble; everything didn't go. We had definitions of what a solo was and how one
approached that solo. Some people thought they were rather strict definitions; I
found that they made the students better players. Once they learned the definitions,
they were on their own to redefine them in their own way. So it was really a situation
where those of us charged with that responsibility of 'teaching' were required to
produce the information directly. No Socrates here.

"All of those teaching devices--the idea of the solos, etc.--came from a viewpoint
that I couldn't stand back and 'see what these students could do'. It was to be assumed
that they couldn't do anything. If they could do something they would be someplace
else, not standing there in the room.
"I never was caught up in the stigma about being a teacher. I think teaching is a
higher calling, but you have to know when you can actually do it. I've told many a
class of mine, 'Hey, get the hell out of here; I'd rather practice. Nothing is
happening here. I take my time seriously, and you want to be bullshitting.' I don't
want to come into the room unless the students are just as excited to get in there as I
am. One has to be able to do that if one knows why one is teaching.
"If someone had given me the best players to work with, I certainly wouldn't have
opted to teach people who couldn't do anything. Once I had people who couldn't do
anything, I certainly wasn't going to lament the fact that I didn't have the best
players. So they became the best players for what I wanted to do. They didn't know
anything, because nothing could interfere. They couldn't say 'Why don't we try it
this way?' They *couldn't* try it that way.

"An improvising musician only improvises because probably the most difficult thing in the world is playing a melody *exactly* as it's given to you. That's hard for exactly one reason: we're all individuals; we all change things. When you give something to a group of new people, they're approaching it from all different directions.

"I couldn't teach Ellington tunes [to the ensembles] the way Duke Ellington *thought* about them, or Coltrane's pieces the way he did. I didn't know that intimately how they thought about them, but I could show them those structures and how to move in and out of them. I found that it was easier for me, however, to make all of my own structures, because I knew how I felt about them, and I could correct them better. So I started from the premise of doing my own work as a framework. Then I made all of the rules about what they could do within these structures, and that allowed me to start to *think* originally, because for the first few years it wasn't about my work, it was about teaching the basics of musicianship. It became easier to invent everything, rather than translate and wait for people to learn how to really play an Ellington piece before they started butchering it as improvisers."

R74-1107   Ensemble IV
November 7, 1974   Carriage Barn, BCVT

-1: BD (p)
-2: Arthur Brooks, Jim Tifft (t); Jeff Hoyer (tb); Marc Long (fl); Susan Feiner
(afl); Don Kaplan, George Menousek (as); Stephen Horenstein, John Love, Nick
Stephens (ts); Jay Ash (barsx); Glynis Lomon, Jane Weiner (cello); Larry Jacobs
(g); Prent Rodgers (elbg); Leslie Winston (p); John Clink, Bill Eldridge,
Jackson Krall, Henry Letcher, Sydney Smart, Dennis Warren (d)

Untitled -1	33:20	BD rec
Untitled -2		--

Having been formally incorporated into Bennington's administrative layout in the
Spring term of 1974, the Black Music Division set forth its *modus operandi* in two
Autumn concert series, represented by this piece and **R74-1206**. Bill Dixon's piece
for the Ensemble IV class (culminating that of the previous two entries) was
performed during the first of "Two Evenings of Informal Concerts by the Black Music
Division" (7:30pm). The same night Horenstein conducted a string ensemble and
Ensemble III. Dixon did not participate as musician or composer in the second night,
November 8, 1974.

One of Dixon's program notes from this period (reproduced in *L'Opera*, p. 46)
connects a 1974 orchestra work to the previous year's as, effectively, Part II of
"Letters to Myself from Others and to Others". The piece under construction from
R74-1017 to **R74-1107** might be that work, as might "Untitled" from the next
entry.

Details from concert program.

R74-1206   Ensemble IV and soloists
December 6, 1974   Carriage Barn, BCVT

-1: BD (p)
-2: ENSEMBLE IV: Arthur Brooks, Jim Tifft (t); Marc Long (fl); Susan Feiner (afl); Don Kaplan, George Menousek (as); Stephen Horenstein, John Love, Nick Stephens (ts); Jay Ash (barsx); Glynis Lomon, Jane Weiner (cello); Larry Jacobs (g); Leslie Winston (p); Prent Rodgers (b); John Clink, Bill Eldridge, Jackson Krall, Henry Letcher, Sydney Smart, Dennis Warren (d)

Vamp till Ready -1	7:34	BD rec
Untitled -2		--

This pair of concerts (see also **O74-1205**) was billed as "Two Late Evenings (10:00pm) of Music", a "student and faculty presentation of the Black Music Division".
The program outline is noteworthy as it was the first end-of-term showcase for the Black Music Division.

"Vamp till Ready" was the functional title for Dixon's introductory piano solos. Concerts of the Division frequently began with a solo piano piece (sometimes unannounced) which functioned as a call-to-order and constituted the first performance of the evening. Many of these pieces overlapped the audience's chatter and concluded after the noise had subsided. This prelude was later referred to (as in **R79-0525**) as "Vamp Till Ready". Dixon: "I had a format: at every concert--if it was a concert of various people, I always played solo piano. It made a good balance for programming instrumental works. From the moment the first note sounded, the concert had begun."
In this evening Peter Dembski and Leslie Winston also performed piano solos. The running order of the entire concert was "Vamp till Ready", Susan Feiner's "Solo", "Anemone" (see **O74-1206**), Winston's solo, intermission, the untitled work, and then probably Dembski's solo.

Another piece on the program, "Solo", featured Susan Feiner's alto flute with a solo dancer, Holly Schiffer. Dixon recalls a similar concert performance in which he and Feiner played the "Density 21.5" of Edgard Varèse. They played the piece as written once (or twice), then Dixon improvised while Feiner played the continuous line, and then Feiner improvised while Dixon played it.

The second piece may be the one referred to in Dixon's 1982 Composition list as "Untitled Orchestra Work".

From Dixon's personal statement in the program:
"[W]hile some of my peers in New York and elsewhere might view this teaching situation as just a... thing to do when [one is] not doing what [he] wants most to do, I...feel that I have the superior knowledge insofar as, at this present moment in history, this is the place where an attitude of what I consider the most contemporary of the music, its teaching, aesthetic and performance, is happening. And while still fraught with travail, history will someday prove me right."

Dixon cited his teaching activities for this term as: orchestration; trumpet, voice, and cello tutorials; and "performance and notational practices as they relate to...Contemporary Black Music Aesthetics".

The concert culminated a week-long exhibit in the campus's Usdan Gallery, "September to December in Black Music: An exhibition of photographs, tapes, slides, films, video tapes, scores, etc." One final concert of the Black Music Division was held in Commons Theater on December 17; it is not known whether Dixon participated directly.

Details from concert program. The goals and methods of this term in particular are discussed in *L'Opera*, p. 3.

R74-9996   Bill Dixon

1974   BCVT

BD (t)

| Tracings | 8:46 | CJR 1025 |
| Solo | | unissued |

CJR 1025 is the second record of a two-LP boxed set on Cadence Jazz Records, CJR 1024/5, titled *The Collection*.

R74-9998   Bill Dixon

1974-75   BCVT

BD (t)

Tracings II	1:15	CJR 1024
Swirls	2:27	CJR 1025
The Long Walk	7:32	CJR 1024
Conncordde	4:36	BD rec

CJR 1024/5 are a two-LP boxed set on Cadence Jazz Records titled *The Collection*. These pieces may not have come from the same session; they are grouped together for convenience.

CHAPTER SEVEN

This Is Our Strategy
1975–1979

R75-0326   Bill Dixon Ensemble IV
March 26, 1975   Carriage Barn: BCVT

BD, Arthur Brooks, Jim Tifft (t); Jeff Hoyer (tb); Susan Feiner (afl); Bill
Bauman, Don Kaplan (as); Stephen Horenstein (ts); Jay Ash (barsx); Glynis
Lomon, Jane Weiner (cello); Larry Jacobs (g); John Squires (elbg); John Clink,
Jackson Krall, Henry Letcher, Dennis Warren (d)

>   1.2.4.1.2.1.1.1.1.   18:15   BD rec

Dixon: "I used to have an arrangement with the principal of Mt. Anthony Union High
School, that we could work there all winter, with the provision that his students could
watch the process, which was what I wanted anyway. Generally those things started
out as exercises--things you're working on--and, as usual, by the time you're midway
through the thing you're working on a piece. Jay Ash was graduating; I arranged the
thing, set it, and we made it a piece for his graduation. That was my <u>traditional</u> way
of doing something. I never started out doing something for a person that way. First
we worked."
Stephen Horenstein's journal documented "a series of workshop-rehearsals directed
by Dixon for a group of his advanced students who chose to spend their [NRT]
working with him. We are rehearsing in the local high school, mainly because

the college cannot pay for fuel to heat an extra room for us to use. The college itself is deserted, but we have all stayed here, all sixteen of us. [T]he players are of different levels of proficiency and of different ages (from 17 to 30)." The youngest were students from the high school.

The following postscript closes Horenstein's journal account of the January 16-February 21 winter session at Bennington: "We went on to further explorations in rhythm and dynamics, while at a point in late February, Bill decided to make a piece out of all that we had done. By sectioning various blocks of material, and by focusing on Jay Ash,...he soon completed a composition for Ash's senior recital."

Dixon: "Jay wasn't a composer; he was a performer. Other people wrote pieces for him; mine was the focal work, because it used everyone. It turned out to be his graduation piece." Some of Dixon's manuscripts for sketches that led up to the final version of this work are reprinted in *L'Opera*. The structure of "1.2.4.1.2.1.1.1.1." is virtually identical to that of the "Piece for Jay Ash" (see **R75-1202**); presumably they are two names for (different stages of) the same work. The two known recordings definitely are different performances. Some lines at the beginning and end of the piece metamorphosed slightly fom one to the next, while the solo sequences remain generally the same.

Ash was also featured in ensemble pieces by Stephen Horenstein and Jeff Hoyer in a concert of the Black Music Workshop Series (probably ca. March 23-26).

Philadelphian saxophonist Jimmy Stewart, a guest artist at Bennington that term, delivered the first of a series of monthly lectures on "Aspects of Contemporary Improvisational Practice" in that series on March 24.

Dixon was on sabbatical and not teaching at Bennington in the Spring term of 1975 (Appearing for Ash's senior recital may have been his only official activity on campus that semester); he named alto saxophonist Jimmy Lyons as a sabbatical replacement. Lyons led ensemble IV on Thursday and Friday evenings every week (see *L'Opera*), ending his term with a performance of his ensemble work, "Something is the Matter" on June 6.

Details from concert program; Horenstein's journal, "Winter, 1975: Bill Dixon in Bennington, Vermont" was partially reproduced in "Le Leçon de Bill Dixon" *Jazz Magazine* no. 239-241: November, 1975, p. 18-19; December, 1975, p. 24-25; January, 1976, p. 16-17; February, 1976, p. 14-15; *Bennington Banner*, March 22, 1975; *L'Opera* p. 70-71; Dixon's voicing sketches in *L'Opera* p. 11.

R75-0454   Les Edwards-Bill Dixon
probably first half of 1975   BCVT

BD (p); Stephen Horenstein (ts)

                                              BD rec

Director Edwards commissioned Dixon to write the score for his documentary film
about Black photographer Chester Higgins, based on a book of Higgins's work.
Once he had conceived, composed, and recorded the music, Dixon then retracted it,
and it was not used in the film.
The recording listed here was probably a worktape or rehearsal; the existence and
whereabouts of an actual "finished" soundtrack tape are not known.
The entire enterprise took place in 1975.

R75-0607   Bill Dixon Group
June 7, 1975   Carriage Barn: BCVT

BD (p, reading); Stephen Horenstein (ts); Henry Letcher (d)

Pages as Pages in a Book		unissued; BD rec
Pages [Part II]	15:54	FORE THREE

FORE THREE (It) titles *Considerations One*
The record contains all of the music from this performance but omits the spoken elements: Dixon begins the piece unaccompanied, reading quotes from texts of Le Corbusier, Louis Armstrong, Frank Lloyd Wright, Charlie Parker (see **R72-0305**), and George Jackson.

In this perfomance the instrumental portion heard on FORE THREE follows seamlessly Dixon's reading of the quotes. The complete title is "Pages as Pages in a Book" [Punctuation uncertain], referring to the entirety (readings and music) of the piece, and the shortened title names only the issued segment. Furthermore, the "ballad" segment for tenor saxophone and piano was separately subtitled "Feelings".

The concert program showed this as an unnamed work in progress, to be played by Horenstein, Letcher, "and possibly others". Two pieces by Jeff Hoyer were presented at the same event.

At the beginning of the concert Dixon directed a word of acknowledgement to those students and members of the division who had "made it possible" for him to become a tenured faculty member. Dixon was denied tenure during his sabbatical term, so he was not present to comment on the decision. Instead, groups of Dixon-loyal students and faculty staged a campus-wide demonstrations denouncing the administration's action. Video-taped statements by representatives of both pro- and con- factions were screened continuously at public viewing stations on the campus, and eventually a highly prized statue was held hostage in protest. Finally the administation recanted, and Dixon was tenured. By that autumn, the Black Music Division had solidified to include Dixon as a fully tenured faculty member, Horenstein as full faculty, and Jay Ash and Arthur Brooks as teaching assistants (George Barrow was no longer a regular in the program).
In the same prefatory statement, Dixon noted that the music in "Pages" (like that of Jay Ash's senior recital) was derived from the winter's work at Mount Anthony Union H.S., and that it prefigured Letcher's upcoming senior concert.

Jimmy Lyons's orchestra work (performed on June 6; see **R75-0326**) and Dixon's performance here were both apparently rescheduled from May 30 and 31 to one week later.

R75-0628   Bill Dixon
June 28, 1975   Jennings Hall: BCVT

BD (t); Stephen Horenstein (p)

Untitled #1	7:45	Uniss; BD rec
Untitled #2	8:07	--
Untitled #3	8:14	--
Untitled #4	5:57	--
Bennet	10:16	FORE unissued
Sotto Voce	3:38	--

Tracks one and two were proposed for issue on *In the Sign of Labyrinth*; see
R73-1100.
If not from the same day of recordings, these at least come from the same general
period.

These pieces were recorded after Dixon had removed the recording apparatus described
before **R73-0197** from the studio.

When Dixon turned 50 on October 5, 1975, his students and colleagues presented him
a check with which to purchase a custom-made Schilke trumpet and an airline ticket to
Chicago where it would be made. (Dixon had in fact designed it: "I told him what I
wanted was a horn with the flexibility of the Martin Committee, but with the darker
sound of the Conn. I never went to Chicago; I did it all on the telephone and sent him
drawings.") He continues to use that instrument (among others) at this writing.
"I bought my first Conn around 1960 or 1961. I got it because of its larger bell and
bore--the largest then available--and because of the trigger [that allows the 7th valve
position to play more in tune by just depressing the first and second valves].
Periodically I have used the Schilke horn, but I have never stopped using the Conn.
"Before I had the Conn, I played the Martin Deluxe Committee--the one that Dizzy
played. I got that when I was in school; I had to save for it. (Years later, when I had
the Schilke trumpet made, I found out that Schilke had designed the Martin
Committee.) At the time I bought the Martin, Miles Davis, Fats Navarro, Dizzy, and
(I think) Howard McGhee played it. That was the way you measured it: if those guys
were playing that horn, there had to be something to it. Before the Martin I played a
Reynolds horn.
"I started playing the fluegelhorn about 1953. There were two players I had heard
playing it: Shorty Rogers and Roy Eldridge. I rented one once while my horn was
being repaired, and I bought my first one around 1958. A lot of trumpet players use
the trumpet mouthpiece with it; I use the fluegelhorn mouthpiece."
Dixon played using a Bach 10C mouthpiece on the trumpet until the early Sixties,
when he met the trumpeter and instrument maker Frank Zottola, whose mouthpieces
he has used exclusively since then.

R75-0800   <u>Bill Dixon</u>

ca. 1975?   BCVT

BD (t)

[interpolates "It Never Entered My Mind"]	5:30	BD rec
	5:11	--
	2:12	--
It Never Entered My Mind	2:56	--
	3:03	--
	8:15	--

R75-1202   <u>Bill Dixon Ensemble</u>

December 1975   probably Commons Theater, BCVT

BD?, Arthur Brooks, Jim Tifft (t); Don Kaplan (as); Stephen Horenstein (ts);
Jay Ash (barsx)

Piece for Jay Ash   22:00   BD rec

Jay Ash had studied with Dixon since the fall 1971 at UWM. After returning with
Dixon to Bennington, he enrolled at the college for two years to finish his degree
program in the spring of 1975. Subsequently, he became a teaching assistant in the
Division, remaining active in that capacity through 1978.

Though a different performance, this recorded "Piece for Jay Ash" is structurally
almost identical to Dixon's feature for Ash, "1.2.4.2.1.2.1.1.1.1." (**R75-0326**).
The concert seems to have been given during the *Winter Festival*, November
28-December 3, presenting works by faculty and graduating seniors.
Ash also played a piece (unaccompanied?) on December 6 in the fall Semester
workshop series [see **R75-1207**].

Clues in concert series poster.

R75-1207   Bill Dixon Ensemble
December 7, 1975   Carriage Barn: BCVT

BD, Arthur Brooks, Jim Tifft (t); Jeff Hoyer (tb); Adam Fisher (fl); Susan
Feiner (afl); Don Kaplan (as); Stephen Horenstein (ts); Jay Ash (barsx); Dor
Ben-Amotz, Gregory Brown, Larry Jacobs (g); Jane Weiner (cello); Buddy
Booker, John Squires, David Warren (elbg); Leslie Winston (p); Henry Letcher,
Dennis Warren (perc); Paul Austerlitz, Shelley Bakke, Chip Haggerty, Beth
Howard, Lilian Poole, Bob Sisk, David Smith, Leigh Strimbeck, Naomi
Solove, Julie White (voice)

Larry Neal (reading)

   Bird's Word   c29:00   BD rec

This was the final realization of Dixon's fall ensemble piece, presented in the
end-of-season showcase called *SEPTEMBER 11-DECEMBER 7, 1975 in BLACK
MUSIC* (December 4-7, 1975). The series also included "Motions for L.J." by Arthur
Brooks, "E" by Stephen Horenstein, and other workshop pieces.

8:15pm. From the program notes: "A work-in-progress by Bill Dixon as performed
by Ensemble IV with Larry Neal, poet, critic, essayist. An open discussion
concerning the work of the division and its students will follow."
The piece was untitled as concert programs went to press, taking its name finally
from Neal's text. Likewise, Dixon's phrase's, *"This...is our strategy"*, which Larry
Neal repeats several times toward the end of the work, became the title of the next
term's ensemble work, cf. **R76-0522**.

At least eight undated rehearsal tapes exist for "Bird's Word".
Details from concert program.

R75-1289   Lisa Sokolov
[probably late] fall, 1975   BCVT

BD, Jim Tifft (t); Lisa Sokolov (voice); Mark Preising (ts); Buddy Booker
(elbg); Henry Letcher, Dennis Warren, and unknown others (d, perc)

   Unknown   private tape

Sokolov graduated in the spring of 1976 and had her concert in the prior term. It used
her trio (with Derrik Hoitsma and Peter Dembski) and a larger ensemble performing at
least one original work by Henry Letcher and Mingus's "Eclipse". Dixon presumably
played only for Letcher's piece.

R75-9995   Bill Dixon
1975   BCVT

BD (t)

    Momenti   2:35   CJR 1024

CJR 1024 is the first record of a two-LP boxed set on Cadence Jazz Records, CJR
1024/5, titled *The Collection.*

R75-9997   Bill Dixon
1975-76   BCVT

BD (t)

    Requiem for Booker Little   4:59   CJR 1025
    Masques I   8:35   --
    Unknown and possibly inc   c6:00   BD rec

R76-0200   Bill Dixon
February 1976   BCVT

BD (t)

    Stanza   4:40   CJR 1024

R76-0300   Bill Dixon
March 1976   BCVT

BD (t)

    When Winter Comes   8:07   CJR 1024

R76-0507   Bill Dixon Ensemble
May 7, 1976 et seq.   BCVT

BD, Arthur Brooks, Jim Tifft (t); Jeff Hoyer (tb); Susan Feiner (afl); Don
Kaplan (as); John Love (ts); Glynis Lomon (cello); Leslie Winston (p); Henry
Letcher [and one other] (perc); Ariel Ashwell, Dan Lilienstein, Lisa Sokolov
[and 3 others?] (voice)

This /// is our Strategy: Q	18:36	BD rec
This /// is our Strategy: PSL	45:00	--
This /// is our Strategy: KT	c55:00	--

Rehearsals of this work-in-progress (See **R76-0522**) were recorded on at least May
6, 7, 13, and 14, 1976; and five other (or overlapping) rehearsals were taped on
cassette. They are identified here with letter codes only for ease of differentiating.

R76-0522   Bill Dixon Ensemble IV
May 22, 1976   Carriage Barn: BCVT

BD, Arthur Brooks, Jim Tifft (t); Jeff Hoyer (tb); Susan Feiner (afl); Adam
Fisher (ss); Jimmy Lyons, Don Kaplan (as); John Love, Stephen Horenstein
(ts); Jay Ash (barsx); Glynis Lomon (cello); Larry Jacobs (g); Dor Ben-Amotz,
Buddy Booker, John Squires (elbg); David Warren (elbg, b); Leslie Winston (p);
John Clink, Henry Letcher, Jeff Locklin, Dennis Warren (d, perc); Ariel
Ashwell, Jackie Kramer, Dan Lilienstein, Lisa Sokolov (voice); Laurence
Andreas, Hillel Krauss, Sara Matthiesen, Kathryn Thomas, Robin Wilson
(movement)

Camille Paglia, Richard Tristman, Susan B. MacGregor (reading)

This////Is Our Strategy	c47:00	BD rec

An excerpt (18:25) of TIOS (presumably from this performance and recording) was set
to be included in the 4-LP box set produced by FORE records, *In the Sign of
Labyrinth*. See **R73-1100**.

The concert was also video-recorded, but with technically poor results.
Though it had been assembled in a series of rehearsals open to the public, this was
the only concert performance of "This//// Is Our Strategy" [hereinafter "TIOS"], and
the only episode in which Jimmy Lyons appeared.

MacGregor, Paglia, and Tristman were among the participants planted in the audience to stand from their seats and recite the Charlie Parker quote with the ensemble. One segment of the work also features a tape collage of telephone conversations. TIOS was last in the sequence of orchestra pieces: "Letters"--"Untitled" from **R74-1206**--"Bird's Word"--"TIOS" that helped to establish the *modus operandi* for Dixon's work in the Division. The ensemble's personnel for the four successive pieces was also fairly constant, numbering both the players who had been part of the Madison BME (Ash, Horenstein, Hoyer, Tifft) and some of the first stalwart Bennington students in the Division (Feiner, Jacobs, Lomon, Winston).

"This Is Our Strategy" would have been a suitable collective title for that series of pieces, just as it amounted to a manifesto for the educational and organizational platform Dixon designed, which developed on a parallel course. The Black Music Division was spawned at the May, 1973 Festival, gained a regular faculty that autumn, initiated its curriculum, and then was officially installed as a College Division in the fall of 1974; the next year Dixon received tenure on the faculty. But just as all of the other advances in the program's development had been fought for (rather than granted), the TIOS final performance came in the midst of a campuswide controversy involving the dedication of a new building for the Visual and Performing Arts.

Camille Paglia's notes in the concert program addressed that topic, pointing to the centrality of uncompromised avant garde aesthetics to the cultural mission of Bennington, in the face of many months of attacks and usurpations of the Black Music program and the half-triumph of completing the VAPA.

(See also **Robeson**, p. 239.) Meanwhile, then-First Lady Betty Ford and Jackie Kennedy were visiting the campus on the same day to adorn the VAPA opening ceremonies. Mrs. Ford was given a Bill Dixon T-shirt by guitarist Larry Jacobs, with the explanation that this was the only way a Black man would get into the White House.

Details from concert program; Wendi Gross "Silver Flakes for Saturday Night" *Quadrille* Summer, 1976, p. 23.

76-0803   Alan Silva Ensemble

early August, 1976   IACP: Paris

BD (cond); others unknown

"When Alan was opening his school in Paris, he asked me to do a workshop, for which I wrote a piece the night before. The performance of it was held in conjunction with my lecture on the Jazz Composers' Guild. That piece was *dense*." While the lecture was definitely recorded, the concert *may* have been, but a tape is not known.

Dixon was in Paris at this time just prior to traveling to Vienna for the recording with Franz Koglmann.

score in *L'Opera*, p. 124.

R76-0806   Franz Koglmann-Bill Dixon
August 6, 1976   Studio Heinz: Vienna

BD, Franz Koglmann (t); Stephen Horenstein (ts); Alan Silva (b); Muhammad
Malli (cymbals)

      For Franz   19:53   Pipe PR 152

Pipe Records PR 152 (Austria) titled *Opium/ For Franz*
Bill Dixon does not appear on the opposite side of Pipe PR 152, which features the
Steve Lacy composition "Opium" recorded on another occasion by a different
Koglmann group.

"There are certain figures in some pieces that (for whatever reason) I used in a variety
of circumstances. One was the piece originally called 'For Franz', which then went
through a myriad of [versions] because I liked that shape and contour."
Cf. **R79-0525** and **R80-0611a**.

Koglmann and Dixon had corresponded toward the beginning of the Viennese
trumpeter's career, and Dixon eventually spent the summer of 1976 in Vienna in a
situation Koglmann put together. He appeared on record and in performance with a
Koglmann group of hybrid personnel: Arriving in Austria Dixon sent to Paris for
Alan Silva to make the recording. Dixon wrote "For Franz" for the date, arranging it
even to the point of writing out Koglmann's solo. The chosen version was heavily
edited to its issued length, though that take unedited may exist on tape.

Malli is now professionally known as Walter Malli.
One segment of the score is printed in *L'Opera*, p.109 and in *Jazz Op. 3: Die Heimliche Liebe des
Jazz zur Europaischen Moderne* (Wien: Löcker Verlag, 1986), p. 15.

R76-0807   Franz Koglmann-Bill Dixon
August 7, 1976   Arena Sankt Marx: Vienna

BD, Franz Koglmann (t); Stephen Horenstein (ts); Alan Silva (b); Muhammad
Malli (cymbals)

      For Franz   29:14   BD rec

The group from the previous day's recording session performed during the sixth
weekend of summer programs held in an attempt by local artists to stake a claim to
the outdoor Arena, a multi-disciplinary art space. In spite of these well-received
demonstrations, the facility was subsequently taken out of service by the city
government.
from the "Kultur" section of a Viennese newspaper dated August 10, 1976, p. 15.

In the early 1970s, Dixon began making regular trips to Europe, often in the summers off from Bennington. Normally he took William II, then in his early school years, and Stephen Horenstein. But in 1976 an invitation to perform at the Festival D'Automne (**R76-0928** et seq.) provided Dixon's first engagement to play his music outside of North America since **62-0725**.

Coincident with his Autumn Festival appearance, a group of the BCVT ensemble members spent some of their term in Europe also, performing and studying as a large ensemble: "This was a class project for Henry Letcher and he wanted to take a bunch of students on a tour: Buddy Booker, Leslie Winston, Jeff Hoyer, Lisa Sokolov, Peter Dembski, Jim Tifft, probably Derrik Hoitsma... Telling the people it would be a good experience, I lent them a lot of money, and I got Alan Silva to give them jobs at his school [in Paris] for a while. I arranged for the college to give them a term's credit, but not everyone received it because there were certain requirements they had to fulfill. The tour never really got off the ground", though the musicians did go to Europe.

While the Autumn Festival appearance was a major musical success, this semester loosely mearks the end of a major fruitful period for the Bennington ensemble program, loosely framed by Dixon's return to BCVT in 1972 and the triumph in "This Is Our Strategy" of the spring of 1976. Though the ensemble continued to function, some of its strongest members--the fellows and fellow travelers--were on the way out, leaving the bulk of the ensemble membership to the enrolled students proper. Meanwhile, Dixon was piloting a new concentration on small group performance that continued for the next two decades. Unlike the previous four years, there appears to have been no major Dixon ensemble work in 1977 or 1978. And even as the newly-recognized Black Music program at Bennington was gaining cohesion, its establishment emphasized the artistic and professional differences among the faculty members.

R76-0928   Bill Dixon Trio
September 28, 1976   Musée Galleria, Paris

BD (t -1, p -2); Stephen Horenstein (ts); Alan Silva (b)

Entrances		French Radio rec
-Unknown -2	27:01	
-Places & Things -1	9:55	
-Unknown -2	8:04	

First of five nights of a work commissioned for the Festival D'Automne in Paris,
September 28-October 2, 1976

"My group for the Festival was planned as a quartet with Glynis Lomon but at the last
minute some personal matters intervened and she opted not to go. By the time we
arrived, I hadn't done anything except think about what I wanted to do I hadn't
written any music. I knew I wanted to do a work that would take x amount of days to
develop, and I still wanted the quartet situation. The afternoon that we were setting
up I gave the material to Steve and Alan.
"The way the festival was organized, I chose the venue, and the Musee Galleria was
the one I selected. The theater sat comfortably about 200 people, which was the size
I had asked for, but then we had about a thousand show up. The courtyard was filled
with people, and they had put speakers in the courtyard so people could hear it
outside. We could hardly get in to play they concert.
"The stage was on floor level--not a proscenium stage--so all of the intimacy went,
and there were just too many people (for me). You cannot communicate with a
thousand people playing those subtle, small things. Momentarily, I had to regroup,
and it's one of the few times I've had to do that. In these situations you have a
choice, and my feeling in Paris was: "It doesn't make any difference, because it can't
make any difference. Fortunately for me, the piano was good; fortunately, Steve and
Alan played well, and that was it. But it was touch-and-go at the very beginning,
because that layout wasn't what I wanted.
"There can't be a rehearsal for something, when you play publicly the limited number
of times that I do. In a certain way, even my public performances are 'studio
recordings', because I can't afford to be precious about getting the situation 'just so',
and over the years this attitude has gotten so that it works."

Dixon's group was well-received but the first night caused a stir when, as Horenstein
put it, "People had come from all over France to see this concert and we played for 36
minutes and then packed up." The festival organizers were quick to issue disclaimers
to patrons regarding the subsequent nights (as did Dixon from the stage at
R76-0929), though almost all ran longer.

The series of Autumn Festival performances truly represent a thorough investigation
of a relatively small amount of composed matter. The two-parted theme issued as
"Places and Things" was given a different treatment (in whole or in part) nearly every
night, as were two motives that Dixon played from the piano, one including long
solos by Horenstein and Silva (arco).

The performances were audio taped by French Radio. Dixon chose to issue a portion of the second night's concert on the first of the two FORE Records compilations.

"All of those concerts in Paris I played on the Schilke trumpet. I didn't even take the fluegelhorn, and probably not the Conn."

Ted Joans "Bill Dixon: The Intransigent Black Musician Arrives Very Much Alive In Paris" *CODA* No.152 (December 1976) p.10-11; *Jazz Magazine* No. 247 (September, 1976) p. 36-37. "Bill Dixon" Susan B. MacGregor CODA January/February 1977, p. 33-34; A segment of the score is printed in *L'Opera*, p.108.

R76-0929   Bill Dixon Trio
September 29, 1976   Musée Galleria, Paris

BD (t -1, p -2); Stephen Horenstein (ts); Alan Silva (b)

Places and Things -1	12:42	FORE Three
Unknown -2	24:20	French Radio rec
Unknown -1	6:40	-- --

FORE THREE titled *Considerations 1*
Second of five nights of a work commissioned for the Festival d'Automne. Both this night's performance and the issued title are referred to as "Places and Things".
For bibliographic citations, see **R76-0928.**

R76-0930   Bill Dixon Trio
September 30, 1976   Musée Galleria, Paris

BD (t -1, p -2); Stephen Horenstein (ts); Alan Silva (b)

Letters that Illuminate		
-starts with SH, AS solos -1	22:32	French Radio rec
-starts with BD solo -2	22:34	-- --
-Unknown -1		

Third of five nights of a work commissioned for the Festival d'Automne.
For bibliographic citations, see **R76-0928**; score printed in *L'Opera* p. 179.

R76-1001   Bill Dixon Trio

October 1, 1976   Musée Galleria, Paris

BD (t -1, p -2); Stephen Horenstein (ts); Alan Silva (b)

> Places and Things #2
>> -Unknown -2   20:58   French Radio rec
>> -starts with SH, AS solos -1   21:19   --   --
>> -Places and Things   7:19   --   --

Fourth of five nights of a work commissioned for the Festival d'Automne.
For bibliographic citations, see **R76-0928.**

R76-1002   Bill Dixon Trio

October 2, 1976   Musée Galleria, Paris

BD (t -1, p -2); Stephen Horenstein (ts); Alan Silva (b)

> Exit
>> -Unknown -1   5:00   French Radio rec
>> -starts with SH, AS solos -1   20:53   --   --
>> -starts with BD unacc -2   22:33   --   --
>> -Unknown -1   6:35   --   --

Fifth of five nights of a work commissioned for the Festival d'Automne.
For bibliographic citations, see **R76-0928.**

R76-1003   Bill Dixon Trio

probably October 3, 1976   probably Musée Galleria, Paris

BD (t -1, p -2); Stephen Horenstein (ts); Alan Silva (b)

> BD muted -1   4:30   BD rec
> starts with SH unacc -2   10:46   --
> Places and Things   7:08   --
> *rehearsal*   --
> Unknown -2   7:40   --
> Unknown -1   7:10   --

A further session with the trio was staged for videotaping; no audience was present,
and the venue is uncertain.
see **R76-0928**; score printed in *L'Opera* p. 179.

R76-1124   Bill Dixon Trio
November 24-December 17, 1976   Carriage Barn, BCVT

BD (t, p); Stephen Horenstein (ts); Alan Silva (b)

   Autumn Sequences from a Paris Diary   BD rec

Silva came to Bennington as an artist in residence for these three weeks in the fall
following the trio's Autumn Festival appearance. At least one concert was held
during this time in which material from the Paris concerts was digested into a single,
continuous performance.

Portions of the themes from "Autumn Sequences from a Paris Diary" were also
orchestrated and played as ensemble material in the fall of 1976, as attested by an
ensemble rehearsal tape from November 5.

R76-1299   Bill Dixon-Lee Edelberg
December 1976   BCVT

BD (t); Lee Edelberg (p)

   Touchings: for Piano and Trumpet   BD rec

Dixon's fully notated piece was written for the senior concert of Edelberg, its
premiere.

The piece was also played by Stephen Haynes at **R80-0519**, on which occasion
Dixon reflected, "That piece was originally called 'Touchings for Piano'. It was
completely notated, composed to give Lee Edelberg a piece to play. But the day of
the concert, he didn't have the confidence to do it, so he asked me if I would come out
and play it with him. As providence would have it, that day I was having an extreme
anxiety attack and I didn't know if I would be able to finish playing. Ultimately it
came out very well. There is something about playing under pain of death: you pick
your notes carefully."

The written part--for piano alone--is printed in *L'Opera* p. 63.

R77-0000   Bill Dixon-Stephen Horenstein
1977   BCVT

BD (el p); Stephen Horenstein (ts)

See **R80-0611a**.

R77-0304   Bill Dixon-Stephen Horenstein
March 4-5, 1977   Carriage Barn: BCVT

BD (t, p); Stephen Horenstein (p, ts)

private video rec

These sessions were held at the Carriage Barn to be videotaped by then-documentarist
and researcher Alex Wilkerson, who eventually compiled excerpts of this
performance and other footage from Bennington into a black-and-white presentation.
Parts of Wilkerson's work were subsequently incorporated into Steve Albahari's
video thesis project, also on Dixon's work.

The pieces are duets (not unlike **R70-0615** or **R75-0628**, for instance), but with
little or no gap between them. The March 4 recording includes unnamed pieces of
4:57, 5:03, 7:15, 6:42 and 2:00 durations, plus an excerpt from "Autumn Sequences
from a Paris Diary". Some familiar themes surface on the March 5 segment, including
what sounds like "When Winter Comes" and a reduction for piano and tenor
saxophone of the closing fanfare from "This //// Is Our Strategy".

R77-0423   Margaret Holloway-Bill Dixon

April 23-25, 1977   Lester Martin Theater: VAPA, BCVT

BD (p); Stephen Horenstein (ts)

Julie Miller, Ellen Maxted, Mitchell Lichtenstein (lead actors); Clarke Jordan, Rondi Bergandoff, Christopher Mann, Ed Weiss, Jill Rosenthal, Winston Robinson, and Ron Dabney (supporting cast)

Margaret Holloway (dir)

         Facials   BD rec:

                                                       audio and video

Dixon composed the music to Margaret Holloway's theater piece, the second full-scale play she wrote. (See **R74-0612** for further description of the Holloway-Dixon collaborations.) Holloway directed the 35-character work, returning to Bennington after a year spent in the Yale drama program (1975-76). Holloway from *Quadrille*: "Originally it didn't look like [Bill would] be able to devote too much time to the play. He came in when the play was all blocked...watched a rehearsal, and came back the next night to watch again. Then he went over to the piano and began to play a sound from the image he heard on stage. After that he decided he had to be *in* the play, [to] perform live."
Recordings exist for at least Saturday (23), Sunday, and Monday; the entire run of the work may have included more shows than these.

Tony Carruthers designed the set, and Jan Juskevich the costumes.

The New Paper June 1977, p. 6. BD Composition list 1985; Details from concert program; Alex Brown "Margaret Holloway: Playwright, Director, and Actor" *Quadrille* Volume 11, Number 4, [ca. Summer, 1977], p. 5-9.

77-0517   Jack Moore-Bill Dixon
May 17, 1977   Martha Hill Dance Workshop, BCVT

BD (p); Jack Moore (choreography); Stephen Horenstein (ts); Lyn Bridgman, Susan Brown, Frances Edwards, Wayne Euster, Martha Lee, Shannah Green, Valerie Levine, Kayte Ringer, Kari Reinertson, Nancy Rockland, Anne Soorikian (movement; the dancers also act as a vocal chorus in the piece)

       In the Seventh House   BC Dance video

The work was premiered in this period, if not at this concert.
Lighting designed by Dooley; set by Tony Carruthers, and costumes by Carruthers and Jan Juskevich.

Dixon retains a cassette of an April 11, 1977 rehearsal of the piece, whence the speculative dates above.
The New Paper June 1977, p. 5; BD 1985 Composition list .

R77-0608   Stephen Horenstein Ensemble III
June 8, 1977   BCVT

BD (t); Stephen Horenstein (ts); Paul Austerlitz (bcl); Holly Markush (cello); unknown (b)

       Unknown   BD rcc

Described in the concert program as "A piece for orchestra for Bill Dixon, performed by members of Ensemble III". Dixon is featured repeatedly, soloing over a walking bass figure.

The concert or series seems to have been referred to as "July in Black Music"--a formula in line with the titles often given to the division's seasonal showcases--but , given the date of the concert, may be a misprinting of "June in Black Music".

R77-0617   Jack Moore-Bill Dixon
June 17, 1977   Greenwall Dance Workshop: BCVT

BD (p); Stephen Horenstein (ts);

Jack Moore (choreography); Hillel Krauss, Kayte Bressee, and 8-13 others
(movement)

   Unknown   BD rec

Moore created this senior piece for Krauss and Breesee, the featured dance soloists.

Dixon has cassettes of a rehearsal and the performance, one or both of which must
have occurred on June 17, 1977.

R77-1014   Bill Dixon Ensemble IV
October 14, 1977   BCVT

BD (p); Arthur Brooks, Stephen Haynes (t); Rick Hogarth (frh); Beth Kanter
(afl); Paul Austerlitz (bcl); Stephen Horenstein, Steve Simon (ts); Jay Ash
(barsx)

   Lecture/Demonstration   BD rec

Dixon's 1982 Composition List cites an "ORCHESTRA WORK in progress",
possibly referring to this piece. It was part of a fall concert series including
performances by Nadi Qamar (October 4); Milford Graves (11); Jay Ash and Arthur
Brooks (13) Dixon, and Clifford Jordan (November 9).

Kanter had been a C-flutist, but converted to the alto flute to play in the ensemble.

R77-1119   Margaret Holloway-Bill Dixon
including November 19, 1977   VAPA: Lester Martin Theater, BCVT

BD (t); Arthur Brooks, Stephen Haynes (t); Stephen Horenstein (ts); Charlie
Townsend (vln); Peter Steadman (vla); Holly Markush, Kristin Vogelsang
(cello)

A Season in Hell   BD rec

Margaret Holloway directed this three-act adaptation of Rimbaud's text. Dixon's
music, played uninterruptedly throughout the play's 2-3 hour duration, became the
room's sound and ambience from the moment the audience entered. The music may
also have been subdivided to parallel the play's three acts.

November 18 and 19 are the Friday and Saturday performances from what was
undoubtedly a longer run of several consecutive nights. Materials for this score were
introduced in the ensemble classes as early as October 20, 1977.

R77-1202   Bill Dixon-Larry Jacobs
December 2, 1977   Commons Theater: BCVT

BD (t); Larry Jacobs (g)

Piece for Larry Jacobs   15:58   BD rec

The piece played here was apparently adapted for the ensemble performance at
R78-0324. The two performances share certain figures, notably a returning
ostinato.

R77-1298   Bill Dixon-Leslie Winston
December 1977   BCVT

BD (t); Leslie Winston (p); Stephen Horenstein (ts); Jay Ash (barsx); others
drawn from ensemble

Unknown   39:58   BD rec

possibly the senior recital of Leslie Winston; definitely a public concert.
Dixon orchestrated lines written by Winston for the ensemble: Winston is the
primary soloist and also plays ostinati with the solos of Dixon, Ash and Horenstein.

78-0000   Derrik Hoitsma
prob ca. 1978   BCVT

BD (t); Derrik Hoitsma (vln); Clare LeMessurier (movement)

      Listen

From Hoitsma's senior concert.

"If you define music as something that people do, and have the different categories of it, then the problem wth expressive music--especially with the newer generation--is that they're quick to say 'I want to do <u>my</u> music.' Then you have to ask 'But do you have any?' With them it's not an evolutionary process. Their idea of doing music (and, ultimately, of how one plays an instrument) is different".

R78-0324   Bill Dixon: Ensemble IV
March 24, 1978   Commons Theater , BCVT

BD (t, p); Arthur Brooks, Stephen Haynes, Devon Leonard (t); Rick Hogarth
(frh); Paul Austerlitz (bcl); Stephen Horenstein, Steve Simon (ts); Jay Ash
(barsx); Holly Markush, Charlie Townsend (cello); Buddy Booker (elbg?);
Xtopher Faris (b); Leslie Winston (p); Jean Barnet (vibes); Lulu Nelson,
Lorraine Steiner, Ellen _____ (voice)

preamble		BD rec
Rehearsal		--
Piece for Larry Jacobs	24:46	--
Rehearsal		--

Dixon's "Piece for Larry Jacobs" has some similarities to the piece with the same
name performed in a duo with Jacobs at **R77-1202**. The 24:46 final reading of the
piece is uninterrupted, though this was an open rehearsal for a work-in-progress. The
layout for this event illustrates some regular attributes of the ensemble meetings. In
attendance were students, faculty, and other interested parties, whom Dixon addresses
in a prefatory remark about the method and content of the music:
"This won't be in the traditional sense a 'concert' because this...work...is near 90%
complete; it's only an idea at this particular point. So we will work; this is a
rehearsal. This is a piece of music for the senior recital of Larry Jacobs. But as is the
case with every piece of music I do, it is also for all of these people, and before it's
for any of them it's for myself.
"It's one of the first times I've extrapolated from other pieces of music that I've done.
In fact I just may have at this point found it impossible to be inventive. So I'm
going to be stealing some things from myself--literally. This is a complicated work.
You will hear it tonight and we'll expose ourselves. And at the end of the term you
will hear it again. If you can remember then, you'll see what didn't work or
conceivably how we have made some things work that don't come off tonight. The
only thing we won't have tonight is the chorus. This is a piece for small orchestra,
various people who will solo, piano, voice, and spoken word. As with much of this
music it is more interesting for us to perform it than it is for some of the listeners to
be assaulted by the sounds.
[To the ensemble]: I'm going to give you most of the things from the piano, except
what you have [a series of block chords indicated by roman numerals]."

In the same introduction, Dixon seems to refer to the UOTS piece (**R68-0000** and
R68-0715) as "the last time I did an orchestra piece", perhaps drawing on the
connection of a ten-year mark since that piece was created. However, the "Piece for
Larry Jacobs" has no discernible relationship to that music.

The ensemble meeting is then conducted without attention to the audience. Some
sections of the piece are played, then the entire work. Dixon then inquires of the
audience whether there are any questions about the proceedings, or how the event was
organized. Then he identifies certain sections that need more work, and they are
rehearsed.

Note also that this event was held fairly early in the spring semester. The Bennington College calendar includes a long winter session (the NRT) to accommodate both the need of students to spend a few months of fieldwork in other (usually less remote) circumstances than Bennington and the general desire of the College community not to have to battle the Vermont winter on a daily basis. Thus the fall term runs from mid-September through December, and the spring term from the end of February into early June.

R78-0421   Bill Dixon Ensemble V

April 21, 1978   Putney, Vermont

Arthur Brooks, Stephen Haynes (t); Stephen Horenstein (ts); Jay Ash (barsx); Leslie Winston (p); Larry Jacobs (g); Xtopher Faris (b)

> BD audio rec;
> BC Dance video

While the video-taping of this performance may have been successful, it was recorded with no sound.

78-0519   Frances Edwards-Bill Dixon

May 19-20, 1978   BCVT

BD (p); Frances Edwards (choreography, movement); Stephen Haynes (t); Stephen Horenstein (ts)

> Solo

Dixon wrote the music for Edwards's solo dance piece.

A recording of a rehearsal/preparation for this collaboration exists; it includes only Haynes and Horenstein's parts.

This piece (or **R78-0525**, or neither) may have used the music recorded on Dixon's unexplored tape labeled "Dance Piece-1978".

Frances Edwards also did some informal voice-piano duets with Dixon.

Details from concert program.

R78-0523   George Barrow-Bill Dixon
probably ca. May 23, 1978   Commons Theater, BCVT

BD (t); George Barrow (ts)

-1: *add* Nadi Qamar (p); Chuck Israels (b); Warren Smith (d)

    Untitled Duet   BD rec
    Unknown -1   --

Barrow had been an "extra-divisional faculty" member at Bennington in 1973-74 and
returned in 1978 as a Hadley Fellow, which entailed that he give at least one
campus-wide presentation. (Earlier in the Seventies, the poet Ted Joans and
critic/writer Clayton Riley had been Hadley fellows in Black Music.)
The untitled duet was the first event of that presentation, followed by Dixon's spoken
introduction of Barrow. The event showcased Barrow discussing his work, playing
several different pieces out of the literature and (-1) in the quartet formation. Dixon
joined for this last piece, an original by Warren Smith.

Barrow was definitely on campus for the Spring Festival of May 23?-??, 1978. His
public appearance in that time is thought to be the Hadley lecture/demonstration.
The event was definitely audio- and probably video-recorded. The same is true for the
several ensemble performances from the same festival week: Dixon's, Graves's,
Brooks's, and others. Then-Bennington student Maria Stevens was at the time
compiling a video thesis on the Division using taped concerts and conversations
with its members--probably inclusive of the Barrow demonstration.

R78-0525   Trina Moore-Bill Dixon
May 25, 1978   BCVT

BD (probably p); Trina Moore (choreography, movement?); others unknown

                                                               BC Dance video?

Dixon recalls a work with Moore at Bennington; the specifics are entirely uncertain.
It seems that the still-extant tape recording was set aside as scrap--perhaps it was
unsuccessfully recorded. This piece (or **78-0519**, or neither) may have used the
music recorded on Dixon's unexplored tape labeled "Dance Piece-1978".

Moore, a Bennington student had taken one of Dixon's classes.

78-0601   Margaret Holloway-Bill Dixon
June 1-4, 1978   "The Loft": Bennington

BD (p); Stephen Horenstein (ts)

    Facials

The Green Mountain Arts Collective presented Facials in an off-campus run a year
after its premiere at BCVT (**R77-0423**).
From the *Bennington Banner*: "The cast of 'Facials' includes area residents and
Bennington Alumni and current students. Approximately 30 characters appear in
Facials, many of the actors double cast. The play's score is performed live each night
by...Dixon and...Horenstein.
"Holloway received a master's degree in drama from Bennington last year. This fall
she will attend Yale University's graduate program in directing."

Set design: Tony Carruthers; Choreography: Ron Dabney; Lighting: Melissa Walz.
Bennington Banner June 2, 1978, p. 8. BD 1985 Composition list .

78-1201   Jack Moore-Bill Dixon
December 1, 1978   BCVT

BD (p); Jack Moore (choreography); Barbara Roan (movement)

    Tea Dust at 5:43pm

The work is cited as a 1978 composition (another reference shows 1979), and it was
definitely created for Roan to perform, hence this listing.
Pants "executed" by Joselyn Muhleisen; costume and set designed by Jack Moore.
This performance comes from a Judith Dunn tribute concert.

For any number of reasons--which may never fully be known--Dixon's musical
activities in the late Seventies focused more heavily on the composition and
refinement of his own songs--short pieces with and without words. As Dixon signals
in the liner text accompanying **R88-0628**, Jack Moore's solicitation of short
scores to his dance solos "Tea Dust...", "Autumn's Chant", "Waltz", etc. may have
contributed to that concentration.
The paucity of stable ensemble players likely also began to diminish the importance
of that outlet for Dixon's composition and performance. (Former teaching assistants
and ensemble regulars Jeff Hoyer and Jay Ash had departed Bennington by 1978 and
79 respectively.) Concurrently, Dixon instructed some serious music students whose
interests lay more in creating or singing songs; the pianist and show composer
Diedre Reckseit and singer Shellen Lubin (see **O81-1203**) are representative of this
group.
Setails from concert program.

R78-9993   Bill Dixon-Milford Graves
ca 1978   BCVT

BD (t, p); Milford Graves (d, perc)

c50:00   BD rec

"For an entire term, Graves and I taught a class together, 'The Percussionist as Soloist'. My feeling was that he was a soloist, and I came up with this idea for the class. We came into the room and we would discuss various things and then play. I used the piano and trumpet throughout the course".

R79-0400   Hillel Krauss-Bill Dixon
probably spring term, 1979   VAPA: BCVT

BD (p); Hillel Krauss (movement)

Dixon consented to undertake a duo tutorial with Krauss, who was otherwise on his way out of the Dance program. One term's work led up to a final concert. Some video recordings of the episodes, in which Dixon played a version of the music used for Jack Moore's "Tea Dust at 5:43pm", are now held in the Dance Department Archives. The recordings are from a fairly advanced moment in that term.
"Dancers in general talk too much about what they're doing--so they end up *not doing* it. For the first three sessions Krauss and I had, we came into the room and stayed a couple of hours: I played and he moved. Then the fourth or fifth time I gave him a little correction or mentioned something."

R79-0428   Barbara Roan
April 28, 1979   American Theater Lab, NYC

BD (p); Jack Moore (choreography); Barbara Roan (movement)

Tea Dust at 5:43pm   c. 13:00   BC Dance video

Video recording held at the Jerome Robbins Dance Collection of the New York Public Library. There is also some evidence that these performances were carried on television.
Dance Magazine July, 1979, p. 23, 26-9; entire series (April 26-29) was reviewed as well.

R79-0428   Barbara Roan

April 28, 1979   American Theater Lab, NYC

BD (p); Jack Moore (choreography); Barbara Roan (movement)

  Tea Dust at 5:43pm   c. 13:00   BC Dance video

Video recording held at the Jerome Robbins Dance Collection of the New York Public Library. There is also some evidence that these performances were carried on television.

Dance Magazine July, 1979, p. 23, 26-9; entire series (April 26-29) was reviewed as well.

79-0511   Bill Dixon Quartet

May 11, 1979   Greenwall Music Workshop: BCVT

BD (p); Stephen Horenstein (ts); Jennifer Keefe (voice); Katherine Ringer (movement)

  Places

Dixon's composition premiered at this concert, held in celebration of Erik Satie's birthday (17 May 1866). Other works on the program were composed by Alexis Emmanuel Chabrier, Virgil Thomson, and Vivian Fine, who staged the concert.

Keefe sang a wordless vocal here, in contrast to Shellen Lubin's later vocal version. Dixon: " 'Places' was written for Keefe as an exercise for things she was deficient in. What I would do in those days was collect all the things that a person couldn't do well into a piece. The exercises were always musical."

Details from concert program

R79-0520   Black Music Faculty and guests Quartet

ca. spring, 1979   Paul Robeson House: BCVT

BD, Stanton Davis (t); Nadi Qamar (p); Sonny Brown (d)

  Without a Song [inc]   BD rec

Dating relates to the presence of Brown and Davis, both of whom are known to have been at Bennington for (extended or less so) stays that included **R79-0525** and **R79-0526**).

During Milford Graves's sabbatical term, Nadi Qamar was brought to the campus as a teaching assistant. He would later join the regular faculty of the Black Music Division until its demise in the mid-Eighties.

R79-0525   [Various Groups]

May 25, 1979   Paul Robeson House: BCVT

-1: BD (p)
-2: *add* Stanton Davis (t); Stephen Horenstein (ts); Sonny Brown (d, perc)
-3: *add*: Arthur Brooks (t); Holly Markush (cello)
-4: BD (t, flgh; no p); *add* Stephen Haynes (t); Rick Hogarth (frh); Paul
Austerlitz (bcl); Larry Jacobs, Robert Lavin (g); Carl Landa, Noah Rosen (p);
Kevin Campbell (d, perc)

		BD rec
Vamp Till Ready -1		
Places -2	c14:00	--
I Wonder if She'll Speak to Me -3	c7:00	--
Orchestral Setting/For Franz -4		--

All are Bill Dixon compositions.
"Vamp Till Ready" is a band call that began while the audience was still gathering and
milling. (see **R74-1206**)
"I Wonder if She'll Speak to Me" was also played by Haynes and Linda Dowdell at
O80-0519
"Orchestral Setting/For Franz (Night and Day)" was recorded the following day with
roughly the same personnel (see **R79-0526**). It's precursor was **R76-0806**.
These four works and a solo guitar performance by Larry Jacobs comprised the final
concert in the Black Music Division's Spring Festival Week (May 21-25).

Davis and Sonny Brown were at Benninton for a significant part of this semester,
assisting with ensemble and instrumental instruction. Brown's composition for
ensemble was performed in this series, either the same or the previous night.

In addition to the week of performances, The Black Music Division arranged a series
of residencies, master classes and guest appearances, including Stanton Davis (March
26-29), Brass Proud (April 10-11), Dave Baker (April 17), the photographer Arnold
Hinton (May 1), poet Malika Mbuzi (May 5-7); and Jeanne Lee (May 15-18).

Though the exact details of their activities is not known, trumpeters Ted Daniel and
Alan Shorter (in the fall of 1976) also spent time at Bennington in the Seventies in
workshops or residencies.

Details from concert program.

R79-0526   Bill Dixon Orchestra

May 26, 1979   Robeson House lecture room: BCVT

BD, Stephen Haynes (t, flgh); Arthur Brooks, Stanton Davis (t); Rick Hogarth (frh); Paul Austerlitz (bcl); Stephen Horenstein (ts); Holly Markush (cello); Larry Jacobs, Robert Lavin (g); Carl Landa (p); Kevin Campbell (d)

Orchestral Setting/For Franz		BD rec
orchestra rehearsal take	1:18	--
Part I: take -1 ct	3:06	--
Part II: take -1 bd	1:05	--
Part II: take -2 ct	2:58	--
Part II: take -3 ct	3:28	--
Part III: take -1 bd	4:35	--
Part III: take -2 ct	9:31	--
Part IV: take -1 bd	3:08	--
Part IV: take -2 ct	4:23	--

Part V: take -1 ct	3:55	BD rec
Part V: (ts) solo only	1:42	--
Part VI: take -1 ct	1:37	--
Part VI: take -2 ct	2:07	--
Part VI: take -3 ct	2:05	--

Roman numerals above indicate Dixon's subdivisions of a large orchestra work intended to be sewn together (à la "Metamorphosis" and "Voices") as the continuous work, "For Franz".

The piece is a reorchestrated version of "For Franz" from **R76-0806**, interpolating "Night and Day" as a bass clarinet feature in the middle of section IV. It also relates to the "For Cecil Taylor" of **80-0610a**.

"Orchestral Setting/For Franz" had been performed in a concert the prior evening (cf. **79-0525**), and Dixon made arrangements for this sunny Saturday morning recording session to be professionally recorded. It was never issued, in fact not heard again by Dixon until 1993. Consequently, he has never designated the "master takes" of each section.

The three takes of Part VI were inexplicably slated on the tape as -6, -7, and -8 respectively.

tangentially in program to concert at **R79-0525**.

R79-0609   Bill Dixon Ensemble IV
June 9, 1979   BCVT

BD (t); Arthur Brooks, Stephen Haynes (t); Paul Austerlitz (bcl); Stephen
Horenstein (ts); Holly Markush (cello); Larry Jacobs (g); Spin Dunbar (b); Carl
Landa or Linda Dowdell (p); Kevin Campbell (d)

        Untitled   c18:00   BD rec

apparently a class/workshop/lecture/demonstration

79-0699   Margaret Holloway-Bill Dixon
probably June, 1979   presumably VAPA: BCVT

BD and/or Susan Barry (p); Arthur Brooks, Vance Provey, Stephen Haynes (t);
Stephen Horenstein (ts); Holly Markush (cello); *probably* Spin Dunbar (b)

actors: Laura Shelton (title role); Donna Jordan, others unknown

        Penthesilea   BD originals

Kleist's play, adapted and directed by Margaret Holloway was performed nightly
Wednesday through Sunday, with two shows on Saturday.
Barry played piano at the first performance and the one on Saturday afternoon.
Dixon's composition "Penthesilea" from the *November 1981* recording has no direct
musical relation to his score for Holloway. Rather, he wrote that piece with
Shelton's performance of her role in mind. "When we got ready to do this quartet tour
a few months later, while [the quartet piece was] not deliberately derivative--I just
couldn't shake those ideas. After [the recorded version] was finally done most of the
people who heard it were remarking at how well I had made a 'reduction'; that wasn't
the intent at all."

Holloway was apparently on faculty at Yale at this time, returning to BVT as guest
director of the play.

Provey was not enrolled at Bennington but took part in the ensemble workshops
while a teaching fellow. He was, in Dixon's words, a gifted teacher and active as a
teaching assistant in Dixon's ensemble from this point at least through fall, 1982.

R79-0799   Bill Dixon Trio

summer, 1979   Bim Huis: Amsterdam

BD (t-1, p-2); Stephen Horenstein (p-1, ts-2); unknown (d)

Autumn Sequences from a Paris Diary -2	19:32	BD rec
Unknown -1	9:24	--
spoken interlude		--
Unknown -1	7:17	--
Unknown -2 *inc.*	11:49	--
Unknown -2	15:48	--
Unknown -2	13:45	--
Unknown -2 *inc.*	8:40	--

The Bim Huis had earlier tried without success to engage Dixon to play there, but he and Horenstein accepted the offer for this one night performance while traveling in Europe. They did not perform anywhere else on the trip. The drummer was an Amsterdam musician with whom Dixon was not acquainted before this performance.

Dixon gave at least one interview during the trip, published in full in a Dutch magazine in 1980.

79-0967   Bill Dixon

probably early fall, 1979   BCVT

BD (p)

Dixon apparently played a solo for this Music faculty concert held at the beginning of the new school year.

Robeson

"When I first came to Bennington in 1968, I was given a copy of the plans for the new performing arts building. It had been proposed in 1964, and by 1968 they were still just discussing it. So until that time there were two performance spaces: Commons Theater upstairs was the performing space for dance (there may have been some drama things there), and there was what they called the Barn Theater, where most of the theater/drama events were held.

"The downstairs space of the Carriage Barn had been used previously for dance. In fact the floor was still a dance floor, but it was now a concert space for the music department. The upstairs room of the Carriage Barn had been the gallery for the art division.

"When I came back from Wisconsin [see p. 162 et seq.], in order to do any work done at all, my ensemble used to meet in the music building [Jennings Hall], in a small room on the ground floor, room 136. (The first "Letters" [**R73-0519** et seq.] was rehearsed there exclusively). I also had some time for my classes scheduled in the Carriage Barn. Then when my ensemble and classes became more intact, I could "borrow" a night for my class from the Dance Department, and use the Commons Theater.

"Once they started to build the new building, VAPA [Visual and Performing Arts--finished in the mid-Seventies, see **R76-0522**], they made provisions for all of the departments except Black Music; I was given no space. The Dance, Drama, and Music Departments each had a new performance space. In addition, Dance kept the space upstairs in Commons. The Music Department kept the Carriage Barn. I would have to be on a schedule where the Music Department would let me use the Carriage Barn two days a week and at other times I would borrow from Dance. On days that we had the Carriage Barn, if the Music Department wanted something else to happen, they would pre-empt [my classes].

"In reaction to that, while I was on sabbatical [in the spring term of 1975], the Division opted to cancel all classes until they had a legitimate space. Subsequently, the college administration made a proposal to me--as chairman--to fix the upstairs of Commons so I could use it. We went over what would be needed, and how much it would cost, and then they decided they didn't want to do that. One morning I got a call from the president, Joe Murphy: 'Would the Carriage Barn be all right for Black Music?' I told [him] what I needed to fix it up, and that's how we got the space, after much, much scuffle.

"Then I got permission from the Dean of Faculty to rename it. It had never been named for anyone. I held a meeting of all the people taking classes in Black music to submit names. The votes came in, and the students wanted to name the building for me. (You can imagine what that would have done...) I immediately squelched that. I told the people that wasn't it; the voting was over, and I was naming the place for Paul Robeson. We had a big opening ceremony."

Some of that ceremony was incorporated into the *Works/Fall '79* series on campus, showcasing Black Music projects: ABC Television producer Gil Noble attended on December 3 to introduce The Tallest Tree, a 90-minute film on Robeson.

Dixon: "It would be ideal if I could carry the sound of the Carriage Barn when there's no one in there with me: over the years, that has become *the* sound for me. When you put people in there, it starts to crowd the sound a little. If I could play within that kind of ambience, I wouldn't need amplification. Once I began to use the Carriage barn more, I didn't really need that amplification set-up.

"I can't play in the street; the sound doesn't stay there long enough for me to even know I've done anything. Amplification for me lets me hear intimately each one of the details as I want to hear them. The sound lingers just enough for me to be able to do something. I'm not a very good cornet player, because the instrument is too short, and the sound never travels long enough before it's out of the horn.

"More traditional players might say that those are idiosyncrasies I can't afford to have. I could afford to have them, because I wasn't doing anything else. If someone had always been calling me to work jobs and I was of the temperament and musicality to do those things, I would never have developed this approach to playing. I wouldn't have been allowed to. But in doing my own work, I could select what I wanted to do, and how I wanted to do it, and I developed that over the years."
Bennington Banner December 1, 1979.

R79-1207   Bill Dixon Ensemble IV
December 7, 1979   Paul Robeson House: BCVT

BD (t, flgh?); Other members likely from ensemble of that semester

    Haiku Pieces   30:00   BD rec

Despite the title, the (apparently two) pieces on this cassette run nearly 30:00.

This concert culminated the Autumn series *Works/Fall '79* that began on December 3.
From the *Banner*: "Included in this presentation will be a lecture on the philosophy,
aesthetics and methodology with excerpts from past works used as examples and
reference points. The second part will include new works for large ensemble, as
performed by members of the class 'Introduction to the Art of Ensemble Performance'
(Dixon's Large Ensemble)."
Bennington Banner December 1, 1979.

79-9998   Sandye L. Wilson
ca. 1979   BCVT

BD (p); Vance Provey (t)

    Somethin' to be Recalled

Wilson's theater presentation was staged in fulfillment of a B.A. in Drama. She wrote
and performed the piece, directed by Judy Dennis, and Dixon composed the music.

Dixon was on sabbatical from teaching at Bennington in the Spring term, 1980.
Details from concert program.

CHAPTER EIGHT

Trio/Quartet
1980–1982

R80-0519   Stephen Haynes-Bill Dixon
May 19, 1980   Paul Robeson House: BCVT

-1: BD (p) Stephen Haynes (t)
-2: BD, Stephen Haynes (t); Linda Dowdell (p)

Untitled -1	6:30	private tape
Touchings for Piano and Trumpet [II] -2	8:04	

Haynes's term of study in the Black Music Division ended with this senior concert.He
was among the first students to have started and graduated as a major from the
program.

Further sections of this concert are listed in **O80-0519**, whence also the other
version of "Touchings for Piano and Trumpet".

Details of concert program.

R80-0606   Bill Dixon Sextet
June 6, 1980   Teatro Romano, Verona

BD (t-1, p-2); Arthur Brooks, Stephen Haynes (t); Stephen Horenstein (ts); Alan
Silva (b); Freddie Waits (d)

Summer Song/Two/Evening -1	13:22	BD rec
For Cecil Taylor -2	9:44	Nettle NTL 001
Sketch/Firenze -1	4:44	BD rec
like Summer Song/Three/Aurorea	20:25	--

Nettle NTL 001 titled *Verona Jazz*, contains a 9:06 excerpt of the piece. The CD was
released in conjunction with the June, 1996 issue of the Italian periodical *Musica
Jazz*, an anniverary reflection on the 15 years since the first Verona Jazz Festival.
Dixon's Sextet took part in that first festival (he also appeared there at **R88-0626**
and **R92-0625**).

All pieces begin as duets for Dixon and Silva. These titles for "Summer Song/Two..."
[the longer version for sextet, as on SN1008] and "Sketch/Firenze" are based on
similarities to the Soul Note studio recordings (**R80-0611a**); the second piece is
unmistakably "For Cecil Taylor", with a slightly different arrangement in which
Silva solos before Horenstein.
Horenstein may also play baritone saxophone.
In the fourth piece there is a pause (perhaps reflecting the "Dusk/Daybreak"
subsections) at 6:37 and the recording drops out for :04 but resurfaces after having
omitted more music than that.

The 9:00pm Verona concert initiated Dixon's first performing tour of Italy and
Switzerland, which entailed at least 7 stops: two in Verona, then Via Reggio,
Florence, Monselice, Bellinzona, and Milan. A proposed concert in Vincenza
appears not to have materialized.
The horns come from Bennington, Silva joined the band coming out of Paris, and
Waits was Dixon's choice. They had met for the first time shortly before the tour.
Dixon's original plan was to include Jimmy Lyons and Art Davis in the group, and
publicity was distributed to this effect, but both Lyons and Davis cancelled just prior
to departure. Freddie Waits arrived in Italy on the day of this performance.

Dixon dedicated the performance to Miles Davis.

Outdoor photographs seen in the inserts to *Bill Dixon In Italy Vol. 1* and *Vol. 2*
(**R80-0611a and -b**) were taken at the sound check for this event.

Il Teatro Romano: la Storia e gli Spettacoli (Verona: Cura Dell' Offticio Stampa del Comune di
Verona, 1991?), p. 154.

80-0607   Bill Dixon Sextet/ Andrew Hill
June 7, 1980   Can de la Scala, Verona

-1: BD (t, p); Arthur Brooks, Stephen Haynes (t); Stephen Horenstein (ts, barsx); Alan Silva (b); Freddie Waits (d)

-2: BD (t) on first portion only; Andrew Hill (p); Alan Silva (b); Freddie Waits (d)

11:30pm
"Andrew Hill was in Verona to play the festival as a soloist. [Soul Note Records producer]Giovanni Bonandrini wanted to do a recording with him, but did not arrive at the Verona festival until after Andrew's set. I was playing a concert with the sextet at the hippest club--a three-story club--in Verona, so during the intermission it was arranged that Andrew would play and Bonandrini could have another opportunity to hear him.
Andrew didn't have a band, so he asked me if he could use Alan Silva and Freddie Waits--perfectly all right with me. He also asked me to play with him that night. I told him I wouldn't play the whole set with him, but I would play the beginning of a piece (maybe the first ten minutes) that the trio could work into a set. He and I played a duet with no written music; then Silva and Waits joined in, and they carried on as I left the bandstand. It worked very well, and we had a certain affinity. But in all this time I've known Andrew, we've only played for those ten minutes, though we talked about it ever since the days of the Cellar Cafe."

80-0609   Bill Dixon Sextet
June 9, 1980   Hop Frog Club: Via Reggio, Italy

BD (t, p); Arthur Brooks, Stephen Haynes (t); Stephen Horenstein (ts); Alan Silva (b); Freddie Waits (d)

Program is unknown and likely similar to **R80-0611a** and -b .
9:00pm
Details from concert poster.

R80-0611a   Bill Dixon Sextet
June 11-13, 1980   Barigozzi Studio, Milan

BD (p); Arthur Brooks, Stephen Haynes (t); Stephen Horenstein (ts, barsx);
Alan Silva (b); Freddie Waits (d)

Sketch/Firenze	14:54	SN 1011
Firenze	4:45	SN 1008
Dance Piece	12:50	SN 1011
--Places		
--For Jack and Barbara		
--Autumn Sequences from a Paris Diary		
For Cecil Taylor	19:55	SN 1008
--Almost Anacrusis		
--Conversation		
--New Slow Dance		

Soul Note SN 1008 [LP] titled *Bill Dixon in Italy Volume one*=CD 121008-2
Soul Note SN 1011 [LP] titled *Bill Dixon in Italy Volume two*=CD 121011-2

"Giovanni Bonandrini also came from Milan to Verona to hear our performance there.
I was supposed to do one record; once he heard the group he told me he wanted two
records. I said I didn't have enough material for two records. He came back the next
day with a sizeable advance and a contract and so we did two volumes. That's why
there's a repetition of the material. Alan Silva and I could have played duets for ten
years, but that wasn't representing what the group was about. On the first day of
recording, Waits didn't like the drums, so Bonandrini took a train to Rome to pick up
another set."

"For Cecil Taylor" for the sextet was scored on paper before the performances: "This
line--exactly like this--had already been done half a dozen times (The original was
written for electric piano and tenor saxophone [see **R77-0000**]), except that here I
wrote out the full notation where otherwise I might just show the tenor pitches and
indicate what was to be held, etc. Steve already knew how it went." The piece also
relates to "For Franz" from **R76-0806**.
"Once I got ready to do it with the sextet, I wrote a score in order to generate the
individual parts for the horns. I had memorized it and didn't use the score. If you'll
notice the key signature, it shows A-flat and D-sharp."

One segment of "For Cecil Taylor" played by Stephen Haynes is printed in *L'Opera* at p. 125, and
a segment of the full score at p. 171-74.

R80-0611b   Bill Dixon Sextet

June 11-13, 1980   Barigozzi Studio, Milan

BD (t-1, p-2); Alan Silva (b);
-1: add Arthur Brooks, Stephen Haynes (t); Stephen Horenstein (ts);Freddie
Waits (d)

Summer Song/One/Morning -1	4:10	SN 1008
Summer Song/Two/Evening -1, 2	12:45	-- --
Summer Song/Three/Aurorea -1	6:00	SN 1011
--Daybreak	(3:20)	-- --
--Dusk	(2:36)	-- --
Summer Song /Two/Evening [vers. 2] -1	7:30	-- --

Soul Note SN 1008 [LP] titled *Bill Dixon in Italy Volume one*=CD 121008-2
Soul Note SN 1011 [LP] titled *Bill Dixon in Italy Volume two*=CD 121011-2

R80-0615   Bill Dixon Sextet

June 15, 1980   Piazza del Annuciata, Florence

BD (t, p -1); Stephen Horenstein (ts, barsx) -1; Alan Silva (b); Freddie Waits (d)

-2 add Arthur Brooks, Stephen Haynes (t)

(Sketch/?)Firenze	6:10	BD rec
Untitled Quartet *and* For Cecil Taylor -1,2	31:45	--
Autumn Sequences from a Paris Diary -1	4:50	--
Sketch/Firenze -1, -2	6:10	--
like Almost Anacrusis -1	5:49	--
Summer Song/Two/Evening -2	13:21	--

The second piece begins as a duet for Dixon (p) and Horenstein (ts), becomes a quartet with Waits and Silva and bridges into "For Cecil Taylor" with no pause in the music, though there is applause. The other trumpets join at that transition and Dixon is the second trumpet soloist. Horenstein plays some ensemble parts on baritone saxophone.

The venue for Dixon's 9:30pm engagement was a large piazza in view of Il Duomo.

80-0616   Bill Dixon Sextet

June 16, 1980   Monselice, Italy

BD (t, p); Arthur Brooks, Stephen Haynes (t); Stephen Horenstein (ts); Alan Silva (b); Freddie Waits (d)

Program is unknown and likely uses material related to **R80-0611**.
Details from concert poster.

80-0617   Bill Dixon Sextet

June 17, 1980   Bellinzona, Switzerland

BD (t, p); Arthur Brooks, Stephen Haynes (t); Stephen Horenstein (ts); Alan Silva (b); Freddie Waits (d)

Unknown; likely similar to **R80-0611**   see below

Program is unknown and likely uses material related to **R80-0611**.

R80-0618   Bill Dixon Trio

June 18-22, 1980   La Chapelle des Lombards, Paris

BD (t); Kent Carter (b); Oliver Johnson (d)

BD rec

This week's residency was spun off the tour to Italy. While on that trip, Dixon envisioned playing in Paris with the sextet but financial circumstances prevented it. Instead, he traveled there as a single, where the concert organizers arranged for the "best bassist and drummer in Paris".

Steve Lacy was apparently not working at that moment; hence, Carter and Johnson (members of his working group) were available. Dixon knew the bassist from years before, but played here for the first time with Johnson.

Dixon's erstwhile sextet members came to Paris to see this music and eventually took part (**R80-0624**).

Each concert started at 8:30pm. The first night was begun flat-footed, without the planned rehearsal. Dixon recalls this as a solid working relationship--different in character and aesthetic from the sextet's music--that got better with each night (**R80-0624** was the last).

Jason Weiss "Bill Dixon Chapelle des Lombards, Paris, June 18-24, 1980" *CODA* #174, September, 1980) p. 35.

R80-0623   Bill Dixon Trio

June 23, 1980   La Chapelle des Lombards, Paris

BD (t); Kent Carter (b); Oliver Johnson (d)

trio (starts with BD unacc.)	20:00	BD rec
trio (starts with KC unacc)	9:10	--
BD solo	2:15	--
trio (starts with BD unacc.)	17:10	--
trio	3:40	--
trio	11:45	--
BD solo	1:00	--

This night's performance is listed separately, the only one of which a full recording is verified.

see **R80-0618**.

R80-0624   Bill Dixon Trio and guests

June 24, 1980   La Chapelle des Lombards, Paris

BD (t, p); Arthur Brooks, Earl Cross, Stephen Haynes (t); Arthur Doyle, Stephen Horenstein (ts, barsx); Kent Carter, Alan Silva (b); Oliver Johnson (d)*

BD rec

The final night of a week's stand for the Dixon-Carter-Johnson group at this location (see **R80-0618**) was opened up to a number of musicians who were, respectively visiting (Cross: in London and the continent for some six weeks by that point), stranded (Doyle), and in Europe from the Dixon Sextet appearances of earlier in the month (Brooks, Haynes, Horenstein).

Much of the music performed on this occasion derived from the Sextet repertoire played in Italy. Earl Cross apparently sat in toward the earlier part of the evening and does not appear on the recording (which likely covers only the second set). Dixon began the first set on piano, introducing a setting that (apparently) was to include Horenstein in a duet. Horenstein was without his tenor mouthpiece and therefore left the concert (in search of it) for much of the set, entering late on baritone saxophone. He plays tenor in the second set.

see **R80-0618**.

R80-0831   Bill Dixon Trio

August 31, 1980   Institute of Contemporary Arts: London

BD (t, p); Kent Carter, Alan Silva (b)

      Unknown   22:50   BD rec

Dixon returned to Europe separately from the June sequence of concerts to perform at
the Actual 80 festival. The program was short; Kent Carter became indisposed toward
the close of the concert. Dixon began unaccompanied on trumpet, switched to piano
ca. 14:00 for Silva's solo, then back to trumpet.
The Actual 80 Festival included an international roster of improvisers. Dixon also
gave a talk for the festival audience opposite saxophonist Evan Parker on August 30.
Details from a general poster for the entire event; Valerie Wilmer "Dixon: Keeping On Doing It"
Time Out London August 22-28, 1980, p. 17; Ken Ansell "Getting It Together" *Jazz Journal
International* November, 1980, p. 21.

In the fall term of 1980, Horenstein took his sabbatical in Jerusalem, after which he
was not reappointed. He effectively stayed in Israel from that point, eventually
becoming the head of the Jerusalem Institute of Contemporary Music (See
R90-0322).

81-0098   Bill Dixon-[James Baldwin]
1981   BCVT

BD (p);
unknown (reciting voice/s)

      Sonny's Blues

On at least two occasions Dixon staged a reading of James Baldwin's short story,
once using music that he had composed. The other is in **R73-1200**.
Details from BD composition list.

81-0099   Jack Moore-Bill Dixon
1981   BCVT

BD (p); Jack Moore (choreography); Rick Shaw (movement)

          Tea Dust at 5:43pm

This title is listed in the Jack Moore Memorial program (**R88-1112**), as opposed to "Teadust at 5:45pm" shown in Dixon's composition list of 1985. Date comes from that source.
Other performances include **79-0428**, **R82-1209**, and **R88-1112**.

Dixon: "Everything Jack did he tailored to the physical aesthetic of the people he was composing for, so he could make things at times for people who really couldn't dance."
BD composition list of 1985.

R81-0206   Bill Dixon Trio
early February 1981   McClear Place Studios, Toronto

BD (t); Art Davis (b); Freddie Waits (d)

Excerpt #1	5:37	Imagine the
Excerpt #2	c6:23	Sound

Film footage with sound was taken in studio for use in the Bill Smith-Ron Mann film, Imagine the Sound. The film uses music and picture from this studio performance, and footage of Dixon being interviewed by Bill Smith, in the presence of Davis.
It also documents the music of Cecil Taylor, Paul Bley, and Archie Shepp, who are interviewed as well.

Dixon recalls playing in the studio many hours. Joe Medjock, in an essay that accompanies at least the LaserDisc issue, reports that "the musicians were asked to perform pieces which were less than ten minutes long--the length of a standard film magazine--so that editing of the music was not required."
Imagine the Sound was later released on VHS videocassette and then LaserDisc by Voyager Press.
cf. also **81-0208**.

81-0208   Bill Dixon Trio

ca. February 8, 1981   The Edge, Toronto

BD (t); Art Davis (b); Freddie Waits (d)

      Unknown

This one-night engagement was organized to coincide with the recordings for *Imagine the Sound* (**R81-0206**). Dixon favored this live performance (probably recorded and possibly filmed) over the studio recordings eventually used in the film.

During this trip Davis and Waits recorded with Canadian guitarist Peter Leitch on February 9 and 10.

Jack Litchfield: *The Canadian Jazz Discography 1916-1980* (Toronto: University of Toronto Press, 1982) p. 416.

R81-0516   Bill Dixon-Judith Dunn
May 16, 1981   Martha Hill Dance Workshop: BCVT

Bill Dixon (t); Judith Dunn (choreography); Arthur Brooks, Stephen Haynes,
Vance Provey (t); Holly Markush (cello); Spin Dunbar (b); Penny Campbell,
Cheryl Lilienstein, Marjorie MacMahon, Cherri Phillips, Emily Schottland
(movement)

Summerdance	26:15	BD video rec
Summerdance	27:02	--

This and **R81-0524** re-created the summer 1971 dance-music collaboration
"Summerdance" (**R71-0714**)--originally choreographed by Judith Dunn and
reconstructed here by Dunn and Cheryl Lilienstein [née Niederman], who had been a
member of the Dixon-Dunn company that premiered it.

The 1981 staging was rehearsed in Burlington, Vermont. Of the four versions
recorded to video tape, it appears that two came from this day and two from
R81-0524, though it is not clear which performances come from which venue. The
May 16 BCVT performances were held during Alumni Reunion Weekend at
Bennington.
Dixon: "In certain ways the original one was more exciting to do. Time had passed,
certain things were now in the air, and the players thought they knew more. The feat
of the "Summerdance" recreations was that this woman [Dunn] could teach the
movements to the dancers from a wheelchair.
"One problem with playing in Martha Hill was that, while the audience can hear very
very well, you as a player cannot hear the sound--like playing into a cloud of cotton.
You have to imagine what it sounds like as the notes escape from the horn."

This performance of "Summerdance" was the first of at least three re-stagings of
Dixon-Dunn pieces in her last years (the others are **81-0524** and **82-0415**). By
the 1980s, Judith Dunn's mobility had been seriously impaired by a malignant cancer
centered on a brain tumor, which eventually took her life in July, 1983. Increasingly
distanced by that illness from her artistic careers in dance and, later, film, she
expressed her creativity in needlepoint and the sewing crafts from a wheelchair.
After Bennington, Dunn lived in upstate Vermont, from which she had been in touch
with Dixon continuously since the period of their collaboration (1966-72). [Dixon
also organized a day-long salute at Bennington to Judith Dunn's work, and to her
presence at the college: See **X83-0613**.]

Details from concert program;
Dunn obituaries in *Ballet News* October, 1983, p. 31; *Dance Magazine* September, 1983, p. 120,
127; *New York Times* July 3, 1983; *Variety* July 20, 1983;

R81-0524   Bill Dixon-Judith Dunn
May 24, 1981   Burlington, Vermont

Bill Dixon (t); Judith Dunn (choreography); Arthur Brooks, Stephen Haynes,
Vance Provey (t); Holly Markush (cello); Spin Dunbar (b); Penny Campbell,
Cheryl Lilienstein, Marjorie MacMahon, Cherri Phillips, Emily Schottland
(movement)

Unknown		
Summerdance	25:51	BD video rec
Summerdance	26:00	--

The Bennington "Summerdance" re-staging (**R81-0516**) was repeated the next week
in Burlington's Edmunds Jr.High School. Of four versions recorded to video tape, it
appears that two came from this day and two from Bennington (**R81-0524**), though
again it is not clear which performances come from which venue.
A Burlington performance--presumably this one--is thought to have been
video-recorded (and broadcast) by WCFE-TV in Plattsburgh, New York.

From the program: "A piece composed and directed by Bill Dixon will precede the
performance of SUMMERDANCE." No further details are known about that piece;
probably most or all of the musicians were used, and none of the dancers.
See also **O81-1108**.

The Vermont Vanguard Press May 29-June 5, 1981, p. 17; reviewed in *Burlington Free Press* [date
unknown]; details from concert program.

R81-0615   Bill Dixon

June 15, 1981   Worcester, Massachusetts

BD (t); Mario Pavone (b); Lawrence Cook (d)

Unknown ["Play your open 'E'..."]	14:18	BD rec
Unknown [starts with BD unacc]	18:18	--
Unknown [starts with BD unacc]	10:47	--
Unknown ["...Latin..."]	6:22	--
Unknown [starts with BD unacc]	8:26	--

The concert in the New England Repertory Theater comprised two sets separated by an intermission.

Dixon's trio with Pavone and Cook debuted at this engagement.
"I had to do this concert in Worcester for the radio station, and they wanted a trio. So on the spur of the moment, I called Laurence in Boston, asked him if he wanted to work in Worcester and if he could get Mario. It worked so well, that was it."
Dixon explains part of the high level of this music through Cook's and Pavone's attentiveness in this new situation. There was no rehearsal for the concert.

Dixon's minimal verbal instructions (as above), hand signals, figures implied in his playing, and eye contact often represented the only notation or instructions for pieces the group played. He occasionally wrote out parts for Pavone.

The trio concept stuck immediately and (in one form or another) became Dixon's *modus operandi* for playing in and outside of Bennington for most of the next seven years.
"Every year during the existence of the Division, I would do 2 or 3 concerts. If I wanted to rehearse something, I would have Cook and Pavone come up on an honorarium. That kept the group together, and it let me work, but it wasn't just a selfish endeavor. I wanted students to see a working group. As an artist who happens to be a teacher, it was necessary for students to see me play 'seriously' (In fact, although they might not have thought of it that way, I was just as serious playing with them as I was with Mario and Laurence.) Sometimes I would have a workshop for students with the trio. Overall it worked very well."

R81-1105   Bill Dixon Quartet
November 5, 1981   Cinemateatro CIAK, Milan

BD (t, flgh); Mario Pavone, Alan Silva (b); Lawrence Cook (d)

BD solo	2:31	BD rec
Unknown	19:00	--
Unknown	9:14	--
Unknown	17:30	--
like Penthesilea	16:10	--

See also **R81-1106**. This and the following entries document a quartet tour by van through Northern Italy and Switzerland.

The trio that Dixon had premiered in Worcester in June became a regular working formation, but most often with a second bass instrument added--Alan Silva, Joe Fonda, John Voigt, William Parker, and tubaist John Buckingham were those second bass voices. However, the progression of two-bass quartets continued with a substantially different group through **R94-1109**.

"I liked all of those basses because the bass can do practically anything. Get a couple of basses and a sensitive drummer: they cover all of the areas, and if they're good--if they listen--there's no duplication."

Details from concert program.

R81-1106   Bill Dixon Quartet
November 6, 1981   Cinemateatro CIAK, Milan

BD (t, flgh); Mario Pavone, Barre Phillips (b); Lawrence Cook (d)

Unknown	9:00	BD rec
Unknown	7:42	--
Unknown	10:30	--
Unknown	2:58	--
Unknown	12:50	--

Dixon introduced Barre Phillips as a special guest: "There's a change in our program tonight. Alan Silva is in Berlin..." Silva left the tour briefly to play at an FMP event.
The quartet appears on all selections, although each piece begins with an unaccompanied statement by one of the members of the group.

In an afterword from the stage, Dixon dedicated the concert to Mrs. Nuncia Barrazzetta and Ms. Linda Barassi, whose husbands (Italian critical writer Giuseppi Barrazzetta and Dario Barassi, owner of FORE) were instrumental in sponsoring the FORE records releases, *Considerations 1* and *2*.

see also **R81-1105**.
Details from concert program.

81-1107   Bill Dixon Quartet (?)
possibly November 7, 1981   Whiskey Club: Milan

BD (t); Mario Pavone (b); Laurence Cook (d)

Dixon was hesitant to play in a "club" establishment, particularly one with this name.

R81-1108   Bill Dixon [Quartet]
November 8, 1981   Volkshaus, Zürich

BD (t); Mario Pavone, Alan Silva (b); Lawrence Cook (d)

[BD Spoken] *Announcement*	1:13	Soul Note 1038
Webern	1:24	--
Windswept Winterset	15:42	--
Velvet	6:44	--
Llaattiinnoo Suite	15:24	--
[BD spoken] *Announcement*	1:40	--

Soul Note 1038 is one half of the 2 LP set *November 1981* (1037/38) also issued on
Soul Note CD 121038-2.
Final announcement includes Dixon's introduction of Cecil Taylor, who played next
on the program.

R81-1110   Bill Dixon Quartet
November 10, 1981   Sala-Teatro Pio IX: Padova, Italy

BD (t, flgh); Mario Pavone, Alan Silva (b); Lawrence Cook (d)

Unknown	13:50	BD rec
Unknown	17:08	--
Penthesilea	12:20	--
Fragment	1:48	--
Unknown	10:47	--
Unknown	11:04	--
Unknown	6:32	--
Unknown [inc.]	15:32	--

The name of the performance space has also been given as "Il Cinema Teatro".
The third piece seems to be the same melody as the issued "Penthesilea" but a
different rhythmic scheme. Dixon is heard singing the rhythm he wants to the rest of
the group during the piece, and (later) indicating a pulse for the next piece.
The music of this "Penthesilea"was not identical to **R79-0699**, q.v.

The fourth and eighth pieces here may run longer on other tapes of the concert.

The quartet performs on all selections.
Details from concert program.

81-1111   Bill Dixon Quartet

November 11, 1981   Centro Jazz: Torino, Italy

BD (t, flgh); Mario Pavone, Alan Silva (b); Lawrence Cook (d)

A promotional handbill for the concert exists.

81-1112   Bill Dixon Quartet

November 12, 1981   Genova, Italy

BD (t, flgh); Mario Pavone, Alan Silva (b); Lawrence Cook (d)

While scheduled to have occurred in Genova, this stop on the tour may have been changed, in which case the group would have performed in Florence.

81-1113   Bill Dixon Quartet

November 13, 1981   Piacenza, Italy

BD (t, flgh); Mario Pavone, Alan Silva (b); Lawrence Cook (d)

R81-1115   Bill Dixon Quartet

probably November 15, 1981   Milan

BD (t); Mario Pavone, Alan Silva (b); Laurence Cook (d)

A one-hour Italian television program compiled footage from Dixon's Milan concert(s) and a studio performance by the quartet (probably on the date above) with an interview of Dixon by the Italian journalist Pino Candini.

Around the time of this television broadcast, Dixon was presented the Giancarlo Testoni award by the Italian Discographical Critics Association in Milan.

R81-1116   Bill Dixon Quartet
November 16-17, 1981   Barigozzi Studio, Milan

BD (t); Mario Pavone, Alan Silva (b); Lawrence Cook (d)

November 1981	10:40	Soul Note 1037
Penthesilea	10:10	--
The Second Son	5:10	--
The Sirens	7:05	--
Another Quiet Feeling	6:48	--

Soul Note 1037 is one half of the 2 LP set *November 1981* (1037/38) also issued on Soul Note CD: 121038-2.

"Another Quiet Feeling" refers in its title to "Four Quiet Feelings", **O72-0423**.
see **R81-1108**.

R81-1205   Bill Dixon Trio
December 5, 1981   BCVT

BD (t); Mario Pavone (b); Laurence Cook (d)

                                                                 BD rec

Both this performance and **O81-1203** were probably part of an end-of-term festival cursorily described in *L'Opera*.
L'Opera, p. 81.

R82-0200   Bill Dixon
ca. 1981-82   BCVT

BD (t)

Flame	3:10	BD rec
Meta-Pedal	6:14	--

Durations for these (sometimes incomplete) pieces are as follows: 3:10, 4:29, 9:41, 0:57, 2:33, 3:36, 5:57, 2:45, 7:59, 4:21, 0:50, 2:18, 1:07, 10:22, 0:17, and 8:23.

R82-0415   Bill Dixon-Judith Dunn

April 15-6, 1982   St. Mark's Church, NYC [Danspace]

BD (t, flgh); Judith Dunn (choreography); Cheryl Lilienstein (movement)

    Dew Horse   c28:00   NYPL rec

"Dew Horse" was part of a series of Judson Dance Workshop re-creations, staging
some of the more memorable works from that program. All were recorded and are now
held by the New York Public Library's Jerome Robbins Dance [image] Collection in
Lincoln Center. Judith Dunn, a founding member of the Judson Dance community,
attended the concert in a wheelchair. The dance was created in 1963 and first
performed by Dixon and Dunn collaboratively at **R66-0711**, q.v. Here Dixon and
Lilienstein performed three sequences of alternation between music and dance.

Details from video tape annotations; Dixon's program note to this concert is reprinted in *L'Opera*
p. 53-55; reviewed in *New York Times* by Anna Kiffelgoff April 18, 1982 and in the *Village
Voice* by Deborah Jowitt May 4, 1982.

R82-0508   Bill Dixon Trio

May 8, 1982   Third Street Music Settlement, NYC

BD (t); Mario Pavone (b); Lawrence Cook (d)

like Penthesilea	10:00
starts with arco bass	6:22
	7:12
BD talks	
starts with pizzicato bass	10:02
	8:35
ends with BD unaccompanied	11:41
	7:36
starts with BD unaccompanied	8:17

One in a series of performances at this site curated by Judy Sneed; Mal Waldron
performed in another concert of the series.

Steve Albahari's 1982 photographs of a New York concert (printed in *L'Opera*)
presumably pertain to this event.

down beat (October, 1982) p.57 [photo in this article from ca.1966]; *L'Opera* p. 185, 187, 189.

R82-0626   Bill Dixon

June 26, 1982   Ferrari Gallery, Verona

BD (t)

-1: add Bruno Marini (bcl)

> Webern   filmmaker's
>
> Places and Things -1   rec

Dixon performed solo at the gallery on the opening day of his first show of paintings there, which coincided with the Edizioni Ferrari record release (see **R70-0428** and **R73-0197**).

Several recordings from the proposed/planned 4-LP set, *In The Sign of Labyrinth* (see **R73-1100**), were registered with BMI around this time, suggesting that he may have spent a part of this or subsequent trips to Italy (see next) shoring up plans for that project.

Dixon recalls this gallery opening as roughly one year before **82-1021**, but not during the November 1981 tour. A director from Rome filmed the event.

Details from Composition list; *Musica Jazz* August/September, 1987, p. 15-16.

82-0707   Jack Moore-Bill Dixon

July 7-10, 1982   St. Marks Church [Danspace]

BD (p); Jack Moore (choreography, movement); *Other dancers include one or more of the following*: Ronald Dabney, Reuben Edinger, David Hurwith, David Malamut, Erin Martin, Barbara Roan, Richard Shaw

> Cool

The collaborative composition of Moore and Dixon was performed during a week-long series of Moore's work, called *Snow Shadow Garden and Some Other Pieces*. Shaw is the same dancer Rick Shaw who premiered Moore's work "Autumn's Chant" (**R82-1209**).

July 7-9 at 8:00pm and July 10 at 5:00pm

Details from series poster and 1985 Composition list.

R82-0930   Bill Dixon Quartet
September 30, 1982   BCVT

BD (t); Joe Fonda, Mario Pavone (b); Laurence Cook (d)

                                                    BD rec

Dixon's brief description of this event read: "concert /informal/ with introduction pertaining to improvisation".

After the November, 1981 performance tour with a two-bass quartet, Dixon wanted to maintain that configuration in the US, which was not possible with Silva living in Europe. Dixon took up Mario Pavone's suggestion to use Joe Fonda as the second bass player, and the group played exactly twice with that lineup. Fonda's successors in that position were John Voigt, William Parker, and, briefly, the tuba player John Buckingham.

82-1021   Bill Dixon
October 21, 1982   Brescia, Italy

BD (t)
-1: *add* (flgh)

           Webern Work/Study   rec uncertain
           Dew Horse -1
           Sotto Voce

Dixon's performance in the Multimedia Arte Contemporary Gallery coincided with the opening of a show of his paintings there (October 21-November 18).
Attro [Italy] #9 (October, 1982) p.20; details from concert announcements.

R82-1123   Barbara Roan-Jack Moore
November 23-24, 1982   Martha Hill Dance Workshop: BCVT

BD (probably p); Barbara Roan, Jack Moore (choreography, direction); other personnel and instrumentation unknown

           Dream Song   BC Dance video

Dixon contributed only this piece to *Scraps and Peels (A Revue of Sorts)* which combined music from many different sources--live and pre-recorded. Though both nights were audio/video recorded by the Dance department, music from "Dream Song" is included on none of the tapes, and there is no substantive information about the instrumentation, etc.
Details from concert program.

R82-1203   <u>Bill Dixon Quartet</u>
December 3, 1982   BCVT

BD (t); Joe Fonda, Mario Pavone (b); Laurence Cook (d)

                                                        BD rec

Acoustic differences between this and **R82-0930** suggest that they *may* have been
held in different locations.

R82-1209   <u>Jack Moore-Bill Dixon</u>
December 9-11, 1982   Martha Hill Dance Workshop: BCVT

BD (p); Jack Moore (choreography)

-1: Rick Shaw (movement) Jennifer Wollerman (voice)
-2: Barbara Roan (movement)

> Autumn's Chant -1   10:44   BC Dance video
> Tea Dust at 5:43pm -2   11:30   --

Printed in the program to this Faculty Dance Concert as "Autumn's Chanting", it
appears instead that the title is correct as given above.
Wollerman contributes a wordless vocal to the lines with Dixon. Other text
vocalized in the performance may have come from Ben Belitt's poem for Jack Moore.

Raymond J. Dooley: lighting; Jack Moore: costume.

82-9998   <u>Jack Moore-Bill Dixon</u>
1982   BCVT

BD (p); Jack Moore (choreography, movement); unknown (voice)

> Cool

See **82-0707**.
BD 1985 Composition list.

CHAPTER NINE

Thoughts 1983–1988

R83-0508   <u>Bill Dixon Quartet</u>
May 8, 1983   Paul Robeson House: BCVT

BD (t); Mario Pavone and *probably* John Voigt (b); Laurence Cook (d)

BD rec

The concert was held to benefit the college's student publication *SILO*.
The first piece began with Dixon unaccompanied. Bostonian bassist Voigt,
introduced to Dixon by Laurence Cook, joined the group as a second bassist for at
least four performances in 1983.

MIT Master's Student Steve Albahari taped the concert while at Bennington
compiling a video thesis project on Dixon's work.

R83-0514   Bill Dixon Trio
May 14, 1983   BCVT

BD (t); *probably* Mario Pavone (b); Laurence Cook (d)

    Penthesilea   BD rec
    The Second Son   --

Dixon's group here played the last part of a long Black Music Division concert, at
the conclusion of which Dixon identified these pieces. Either the concert--or simply
Dixon's portion--was titled "Moment".

R83-0610   Jo and Martha Wittman
June 10-12, 1983   Martha Hill Dance Workshop, BCVT

-1: *on tape* BD (t); Spin Dunbar (elbg); Ben Wittman (d)

-2: BD (t); Jo Wittman (p)

    East West Traveling Dances: Section 1 -1   BC Dance video
    East West Traveling Dances: Section 6 -2   --

All performances at 8:00pm
The piece was so named for its use of dancers from the University of California and
Bennington.

The interior sections (2-5) included sound from other sources in which Dixon did not
participate. The three players in -1 recorded their parts independently before the
concert. Those channels were manipulated on tape by Jo Wittman for the resulting
audio track. See also **R87-0501**.

On August 1, 1983, Dixon tendered to the trustees and administration a detailed
proposal for an autonomous Black Music Institute within the Bennington College
community. Like its predecessor of a decade before, this plan was rejected.
Details from concert program.

R83-1027   Bill Dixon Quartet
October 27, 1983   Paul Robeson House: BCVT

BD (t -1, flgh -2); Mario Pavone, John Voigt (b); Laurence Cook (d)

starts with BD unacc -1	23:32	BD video rec
starts with Pavone pizz. unacc. -2	14:09	--
starts with Pavone arco [inc] -2	5:40	--
BD talks	5:40	--
starts with BD solo -1	19:19	--
starts with BD solo -1	5:15	--
-2 [inc]	4:04	--
starts with both basses pizz -1 [inc]	3:29	--
BD talks		--
-1	4:34	--

R83-1028a   Bill Dixon Quartet
October 28, 1983   Wesleyan University: Middletown, CT

BD (t, flgh); John Voigt, Mario Pavone (b); Lawrence Cook (d)

starts with BD solo	7:27	BD rec
	6:21	--
arco bass continuo at head and throughout	6:48	--
pizzicato bass at head	9:19	--
pizzicato at head	7:37	--
BD solo	1:20	--

The exact venue was the World Music Hall on the campus at Wesleyan. First half of the concert described here; the second half at **R83-1028b**.

Titles given in Dixon's composition list ("Windswept Winterset", "Penthesilea", "The Second Son" and "Another Quiet Feeling") identify some of the musical materials that went into this concert, though there is seemingly not a one-to-one correspondence.

Pavone and/or Cook began cracking under the strain of having no written guidelines for each piece or performance (see also **R81-0615**). Dixon: "They eventually [after October, 1985] reached the limit of what we could do as a group. Their influences with other people [i.e., pulsative time] were starting to creep over into my music. Mario was more comfortable with certain things in a more traditional framework. I had been through that already and didn't need to pass out parts to people on a concert just so that they could see that I was literate musician.".

Vernon Frazer "Around the World" *CODA* #194 (February, 1984), p. 32.

R83-1028b   Bill Dixon Quartet

October 28, 1983   Wesleyan University: Middletown, CT

BD (t, flgh); John Voigt, Mario Pavone (b); Lawrence Cook (d)

BD spoken introduction	6:36	BD rec
unknown	14:53	--
pizzicato solo at head	12:51	--
drum solo at head	8:27	--
BD solo	1:47	--

The exact venue was the World Music Hall on the campus at Wesleyan. These pieces formed the second half of the concert whose first half is listed as **R83-1028a**. see **R83-1028a**.

R83-1110   Bill Dixon Ensemble

November 10. 1983   BCVT

BD (t); Arthur Brooks (t: muted); Vance Provey (t: open); Keshavan Maslak (as); unknown (g); Whit Dickey (d)

Untitled	35:30	BD rec

Maslak assayed to become a teaching fellow at BCVT, and thus was present for the weekend and this Friday informal workshop/rehearsal.

84-0003   Bill Dixon Quartet

1984   BCVT

BD (t, flgh); Mario Pavone and *probably* John Voigt (b); *probably* Lawrence Cook (d)

New Slow Dance
Octobersong
Velvet
Windswept Winterset

There is no conclusive evidence that this concert is distinct from **R83-1027**; however, since they are shown in different years, this is listed separately. All data from 1985 composition list.

R84-0531   Bill Dixon and Arthur Brooks
May 31, 1984   Paul Robeson House: BCVT

-1: BD (t, flgh); Mario Pavone, John Voigt (b); Laurence Cook (d)

-2: BD (flgh); Arthur Brooks (t); Jeffrey Taylor (ts); Pilar Castro (cello); Eric
Zinman (p); Andy Dillon, Rick O'Neal (perc)

      Stations -1   BD rec
      Maze -2   --

In a concert dedicated to Jesse Jackson, Arthur Brooks's "Maze" was performed by his
ensemble, with Dixon as a guest. The 1985 Composition List cite to a Dixon
composition of the same name (formerly **R84-0001**) is erroneous, and should
indicate instead his work, "Stations".

Pianist Zinman studied composition with Dixon for a year, probably up to his senior
concert April 2, 1985.
Details from concert program.

84-0601   Barbara Ensley-Bill Dixon
June 1-2, 1984   Washington Square Church, NYC

BD (t, flgh, p); Barbara Ensley (choreography, movement); Felicia
Moseley-Whittington, Cathy Singer, Luis Viana, Mei Wu (movement)

      Groundflight

Ensley dedicated this work to the memory of Judith Dunn.
Details from concert program and Dixon's 1985 Composition List.

R84-0602   Bill Dixon Quartet

June 2, 1984   Cuando Community Ctr: 9 2d Av, NYC

BD (t, flgh); Mario Pavone, John Voigt (b); Laurence Cook (d)

Another Quiet Feeling	BD rec
Webern	--
Octobersong	--

Dixon's set was part of the first *Sound Unity Festival* staged by William Parker and Peter Kowald, with financial assistance from painter A.R. Penck and in association with the New York City Artists Collective.
Dixon's quartet set began behind schedule; the group had rehearsed for roughly two minutes before taking the stage, with minimal instructions.

Bill Dixon also led a workshop at the festival, which--in the absence of Pavone and Cook--developed into a demonstration for the many trumpet players in attendance. Dixon's topic was "How I Practice". Many musical sets at the festival were filmed by Ebbe Jahn for her documentary Rising Tones Cross. Neither Dixon nor his music are featured in the film, and it is not clear whether his sequence was filmed at all.
Details from BD composition list and concert advertising.

R84-0615   Bill Dixon Quartet

June 15, 1984   Paul Robeson House, BCVT

BD (t); Marco Eneidi (as); William Parker (b); Laurence Cook (d)

evolves from [A440] tuning tone	29:06	BD rec
BD solo at head	10:52	--
crashing start	1:30	--
BD solo	1:54	--
BD unaccompanied to start, then add WP	5:28	--
Unknown	10:25	--
WP arco at head	2:50	--

Original tapes are labeled (in unfamiliar handwriting probably belonging to the recordist): "Demo TAPE ONE AND TWO"

Eneidi hitchhiked to Bennington to play with Dixon in the first part of 1984. He and William Parker were invited back in June of that year for this session coincident with the campus graduation dinner. Eneidi stayed at Bennington for most of the ensuing year, playing in Dixon's ensemble and acting as a teaching assistant in the Division.

84-0899   Bill Dixon-Milford Graves
prob summer, 1984   Top of the Gate, NYC

BD (t); Milford Graves (d)

The concert was produced by Reggie Workman and apparently dedicated to Jesse Jackson in the election year. "Graves was going to do a drum solo, but I said: 'I'll be there; why don't we do a duet?' "

84-1095   Bill Dixon Quartet
probably fall, 1984   BCVT

BD (t); *and probably*: John Voigt, Mario Pavone (b); Lawrence Cook (d)

>   Velvet
>   Llaattiinnoo Suite
>   The Sirens

All info extrapolated from 1985 Composition list, which may mean to attach these titles to **R84-0615**. The second bass player could with equal likelihood have been Voigt or William Parker. While it is plausible that these titles apply to one of the 1984 concerts listed with a specific date on adjacent pages, there is no clear correspondence based on the number of pieces or the number of players.
1985 Composition list

R84-1110   Bill Dixon Quintet
November 10, 1984   Paul Robeson House, BCVT

BD (t); Marco Eneidi (as); Peter Kowald, Mario Pavone (b); Laurence Cook (d)

BD spoken introduction	3:30	BD rec
featuring ME	9:10	--
Unknown	19:55	--
ends with BD solo	9:17	--
ME solo at head [interruption mid-piece]	11:43	--
Bass solo at head	6:05	--

This was the last of a (week-long?) series of fall concerts, as implied in Dixon's prefatory remarks which also noted the 20th anniversary of the October Revolution. In the same introduction, he mentions having first heard Peter Kowald playing the previous June at the *Sound Unity Festival* (see **R84-0602**). Dixon dedicated the concert to his two (by then deceased) brothers.

R85-0130   Music Is an Open Sky
January 30, 1985   Sweet Basil, NYC

BD (t); David S. Ware (ts); Peter Kowald (b); Andrew Cyrille (d)

                                                                    private tape

Dixon played as part of this 10:00pm "collaboration" at the *Music Is an Open Sky*
series (January 28-February 11) on his way out of the country.

This concert was definitely recorded.

The folowing day Dixon, Arthur Brooks and Marco Eneidi flew to Vienna for
R85-0209, stopping en route in Verona but not playing there.
Details from schedule/handbill

R85-0209   New Jazz Workshop
February 9, 1985   Museum des 20. Jahrhunderts, Vienna

BD (p, t); Arthur Brooks, Willibold Gföhler, Klaus Peham, Paul
Schwingenschlögl (t); Richard Isaiah, Jacques Nobili (tb); Elisabeth Matzka (fl);
Hans Steiner (bcl); Marco Eneidi, Harald Meier, Max Silye (as); Harri Sjöstrom
(as, ss, fl); Helmut Strobl (as, cl, ts); Stefan Slupetzky (ts); Peter Jandl, Peter
Machacek (ts, ss, fl); Hermann Simböck (vln); Stephan Suchy (cello); Erich
Einzinger, Alfred Freundlinger, Peter Lemberg, Burkhard Stangl, Helmut
Wilfinger (g); Rudolf Görnet, Volker Kagerer, Harry Klaffenböck (b); Robert
Beirer, Adriane Muttenthaler, Elisabeth Stein (p); Peter Barborik, Gerhard
Scheider, Paul Skrepek (d); Georg Melchart (perc)

Tutti	Video rec
6[HKb/JNtb/GSd/PSt/HSs/HSs]	--
7[WGt/RGb/PLg/KPtpt/PSd/SSs/ESp]	--
6[PBd/ABt/MEas/VKb/AMp/HSs]	--
5[RBp/AFg/HSJs/SSs/HWg]	--
6[VKb/EMfl/HSvln/ESp/HSs/SScello]	--
5[RGb/GSd/PSt/PSd/BSg]	--
7PBd/?H?/HKb/HMs/GMperc/JNtb/MSs]	--
3[JNtb/PSt/HSs]	--

Tutti	Video rec
6[4[BDt?/VKb/GSd/ESp]	--
BD (t)	--

Dixon was invited to lead this 5-day workshop and brought Brooks and Eneidi to take part. The three did not play together on the trip apart from this final performance/showcase.

"I arrived a couple of days early, knowing in advance the instrumentation of the group. I was staying in this beautiful hotel--stayed in the room for two days and two nights copying out the parts.

"So I walked in that day with the 'Fourth Sketch for Orchestra'. The musicians took out the parts to look at them; I looked at their faces, and said to myself 'I'm not going to do this to these people'. I knew they were never going to be able to perform that piece of music I had written, since I was only going to be there a week. George Russell had been there two years earlier, then Mike Mantler, both bringing all of this complicated music. The people had been miserable trying to do that, and they couldn't really do it anyway. So I had all of these musicians who wanted to play and had a miserable time the two years previous. I had them pass in the parts and said 'OK, now let's start'. They were so relieved when I tore that music up in front of them.

"I broke them up into groups so everyone could play and made things for them to work on. Then for the concert I made segues on the piano and only played the trumpet (I knew people wanted to hear me play it) in the last minute and a half. I put all of that together as a workshop.

"I think I kept the same title ["Fourth Sketch for Orchestra"] for the whole concert."

The piece was immensely successful in Vienna; it was also filmed for television.

"The students from the orchestra (and some other people who heard about it) asked me to do a brass workshop as part of the five days. It started at 10:00 that night and went on until about 6:00am. Then the saxophones requested a workshop, so I had to give one for them too."

This series of workshops acted as a blueprint for Dixon'a master class engagements away from Bennington. Further refinements to his approach are visible in the ventures to Nuremburg (**R90-0319**), Jerusalem (**R90-0321/2 6**), Villeurbanne (**R94-1107/08**) and New York University in a one day episode of November 23, 1996.

The trip to Vienna also afforded Dixon the opportunity to develop some etchings at Kurt Zein's studio, where he had last worked in the summer of 1976.

Details from program for this night and poster for the entire workshop; Paul Schwingenschlögl "Bill Dixon à Vienne" *Jazz Magazine* # 340 (June, 1985); Robert Bilek "I Am an Artist" Kultur Falter February, 1985, p. 21.

85-0405   <u>Bill Dixon Group</u>
April 5, 1985   BCVT

BD (t); John Buckingham (tu); Marco Eneidi (as); Stephen Horenstein (barsx); William Parker, Mario Pavone (b); Laurence Cook (d)

> For Nelson and Winnie

Dixon's 1985 Composition List supplement labels this performance "I", the **R85-0516** recording "II", and both as premieres--possibly indicating that they were substantially different.

The concert may have been held as part of Bennington's Spring Festival in which groups of Milford Graves, Eneidi and visiting pianist Clyde Criner also took part. Horenstein was an artist-in-residence at Bennington for a week after having completed a residence at Middlebury College that spring. He subbed on baritone saxophone for the bassist Peter Kowald, who had been scheduled to make this performance but was unable. While in the US, Horenstein was invited to be in the *Thoughts* recording (see next entry) but was not able to participate.

In the same term, Dixon was honored at a ceremony in New York as one of 219 BMI Jazz Pioneers; names of the honorees were also read into the *Congressional Record*.

In the *Bennington Banner* Lyle Glazier reported this concert in relation to the dissolution of the Black Music Division, which apparently became final at the same point.
Some of the same factors that had forced the Jazz Composers' Guild to disband twenty years earlier hastened the demise of the Black Music Division. Differences of philosophy and method among the members of the Black Music faculty, which were negotiable on issues relating only to the program, eventually prevented the Division from maintaining a united front to the perpetually unsympathetic majority represented by the "legitimate" Music Department and College administration. The Division's curriculum and faculty were retained and inneffectively subsumed into the Music Department at Bennington. Arthur Brooks, Dixon, Milford Graves, and Nadi Qamar were all subsequently considered members of the general music faculty.

"Everyone on that campus knew and acknowledged that the Black Music Division the way I ran it (and I *ran* it: there was no rotating chairmanship every year where you have some people who can only open the mail and call the meeting to order...) was a superior teaching division, even with our resources, which were a pittance compared to what the other divisions had.
"You see, if you're not too sure you're right, and if other people can point out where you may not be, then compromise is your only logical choice. But I don't know how it is possible to compromise if you know and everyone else knows that you're right. So it was just a matter of time."

Dixon also addressed at length the topic of the Division's dismantling in a letter reprinted in *L'Opera*.
Lyle Glazier *Bennington Banner* April 16, 1985, p. 8; *L'Opera*, p. 33-40.

R85-0516a   Bill Dixon Septet

May 16, 1985   Paul Robeson House, BCVT

BD (p); Marco Eneidi (as); John Buckingham (tu); Peter Kowald, William
Parker, Mario Pavone (b); Laurence Cook (d)

Windows-1	ct	2:30	video original
Windows-2	ct	5:20	--
Windows-3	ct	3:30	--
Windows-4	mst	4:40	Soul Note 1111
Windows-5	ct	4:40	video original
Time I -1	ct	6:15	--
Time I -2	mst	4:04	Soul Note 1111
Time II-1	ct	5:30	video original
Time II-2	mst	5:09	Soul Note 1111

Soul Note SN 1111 titled *Thoughts*, also on CD 121111-2.

Session continues on **85-0516b**; all takes on video original
All pieces here were played from written parts. They are listed in the sequence in
which they were played at the session. "Time I" and "Time II" are the first and fourth
parts of the suite "For Nelson and Winnie". Though listed on side A of the LP, "Time
II" occupies the first band on the record's B side.

The basses were independently recording-baffled to isolate their sounds.

R85-0516b   Bill Dixon Septet

May 16, 1985   Paul Robeson House, BCVT

BD (t); John Buckingham (tu); Marco Eneidi (as); Peter Kowald, William
Parker, Mario Pavone (b); Laurence Cook (d)

Thoughts	11:20	Soul Note 1111
Song For Claudia's Children	8:30	--
Brothers	8:30	--
Points	8:45	--
Essence	4:30	--
Transfiguration	5:10	--

continued from **85-0516a**.

All are first-and-only-takes.

"Essence" and "Transfiguration" are parts 2 and 3 of the four-part suite "For Nelson
and Winnie".

"Brothers" on SN 1111 is edited from an original ca. 9:00. Dixon's fluegelhorn solo
is incomplete due to a tape switch on the video original, but that tape still holds
roughly 30 seconds following his first phrase that do not appear on the record.
The video version of "Points" plays 9:15, whereas the LP timed at 8:45. That piece
too was probably edited for *Thoughts*.

See **R85-0516a**

R85-0608   <u>Bill Dixon</u>

June 8, 1985   Greenwall Music Workshop, BCVT

BD (p and voice on tape)

    Waltz   6:23   BC Dance video

"Waltz" (also referred to as "Linda's Waltz") was indirectly composed for dancer Linda
Tarnay, in a work to be choreographed by Jack Moore. Dixon: "Linda had asked
[Moore] if he could get me to write a waltz for her. Even when Jack approached me
about it, my response was something like 'Come on, man; get real'. But I did this
piece and, like all these pieces it was very very good for me because it was utilitarian.
I made something that was rhythmically intact so that he could do what he was doing,
but melodically, harmonically, and spatially interesting for me. That was the way I
wrote a lot of songs in those days. None of them were abstract.
"So after I had done it and he had made this fantastic dance, he told me that it was for
someone else. In the end I never gave the piece to her." It was therefore never
performed in that form.

For this concert commemorating Jack Moore's retirement from Bennington after 24
years on faculty, Dixon pre-recorded some spoken reflections on working with Jack
Moore. [The text he read appears in *L'Opera*.] That tape was played back
continuously as Dixon performed his own music from "Waltz" live in the hall. "I was
trying to sum up the things I had done with him. I had written out the text, and then
taped myself speaking it, and I tried to make it so that it sounded like I was speaking
to him. It was all very staged: I was dressed in suit and tie. I came out to get situated
at the piano, and then before I played, the voice part began. At that time Jack had
never heard this himself. It was beautiful."

Bill Dixon was on sabbatical from Bennington in the fall term, 1985; pianist Clyde
Criner was his sabbatical replacement for the semester.
L'Opera, p.128-30.

86-0000   Art Davis Workshop
1986   BCVT

BD (t); Art Davis (b); John Schenck (cl); Rachel Neill (ss); others unknown

Davis came to Bennington earlier in the 80s to lecture on his early-Seventies case
with the Human Rights Commissions against the New York Philharmonic. Here, he
returned to give a workshop with Dixon's ensemble, at the conclusion of which he
and Dixon performed a brief duet

Though certain members of the group have remained active and successful in music,
Dixon recalls this as a particularly low point for the ensemble, notably after the
disappearance of the Black Music Division.
"The only thing the ensemble members had going for them was this (I think this is
what happens a lot in the university today): Young people are made to think that they
are significant simply because they live and breathe, and in that instance they are,
but not because of what they say. There is no profundity if you open your mouth just
to 'rap' and can't back it up with knowledge or experience or ability or erudition or
the imagination. But we allow that; we permit it".
Dixon's description of the event points to further factors in the decay of the Black
Music Division. "It was almost embarrassing. Here's Bennington, posturing itself
as a vanguard institution in the Arts. Here was Art Davis, coming up to do a
workshop. First of all there weren't half a dozen competent bassists on the campus
who could benefit from what he's talking about. So here are these kids, here I am,
Bill Dixon, and here's Dr. Art Davis. He did a very good elementary thing--he tried to
get them to play a 12-bar blues, and he had to sing the cadential parts--and they
couldn't even do *that*. Here were these 'thinking, questioning' intellectuals, and they
couldn't do it."

R86-0399   Bill Dixon--Matt Henderson
Spring 1986   Jennings Hall, BCVT

BD (t); Matt Henderson (g)

                                             BD rec

Henderson was a masters student in the Music Department at Bennington.
Informal sessions.

R86-0509   Maureen Riva Ellenhorn
May 9-11, 1986   Possibly Greenwall Auditorium, BCVT

BD (acoustic and Fender-Rhodes p); Maureen Riva Ellenhorn (choreography, movement); Sandra Burton, DD Dorvillier, Erin Fitzgerald, Maiya Greaves, Janet Schuman (movement)

A Field Called No-time   8:06   BC Dance video

Part of a Martha Hill dance performance presented by the BCVT Dance Department. 8:00pm on each of three consecutive nights; probably the same program ran each night.

Dixon wrote and performed the music for Ellenhorn's dance, which was played back from a tape at the event. He recorded one track of the piano, then the other on electric piano, and synchronized them to generate the tape played back in performance. Details from concert program.

86-0515   Bill Dixon Quartet
May 15, 1986   BCVT

BD (t, flgh); William Parker, Mario Pavone (b); Laurence Cook (d)

add Matt Henderson (g) and Michael Downs (voice) for one piece

Dixon's quartet, in addition to playing his own music, was joined by two student musicians to perform a piece written by Dixon's composition student, John Bepler.

R86-0516   Bill Dixon Trio
May 16-17, 1986   Charlie's Tap, Boston

Bill Dixon (t); Mario Pavone (b); Laurence Cook (d)

BD rec

Details from concert listings and tape boxes; Michael Ullman "Blowing Mild: Still Quiet on the Dixon Front" *The Boston Phoenix* May 27, 1986, section three, p. 9.

R86-0901   Bill Dixon Quartet
circa September 1, 1986   Lexington, New York

BD (t); William Parker, Mario Pavone (b); Laurence Cook (d)

		11:47	BD rec
BD solo		0:33	--
starts with BD solo		10:13	--
		7:23	--

The Lexington organization "Art Awareness" sponsored this Labor Day weekend concert.

R86-1010   The Collaborative Process
fall term, 1986; esp. October 10   Martha Hill Dance Workshop: BCVT

BD, Arthur Brooks (t); Marco Eneidi, Rachel Neill (as); Elizabeth Brunton (cello); Matt Henderson, Tony Wilson (g); *probably* Claudia Friedlander (voice); Nina Galin (unknown); Hope Clark, DD Dorvillier, Audrey Kindred, Chivas Sandage, Gertrude Saunders, Allison Tardell (movement)

an improvisation   BD video rec

"The Collaborative Process is an old class that I taught periodically. Judith Dunn and I used to teach it under the same name (see **R68-0916**). Every dancer had to have his or her own musician; the two collaborated. Anyone could take it who wanted to work. It required at least eight or nine people in the class interacting to make it work. Each class meeting included all of the dancers and the musicians with whom they were collaborating." This October 10 meeting was referred to as an improvisation and consisted of a continuous interplay between musicians and dancers in the same space simultaneously. It was very rigorous and I could never get people to commit to it, so I didn't teach it that much. In fact, that was the last year I taught it, at the request of Chivas Sandage.
"I gave them exercises to do, and they had to show something. Every day, each musician had to learn a phrase of some kind; each one would determine what it was. They had to be able to play it in any way. Every dancer had to learn four movements--again, it could be a gesture, anything--and likewise they had to be able to do theirs in any way and recall them. By the end of the term, they had all of this material. And they also learned how to speak the language of the other discipline. I suggested that they spend time together, listen to music and watch things together, and so on. Everyone kept a daily journal and at the end of the term they each made a presentation."

Brooks and Eneidi assisted in teaching this course.

R86-1015   Bill Dixon-Tony Widoff

October 15, 1986   Greenwall Music Workshop, BCVT

BD (t, flgh); Tony Widoff (keyboard synthesizer)

      October: 1986   BD rec

The work (and this duo) was premiered here at "A Concert for Lionel--music by Lionel Nowak and Friends". Nowak had been a member of the College's music faculty since 1948.

Dixon and Widoff made other non-public sessions on October 1, 31; November 5, 15, and 16, 1986; and June 1, 1987. Six further, undated tapes are also extant.

" 'Concert for Lionel' Airs Works by Friends" *Bennington Banner* ca. October 10, 1986.

R86-1022   Bill Dixon Quartet

October 22, 1986   Middlebury College, Vermont

BD (t); William Parker, Mario Pavone (b); Laurence Cook (d)

starts with BD unaccompanied	11:50	BD video rec
Untitled	14:05	--
Untitled	2:35	--
starts with BD unaccompanied	16:21	--

Dixon spent a week (October 21-26) as a "Distinguished Visitor in the Arts" at Middlebury, during which his activities included (in order):

-a radio interview on the college station (October 21)

-a master class with the jazz band

-a master class with the symphony orchestra

-this open quartet rehearsal (October 22)

-master classes in Dance (probably October 23)

-a college-wide lecture (October 24)

-a quartet performance (October 25) adding Penny Campbell **R86-1025**

Bill Dixon "To Whom It May Concern Nineteen Years Later" *CODA* December 1986/January 1987, p. 24.

R86-1025   Bill Dixon Quartet
October 25, 1986   Middlebury College, Vermont

BD (t, flgh -2); William Parker, Mario Pavone (b); Laurence Cook (d); Penny
Campbell (movement)

rehearsal:	22:19	BD video rec
rehearsal:	1:55	--
rehearsal:	27:36	--
First concert:		
	34:54	--
-2	22:08	--
Second concert:		
	24:10	--
switches to -2 at 21:00	27:08	--

From Dixon's week spent as a Distinguished Visitor in the Arts; see **R86-1022**.
See **R86-1022**.

R86-1116   Bill Dixon-Tony Widoff
November 16, 1986   Carriage Barn, BCVT

BD (t); Tony Widoff (synthesizer)

Unknown	14:58	BD rec

This was the first of two senior concerts Widoff played (the other is **R87-0299**),
both including duets with Dixon.

"After playing vigorously for a week at Middlebury [**R86-1025**], I came back, did a
concert, and noticed something a little tense in my playing, so I moved something
very slightly in my embouchure. I'm only now [1991] finally getting comfortable
with that embouchure change. Of course I can play, but in the beginning I wasn't
playing with the kind of ease that I like."
Details from concert program.

86-1205a   Bill Dixon
December 5, 1986   Carriage Barn, BCVT

BD (t, flgh); Tony Widoff (synthesizer); William Parker, Mario Pavone (b); Laurence Cook (d); Penny Campbell (choreography and movement)

This evening was billed as "Bill Dixon in Concert"; the program lists works for "solo piano; ensemble; ensemble and dancer; trumpet and synthesizer", although the music may not have taken exactly that form.

This 9:00pm concert did not conflict with **86-1205b**, held on the same night with Dixon's music from a pre-recorded tape.

From *Bennington College Week*: "This event, which commemorates Mr. Dixon's Fortieth Anniversary in music, will consist of: three new compositions in music; the unveiling of three paintings [ca. 1983 and 1985] (not previously, publicly exhibited); the METAMORPHOSIS MUSIC publication of *L'Opera, Volume One*, a collection of writings, drawings, music manuscript and photographs--covering the period 1962 to 1986; and the release of *Thoughts*, Mr. Dixon's latest recording, being internationally released in January 1987 on LP, cassette, and compact disc."
Details from concert program and *Bennington College Week* Vol. LXXXV No 13, December 1-7, 1986.

R86-1205b   Chivas Sandage-Bill Dixon
December 5-7, 1986   Martha Hill Dance Workshop, BCVT

BD (p); Chivas Sandage (choreography, movement); Rachel Goldberg, Anne Hubbard, Teresa Smith, unknown (movement)

   Rushing at the Shift, Dusk   11:44 BC Dance video

For the first night, Dixon's music for this event was played from a tape and not live. See **R86-1205a**.

Recordings exist for all three nights. The given timing is specific to December 5, but durations of the other performances are presumed similar.
Details from concert program.

R87-0299   Bill Dixon-Tony Widoff
February 1987   Greenwall Music Workshop, BCVT

BD (t); Tony Widoff (synthesizer)

>   Unknown   >6:00   BD rec

From Widoff's second "Senior concert"; see also **R86-1116**.
Details from concert program.

R87-0501   Martha and Jo Wittman
May 1-3, 1987   Martha Hill Dance Workshop, BCVT

on tape: BD (t); Spin Dunbar (b); Jo Wittman (keyboards); Ben Wittman (d);
Martha Wittman (choreography, movement)

>   Landscape   BC Dance vid

"Landscape" was part of the program *Three Excerpts from East-West Traveling
Dances 1982-1983* (see **R83-0610**), of which the other two were "Women's Solo
and Quartet" and "Lament". All were presented as the first in a series of concerts in
honor of Jo Wittman's retirement from the Dance Department.
Each musician above recorded independently prior to the peformance; their
contributions were combined and sequenced on tape by Jo Wittman for the final order.
He is credited in this production with "soundscore" and Martha Wittman as
choreographer.
It is not clear whether this performance used an identical, reconfigured, or totally
different layout from **R83-0610**.
Recordings are known for the first two nights.
Details from concert program.

R87-0515   Sandra Burton-Bill Dixon
May 15-17, 1987   Martha Hill Dance Workshop, BCVT

BD (p); Sandra Burton (choreography, movement, text collage, voice); Anya
Clarke, Nicole Claro, Shaunna Gray, Gibbs Saunders (movement)

>   Dragon Ladies Demise   BC Dance video

Set and lighting by Jane Kocol; Burton designed the costumes.

Burton's narrative piece--probably created for her master's degree thesis--concerned
three women, one of whom was Emelda Marcos.

87-0967   Bill Dixon

probably fall term, 1987   Greenwall Music Workshop, BCVT

BD (t and/or flgh)

Dixon played solos in this concert and at least one other Music Faculty Concert (probably more) in the late 80s or early 90s.

R87-1017   Sage City Symphony Orchestra

October 17, 1987   Greenwall Auditorium: BCVT

John Tisbert, Ed Keogh, Susan Newton (t); John Howland, Gerry Cohen, Maria Lattimore, Elizabeth Hadlock (frh); Doug Personette, Chris Hoder, Ron Woodworth (tb); Ed Lawrence (tu); Gail Albright (picc); Christine Graham, Manny Kent (fl); Zeke Hecker, Fred Meyer (ob); Yuji Shinozaki (engh); Charles Thompson (bsn); Ellen Sager (concertmaster); John Swan, Debbie Cunningham, Kathy Cunningham, Jane Hanks, Judy Manes, Suzy Reiss, Jane Rink, Marjorie Sherman, Harriet Welther (1st vln); Elaine Beckwith, Nora Stevenson, Annemieke tem Bokum, David Bort, T-Kay Damon, Adelaide Fine, Becky Hong, Becky Howland, John Kuegel, Max Putnam, Richard Sager, David Scribner (2d vln); Joe Schaaf, Alice Wu, Lorelei Bond (vla); Bill Peck, Robert Nowak, Daniel Cunningham, Oakley Frost, Petra Levin, Max Weiss (cello); Jim Fitzgerald, Bart McLean (b); Ehran Elisha (tymp); Margie Rooen, Brian Cason, Janet Gillespie (perc); Michael Downs (voice); Lou Calabro (cond)

Quinacridone: For Nelson and Winnie   BD rec

Dixon's composition was commissioned by the symphony and rehearsed with Calabro conducting.

The concert, presented in conjunction with the Vermont Academy of the Arts and Sciences, also featured works of Rimsky-Korsakoff and Vincent Persichetti, to whose memory the concert was dedicated.

Dixon: "I took the speech that Nelson Mandela made when he was being sentenced and wrote that out for a baritone voice [Downs]. You can't bypass the words."

In his 1986 *CODA* article, Dixon refers to a "full length work for orchestra that will be premiered in the Spring of 1987", presumably meaning "Quinacridone", though it actually premiered in the fall. The same article indicates that "For Nelson and Winnie" from **R85-0516** was excerpted from the orchestra piece.

Details from concert program; "To Whom It May Concern Nineteen Years Later" *CODA* December 1986/January 1987, p. 24.

88-0402   Bill Dixon

April 2, 1988   Martha Hill Dance Workshop, BCVT

BD (t); Tony Wilson, Matt Henderson (g)

> Linear & Density-Sketches for Small Ens.

Part of a memorial concert for Bennington Dance Division faculty member Jo(sef) Wittman (1919-1987).

Details from concert program.

88-0403   Bill Dixon

April 3, 1988   Greenwall Music Workshop, BCVT

BD (probably p)

> A Song: one & two

Part of the "Spring Sampler" concert of the Music Department, with mainly faculty as composers and performers. The program also included Dixon's student, drummer Ehran Elisha, though he probably has no connection to the piece.

Details from concert poster.

R88-0417   Bill Dixon Ensemble

April 17, 1988   The Kraine: 85 East 4th Street, NYC

BD (cond, t); Arthur Brooks, Roy Campbell, Leo Smith (t); Bill Lowe (tu); Karen Borca (bsn); Jemeel Moondoc (as); Glenn Spearman, David S. Ware (ts); William Parker, Mario Pavone (b); Laurence Cook (d)

> Sisyphus   BD rec

Dixon's ensemble composition, part of the *Second International Sound Unity Festival*, was given a single performance after rehearsals at Jemeel Moondoc's loft on at least the days of and before the concert. According to Dixon, the piece would have benefited from further and more focused rehearsals.

"At the first rehearsal, everyone wasn't there--and they were being paid for these things. At the second one, some of the people who had been there the day before sent substitutes. I was ready to go right back to Vermont; I can't deal with that kind of thing where everyone sight reads a part, then struts out and does a funny solo, and thinks they're into something. I come from a different tradition where a thing has to be *definitive.*"

LP liner notes to *Son of Sisyphus* (**R88-0628**); some details from the leaflets for the series; also announced in *Jazznews* [Dublin] July/August 1988.

R88-0517   Ehran Elisha-Bill Dixon
May 17, 1988   Carriage Barn, BCVT

BD (t); Ehran Elisha (d); Jeremy Harlos (b)

     Masada Echoes   BD rec; also
                                                           video rec

Ehran Elisha later performed this work many times (eventually adopting the title
above) although this was the only performance to feature Dixon, and the piece had no
title for this concert. Elisha had undertaken a term's tutorial with Dixon that
culminated in this senior concert. Their duet was the last piece on the program. This
event is not to be confused with Elisha's other graduating concert, held in the
Greenwall Auditorium, in which he performed as the soloist in a piece written for him
by his father.

"I started doing pedal tones so that I could play longer. When you play the trumpet,
if you're using too much pressure, the blood goes out of your lip, so it won't vibrate
when the air passes through. So a lot of guys buzz and do things like that to warm up,
but I had to find a way to be able to do that and play. To play pedal tones you have to
be completely relaxed, and I found that I could do them and start the blood to
recirculating immediately. I then began making that into a musical component. It
wasn't to be slick. Like everything I've done it's been utilitarian in the beginning
and has allowed me aesthetically to do *something* else."

R88-0622   Bill Dixon Quartet
June 22, 1988   Knitting Factory: 47 E Houston, NYC

BD (t); John Buckingham (tu); Mario Pavone (b); Lawrence Cook (d)

     [all untitled]   10:10   BD rec
                                                    17:25   --
     inc.   frag.   --

Dixon elected to make this appearance in the Knitting Factory's "Comprovisations"
festival as a last opportunity for the quartet to play before going on tour to Italy.
They departed June 23 to play the events that appear on subsequent pages.

Buckingham was present but he is almost inaudible on the recording; apparently he
had pushed away the microphone in getting situated on stage and never returned it to
recording position. A formal multitrack recording was made by the Knitting Factory.
While one segment of it survives in Dixon's possession, the club denies any
knowledge of the whereabouts of the remainder.
Details from Knitting Factory program schedule.

R88-0626   Bill Dixon Quartet
June 26, 1988   Teatro Romano: Verona, Italy

BD (t); John Buckingham (tu); Mario Pavone (b); Lawrence Cook (d)

BD Spoken intro	1:30	BD rec
like Mandala per Mandela -1	15:33	--
Vecctor	11:00	--
Molti Molti Anni Fa...	10:34	--
Unknown ["one more short number"]	5:36	--

This Verona Jazz Festival engagement was apparently also video-recorded. Titles
above are based on comparisons with the Soul Note recordings (**R88-0628**):
The first piece also has some similarities to "Schema VI-88"; however,
Buckingham's ostinato in that work and in "Molti Molti Anni Fa..." have no
counterpart in the *Son of Sisyphus* studio recordings.
Dixon dedicated this performance to Winnie and Nelson Mandela.

From *Son of Sisyphus* notes: [Jack Moore] died on the 23rd of June and I was on a
flight to Italy, first to perform in Verona and Bolzano, and then to make this
recording in Milan."
Musica Jazz August/September, 1988, p. 12.

R88-0628   Bill Dixon Quartet
June 28-29, 1988   Barigozzi Studio: Milan, Italy

BD (t, p-1); John Buckingham (tu, except -1); Mario Pavone (b); Lawrence
Cook (d, except -1)

Silences for Jack Moore -1	2:18	SN 121 138-1
Vecctor	1:55	--
Son of Sisyphus	7:19	--
Schema VI-88	3:10	--
Fusama Codex	5:23	--
Mandala per Mandela	3:50	--
Sumi-E -1	2:58	--
Negoro Codex	4:28	--
Molti Molti Anni Fa	7:40	--

Also released on compact disc and cassette as 121138 -2 and -4, respectively; all
titled *Son of Sisyphus*.

88-0701   Bill Dixon Quartet
July 1, 1988   Bolzano, Italy

BD (t); John Buckingham (tu); Mario Pavone (b); Lawrence Cook (d)

88-1112   Jack Moore-Bill Dixon
November 12, 1988   Martha Hill Dance Workshop, BCVT

BD (p); Jack Moore (choreography)
-1: Nancy Peck (movement)
-2: Barbara Roan (movement)
-3: Rick Shaw (movement)

> Collage of Excerpts #2 including: 30:27   BC Dance video
>   Unknown
>   Unknown -1
>   Tea Dust at 5:43 pm -2
>   Unknown [probably "Fire"]
>   Autumn's Chant -3

The Jack Moore Memorial Concert presented excerpts of many of the
choreographer's works, including "Tea Dust at 5:43 pm" (**78-0099**) and "Autumn's
Chant" (**R82-1209**), collaborative works from earlier years for which Dixon wrote
the music. At the concert Dixon played piano for the entire Collage of Excerpts # 2.
The three unkown pieces are definitely Moore's "Assays", "Opticon", and "Fire";
"Assays" and "Opticon", Moore pieces from the early Sixties, are likely the first two.
Dixon played the original music for "Tea Dust..." and "Autumn's Chant" and
improvised a suite for the other works that briefly interpolated themes from "Autumn
Sequences from A Paris Diary" and *Thoughts*.

Details from concert program.

CHAPTER TEN

Round Up the Usual Suspects 1989–1997

88-1120   <u>Bill Dixon Quartet</u>
November 20, 1988   Vienna

BD (t, p); Leslie Winston (p, Yamaha DX7); Klaus Koch (b); Sydney Smart (d)

Unknown	29:00	BD cassettes
Dixon (p) solo	2:35	
Unknown	11:24	

Dixon switches to piano (as Winston lays out) for the last third of the first piece.

This performance was part of the *Cool Noir* series curated in memory of Chet Baker [he had died May 13 of that year] by the Wiener Musik Galerie, which set out to "show the influence of 'Cool Jazz' on the modern development of American and European music" according to the series program [BY trans.]. The festival

encompassed performances by the Jimmy Giuffre Quartet, Anthony Braxton and Marianne Schroeder, Franz Koglmann's Pipetett with Ran Blake, Jeanne Lee and Ran Blake, and of Morton Feldman's *Untitled Composition for Piano and Cello*.
All concerts in the series were held at the Österreichischen Museum für angewandte Kunst.

Here was Dixon's first meeting and performance with Klaus Koch, who was recommended from the German Radio Orchestra of Köln.
Dixon's remarks in introducing the musicians are indicative of a conscious turn in his music away from the trio and quartets with Pavone and Cook, following their tour of the previous summer. To date, that group has not reunited as such.
Details from exhibit-book; Peter Niklaus Wilson " 'Cool' als Lebensgefühl" *Neue Zeitschrift für Musik* February, 1989, p. 39-40.

R89-0399   Bill Dixon-Leslie Winston-Xtopher Faris
Spring 1989   Carriage Barn, BCVT

BD (t); Leslie Winston (keyboards *including* Yamaha DX7); Xtopher Faris (b)

    Unknown   c8:00   BD rec

Certainly other pieces than this one were recorded at the session.

89-0401   Bill Dixon-Laura Chapman
April 1, 1989   Martha Hill Dance Workshop, BCVT

BD (p); Laura Chapman (choreography, movement); David Stickford (movement); Joel Hauserman (slide projection)

    Transparencies

Dixon created the music for this multimedia event. Two of six segments of the work (which had premiered in Cleveland) were performed in this concert of the Spring Alumni Dance Series, dedicated to Jack Moore and Jo Wittman, both recently deceased.

89-0415   Sage City Symphony

April 15, 1989   Shaftsbury Elementary School, VT

John Materno, Gary Sharon (t); John Howland, Marie Cox, Maria Lattimore,
Elizabeth Hadlock (frh); Doug Personette, Jerry Zaffuts (tb); Ed Lawrence (tu);
Gail Albright (picc); Lauren Cale, Manny Kent (fl); Cindy Campbell, Betsy
Colt (ob); Glenn Beard, Zafer Ponter (bsn); Ellen Sager (concertmaster); John
Swan, Guy Rauscher, Marcella Rauscher, Tommy Wallace-Senft, Suzy Reiss,
T. Larry Read (1st vln); John Kuegel [principal] , Elaine Beckwith, David Bort,
Adelaide Fine, Jane Hanks, David Scribner (2d vln); Louis Tavelli [principal] ,
Joe Schaaf, Nora Stevenson, Alice Wu (vla); Bill Peck, Daniel Cunningham,
Martha Hardy, Mimitria Koninis, Emily Sprague (cello); Jim Fitzgerald,
Xtopher Faris (b); Margie Rooen, Brian Cason (tymp/perc); Lou Calabro (cond)

      Anniversary Overture

Bill Dixon was one of 8 composers commissioned to write a finite segment of music
(32 bars, apparently), all of which pieces would be linked end to end and played
continuously as the Overture, recognizing the 16th anniverary of the founding of the
Sage City Symphony. The other segments of the piece were written by (in sequence):
Lou Calabro (music director for the orchestra), Thomas Read, Ed Lawrence, Susan
Hurley, Jeff Levine, Allen Shawn, and Maria Lattimore.

Dixon, regarding his portion: "I tried to imagine how the rest of the composers would
go about doing their segments, and in that instance I decided to try to deal with a
mass of dense sound for the orchestra. Since I didn't attempt to write anything for the
rhythm or percussion, and since the rhythmic figure seemed to be something that
everyone would use, I tried to designate the mass of sound as something that would
'ride over' that rhythmic thing."
Details and quote from concert program.

89-0521   Bill Dixon

May 21, 1989   St. Marks Church, NYC

BD (t)

"A Celebration in Memory of the Life and Work of Jack Moore (1926-1988)", held
under the auspices of the Danspace project at the church.

Dixon performed an untitled trumpet solo, as there was no piano available.
Details from concert program.

89-0908   Bill Dixon-Xtopher Faris
September 8, 1989   Greenwall Music Workshop, BCVT

BD (t); Xtopher Faris (b)

Part of a "Pre-Registration Concert" for the entering class at Bennington, featuring
music of faculty members and others, largely played by students.
Details from concert program.

R89-1099   Bill Dixon-Ehran Elisha
fall, 1989   Wesleyan University

BD (t); Ehran Elisha (d, perc)

                                                          private tape

Dixon performed this duet at the memorial service for tenor saxophonist Bill Barron,
a Wesleyan faculty member who died September 21, 1989. Elisha, a recent alumnus
of Dixon's program at Bennington, was at this time in graduate studies at Wesleyan.

90-0307   Bill Dixon-Xtopher Faris
March 7, 1990   Greenwall Music Workshop, BCVT

Bill Dixon (t, flgh); Xtopher Faris (b)

          For Beauford Delaney

Concert titled "Music by Faculty Composers"

"In the Seventies when I was going back and forth to Paris a lot, I would see [the
Black painter Beauford Delaney], and we had peripheral conversations sitting there in
Saint-Germain. I didn't know who he was, and then I read an obituary and realized
that this was the same man. I was asked to do something at this faculty concert and I
was working on some things with Chris, so I decided it would be a piece for him".
Details from concert program.

R90-0310   Bill Dixon-Xtopher Faris
March, 1990   Southern Vermont College: Bennington

BD (t, flgh); Xtopher Faris (b)

BD video rec

This "Duo Concert of Untitled Compositions" was a lecture-demonstration dealing with Dixon's work and improvisation vis-à-vis notational composition. Dixon: "That was another opportunity to get Chris ready for the work we were going to do in Nuremburg".
Details from concert program.

R90-0314   Bill Dixon Trio
March 14-18, 1990   Nuremberg, Germany

BD (t?); Xtopher Faris (b); George Buckner (d)

video rec

Dixon's trio appeared was one part of a week (14-18) of Black Music demonstrations. He had a show of paintings, gave the concert (above) and a public reading of some segments of *L'Opera*, and held an ensemble workshop (**R90-0319**). Buckner is an American drummer now living in Germany.
Details from concert poster and program.

R90-0319   Bill Dixon Trio
March 19, 1990   Nuremberg, Germany

BD (t?); Xtopher Faris (b); others unknown

video rec

The ensemble workshop, with mostly string players participating, was added on the last day of Dixon's stay in Nuremburg.

Dixon traveled directly from Nuremberg to Jerusalem; Faris returned to the US.
Details from concert poster and program.

R90-0321 Workshop Ensemble of the Institute of Contemporary Music
March 21, 1990 Cinematheque, Jerusalem

BD (p); Rafi Malchiel (tb); Shachar Cohen (fl); Yoni Dror (ss); Gan Lev (as, ss); Al Kostin (ts); Stephen Horenstein (ts, ss); Elan Arad (barsx); Amos Hoffman (g); Ayal Gan-Or (b); Shai Bachar (p); Noam David, Avi Yshay (d); unknown (hand drums)
-2: BD (t, flgh)

Large Ensemble Work [Dixon]	28:15	video rec
Large Ensemble Work [Horenstein]		
Jerusalem -2	27:00	

Dixon arrived in Israel on a Monday, giving a Tel-Aviv press conference the same day. The following day, he was involved in this Tuesday performance.
Dixon conducts from the piano throughout the solos and group figures of his piece. This performance preceded all of the rehearsals with ensemble members from the ICM, including a larger group.

He used two microphones in the solo performance, both carrying effects; direct sound is unamplified. In prefatory remarks for the concert, Dixon dedicated that piece to the people of Jerusalem.

The same concert included music organized by Jeremy Montague.

The following night, Dixon, Horenstein, Jeffrey Kowalsky, and others participated in a panel discussion on improvisation at another venue in Jerusalem.

R90-0322   Workshop Ensemble of the Institute of Contemporary Music
March 22-24, 1990   Inst. of Contemporary Music, Jerusalem

BD (p); Rafi Malchiel (tb); Shachar Cohen (fl); Yoni Dror (ss); Gan Lev (as, ss); Al Kostin (ts); Stephen Horenstein (ts, ss); Elan Arad (barsx); Amos Hoffman (g); Ayal Gan-Or (b); Shai Bachar (p); Noam David, Avi Yshay (d); unknown (hand drums)

     workshop rehearsals   video rec

Stephen Horenstein, Dixon's former pupil and assistant at Bennington, invited him to conduct an instructional and performance series at the Jerusalem Institute, where Horenstein headed a Black Music program modeled after Bennington's. Dixon thus led several days of workshops (Wednesday, Thursday, and Friday), culminating in the concert performances of **R90-0326**.

R90-0325   Workshop Ensemble of the Institute of Contemporary Music
March 25, 1990   Jerusalem Theater, Jerusalem

-1: BD (p); Rafi Malchiel (tb); Shachar Cohen (fl); Yoni Dror (ss); Gan Lev (as, ss); Al Kostin (ts); Stephen Horenstein (ts, ss); Elan Arad (barsx); Amos Hoffman (g); Ayal Gan-Or (b); Shai Bachar (p); Noam David, Avi Yshay (d); unknown (hand drums)
-2: BD (t, flgh, p); Stephen Horenstein (bfl, ts, barsx, p)

     Ensemble Piece [Dixon] -1   video rec
     Ensemble Piece [Horenstein] -1
     Duets -2

Saturday night

R90-0326   Bill Dixon-Steve Horenstein-Jeff Kowalsky
March 26, 1990   Cinematheque?, Tel-Aviv

-1: BD (p); Rafi Malchiel (tb); Shachar Cohen (fl); Yoni Dror (ss); Gan Lev (as,
ss); Al Kostin (ts); Stephen Horenstein (ts, ss); Elan Arad (barsx); Amos
Hoffman (g); Ayal Gan-Or (b); Shai Bachar (p); Noam David, Avi Yshay (d);
unknown (hand drums)
-2: BD (t, flgh, p); Stephen Horenstein (ts, barsx, bfl, p); Jeffrey Kowalsky
(perc)
-3: BD (t, flgh, p); Stephen Horenstein (ts, barsx, bfl, p)

Ensemble Piece [Dixon] -1		
Ensemble Piece [Horenstein] -1		
Duet #1 (p, ts) -3	3:45	BD rec
Duet #2 (flgh, p) -3	>4:19	--
Duet #3 (flgh, bfl) -3	2:20	--
Duet #4 (t, barsx) -3		--
Duet #5 (p, p) -2	3:00	--
Trio (t, ts) -2		
Trio (t, barsx) -2		
Trio (t, p) -2		

All above are from the same Sunday night concert.
Kowalsky was a concert percussionist with the city symphony in Jerusalem.

Dixon also gave a radio interview in Tel-Aviv.

90-0520   David S. Ware Quartet
May 20, 1990   Knitting Factory, NYC

BD (t); David S. Ware (ts); Matthew Shipp (p); William Parker (b); Marc
Edwards(d)

advertised in *Village Voice* May 22, 1990, p. 119.

90-0613　　　　Bill Dixon-Xtopher Faris

probably June 13, 1990　　　　　　　　Carriage Barn, BCVT

BD (t); Xtopher Faris (b)

10:37

20:11

16:39

c.14:30

Dixon and Faris recorded on this occasion; July 25 and 30, 1989; and twice in the fall of 1990. A total of 27 known cassettes from this period contain Dixon's duets with Faris or bassist Jeremy Harlos.

In the early Nineties, Dixon compiled on cassette and duplicated a tape of recent works. It included one or more duets with Faris, work with Leslie Winston--with or without a bass player--and other duo and trio recordings. Copies of the tape were given to some of Dixon's friends and followers of his music; it was also often sent as a reply to admirers writing to inquire where Dixon's latest work was available. "The initial idea was to do a limited edition of cassettes. I didn't want exact duplicates. The covers were all hand-designed; everything was done by hand." Possible sources of the music also include **R89-0399** and **R92-1204**.

Details from concert program.

R90-0999   Bill Dixon Ensemble
fall 1990   *probably* Carriage Barn BCVT

BD (cond, t); Arthur Brooks (t); Rebecca Rodriguez (bcl); Jason Zappa (barsx);
Justin Perdue (g); Xtopher Faris, Mark Leonard, Jeremy Harlos (b); John Blum,
Michael Johnson (p); Rich Hauver (vibes)

rehearsal for Letters: Round Up the Usual..   BD rec

This excerpt from one of the ensemble class's regular meetings includes two readings
of the bass figure that is central to the "Letters: Round Up The Usual Suspects"
orchestra work.
"There's a beautiful part in [that piece] with the arco basses--that sweeping
movement [an ascending glissando through the instrument's entire range]. When we
were working on that I told them 'I want a thing going in there'. I had played
something on the horn, and on the piano, so I had set the ambience in the room.
Then Chris Faris was messing around and all of the sudden made this sound... 'THAT's
what I want! Do it just the way he did it'. What I wanted was to have all of them do
that figure with an uneven unison setting in, because [they wouldn't all gliss up
exactly together]."

This rehearsal presumably precedes **R90-1005**, although the piece was undoubtedly
explored in the interim between that performance and **R90-1207**, and the
differences between these two major concerts demonstrate a certain flux of musical
materials.

R90-1005   Bill Dixon Ensemble
October 5, 1990   Carriage Barn, BCVT

BD, Arthur Brooks (t); Rebecca Rodriguez (bcl); Bill Cole (nagaswaram, shenai, and other double reeds); Gan Lev (as); Jason Zappa (barsx); Justin Perdue (g); Mark Leonard, Jeremy Harlos, Xtopher Faris (b); John Blum, Michael Johnson (p); Rich Hauver (vibes)

Brooks Ashmanskas, Beau Friedlander, Robert Sugerman, Sharon Vogel (reading)

Letters: Round Up The Usual Suspects   1:29:05   BD video rec

A first realization of the fall orchestra piece, "originally done to support the class, *Composition, Improvisation, Performance*. So it came about for highly utilitarian purposes.
" 'Round Up The Usual Suspects' for me is a classic, because I do my orchestration right there--I can constantly change the orchestration. I could do that piece seven nights in a row. While the flavor and the intensity would be alike, I could change the orchestration.
"I gave all the elements to the players: some are written, some given verbally.   They know the shape or the contour of that line; I don't have to tell them what to play. Or I can point--that means go an octave higher, over the line. Or if I do a wavy figure, that means to flitter through the line.
"No one listening to it would know what is written (in the narrow way we define 'written'). I don't really think something is an especially good piece of music if you know from hearing it what's written and what's improvised. Music that works like that has already been done definitively. I'm not saying that you don't sometimes just want that, but [the method employed in this piece] is supported by the tradition of the music going constantly forward.
"I didn't tell Bill [Cole] how to play, but I was able to surround his sound with other colors. I used Arthur Brooks almost exclusively in the mute. I could also play something when I wanted to, to suggest something, to signal someone to play with me, in unison, or opposed to me. The conductor also is a player; to shape the tone I have to play.
"This is the kind of piece I could do anywhere, with any group of people. The workshop would be, finally, after you've gone through the teaching, etc., to do this piece for maybe three nights, with six different people conducting. Each conductor would have to play--preferably a linear instrument to create lines, not the piano. Select six people out of that workshop who have the ability and their own aesthetic about shaping and voicing.
"This allows anyone who is doing that piece of music--irrespective of the composer--to orchestrate right on the spot, if (s)he understands what those instruments do, and how those players move...and you can hear it.
That's what excites me about the large ensemble, which is different from the ensemble pieces of the 70s and 80s.
"In this performance the voices didn't understand or become comfortable until the end of the piece. The second time, a couple of months later [**R90-1207**], they started off with a better understanding. So in the beginning, there is that deep, ominous

sound from the bass, the occasional cluster from the vibes, and then you have these voices. It plays out and plays out until the audience has heard just the letters being read, and they think it's going to go on that way.

"But the technical problem--and I was not able to do it--was for each voice to have its own amplification system, so that they could raise their level if I told them I wanted them to scream out over anyone. When I do it the next time, I'm going to have that. I would only want four voices, otherwise it becomes a chorus. The principle is not the voice as a voice: it's the voice as an instrument, doing exactly what these other instruments do."

R90-1130   John Blum-Bill Dixon
November 30, 1990   Carriage Barn, BCVT

BD (t); John Blum (p)

     Untitled Duet

This duet from Blum's senior concert was reflective of the work the two had done in duet tutorials since 1988, which were carried out in class time, summers, and the NRT.

Blum also was involved in a latter-day episode of "The Collaborative Process" (see **R68-0916** and **R86-1010**) in which he and one classically-trained dancer participated.

R90-1199   Bill Dixon-Bill Cole
Fall 1990   Carriage Barn, BCVT

BD (t); Bill Cole (nagaswaram, shenai, and other double reeds)

                                                        BD rec

Informal sessions; note the relationship to Cole's appearance in the second performance of "Round Up the Usual Suspects". Throughout this term Cole was in the throes of a highly publicized discrimination suit with the administration at Dartmouth College (where he was a faculty member) that culminated in the loss of his position there.

R90-1207   Bill Dixon Ensemble
December 7, 1990   Carriage Barn, BCVT

BD (t); Rebecca Rodriguez (bcl); Bill Cole (nagaswaram, shenai, and other double reeds); David Bindman (ts); Jason Zappa (barsx); Justin Perdue (g); *probably 2 of the following*: Mark Leonard, Jeremy Harlos, Xtopher Faris (b); John Blum, Michael Johnson (p); Rich Hauver (vib); Ehran Elisha (d);

Brooks Ashmanskas, Beau Friedlander, Robert Sugerman, Sharon Vogel (reading)

Letters: Round Up The Usual Suspects   1:20:17   BD video rec

Elisha, an alumnus of the Black Music program at Bennington, returned as a visitor while in graduate studies at Wesleyan University.
Unlike the earlier concert of "Letters: Round Up The Usual Suspects", there were some written elements to this performance, notably Bindman's playing of Letter **C** from "Metamorphosis" (**R66-1010**).
Dixon selected David Bindman as a sabbatical replacement to lead his ensemble classes in the spring term 1991 (Bindman had been an occasional guest to those classes in earlier months).

Dixon was invited by Stephen Horenstein to spend his January-September, 1991 sabbatical in Israel, but trepidation resulting from the conflict with Iraq in Kuwait caused the hosts to reconsider the trip, and Dixon did not go.

R91-0628   Sound Unity
June 28, 1991   The Kitchen: 512 W 19th Street, NYC

BD (t, flgh); Butch Morris (c); Alan Silva (electronic keyboards); *probably* Frank Wollny (elbg); A. R. Penck (d)

private tape

An unrehearsed and unpublicized session organized by Penck, the patriarch of the *Sound Unity Festivals*. See also **R91-0629**.
Dixon played using his preferred amplification system.
Butch Morris left this performance early to lead his own concert at the Knitting Factory.

R91-0629   Sound Unity
June 29, 1991   The Kitchen, NYC

BD (t, flgh); Butch Morris (c); Frank Wollny (elbg); Alan Silva (electronic keyboards); A. R. Penck (p); Rashied Ali (d); Jeanne Lee (voice)

private tape

The situation for this performance mirrored that of **R91-0628**, except for the stated changes in personnel and the fact that Morris stayed for the entire concert. Ali attended as a spectator, but Penck's absence at start time prompted him to sit in on drums. Penck therefore entered on piano and may have played no drums this night.

R91-0719   Bill Dixon Group
July 19, 1991   Nuorisokeskus: Pori, Finland

BD (t); Jari Mougita (tb); Harri Sjöstrom (ss); Ulf Åkerhielm (b); J.R. Mitchell (d)

IROP   44:44   BD rec

Dixon's performance here at the Pori Jazz Festival was preceded by a rehearsal in the hall of the concert.
He apparently remained in Europe from mid-July through August 6, 1991, giving a radio interview for KUULAA while in Finland.

"That was the first time I traveled to Europe without a group to perform. I had gotten tired of all of the faxes back and forth, and everyone crying about the airfares, etc."

R91-0911   ABG and Bill Dixon-Allen Shawn
September 11, 1991   Greenwall Music Workshop, BCVT

-1. Bill Dixon, Arthur Brooks (t); Gary Sojkowski (d)

-2. Bill Dixon, Allen Shawn (p)

    ABG Part One -1   BD rec
    Collaborazione -2   --

-1 is the one Bennington concert performance by this trio known to have been recorded.

This "Informal Post-registration Concert" also included music by faculty members Shawn, Lou Calabro, Lionel Nowak, Peter Golub, and Gunnar Schonbeck, in addition to Max Reger and Paul Hindemith.
Details from concert program.

R92-0107   Bill Dixon-Arthur Brooks-Gary Sojkowski
January 7, 1992   Jennings Hall, BCVT

Bill Dixon, Arthur Brooks (t); Gary Sojkowski (d)

                      BD rec

An informal session at Bennington

R92-0116   Bill Dixon-Arthur Brooks-Gary Sojkowski
January 16, 1992   Jennings Hall, BCVT

Bill Dixon, Arthur Brooks (t); Gary Sojkowski (d)

                      BD rec

The same situation as **R92-0107**

R92-0229   Bill Dixon-Bill Cole
February 29, 1992   St. Marks Church, NYC

BD (t); Bill Cole (Ghanaian wood flute, zuona, rain stick, hojo)

Untitled duet	51:22	WKCR rec
BD talks	3:41	--
Untitled duet	0:39	--

For this concert and the following night, Dixon played two trumpets: a beryllium
Schilke horn (in the first 25:00), and one designed by Jerome Callett (later), which
Dixon acquired in the last quarter of 1991. Though little documented in prior or
subsequent entries, using both was by this time common practice for his
appearances.
Bill Cole played the above instruments in the order in which they are listed.
Dixon and Cole played these duets from opposite ends of the performance floor at St.
Marks.
This was the second of three nights of concerts. First was Cole's Untempered Trio;
the third follows on **R92-0301**.

R92-0301   Bill Dixon Quartet
March 1, 1992   St. Marks Church, NYC

BD (t, flgh); Arthur Brooks (t); J.R. Mitchell, Gary Sojkowski (d)

Negoro Codex I	38:57	WKCR rec
Negoro Codex II	8:01	--
Negoro Codex III	8:27	--
Negoro Codex IV		

The quartet rehearsed at the church before the concert.
Titles are taken from the concert program. In the actual musical layout there were not
four but three distinct segments. Dixon announced at the concert that only the fist
half of the second concert would be performed, whence the attribution of times above.
The drummers played from opposite corners of the stage. Dixon played from center
stage using his amplification set-up of choice, with Brooks moving about the stage
area unamplified.
See also **R92-0229**.
The trio without Mitchell had played at informal sessions at Williams College (in
addition to **R92-0107** and **R92-0116**) throughout the foregoing months, and
continued to do so (publicly at least once) throughout 1992.
Details from concert program.

R92-0516   Jack Moore-Bill Dixon
May 16-18, 1992   Martha Hill Dance Workshop: BCVT

BD (p); Jack Moore (choreography); Jason Zappa (barsx); Andrew Grossman
(movement)

Tea Dust at 5:43pm   BC Dance video

Part of a series of concerts held in fulfillment of Grossman's Master's degree in
Dance. The others are **R92-0605** and **R93-0514**. For this concert, "Tea Dust..."
was listed as a 1979 composition, contradicting to the information that generated
R78-1201.
Jack Moore also designed the costume for this dance; in fact, Grossman wore the
same outfit that Barbara Roan had worn to premiere it.
Details from concert program.

R92-0605   Andrew Grossman-Bill Dixon
June 5-7, 1992   Martha Hill Dance Workshop: BCVT

BD (t); Andrew Grossman (choreography, movement)

Charybdis [Spectre]   BC Dance video

Part of a series of concerts held in fulfillment of Grossman's Master's degree in
Dance. The others are **R92-0516** and **R93-0514**.
The work was premiered on this occasion, uniting Grossman's dance, "Charybdis"
with Dixon's music "Spectre". Lighting and costumes were designed by
Cinnamon-Anne Booth.

"I think the piece was very successful; of course, very few people understood it. I had
watched Grossman since the first time he walked on a dance floor [Grossman had
studied at BCVT as an undergraduate as well], when he was the most awkward and
gangly person you could imagine. I watched him develop at Bennington into a very
fine dancer, a very strong performer."

R92-0625   Bill Dixon-Cecil Taylor
June 25, 1992   Teatro Romano: Verona, Italy

BD (t, flgh?); Cecil Taylor (p)

41:00	BD rec
7:38	--
2:06	--

This performance was beset by amplification problems.
"Prior to this tour we had been supposed to travel to Vienna to do duets. I really
wanted to do that, but the presenters balked at the money. I was first asked to play
duets with Taylor by Nicola Tessitore about five years ago, but I was still working
on--and wanted to finish--my work with the two basses and drums. This year I felt
that now was the time."
Musica Jazz August, 1992, p. 17; "Spettacoli" *Veronasette* July 3, 1992 p. 67-68.

R92-0629   Bill Dixon-Cecil Taylor
probably June 29-30, 1992   École Nationale de Musique: Villeurbanne

BD (t, flgh); Cecil Taylor (p)

                                                            BD/CT rec

A formal studio recording (there was no concert held in Villeurbanne) was another
component of the Dixon-Taylor tour together.
The recordings were undertaken over 2 days.

R92-0701   Bill Dixon-Cecil Taylor
July 1, 1992   Vienne, France

BD (t, flgh); Cecil Taylor (p)

                                                            BD video rec

R92-1031   Bill Dixon-Arthur Brooks-Gary Sojkowski
October 31, 1992   Carriage Barn: BCVT

Bill Dixon, Arthur Brooks (t); Gary Sojkowski (d)

                                                    BD rec

An informal session at Bennington: not a performance.

92-1121   Christina Montoya-Bill Dixon
November 21-22, 1992   Martha Hill Dance Workshop, BCVT

BD (p); Christina Montoya (choreography, movement); Spencer Hall (sculptures)

          Woman on the Verge of a _____

Details from concert program.

R92-1204   Bill Dixon-Leslie Winston
December 4-5, 1992   Carriage Barn lecture room, BCVT

BD (t); Leslie Winston (Yamaha DX7 and/or other keyboard synthesizers)

Elegantissimo: a Dance for Carla Facci	9:44	BD rec
[all others untitled]	9:07	--
	5:15	--
	7:08	--
	11:16	--
	9:15	--
	9:13	--
	12:29	--

Dixon played the Schilke trumpet at this private session. At a later point, he and/or Winston sequenced some of the pieces to include three from the second day and two from the first, of which total at least one was realized with delay, one with reverb, and one with a second trumpet line multitracked.

R93-0506   Bill Dixon
May 6, 1993   Carriage Barn Lecture Room: BCVT

BD (t, flgh)

     Untitled solo   9:44   BD rec

Dixon's 2-day exposition on solo-playing was presented in a series of faculty
lecture/demonstrations at BCVT. The first day (May 5) included excerpts from audio
and video recordings of solos, presented in a historical survey. This second day was
based on demonstration and explanation (on theoretical and functional/physical
bases) of playing solos on trumpet and fluegelhorn. Dixon's presentation involved
therefore many fragments and short thoughts, as he illustrated the differences
between instruments. One longer solo for trumpet closed the program; its time is
shown above.
Details from series poster.

R93-0514   Andrew Grossman-Bill Dixon
May 14-15, 1993   Martha Hill Dance Workshop, BCVT

BD (t); Andrew Grossman (choreography); Eva Lawrence (movement)

     Charybdis [Spectre]   BC Dance video

Grossman's dance, "Charybdis" was united with Bill Dixon's music, "Spectre", as
danced here in its second performance by Lawrence.

This, and the concert that premiered the piece (**R92-0605**), were held in fulfillment
of Grossman's master's degree in the Dance Division.

93-0526   Shannon Jones
May 26, 1993   Greenwall Music Workshop, BCVT

BD, Alex Huberty, Mark Sutton (t); Shannon Jones, Kristin DiSpaltro (voice);
Molly McQuarrie (ss); Matthew Hutchinson (p); David Brandt (vib); Matthew
Weston (d); Mohammed Ali (conga)

from Jones's senior concert
Details from concert program.

R93-0529   Molly McQuarrie
late May or early June, 1993   Carriage Barn: BCVT

Molly McQuarrie (ss);

-1: add BD (p); Troy Kinzer (b)

Solo for Soprano Saxophone	private tape
Untitled -1	--

McQuarrie had formally completed her studies in the fall of 1992, culminating in an official senior concert (November 18) with the ensemble class of that term. She chose to hold another senior concert, above, performing the "Solo..." that Dixon wrote for her. It was fully notated music, designed to be interpreted by the performer.

McQuarrie and Troy Kinzer had been playing actively as a duo throughout the previous months; Dixon was invited to perform with them as a special guest. The concert was held on a Thursday, possibly the week before **O93-0603**.

R93-0802a   Bill Dixon
August 2-3, 1993   Barigozzi Studio, Milan

BD (t, flgh); Barry Guy, William Parker (b); Tony Oxley (d)

Moment	4:24	SN 121208-2
Anamorphosis	12:28	--
Viale Nino Bixio 20	9:16	--
Pellucity	9:04	--
Vade Mecum	15:51	--
Twice Upon A Time	13:12	--
Acanthus	13:24	--

The CD-only release Soul Note 121208-2 entitled *Vade Mecum.*

"The reason these pieces are my 'compositions' is that if I hadn't played everything the way I do, the other players wouldn't have played what they did. I know when I want so-called continuity, and I know exactly what to do to make them drift in and out of whatever I want. If you'll notice, the best players don't imitate what you're doing. They know where they have to go; those are your best musicians.
"When a thing was too long, I could play something [as a signal]. I can do it. If I'm playing and you don't even hear me doing it, the players do. That's what made Barry and William so significant in that playing. Both of them discarded their catalogues of singular events and meshed, based on the music of that moment.
"I now think it is time for us to acknowledge that the things they do are theirs, and the things I do are mine, and I did that [in the notes accompanying Soul Note 121208-2]. It takes a long time for someone to do that with confidence, to give up the outward security that people felt like you had as a so-called composer. I am writing this thing down as though on paper but in sound, in the air. It's as formal as any notated music. It's *heard.*"

R93-0802b   Bill Dixon
August 2-3, 1993   Barigozzi Studio, Milan

BD (t, flgh); Barry Guy, William Parker (b); Tony Oxley (d)

-1 one additional layer of all players overdubbed

Valentina de sera	3:07	SN 121211-2
Tableau	10:21	--
Ebonite	15:51	--
Reflections	15:26	--
Incunabula	13:33	--
Octette # 1 -1	11:45	--
		--

The CD-only release Soul Note 121211-2 entitled *Vade Mecum II* .

The overdubbed "Octette #1" was realized with Dixon only hearing the prior layer of recording; the other players heard only the sequence being recorded.

93-1031   Bill Dixon-Joseph Bloom
October 31, 1993   Greenwall Music Workshop, BCVT

BD (t, flgh); Joseph Bloom (p)

'Tis An Evening When the Whole Body is One Sense"

A Halloween Concert of the Music of Charles Ives, presented by the Music Department of Bennington College.
Details from concert program.

94-0299   Bill Dixon-Tchangodei
February 1994   Le Bec du Jazz: Lyon, France

BD (t); Tchangodei (p)

Dixon was invited to the URDLA [Union Regionale pour le Developpement de la Lithographie d'Art] facility in Villeurbanne to create a series of lithographs. While there he spent perhaps as many as ten evenings out of a month-long stay playing informally with Tchangodei in the latter's club in adjacent Lyon.
Dixon's liner essay to *Vade Mecum* (Soul Note 121208-2) describes this period and activity; Francis Marmande "La Vie du Jazz" *Jazz Magazine* #435 (March), 1995.

R94-0520   Ensemble III and guests
May 20, 1994   Carriage Barn: BCVT

BD (t, flgh, p, cond); Arthur Brooks, Alex Huberty (t); Brian Bender (tb); Bill
Cole (nagaswaram, various double reed instruments); Marco Eneidi, Laura Henze
(as); Scott Currie, Jason Zappa (barsx); Mary Springer (cello); Link Smith (b);
Luke Iwabuchi (p); Laurence Cook (vibes, cymbals); Matthew Weston (d)

    Sisyphus II   BD video rec

Audio recording also exists.

R94-0715   Bill Dixon-David Bindman
July 15, 1994   Cotton Hill Studios, Albany NY

BD (p); David Bindman (ts)

Untitled	4:33	BD rec
Untitled	10:55	--
Untitled	6:26	--
Untitled	12:59	--
Untitled	11:47	--

Dixon wrote a piece in several movements for Bindman with this instrumentation.
Piano/flute and piano/clarinet duets were also recorded the same day. It is not known
certainly whether all five items above come from this session, the next, or some
combination of both.
The same work was played live at **R94-1007a**; see also **R95-0225**.

R94-1002   Bill Dixon-David Bindman
October 2, 1994   Cotton Hill Studios, Albany NY

BD (p); David Bindman (ts)

                                                         BD rec

Dixon and Bindman returned to record again at the site of **R94-0715**, though this
session may have included entirely different material.

R94-1005   *Three Days in October*
October 5, 1994   Carriage Barn: BCVT

Impromptu: Bill Dixon (p); Stephen Haynes (t)
then add Gregg Bendian (d, perc)

                                                    BD video rec

This and the following three entries come from the *Three Days in October* festival

R94-1006   *Three Days in October*
October 6, 1994 AFTERNOON   Carriage Barn: BCVT

Impromptu Workshop *begins with* BD (p); Alex Huberty (t);Link Smith (b)
then Eric Zinman (p) *replaces* Dixon; *add* Mary Springer (cello); Gregg Bendian
(d, perc); Scott Currie (as); Stephen Haynes (t);
then add BD (arr, cond);
later omit BD

                                                    BD video rec

R94-1007a   *Three Days in October:* Bill Dixon-David Bindman
October 7, 1994   Carriage Barn: BCVT

BD (p); David Bindman (ts)

          Untitled   15:26   WKCR rec

This is the same work recorded at **R94-0715**, performed here during the *Three Days
in October* (see **U94-1004**).

R94-1007b   *Three Days in October:* Bill Dixon-Ehran Elisha
October 7, 1994   Carriage Barn: BCVT

BD (t); Ehran Elisha (d)

          Untitled duet   3:26   WKCR rec

This duet closed the *Three Days in October* (see **U94-1004**).

R94-1107   Bill Dixon Master Class
November 7, 1994   École Nationale de Musique,Villeurbanne

BD (p); 19 unknown (t); unknown (ts)

Dixon's November, 1994 trip to Europe began in France with this two-day workshop
at the National school of music in Villeurbanne, adjacent to Lyon, France.
The first of those two days of conservatory master classes with students (also
attended by and including a number of faculty members) comprised mostly duo
performances with Dixon at the piano and his spot-evaluations of the trumpeters'
improvisations.
The following three entries describe other stops on this trip.
Jeudi Lyon November 3, 1984, p. 28 and the pamphlet *Bill Dixon À Villeurbanne* announced these
events.

R94-1108   Bill Dixon Master Class
November 8, 1994   École Nationale de Musique,Villeurbanne

collectively: BD (p); 19 unknown (t); unknown (ts); ca. 3 unknown (d); Adam
Lane (b)

École NdM rec:

The second day of Dixon's master class (see **R94-1107**) included:
-some duo performances as on the previous day,
-small groups improvising without Dixon, and group critique thereof, and
-Dixon's orchestral settings for the large group: 19 t, ts, d, and possibly g

On the following day were held a public lecture by Dixon about his art and aesthetics,
and the official opening of a show at the URDLA institute of the lithographs he had
made there in February of the same year (see **94-0299**).
Same as **R94-1107**.

R94-1110   Bill Dixon Quartet
November 10, 1994   Espace Tonkin: Villeurbanne, France

BD (t); William Parker, Barry Guy (b); Tony Oxley (d)

Untitled # 1	29:01	BD rec
Untitled # 2	24:20	--
Untitled # 3	16:58	--

The first and last public performance of Dixon's quartet in this formation.
Announced in the pamphlet, *Musiques à Villeurbanne*.

94-1118   Tony Oxley's Celebration Orchestra with special guest Bill
November 18-19, 1994   rehearsal hall, Berlin

BD (t, flgh); Oxley (d, cond); Ernst-Ludwig Petrowsky, Frank Gratkowski (as, cl); Phil Wachsmann, Alex Kolkowski (vln); Marcio Mattos, Alfred Zimmerlin (cello); Pat Thomas (piano, electronic keyboards); Matt Wand (electronic manipulations); Tony Levin, Stefan Hölker, Jo Thönes (d); Phil Minton (voice)

> The Enchanted Messenger

Based on a graphic (but linear) score by Tony Oxley. Some structural elements and entry points were set or altered in rehearsals.
The first rehearsal consisted of working through the sections in sequence and sharpening transitions and signals among the parts and musicians.

Trombonist Johannes Bauer attended only the second rehearsal.
The second rehearsal began and ended with a full-scale reading of the piece, both of which (particularly the later) were arguably more definitive realizations of the work than the final performance.

R94-1120   Tony Oxley's Celebration Orchestra with...guest Bill Dixon
November 20, 1994   Haus der Kulturen der Welt, Berlin

BD (t, flgh); Oxley (d, cond); Johannes Bauer (tb); Ernst-Ludwig Petrowsky, Frank Gratkowski (as, cl); Alex Kolkowski, Phil Wachsmann (vln); Marcio Mattos, Alfred Zimmerlin (cello); Pat Thomas (piano, electronic keyboards); Matt Wand (electronic manipulations); Stefan Hölker, Tony Levin, Jo Thönes (d); Phil Minton (voice)

> The Enchanted Messenger   SN 121284-2

The CD-only release Soul Note 121284-2 titled *The Enchanted Messenger*.

Following two days of rehearsals, the final performance of this work was held on the last day of the Berlin Jazz Festival. Further details of the structure and evolution of the piece can be found in the liner essay for Soul Note 121284-2.

The performance was also broadcast--possibly in edited form--on Berlin radio (RIAS) and television.
Details from Berlin Jazz Festival program.

R95-0225   Bill Dixon-David Bindman
February 25, 1995   Greenwall Auditorium: BCVT

BD (p); David Bindman (ts, cl)

Untitled [(ts), then (cl)]	38:00	BD rec
Untitled [(ts) only]	8:00	--

Dixon's composition for this duo (performed in **R94-1006** and **R94-0799**) was considered for the content of this performance; Dixon and Bindman decided instead to work without written music.

Concert presented by Congregation Bethel. A May 7, 1995 collaboration between Dixon and writer Jamaica Kincaid--announced in this program--did not take place. Details from concert program.

R95-0418   Bill Dixon-Matthew Weston
April 18, 1995 et seq.   Carriage Barn: BCVT

BD (t); Matthew Weston (d)

BD rec

Weston took a weekly duo tutorial with Dixon his senior year. The later episodes of their duets were recorded, including but not limited to April 18, May 9, May 16, May 30.

By circumstance and not by design, the formula for each day's tutorial was an uninterrupted piece of ca. 35:00, followed by a shorter piece (5-15:00) or two.

95-0691   Bill Dixon-Matthew Weston
probably June, 1995   Greenwall Auditorium: BCVT

BD (p); Matthew Weston (d); other students from Dixon's ensemble classes

Weston's senior concert (here) was possibly the last one to take place under Dixon's aegis at Bennington. In accordance with the mandatory retirement policy of the College, Dixon formally retired at the end of his seventieth year, but for the fall 1995-spring 1996 he opted to have no active teaching responsibilities.

R96-1026   Bill Dixon-Tony Oxley
October 26, 1996   Teatro Colosseo, Rome

BD (t, flgh); Tony Oxley (drums, percussion)
   Untitled   33:09   BD rec

R97-0719   Bill Dixon Trio
July 19, 1997   Nickelsdorf, Austria

BD (t, flgh); Barry Guy (b); Tony Oxley (drums, percussion)
   Untitled   30:30   BD rec
   Untitled   25:20   --

The 18th Nickelsdorf festival--subtitled "Konfrontationen '97--hosted Dixon's Trio.

Dixon plays fluegelhorn exclusively for the first piece, switching eventually to trumpet at 18:11 in the second.

CHAPTER ELEVEN

Bill Dixon's Music Played by Others

O54-0011   <u>Duane and Bobby</u>
probably first half of 1954   NYC

Prior to his tour to Alaska with the Tommy Roberts band (**54-0099**), Dixon wrote a book of the incidental music for this team's act. They rehearsed it on 48th Street.

O61-0115   <u>Ralph Zeitlin</u>
January 15, 1961   Contemporary Arts Gallery, NYC

Ralph Zeitlin (recorder)

        Lament for Solo Recorder

Zeitlin commissioned Dixon to write the piece; other works on the bill (3:00-6:00pm) written by William Ahern, David Amram, Robert Chen, L'Noue Davenport,

Matt Notkins, Hans Ulrich Staepes, and Tui St. George Tucker were played by Zeitlin (recorder) and Ed Brewer (harpsichord).

The Contemporary Arts Gallery (42 Grove Street, across from the Village Art Center) was Bill Dixon's studio space for painting, acquired from folk singer Oscar Brand's wife: she vacated it, Dixon took over the space and opened it to the public on weekends for public viewings of the works, panel discussions, and concerts such as this. During this time, he lived nearby on Bank Street.
"I had a lot of chamber music there--woodwind quintets, etc. I had no Jazz groups there; first of all, I didn't have a piano, and in those days a piano was mandatory for this music. The only piece of music I wrote for that situation was the one for Ralph Zeitlin." Dixon taught "two short courses on music" as announced by *Metronome* (*How to Listen to Music* and *Understanding Contemporary Jazz*) were taught by Dixon.

Zeitlin was in his early 20s at the time of this concert. He and Dixon met while both were working at the UN.
Details from concert program; *Metronome* February, 1961, p. 8.

O63-0627   John Tchicai
June 27, 1963 or later   WBAI-fm: NYC

        Afternoon

Dixon's ballad was written for (and presumably premiered at) one of Tchicai's WBAI appearances--either on this date or July 11, 1963. It apparently was also played on the NYC5 tour to Scandinavia later that year (See **R63-0799** through **R63-1012**).

O64-0395   Don Heckman-Ed Summerlin Improvisational Jazz Workshop
between February and April, 1964   Hardware Poets' Playhouse: NYC

Lew Gluckin (t); Don Heckman (as); Ed Summerlin (ts); Steve Kuhn (p); Steve
Swallow or Ron Carter (b); *probably* Joe Cocuzzo (d); *possibly* Lisa Zanda
(voice); Bob Norden or Brian Trentham (tb)

> All the King's Women   *excerpt*   1:00   BD rec

The excerpt appears on Dixon's Compilation tape B.
Hardware Poets' Playhouse located at 115 W. 54th Street
"First performance" of this piece (the only one) was to be given "later this month",
according to a small, untagged blurb-cum-photo which mentions **64-0204** as
having just happened. This notice describes the piece further as Dixon's "newly-
commissioned short work". He was commissioned by Heckman to create this purely
musical composition.
Zanda is not audible on the recording excerpt.

Though the group existed in whole or part outside this context, "All the King's
Women" was Dixon's only involvement. According to Heckman in a 1967 liner note
for their first self-produced record, "The Don Heckman-Ed Summerlin Improvisational
Jazz Workshop is a laboratory for the continuing exploration of new music. Its
materials include jazz, electronic music, happenings, theatrical events, dance, film,
religious services, written music, improvised music, and chance music."
Dixon: "They rehearsed a lot in a nice little place on 23d Street. Whether I was doing
anything or not, I used to just go to the rehearsals because they were so good. I think
they were planning to do record using 'All the King's Women'."

Dixon's spoken introduction to Compilation Tape B cites the date as 1963.

Dixon's 1968 Account of Career erroneously lists this piece as "recorded for Savoy".

A surviving advertisement but not traceable in origin (*Village Voice* or *Villager* is likely); liner
essay to Ictus Records LP 101, *The Don Heckman-Ed Summerlin Improvisational
Jazz Workshop*.

O65-0702   Jamey Aebersold
early July 1965   Newport Jazz Festival, Rhode Island

Jamey Aebersold (arr, acond); Alan Silva (b)

> Metamorphosis

Aebersold led a youth band in a performance of Dixon's work. When the scheduled
bassist was unable to make the trip, Silva deputized.

O69-0707   Jacques Coursil Unit
July 7 and/or 8, 1969   Studio Saravah, Paris

Jacques Coursil (t); Arthur Jones (as); Beb Guerin (b); Claude Delcloo (d)

      Paper   18:45   BYG 529.319

BYG 529.319 titled *Way Ahead* also was (apparently mis-)printed on some copies
with the title *Way Head*. Dixon's music from the Dixon-Dunn collaboration "Papers"
[**68-0224**] was adapted by Coursil (who had played in presentations of the work in
NYC) for his LP.

O69-1009   Marzette Watts

see **U68-1009**.

O71-0000   Susan Myers
ca. 1971   Commons Theater, BCVT

Susan Myers [*now* Sgorbati] (choreography, movement); Mei Mei Sanford (t)

"Sanford had been at Bennington before I got there. She took a leave, and when she
came back they had me teach her on the instrument. I taught her how to play
half-valve figures and then wrote out a piece based on that type of playing--it sounded
like a modern trumpet piece. They gave quite an outstanding performance."
Details exist in concert programs from this event.

O72-0423   Robert McCurdy
April 23, 1972   Morphy Recital Hall, UWMadison

Robert McCurdy (t); Jim Tifft (flgh); Stephen Horenstein (ts)

      Four Quiet Feelings

This was one of the enduring pieces from Dixon's Madison year, written for
McCurdy's senior concert. He was part of the UWM symphony orchestra, and not
Dixon's Black Music Ensemble.

The piece was scored for trumpet, fluegelhorn, and tenor saxophone, with all of the
parts written.
Details from concert program; the tenor saxophone part appears in *L'Opera*, p. 122.

O72-0513   Pat Lagg
May 13, 1972   Madison, Wisconsin

Pat Lagg (t); Stephen Horenstein (ts); Jay Ash (barsx); John Illingworth (cello)

      Piece for Pat Lagg   6:10   BD rec

Dixon's composition for Pat Lagg was premiered here at her senior concert and
peformed one week later (**R72-0520**). Materials for it had been introduced in
ensemble meetings as early as May 1.

O73-0000   John O'Brien -Tony Ackerman
ca. 1973   BCVT

John O'Brien (t); Tony Ackerman (g)

      Trident II   2:25   FORE Uniss

Proposed for issue on *In The Sign of Labyrinth*; (see **R73-1100**), for the prototype
of which the piece was subtitled "Chapter 8".

O74-0528   Susan Feiner
May 28, 1974   BCVT

Susan Feiner, Stephen Horenstein (afl)

      Cipher for Alto Flute

This was a senior concert piece for Feiner when she graduated in the Music
Department--not officially in the Black Music Division.

Dixon used Feiner's complete name for the cipher that generated the pitches for this
piece.

Details from concert program and 1982 composition list.

O74-1205   Orchestration class members
December 5, 1974   Carriage Barn: BCVT

Arthur Brooks (t); Jeff Hoyer (tb); Susan Feiner (afl); Stephen Horenstein (ts, arr); John Love (ts); Jay Ash (barsx); Prent Rodgers (b)

     Trio

The members of this group took Dixon's class, "Orchestration, Arranging, and Instrumentation"
This first of "Two Late Evenings [10:00pm] of Music" also featured performances by Enembles III, VI, and VII, all exhibiting works and concepts in progress through the fall of 1974. The second night is listed at **R74-1206** and **O74-1206**.
Dixon discusses the goals and methods of this class and term in detail in *L'Opera*.
Details from concert program; *L'Opera*, p. 4.

O74-1206   Ensemble IV members
December 6, 1974   Carriage Barn, BCVT

John Love, Bill Bauman, Stephen Horenstein (ts)

     Anemone   4:56   BD rec

"Anemone" was listed in the program as a 1970 composition (it had indeed been played at **R70-1100**), but also under the 1974 heading in later composition lists, referring to this instrumentation. Some figures from "Anemone" relate to the lines in "Four Quiet Feelings", **O72-0423**.

See also **R74-1206** for more details of this concert.
Details from concert program.

O78-1130   Beth Kanter

November 30, 1978   Commons Theatre, BCVT

Beth Kanter, Stephen Horenstein (afl); Arthur Brooks (t); Stephen Haynes (flgh)

    Nightfall Piece

This was part of a concert of works featuring Kanter, although the concert program makes no note of completing requirements for the Black Music Division B.A., and this might not be her official "Senior Concert".
Kanter adapted this arrangement from the RCA Victor recorded version of "Nightfall Pieces" (**R67-0221**); the program note therefore <u>correctly</u> cites this as the first live performance of the piece. The DTW realization (**67-0211**) and "Reorchestrated Version"s of **R68-1020** through **R68-1128** involved a different musical substance and are considered as separate entities, despite having similar titles.
Details from concert program.

O78-1206   David Segal

December 6, 1978   Commons Theatre, BCVT

David Segal (p)

    Song/Fall '78

Segal was Dixon's piano student and not a member of the ensemble. His senior concert, here, was titled "Postcards of the Hanging".
Dixon's piece was "unpublished" according to his files, where it is cited as only "Song".
Details from concert program; also shown in Dixon's Composition lists.

O78-1208   John McCall Quintet

December 8, 1978   Commons Theatre, BCVT

BD (arr); John McCall (b); Les Finley (t); Stephen Horenstein (ts); Carl Landa (p); Kevin Campbell (d)

    Metamorphosis 1978

From the Senior Concert of John McCall.

Finley was taking a second master's degree at Empire College. Through a cooperative arrangement with Bennington, he studied the trumpet with Dixon and played in the ensemble.
Deatils from program; also listed in compositions file.

O80-0519   Stephen Haynes
May 19, 1980   probably Paul Robeson House, BCVT

-1: Stephen Haynes (t); Susan Barry (p)
-2: Stephen Haynes (flgh); Arthur Brooks (t); Stephen Horenstein (ts)

Touchings for Piano and Trumpet -1   5:10
Four Quiet Feelings -2   10:11

"Four Quiet Feelings" was written for **72-0423**. It indeed comprises four segments, here 2:55, 2:15, 1:50, and 2:33 respectively.
"Touchings for Piano and Trumpet" composed for and premiered at **R76-1299**.
Dixon: "The instructions I gave them for 'Touchings...' were 'She's playing and you happen to hear her.' "
R80-0519 gives further details of this concert and its contents.

The tenor saxophone part shown in *L'Opera* p. 122 relates dimly to that for "Four Quiet Feelings" but is not identical.
Dixon's score to "Touchings..." is reprinted in *L'Opera* p. 63.

O81-0000   Susan Barry-Linda Dowdell
1981   Paul Robeson House, BCVT

Susan Barry, Linda Dowdell (p)

Twoplustwo

score reprinted in *L'Opera* p. 110.

O81-1108 Bill Dixon-Judith Dunn
Nobember 8, 1981 Burlington, Vermont

Bill Dixon (<u>composer only</u>); Judith Dunn (choreography); Arthur Brooks,
Stephen Haynes, Robert Miller, Vance Provey (t); Lizbet Buchal (cello); Spin
Dunbar (b); Penny Campbell, Cheryl Lilienstein, Marjorie MacMahon, Cass
Reep, Nancy Watkin (movement)

>   Summerdance

The Burlington "Summerdance" earlier that spring (R81-0524) was successful
enough to merit a second performance, this time some local dancers to replace
Phillips and Schottland. (Watkin was the director of the local CATCH Dance studio,
which co-sponsored this event.) Again it was held at the Edmunds Jr.High School.
<u>Bill Dixon</u> was away in Europe at the time (see 81-1108) and <u>did not perform at this
concert</u>. Music-and-dance works by other groups were also performed in the concert.
The performance may have been audio-recorded.

Details from concert program; reviewed in *Vermont Cynic* November 12, 1981, p. 21.

O81-1203 Shellen Lubin
December 3, 1981 BCVT

Shellen Lubin, Melody Davis, Michael Edwin, Elsie Keller (voice); Stephen
Haynes (t); Spin Dunbar (b); Linda Dowdell (p); John Shepler (d)

>   Lazy Morning
>   Dusty Rose

Dixon composed the music to these two pieces ("songs") to which Lubin's lyrics
were added independently.

"Dusty Rose" was Lubin's text added to the Dixon composition "Places". She is
known to have performed the piece publicly thereafter as well [including a WBAI
broadcast at June 6, 1983, with Laurence J. Esposito (p); and Bill Hamilton (b)], and
Dixon had the piece registered with BMI including both composer and lyricist.
Dixon also owns cassette recordings of himself rehearsing the piece with Lubin, and
of her performing it away from Bennington.
Remaining works on her program were composed by others. The second half of the
concert was a recital by pianist and then-faculty member Nadi Qamar.

Both this performance and **R82-1205** were probably part of an end-of-term festival
cursorily described in *L'Opera*.

Details from concert program; *L'Opera*, p. 81.

O86-0722   Chivas Sandage
July 22, 1986   BCVT

   Unknown

The already-issued recordings of "Shrike" (**R73-0197**) and "Summer
Song/One/Morning" (**R80-0611b**) were used in a solo dance performance by
Chivas Sandage at the Bennington College July Program, July 22, 1986.
Details from concert program.

O90-0217   Hope Clark
February 17, 1990   Prince George's Public Playhouse, MD

   A Gael

Clark used the issued recordings of Dixon's "Webern" and "Velvet" from **R81-1108**
in her dance.
Washington Post February 19, 1990, p. D7.

O90-1207   Martha Wittman
December 7-9, 1990   Martha Hill Dance Workshop, BCVT

Martha Wittman (choreography); unknown (movement)

   Overlay (Late 20th Century American Folk)

Wittman's piece used a part of "Schema VI-88" from **R88-0628** as its audio
component. The performance was recorded on audio-cum-video tape by the Dance
department.
Details from concert program.

O91-1206   Barbara Roan
December 6-8, 1991   Martha Hill Dance Workshop, BCVT

Roan (choreography); unknown (movement)

   The Black Parade (This One's for Jack)

One segment of Roan's piece called "Black Widow Spider" used a part of "IROP" from
R91-0719 as its audio component. The performance was recorded on
audio-cum-video tape by the Dance department.
Details from concert program.

O91-9999   Marie Fahlin
probably second half of 1991   Finland

Marie Fahlin (choregraphy); Susanne Berggren, Katarina, Anna Koch, Anna
Konrad, Marie Fahlin (movement); E.B. Friedlander (recitation)

  I Tu

Fahlin used a tape recording of Dixon's solo from Jerusalem, **R90-0321** in her
dance work.

Dixon's music was apparently used in a 1990s work by Fahlin performed on October
29-31, which might possibly be the same as this piece.
Details from concert program

O92-0526   Marie Fahlin
May 26 and 27, 1992   Martha Hill Dance Workshop, BCVT

Marie Fahlin (choreography, movement)

  Nightpiece

All music for this performance was taken from issued recordings: "Places and Things"
from **R76-0929**, "Tracings II" from **R74-9998**, "Schema VI-88" from
R88-0628, and "I See Your Fancy Footwork" from **R73-0100**.

The entire concert was apparently titled *We Eat Shadow*.
Details from concert program.

O93-0603   Molly McQuarrie
early June, 1993   Carriage Barn, BCVT

Molly McQuarrie (ss)

  Solo for Soprano Saxophone

McQuarrie performed the piece Dixon wrote for her at the graduation concert for the
class of 1993. See also **R93-0529** and **U94-1007b**.

O94-0508   <u>Mary Springer-Hong Ting</u>
May 8, 1994   Carriage Barn: BCVT

Mary Springer (cello); Hong Ting (p)

        h.t.i.t.b.s

Part of a spring showcase for Mary Springer.
Bill Dixon composed this piece; others in the same program were written by Olivier
Messiaen, Anton von Webern, and Lionel Nowak.
Details from concert program.

O94-1007   <u>Molly McQuarrie</u>
October 7, 1994 EVENING   Carriage Barn: BCVT

Molly McQuarrie (ss)

        Solo for Soprano Saxophone   WKCR rec

CHAPTER TWELVE

Producer

"I've spent my entire career trying to do something for this artform; meanwhile, my contemporaries have spent their careers trying to do something for themselves."

U59-0000

Bill Dixon began working at the UN in 1956. "In that period I spent a lot of time organizing things; I thought it was useful because the more focus there was on the music, the more chance there could be for people like myself to become a part of it. So while I was at the UN, I originally wanted to form a whole band there. I couldn't even get a small group going."
He organized the United Nations Jazz Society in 1959 while working at the Secretariat, though he never performed at the UN on any occasion (apart from sitting in with a band at one UNJS Christmas party).

"I worked 9-to-5 at the UN as one life, and after 5 my other life began. I got in two hours of practicing the horn on the job at the UN. At lunchtime they had a piano I would use to go and practice. I was an extremely efficient person. I learned early on that my in-basket always had to be empty and my out-basket full."

Bill Dixon's concept for the United Nations Jazz Society took root at its first general meeting on March 27, 1959, when a constitution was adopted, along with an administrative structure that made Dixon the president. The next week the society began publishing a newsletter, *Jazz Scene*, and shortly launched a series of Friday lunchtime meetings to listen to and discuss Jazz recordings, with Dixon usually moderating the discussion.

"It wasn't for the public, but for the staff. Naturally the UN had a very international staff (by member countries, there might have been 70 or 80 nations represented), and everyone came to those lectures. We had a small room that sat about 75 people, and a Baldwin baby grand piano. I held the class like I [later] did the Introduction to Black Music [at Bennington College]: I played recordings of the principal people and detailed in them what to look for. People could come on their lunch hour, listen to music and have some one talk--no big deal--so it went over very big. I had access to any records I wanted. Then to buttress that I would sometimes have a pianist just play during the lunch hour, giving a small concert. Cecil [Taylor] did it, Paul Knopf, Hale Smith, and a number of other players.

"I tried to keep everything on a high level. I was really rather fanatical about the music in those days and insistent that people respect it as an art. It was rather like that [interview] sequence from [Imagine the Sound; See **R81-0206**]: I would snatch people and ask 'What's the matter with you? *This* is the music here." I was probably a bit much for people.
"Some people in the UNJS wanted to do things in the Society. Most of the time when I had someone take care of something, it got screwed up so that I had to do it anyway, and then I might as well have done it to start with. So I began getting tired of people accusing me of wanting to do everything. That wasn't the case; I just couldn't trust anyone."

The program of the UNJS expanded again in June, 1959 with a panel discussion on The Future of Jazz. Panelists included Dixon's former teacher, composer Carl B. Bowman, John Benson Brooks, George Russell, Gunther Schuller, Cecil Taylor, and Martin Williams.

Subsequent programs were concerned with Jazz History, beginning with a presentation by guitarist Danny Barker and writer Charles Edward Smith about Jelly Roll Morton. Dixon led several of the summer and autumn history programs in 1959, in an effort to provide a common ground for the membership in understanding the topic of Jazz.
A second panel with the theme "Approach to Modern Jazz" was convened (apparently) in November, including Ornette Coleman, Don Cherry, Art Farmer, Benny Golson, Billy Taylor, Randy Weston, and and NBC *Monitor* interviewer, Mrs. Jo Sherman.
A May 29, 1961 panel discussion united Roy Eldridge, Charles Mingus, Wilbur DeParis, Billy Taylor, Max Roach, Stanley Dance, and Martin Williams in a discussion of "Aspects of Jazz" moderated by Dan Morgenstern.

Among the musicians who visited to speak about their work through 1962 were Leo Wright, Randy Weston and Melba Liston (discussing their recent collaboration on the album *Uhuru Africa*), Junior Mance, Ahmed Abdul-Malik with Kenny Dorham, Dave Bailey, Pepper Adams, Al Cohn, Dizzy Reece, Herbie Mann, Slide Hampton, Clark Terry, John Handy III, Harold Ousley, and Steve Lacy.

Dixon: "I've always known when to cut certain things out. In this case, people were beginning to know me only as an organizer. I had always been good at putting things together, but then I had to ease off of doing things for musicians, beacuse it was backfiring for me".

The UNJS continued an active program of lunchtime lectures and concerts for its members, and panels and full concerts that often drew the attention of the greater Jazz press and public. By 1962, internal politics, the consumption of Dixon's time, and his eventual decision to leave the UN entirely prompted his UNJS activities (See also **62-0799**).
The organization continues its activities into the Nineties, though its name was changed after Dixon's departure to United Nations Staff Recreation Council Jazz Society, as it is today known.

"25 Years of the UNSRC Jazz Society" a special issue of the Society's latter-day newsletter, *World Of Jazz* (New York:: United Nations Publications, 1985); Bill Dixon: "Recollections of Bill Dixon" in *World of Jazz* November 1989: p.2-3. "67 at United Nations Find Jazz a Common Language" *New York Tmes* May 23, 1959.

U59-0900   Freddie Redd Quartet
September, 1959   Fifth Floor Lounge: UNS

Freddie Redd (p); Jackie McLean (as); Michael Mattos (b); Larry Ritchie (d)

Leonard Hicks (reciting)

Presentations of live music in concert by the UNJS commenced in September when
Dixon hosted the Freddie Redd group, then performing in Jack Gelber's play The
Connection. Dixon endorsed the Living Theater production of the play to members
of the UNJS, and personally invited the musician-members of its cast to perform the
music at the UN. Hicks was an actor from the production of the play. As is the case
with all subsequent UNJS concerts (and possibly the foregoing panel discussions)
there remains some chance that recordings are still held in the United Nations
Secretariat sound archives.

The UNJS members were extended invitations to attend a number of recording
sessions in the early part of the 1960s, including a dress rehearsal for the Robert
Herridge Theater television production of *The Sound of Miles Davis* usually dated to
April 2, 1959. Members were also allowed free or discounted entry at various times
to the Cafe Roue, the Phase 2 (August 27, 1960), and the Four Steps Coffee Gallery in
Greenwich Village.

"It was more than just a record club." Renowned correspondent William Otis wrote
the first press piece about the UNJS (or, for that matter, about Bill Dixon) for the
Associated Press. From this publicity, and because the United Nations Jazz Society
was the first *international* Jazz society headquartered at the UN Secretariat, Dixon
gained notoriety overnight.
see **U59-0000**; Phase 2 in *Village Voice* August 25, 1960: p. 12.

U60-0000   Randy Weston Quartet
1960   Fifth Floor Lounge: UNS

Randy Weston (p); Cecil Payne (barsx); Ron Carter (b); Clifford Jarvis (d)

At this first formal concert sponsored by the UNJS, Weston premiered his 4-part suite
"Uhuru Africa". Months later he returned for a discussion of the work with
co-composer, Melba Liston.
see **U59-0000**.

U60-0001

"I forget what the name was--I think it was JAZZ INC--, but I formed a small operation at my house where I would supply any number of musicians for any kind of loft performance, and I did that for a while, but I myself never played. I would send musicians to the garment center for fashion shows, and to play for designers. I would pay the musicians a certain amount. My roster included people like Hale Smith. I ran an ad in the *Village Voice.*

"After I started the lunchtime concerts at the UN Jazz Society [see p. 328], the whole concept took off like wildfire, and Jazz societies from all over would call me to ask if I could come up and bring some players for a lecture demonstration: Queens, Riverdale, all over. I took Cecil Taylor up to play at [the Fieldston School?], at the Ethical ____. I would give the opening lecture as an overview and introduce these people to play. I did no playing; rather, I was *presenting* these people." Dixon's lectures at Forrest House (in the Bronx) and Public School No. 134 cited in his accounts of career may also belong to this round of activities.

"I was confining myself: rehearsing in sessions, but never involved actively in this thing. I started to play when I began to work with John Mehegan [See **X61-0297**]. There I used Al Foster."

U60-0531   Thelonious Monk Quartet/Jimmy Giuffre Quartet
May 31, 1960   Fifth Floor Lounge: UNS

Thelonious Monk Quartet: Thelonious Monk (p); Charlie Rouse (ts); John Ore (b); Al Dreares (d)

Jimmy Giuffre Quartet: Jimmy Giuffre (ts); Steve Lacy (ss); Buell Neidlinger (b); Denis Charles (d)

This performance has been cited (by Steve Lacy, among others) as Lacy's first formal personal acquaintance with Thelonious Monk, though they played on separate segments of this concert program. Lacy performed in Monk's group for the first time later that summer.

Among the audience members for this concert were Ornette Coleman and Don Cherry, Randy Weston, Booker Ervin, and many others.

Both groups were appearing at the Five Spot in this period: the UNJS made an arrangement with the Termini brothers to offer concert appearances to the musical act(s) appearing at the Five Spot or the Terminis' other venue, the Jazz Gallery.
See **U59-0000**; also *down beat* August 4, 1960, p. 11-2; *Metronome* August, 1960; *New York Times Magazine* June 6, 1960, p. 54-5.

U61-0000   Cecil Taylor
possibly 1961   Fifth Floor Lounge: UNS

Cecil Taylor *probably* solo (p)

Taylor "performed a program of his own compositions...". This may be the same
event Dixon mentions on page 334.
See **U59-0000.**

U61-1299   Sonny Rollins Quintet
probably late 1961   Fifth Floor Lounge: UNS

Sonny Rollins (ts); Jay Cameron (barsx); Jim Hall (g); Bob Cranshaw (b);
Walter Perkins (d)

The UNJS 25th Anniversary folio cites this among the earliest of Rollins'
performances after emerging from his two year retirement. He apparently returned to
activity in October, 1961, ending a hiatus begun in 1959.
See **U59-0000.**

U64-0414
mid-April, 1964 forward   Cellar Cafe: 251 West 91st Street, NYC

"I was living on 103d street and doing gospel music transcriptions for Savoy Records (see **R64-0204**). Every now and then I would come out of the house to take a break, and walking the streets I happened to come down to 91st Street and saw the Cellar Cafe. You actually went into the cellar coming off the street. I would have walked on past, but they had a sign up that read "JAZZ TONIGHT", with the name of a very fine musician, [alto saxophonist] Bobby Brown. So I went in, and Bobby Brown never showed. That's how I met [the club's manager Peter Sabino and his partner in managing the Cellar]."
Dixon almost certainly ran across the Cellar during Brown's scheduled Tuesday/Thursday/ Saturday quartet engagement, logically April 14, 16, and 18, 1964. It was the only known [advertised] appearance of Bobby Brown at the venue.

The Cellar had been in business for about five weeks by the time Dixon came across it. Its first mention in the press was a nondescript advertisement in the *Village Voice*, inviting the reader to "take a ride uptown; good coffee; we also have a little food. Open poetry readings Monday 8:30pm." A May 7 advertisement using the contact number for Peter Sabino (and apparently placing him in first person) ran as follows:

Three weeks ago my friend and I opened a coffee shop called the CELLAR CAFE with a 'Hell with the Village' attitude at 251 West 91 St. We have lots of things that the Village doesn't--Films every Fri. nite--great Jazz on Thursday and Saturday nite featuring Paul Bley--mean folk music on Wed. and Mon eves., hot literary debates and readings plus a special surprise on Sun.

Though it had been open apparently since late February, the diversified policy was probably the part that was only three weeks old. Dixon recalls a similar eclecticism: "With the poetry readings and films there, it was really very relaxed, like a Viennese coffee house, lots of things going on.

"Over a period of time I discussed things with the owners and began to produce some music for them. I had let people know when I started doing things at the Cellar that the only groups that I was interested in were those with no other place to play. Almost all of the musicians I knew at that time believed that they were doing something meaningful, and they didn't have to wait for someone to tell them before they knew it. It wasn't that I was completely enamored of what all those groups were into musically--a lot of those people I didn't really *know*-- but if they weren't allowed to work anywhere else, the Cellar was open to them. It wasn't up to me to say that these players were either good or bad. I had to have a place where people could come and hear what the musical ferment of their time comprised. Whether some of them were reviewed in the *New York Times* or went to the Five Spot or Carnegie Hall had nothing to do with it.
"What made the Cellar important when I ran it was that I focused on a certain thing. Before, Sabino was just using Jazz players who were playing all over the place. I

picked only those musicians who didn't have an opportunity to play all over New York. Bobby Brown was a very good player, but he didn't even show up that night because he got a gig somewhere else. That wasn't loyalty; you had to have a stable of people. In those days it didn't make any difference what your name was, because nobody had a name anyway. You had to have two things to run a club successfully: you had to make it so people could afford to go to the place, and so musicians were comfortable enough to play and not bullshit the public. So right away I let musicians play as long as they wanted to make their musical point (I don't believe in [the nightclub concept of a 'set']). That philosophy carried over into our plans for the festival [the October Revolution in Jazz, **U64-1001**]), and for whatever the admission price was, we served free coffee and doughnuts. So the place developed an ambience of the music being carried out with integrity."

The Cellar continued to offer Jazz programs on Thursdays and Saturdays in May, 1964, in a weekly schedule that also included 'Julius Lester on Folk', films on Fridays, and the Blues on Monday nights. The first finite evidence of Dixon's programming activities came in a Sunday afternoon concert series that included some of the musicians who had frequented the Take 3 in prior months (See **64-0295** et seq.). Notably, many of these first Dixon-produced Sunday afternoon concerts were advertised along with the Cellar's evening classic film programs.

One pivotal factor in the success of Dixon's Cellar program was the use of the club by day as an open rehearsal space for whoever might drop in. "There wasn't that much work at the time, but people rehearsed incessantly. Rehearsing *was* the work." Having music going on by day served the three-fold function of providing a much-needed place for composers to work out their ideas, precipitating interaction and communication among musicians, and representing to passersby that the Cellar had an active music program. Members of the public could then drift into the house off the street, providing a makeshift audience that gave the musical proceedings a more 'real' setting. "Tony Williams used to come to nearly all of my rehearsals at the Cellar, and nearly all of Cecil's. He desperately wanted to play with Cecil, and he wanted to play with me. My advice to him was: 'I'm not working; Cecil's not working: why should you give up a chance with Miles Davis?' " Williams became enamored of Dixon's lower register playing, as was Carla Bley who composed a work to feature Dixon in this capacity, "Sotto Voce". Vocalist Patty Waters also visited the daytime sessions.

Village Voice February 20, 1964, p. 8; Bobby Brown ad in *Village Voice* April 16, 1964, p. 14. *Village Voice* ad; May 14, 1964, p. 18. An early article was written about this period of the Cellar by a then-Columbia student, Bob Zelman, presumably under the column titled "Harmonic Highlights" in the *Columbia Daily Spectator*.

U64-0524   Paul Bley Quartet
May 24, 1964   Cellar Cafe, NYC

Paul Bley (p); *probably* Pharoah Sanders (ts); David Izenzon (b); Paul Motian (d)

One of the series of Sunday afternoon (3:00pm) concerts staged by Dixon at the
Cellar. Bley recorded the following day with Sanders, Izenzon, and Motian,
prompting the conclusion that he may have used the same personnel on this
engagement, in the process of preparing for the srudio session.

Advertised in *Village Voice* May 21, 1964, p. 17; Carlos Kase and Ben Young "Discography:
David Izenzon" On Air [WKCR Program Guide] November, 1996, p. 5.

U64-0614   Albert Ayler Trio
June 14, 1964   Cellar Cafe, NYC

Albert Ayler (ts); Gary Peacock (b); Sunny Murray (d)

Prophecy	7:12	ESP 3030
Spirits	7:06	--
Children	6:30	In Respect 39501
Saints	9:50	--
Ghosts [incomplete]	10:41	--
The Wizard {as titled on ESP 1002}	6:31	--
The Wizard {as titled on ESP 3030}	9:09	--
Spirits	7:55	ESP 3030
The Wizard	8:21	--
Ghosts	11:21	--

ESP 3030 [monaural only] titled *Prophecy*; the same music appears in stereo on ZYX
ESP 1010-2 [stereo] (CD).

The two versions of "The Wizard" are not the same composition, but the same title
applied to different pieces of music on two separate ESP issues.
The middle five pieces are mistitled on the unauthorized and inferior In Respect issue.

Paul Bley's group may also have played a set on this afternoon presentation at the
Cellar.

U64-0615   Sun Ra Arkestra featuring Black Harold and Pharoah Sanders
June 15, 1964   Cellar Cafe, NYC

Sun Ra (p, org)

Robert L. Campbell *The Earthly Recordings of Sun Ra* (Redwood, New York: Cadence Jazz Books, 1995), p.

U64-0621   Paul Bley Quartet
June 21, 1964   Cellar Cafe: NYC

Paul Bley (p); *possibly also*: Pharoah Sanders (ts); David Izenzon (b); Paul Motian (d)

Another 3:30pm concert staged by Dixon at the Cellar. Personnel from Bley's previous and next Cellar sessions is presumed to apply here.
Advertised in *Village Voice* June 18, 1964, p. 14.

U64-0712   Paul Bley Quartet
July 12, 1964   Cellar Cafe: NYC

Paul Bley (p); Pharoah Sanders (ts); David Izenzon (b); Paul Motian (d)

A 4:00pm concert staged by Dixon at the Cellar.
Advertised in *Village Voice* July 9, 1964, p. 14.

U64-0726   Free Form Improvisational Ensemble
July 26, 1964   Cellar Cafe: NYC

John Winter (fl); Gary William Friedman (as); Burton Greene (p); Alan Silva (b); Clarence Walker (d)

Another 4:00pm concert staged by Dixon at the Cellar. The FFIE had been giving concerts in Brooklyn and Queens since mid-1963, and in Manhattan clubs including the Cafe Au Go Go through the first half of 1964 with the above personnel. However, it is reported that for the Town Hall concert described in **U64-1024** Clarence Walker was replaced on percussion by Tom Weyburn, who may likewise have appeared with the group at the Cellar.
Advertised in *Village Voice* July 23, 1964, p. 14.

U64-0809   Jimmy Giuffre Duo

August 9, 1964   Cellar Cafe: NYC

Jimmy Giuffre (cl); *possibly* Barre Phillips (b)

4:00pm concert staged by Dixon at the Cellar.
Advertised in *Village Voice* August 6, 1964, p. 14.

U64-0820   Valdo Williams Trio

August 20, 1964   Cellar Cafe: NYC

Valdo Williams (p); unknown (b) and (d)

4:00pm concert staged by Dixon at the Cellar.

The bassist and drummer were likely not Reggie Johnson and Stu Martin, as on Williams's Savoy LP of the time.
Advertised in *Village Voice* August 20, 1964, p. 8.

U64-0906   Sun Ra Sextet

September 6, 1964   Cellar Cafe: NYC

Sun Ra (p); *probably* Pharoah Sanders (ts); others unknown

Another 4:00pm concert staged by Dixon at the Cellar.

One Cellar concert by Sun Ra's organization--possibly this one--was held by candlelight: Sabino and his partner had been occupying the club on a sub- sublease, and when the landlord failed to pay the electric bills, service was disconnected. Eventually the meter was removed just prior to Ra's performance, leaving no recourse available.
Advertised in *Village Voice* September 3, 1964, p. 9.

U64-0913   Paul Bley Quartet

September 13, 1964   Cellar Cafe: NYC

Paul Bley (p); Dewey Johnson (t); Giuseppi Logan (as); David Izenzon (b); Rashied Ali (d)

Another 4:00pm concert staged by Dixon at the Cellar.
Advertised in *Village Voice* September 10, 1964, p. 15.

October Revolution

"I did the *October Revolution* completely by myself--irrespective of what anyone says. I did it for a simple reason. I had a point that I had to prove to people. All these writers--Dan Morgenstern, Martin Williams, etc.--were telling me that this music I saw wasn't worth anything, that no one could be interested in it. I knew people could be interested in anything if it was presented to them in the proper way. I *knew* that. And of the people I admired who were in the first wave of this music, the only person who ever lent any moral or philosophical support for the new music was John Coltrane. The rest of them were negative or jealous; they wouldn't help us or endorse what we did, and they had forgotten that the things they were saying about us had been said about them when they were at those stages, when their music was fresh. They were not only hostile but viciously hostile.
"One day I went to the operator of the Cellar, Peter Sabino, and he and I came up with the idea for this thing. Sabino and I were going to go into business; we would get a liquor license and open this place as a club, and he wanted to do a concert. I told him everyone does a concert; why don't we do a week-long event, a festival? The festival was going to be an official opening for the club. We had no money, so I got on the phone. For that first festival I ran my telephone bill up to an unheard of amount of $500.00 and stalled the telephone company from turning my service off. I went one solid year without paying my rent. I owed every grocer in the West Village. I was a believer; I believed in this stuff and poured everything I could into the festival and (later) into the Guild operation."

The name, dates, and schedule of events of the four-day *October Revolution* were completely solidified in time to be advertised in the third week of September. In addition to marshaling the players, Dixon also arranged and moderated nightly panel discussions at the midnight conclusion of each evening's music. (Neighborhood curfew dictated this end time for the music.) While the performance schedule was restricted to artists who could not play in other venues, these panel discussions were a point of contact with musicians who had some access and acclaim. The first night's panel, for instance, was slated to have Nat Hentoff, Mercer Ellington, and Teo Macero. Throughout the other nights musicians Hugh Glover, Don Heckman, Andrew Hill, Steve Lacy, Rod Levitt, Sun Ra, Archie Shepp, and Cecil Taylor and writers Herb Dexter, Rob Reisner and Martin Williams also took part in the panels.

The schedule of activities at the *October Revolution* accomplished its dual purpose of heightening the public awareness of the music and bringing its players together in an organized presentation. Advance publicity and word of mouth were sufficient to draw overflow crowds each night; patrons lined up outside and waited patiently to be admitted one by one as others left. Sizeable reviews in the Jazz press insured that the reputation and legend of the festival spread to those beyond the relatively small circle who actually witnessed the events.

U64-1001   *October Revolution in Jazz*
October 1, 1964   Cellar Cafe: NYC

Joe Maneri: Maneri (ts); others unknown
Ali Jackson Quartet: Jackson (b); others unknown
John Tchicai/Roswell Rudd/Lewis Worrell: Tchicai (as); Rudd (tb); Worrell (b);
Milford Graves (d)
Paul Bley Quintet: Bley (p); Marshall Allen (as); Dewey Johnson (t); Eddie
Gomez (b); Milford Graves (d)
Jimmy Giuffre: Giuffre (cl, ts) unaccompanied
Charles Wittenberg: ?? (b)

Composer Wittenberg's piece was apparently for solo bass and pre-recorded tape. He
may have been in the audience but was not one of the performers.

Dixon: "With the exception of Barry Milroad, most of those players were just
musicians who turned up at the Cellar." Jimmy Giuffre was another striking
exception to the Cellar's policy of showcasing neglected players. An elder
statesman who had earned both a reputation and a place in Jazz history, Giuffre
nevertheless found little recognition for his increasingly experimental trio music of
the early Sixties.

Performances were scheduled for 4:00pm-1:00am each day.
Village Voice September 24, 1964, p. 30; "Strictly Ad Lib" *down beat* October 8, 1964; Dan
Morgenstern and Martin Williams "The October Revolution: Two Views of the Avant Garde in
Action" *down beat* November 19, 1964, p. 15, 33; also reviewed in *Columbia Daily Spectator*.

U64-1002   *October Revolution in Jazz*
October 2, 1964   Cellar Cafe, NYC

Jo Scianni-David Izenzon: Scianni (p); Izenzon (b)
Julian Hayter Quartet: Hayter (g); others unknown
Martin Siegel Quartet: Siegel (p); *see below*
Bobby Brown Quartet: Brown (as); others unknown
Alan Silva Trio: Silva (b); *possibly* Burton Greene (p); Clarence Walker (d)

Newspaper listings show that Makanda Ken McIntyre's Octet was to perform between the groups of Hayter and Brown; the group's presence cannot be confirmed.

"Hayter came to the Cellar a couple of times and just asked me if he could play. I think he went back to Paris, because he was French. Martin Siegal was a very fluent player, something like Valdo Williams--an excellent pianist. He brought his own group."
Siegel had performed at Carnegie Recital Hall in January with Barre Phillips (b); Charles Moffett (d) and for part of the concert Joel Freedman (cello). The lineup for his Cellar concert may have included some or all of these musicians.
Village Voice September 24, 1964, p. 30.
Martin Siegel concert reported in "Strictly Ad Lib" *down beat* March 12, 1964, p. 41.

U64-1003   *October Revolution in Jazz*
October 3, 1964   Cellar Cafe, NYC

Giuseppi Logan Trio: Logan (ob, as, fl, bcl?); Lewis Worrell (b); Don Pullen (p); Milford Graves (d)
Arthur Keyes Octet: Keyes (p? or saxophone)
Barry Milroad Duo: Milroad (p)
Louis Brown Quartet: Brown (ts); others unknown (*possibly* Larry Willis p)
Bill Dixon Sextet: see **R64-1003**

The name "Barry Milburn" was given in some advertisements for the event, though Milroad seems to be correct. "Milroad was very very limited. His interest far exceeded his ability to stay with it and develop."

"Keyes did a lot of writing for his group--a very competent musician. The group was probably four or five horns and three rhythm."

Advertised in *Village Voice* September 24, 1964, p. 30.

U64-1004   *October Revolution in Jazz*
October 4, 1964   Cellar Cafe: NYC

<u>Valdo Williams Trio</u>: Williams (p); unknown (b); unknown (d)
<u>Ken McIntyre Octet</u>: McIntyre (as, ob, bsn, fl)
<u>Sun Ra Sextet</u>: Ra (p)
<u>Don Heckman Octet</u> [*sic*]: Heckman (as); Don Friedman (p); Alan Silva (b); Joe
Hunt (d); Sheila Jordan (voice)
<u>Midge Pike Duo</u>: Pike (b)
<u>Robert Wales</u>: Wales (p) solo
<u>Free Form Improvisation Ensemble</u>: personnel as **U64-0726**

"Of the people who played at the Cellar--especially the pianists--there were two
people that I really liked: Lowell Davidson and this man Robert Wales (I don't know
what ever happened to him).
"I only saw Robert Wales play that one time, and he played solo. I knew him from
going into a clothing store on Eighth Street where he worked; he was a very elegant
dresser. After talking with him casually (never having heard him) I learned that he
was a pianist and invited him to play."
Dixon recalls an (otherwise undocumented) performance by Lowell Davidson's
quartet--including Michael Mantler (t) and Kent Carter (b)--as a part of the October
Revolution.
"Pike was a white South African and a marvelous bass player; he returned to South
Africa shortly after these events.

It appears also that drummer Charles Moffett, Sr. performed in a group at the series.
Dixon usually cites that he or Rashied Ali was in the Bill Dixon Sextet that played
October 3, and if not there, it is possible that Moffett played in Louis Brown's group
the same night. Moffett had also performed earlier in 1964 at the Cellar with Dixon's
group(s) and others.
Advertised in *Village Voice* September 24, 1964, p. 30.

The Guild

In the wake of the *October Revolution in Jazz*, the next formally announced activity relating to Bill Dixon or the Cellar Cafe was a weekend of music advertised with the following manifesto:

> *THE OCTOBER REVOLUTION CONTINUES: musicians-composers Cecil Taylor, Archie Shepp, Sun Ra, Mike Mantler, Burton Greene, Roswell Rudd, John Tchicai, and Bill Dixon have united as the JAZZ COMPOSERS GUILD with the idea in mind that the music as represented by the above-named and others must and will no longer remain a part of the "underground" scene.*

With the addition of Paul and Carla Bley, the roll called here provided the core and total membership for the Guild in its five-month life.

Despite a passing similarity of nomenclature, Dixon's Jazz Composers' Guild had no connection to the Jazz Artists Guild of 1960 (with members Charles Mingus, Max Roach, Abbey Lincoln, and Jo Jones) that coalesced from opposition to the hiring practices of the Newport Jazz Festival. Dixon draws a stronger connection between the JCG and the actions of a group of painters who worked against the establishment in the previous decade. "At one time in the Fifties, a painter was not considered a painter unless his work showed on 57th Street--that one street. With the shift of manufacturing, former factory and warehouse spaces were becoming available downtown and a number of painters took these spaces as studios. Then someone came up with the idea to open his studio on Sundays and have people come by, and before you knew it, those artists realized that they collectively had a thing going. They recognized their power--the attitude that 'We have the thing that everyone wants. Let them come to us'--and were able to organize, so the people from 57th Street were compelled to come to where these artists were. That was what spawned SoHo and all the rest of the downtown art movements."

"In the Jazz Composers' Guild we were politically aware, meaning that we knew that what we did--whether we were paid equitably or not--affected the entire industry. About the playing no one had a problem, but the issues were: How do you get work and maintain both your sanity and your dignity? How do you withstand the constant, vicious tirades coming from those people in the music trying to protect what they have? I am always talking about the collective musician. As far as I am concerned, the only one who is successful is successful because there's one who's not successful."

"The Jazz Composers' Guild was founded on the principle of the medieval guilds, so that the members were protected: one person couldn't have something that this other one didn't get a part of. I was the one who researched this; the other people had never heard of a guild. I came into the room and presented the idea and so forth. We had some meetings that would last 5, 6, or 7 hours, adopted a name and rules. What we needed was financial support until we got ourselves 'out there' as a constituency. "When we first formed the Guild, there were two civilian people allowed at the meetings: Peter ____ and Bernard Stollman, (at the time he was both Ornette's lawyer and Cecil's lawyer, which I had found out surreptitiously). Peter Sabino never joined, but he was privy. We were looking for people whom we could ask for money, and this Peter person was one of these; Cecil Taylor introduced me to Timothy Marquand, another, who had wanted to study the trumpet just after he came from Antioch. (I never took him as a student, but we struck up a friendship.) Someone had entrée to Harry Belafonte, and suggested that he would be a good person to approach.

"Within those first four or five months, we hadn't been at it long enough to expand [the membership of the Guild]. There were a lot of people who wanted to join; it created a lot of bad feelings, really. I said, unequivocally, 'No: give us some time to become a constituency.' If it wouldn't work on a small scale, then it couldn't work at all. Why do you think there were no famous people in the Guild? Ornette was never asked to join; he was only asked to say when he was interviewed, 'I endorse what these guys are doing.' That's enough. [See **64-9090**.] Trane wasn't asked to join, because that defeats the purpose: it would have looked like we were riding on the coattails of these guys. Albert Ayler was never asked to join the Guild. Don Cherry, likewise, and the same for Steve Lacy. The only prerequisites for joining the Guild would have been to accept the by-laws, but we never got that far. The press tried to build up an us-versus-them opposition, which didn't sit well with musicians. You can imagine what might have happened if the establishment had not been able to use these other musicians' public negative statements to put us down.

"Once the Guild had a foothold, the members began to get offers from the Village Vanguard, the Gate, etc. and began to say to themselves 'Look what this publicity has done for us!...'. So obviously their interest wasn't really with the organization. When Shepp started playing at concerts of the Black Arts Repertory Theater, that was the beginning of the end. He wasn't supposed to; it violated our agreement, constitution, and charter. If anyone even got an offer from outside, s/he had to bring it to the Guild to be discussed and voted on. So if the Village Vanguard wanted Roswell Rudd, which they did at one point, we didn't say he couldn't work, but the proposal had to be brought before the Guild. There was a way for the parent society to handle musicians; they tried to splinter us by offering something to individuals. The Guild countered, saying, 'If they want you, then everybody's got to go in there too.' That's the way to defuse it. If a record company wanted to record one of us, I went as a representative and laid out what terms we wanted and that each one of us had to be recorded. I knew at that time you couldn't tell a record company when to release a record; however, we insisted all the records be released within that year.

"I don't think it was known when the Guild started that Archie had made that first record (*Four for Trane*, recorded August 10, 1964) for Impulse!. (I in fact had told him that he should speak to Trane, because he was so desperate to get a record. I said 'Look, stop talking to Bob Thiele. Talk to John Coltrane; he seems to dig you, you're down there all night, you're a saxophone player, Trane has an allegiance for saxophone players. Trane spoke to Thiele, and that's how Shepp got the date.) If it had been I, once I became involved in the Guild I would have had to table the record date, because otherwise I would have seemed hypocritical. I realize now in hindsight that a lot of people didn't have those kind of convictions.
"The reason we didn't win was no one was really 100% committed to a struggle. They were more committed to making the bread. Everyone would tell you, 'Man, I've got a

wife and kids...'. What made them think that their family situation was more important than somebody else's? I have utter confidence that had the Guild stayed together and carried out its principles, the entire art end of the music business would be different today."

Robert Levin "The Jazz Composers' Guild: An Assertion of Dignity" *down beat*: May 6, 1965, p. 17-18.

U64-1017   Sun Ra Octet

October 17, 1964   Cellar Cafe, NYC

Sun Ra (p); *probably* Pharoah Sanders (ts); others unknown

Two weeks after the October Revolution, the musicians who had joined forces under the banner of the Jazz Composers' Guild offered their first weekend of music, beginning with this Saturday concert, 9:00 to 11:00pm.

Advertised in *Village Voice* October 15, 1964, p. 16.

U64-1018   Roswell Rudd-John Tchicai Quartet

October 18, 1964   Cellar Cafe, NYC

Roswell Rudd (tb); John Tchicai (as); *probably* Lewis Worrell (b); Milford Graves (d)

Sunday 4:00 to 9:00pm.

Advertised in *Village Voice* October 15, 1964, p. 16.

U64-1023   Paul Bley Quintet

October 23, 1964   Cellar Cafe, NYC

Paul Bley (p); *possibly* Marshall Allen (as); Alan Silva (b); others unknown

Three days earlier, according to the latest reports, Bley recorded for ESP-Disk using the group he had led at the October Revolution, including Marshall Allen (as); Dewey Johnson (t); Eddie Gomez (b); Milford Graves (d). Some of those musicians were probably part of his group on this occasion as well.
9:00-11:00pm

Advertised in *Village Voice* October 22, 1964, p. 16; *Columbia Spectator* October 23, 1964, p. 3; Henk Kluck *Bley Play: The Paul Bley Recordings Kraaienveld*, The Netherlands: private edition, 1996, p. 45.

U64-1024   Alan Silva Quartet
October 24, 1964   Cellar Cafe: NYC

Alan Silva (b); *probably* Clarence Walker (d); others unknown

The remaining players may have included Winter, Walker, or Friedman (but probably not Burton Greene) from the Free Form Improvisation Ensemble.
9:00-11:00pm.

Dixon had been one of a handful of audience members at a Town Hall concert of the FFIE (apparently September 21) and was struck by Silva's bass playing. Following that concert, they began discussing a collaboration that apparently first bore fruit at **R65-0295**.
"I knew Alan from Whelan's drug store in the Village, where he worked. I had been told that he was a musician, (if you were down on Eighth street, of course, you must be a musician) but didn't make the connection until I saw him playing. The FFIE played at the Cellar (**U64-0726**) and then at the Town Hall concert."
Advertised in *Village Voice* October 22, 1964, p. 16; *Columbia Spectator* October 23, 1964, p. 3; FFIE at Town Hall reviewed in *Village Voice* October 1, 1964, p. 10.

U64-1025   Roswell Rudd-John Tchicai Quartet
October 25, 1964   Cellar Cafe: NYC

Roswell Rudd (tb); John Tchicai (as); *probably* Lewis Worrell (b); Milford Graves (d)

Sunday afternoon: 4:00-9:00pm.
Advertised in *Village Voice* October 22, 1964, p. 16; *Columbia Spectator* October 23, 1964, p. 3;

U64-1030   Jazz Composers Guild
October 30-31, 1964   61 4th Avenue, NYC

Cecil Taylor Unit
Sun Ra Arkestra
Paul Bley
Archie Shepp Septet
Roswell Rudd-John Tchicai Quartet
Bill Dixon Sextette (see **R64-1030**)
Free Form Improvisational Group

Personnel presumed similar to that documented for the *Four Days in December*
performances (**U64-1228** through **U64-1231**) by the same groups. Dixon's
group is cited in **R64-1228**.

The 9:00pm-6:00am *Pre-Halloween Jazz Party* was put on "to raise funds to provide a
permanent home for the Guild" according to advertising for the event. Dixon recalls
that it also was to generate revenue for staging the more formal Guild showcase at
Judson Hall, the *Four Days in December*. The 4th Avenue setting between 9th and
10th Streets was the loft of vibraphonist Ollie Shearer that the Guild rented.
ad in *Village Voice* October 29, 1964.

U64-1108   Archie Shepp Septette
November 8, 1964   Cellar Cafe, NYC

Archie Shepp (ts); *probably* Marion Brown (as) others unknown

Sunday afternoon: 4:00-9:00pm.
Advertised in *Village Voice* November 5, 1964, p. 12.

U64-1125   Cecil Taylor Unit/Roswell Rudd-John Tchicai Quartet
November 25, 1964   2 Pitt Street, NYC

Cecil Taylor Unit: Taylor (p); Jimmy Lyons (as); *probably* Henry Grimes (b);
Andrew Cyrille (d)

Roswell Rudd-John Tchicai Quartet: Rudd (tb); Tchicai (as); *probably* Lewis
Worrell (b); Milford Graves (d)

"9 pm until..."
This address was probably a dancer's studio in the then-fertile Lower East Side, also

the site of a benefit concert--presumably not Guild-related--on November 15 featuring Shepp's group and violinist Malcolm Goldstein.
The double-bill epitomizes some of the beneficent side-effects for the Jazz Composers' Guild's members:

In the two years prior to the Guild's formation, Cecil Taylor's Unit was presented sporadically in New York Jazz clubs--obscure and "name" establishments that paid a pittance, from the Five Spot to the Take 3 Coffee House. Taylor's profile in the press and industry as a working musician was certainly accelerating due to factors beyond the Guild, but it was through the Guild's and Dixon's sponsorship that he began to appear more frequently in concert than nightclub situations, overcoming what had been perceived as a major obstacle to understanding of his music. Taylor's (near-annual) series of Town Hall appearances was initiated with Dixon's facilitation during the Guild period, and by the Summer of 1965 the Unit performed at the Monterey, *down beat* [Chicago] and Newport festivals. He continued to accept (higher-profile) club gigs in New York, but Taylor's next tour to Europe--unlike his first--included mainly radio and concert hall presentations.

The proto-New York Art Quartet, represented by the Rudd/Tchicai group, congealed in the wake of Shepp's *Four for Trane* recording (August 10, 1964), in which Rudd, Tchicai, and Reggie Workman participated. Though the group performed together in New York at least through December of 1965, nearly all of its first concerts were Guild-sponsored events. Like so many groups in the new music, what the NYAQ needed most in its formative moments was a plenitude of playing opportunities. Following the collapse of the Guild, Tchicai and Rudd used the momentum they had gained to tour Europe in the Spring of 1965. Even in the US, alongside the Jazz Composer's Orchestra, they took the stage at the highly publicized Museum of Modern Art concert series.

down beat reported that Bernard Stollman's series "Jazz in Repertory" was scheduled to run at the Cafe Au Go Go from December 8, 1964 to January 3, 1965. Apparently with the approval of the Guild's membership, Guild members Taylor, Sun Ra, and the Rudd/Tchicai group were among those to be featured. Because the Au Go Go did not serve alcohol, it therefore was exempt from the 4:00am curfew, so Stollman's groups were contracted to play the after-hours set (1:00am until dawn) following the club's major act. Though technically not "bar" performances, the entire booking constituted second-rate treatment (at the hands of a third-party promoter) and was therefore frowned upon as a breach of the Guild's principles.

Village Voice November 19, 1964, p. 19;
Au Go Go in *down beat* January 15, 1965, c. p. 10.

U64-1228   *Four Days in December*
December 28, 1964   Judson Hall: 165 West 57th St, NYC

<u>Cecil Taylor Unit</u>: Cecil Taylor (p); Jimmy Lyons (as); Michael Mantler (t);
Buell Neidlinger (b); Andrew Cyrille (d)

<u>Bill Dixon Sextette</u> *see* **R64-1228**.

Taylor's group and Dixon's (**R64-1228**) opened the *Four Days in December* concert
series, the most visible activity staged by the Jazz Composers's Guild.
Advertised in *Village Voice* December 10, 1964, p. 22 and December 17, 1964, p. 16; *New York Times* December 29, 1964, p.21; *down beat* February 11, 1965 p. 37-38.

U64-1229   *Four Days in December*
December 29, 1964   Judson Hall, NYC

-1: <u>Paul Bley Quintet</u>: Paul Bley (p); Manny Smith (t); Marshall Allen (as);
Eddie Gomez (b); Milford Graves (d)

-2: <u>Jazz Composers' Guild Orchestra</u>: Mike Mantler (t); Willie Ruff (frh);
Roswell Rudd (tb); Steve Lacy (ss); Jimmy Lyons, John Tchicai (as); Archie
Shepp (ts); Fred Pirtle (barsx); Eddie Gomez (b); Paul Bley (p); Milford Graves
(d)

Roast -2	Font 881011ZY
Communications No. 3 -2	unissued

Second night of the *Four Days in December* concerts.

Fontana (NL) 881011ZY=Fontana (NL) 681011ZY=CBS Sony (J) SFON7076
=Fontana [PolyGram] (J) 195J-23, PolyGram catalog number 681 011 on LP and CD.
All issues titled: Jazz Composer's Orchestra *Communication*.

From *Jazz Monthly*, largely paraphrasing Carla Bley's note to the Fontana LP:
"The Jazz Composers' Guild Orchestra was formed by Mike Mantler and Carla Bley in
the autumn of 1964 in New York City. This was an eleven piece orchestra designed
for the performance of new jazz compositions and was one of the eight groups in the
Jazz Composers Guild....
"The...Orchestra commenced rehearsals at the home of painter Mike Snow for their
first Guild concert at the Judson Hall in December, 1964, where 'Communications
No. 3' by Mike Mantler and 'Roast' by Carla Bley were performed. This concert was
musically so successful that the two leaders decided to prepare further compositions
for performances in the three-cornered studio above the Village Vanguard club,
known as the Contemporary Centre [sic], which formed the headquarters for the
Guild."
Advertised in *Village Voice* December 10, 1964, p. 22, and December 17, 1964, p. 16; *down beat* February 11, 1965 p. 37-38; "The Jazz Composer's Orchestra" [uncredited article] *Jazz Monthly* July 1968, p. 7.

U64-1230   Four Days in December
December 30, 1964   Judson Hall, NYC

Free Form Improvisation Ensemble: John Winter (fl); Gary William
Friedman (as); Alan Silva (b); Burton Greene (p); Clarence Walker (d)

Archie Shepp Quartet: Charles Tolliver (t); Benny Jacobs-El (tb); Marion
Brown (as); Archie Shepp (ts); Reggie Johnson (b); Roger Blank (d)

Third night of the *Four Days in December*.

Jerry Newman's stereo recording of this FFIE concert survives.

Advertised in *Village Voice* December 10, 1964, p. 22, and December 17, 1964, p. 16; *down beat*
February 11, 1965 p. 37-38.

U64-1231   Four Days in December
December 31, 1964   Judson Hall, NYC

-1: Sun Ra Arkestra: Chris Capers (t); Al Evans (flgh); Teddy Nance, Bernard
Pettaway (tb); Black Harold (fl); Marshall Allen, Danny Davis (as); Pharoah
Sanders (ts); Pat Patrick (barsx); Ronnie Boykins, Alan Silva (b); Sun Ra (p);
Clifford Jarvis, Jimhmi Johnson (d); Ahrt Jenkins (space voice)

-2: Roswell Rudd-John Tchicai Quartet: Roswell Rudd (tb); John Tchicai (as);
Don Moore (b); Milford Graves (d)

> Space Mates -1
> Other People's Worlds -1
> Water Lillies on Mars -1

Concluding night of the *Four Days in December* concert series. All titles belong to
the Sun Ra set. The third piece was performed with the following preface: "Unlike
Water Lilies anyplace else, water lilies on Mars are about three or four stories high
and about a block long. We will try to musically describe them in our next piece."

Advertised in *Village Voice* December 10, 1964, p. 22, and December 17, 1964, p. 16; *down beat*
February 11, 1965 p. 37-38. **Bob Zelman reviewed this concert under the column titled**
"Harmonic Highlights", presumably in the *Columbia Daily Spectator*.

Contemporary Center

Coincident with the *Four Days in December* series, the Jazz Composers' Guild changed its base of operations. An advertisement in the *Village Voice* proclaimed,
THE JAZZ REVOLUTION CONTINUES. The New Headquarters of the Jazz Composers' Guild Is the Triangle ABOVE THE VILLAGE VANGUARD, 180 7th Ave. So. Every Friday and Saturday night from 9pm, beginning on January 8th. Contribution $2

Dixon: "When we left the Cellar it was because we could no longer afford the rent there. [The club was also served with a summons for presenting music without a license and subsequently closed its doors.] I didn't play as much at the Contemporary Center because I was organizing the stuff; I only played when I had something to play. The groups that played frequently did so because they wanted to. In that way, we had to provide a place so that these guys would't be playing all over town. Right away, we were trying to make people understand the philosophy: 'If you're playing all over town, we can't win.' Because we were in one location, everyone knew 'That's where you go to hear...' "
On the other hand, Dixon opposed adopting this particular site as the Guild's new base of operations. "Why place yourself where people would have to choose [between the Guild and the Vanguard's fare]? Max Gordon's place was the darling of the entire scene; he's advertising, and yet [the other Guild members] wanted to stand upstairs with an empty room and look like fools, whereas they could have found someplace isolated to do what we had to do and drum up our own constituency. Look what happened after they started the programs: it didn't make sense, because most people going to the Vanguard didn't give a shit about the Guild's programs.

"So right from the very beginning, it wasn't like how things had been done at the Cellar. I was beginning to take a dim view of what [the other Guild members] were doing, because there were too many violations. People were beginning to get outside offers. I didn't have too much control over the thing. From that point on, the organization became more and more fragmented and began to lose direction. At any rate I got the thing back together and we continued giving the concerts."

The Contemporary Center (also known as the Contemporary Dance Center, the 'Triangle', and the American Center) was otherwise the loft space of dancer/choreographer Edith Stephen. As early as 1963, the space had been host to performances by the Prince Lasha-Sonny Simmons group and Walt Dickerson. Though billed as at The Contemporary Center, these concerts were independent of the JCG. It may also be the venue LeRoi Jones refers to as "The Center" in *down beat*.

Contemporary Center ad in *Village Voice* December 31, 1964, p. 6; LeRoi Jones "New York Loft and Coffee Shop Jazz" *down beat* May 9, 1963, p. 13 and 42; reprinted in Black Music (New York: William Morrow & Co [Apollo ed.]: 1968), p. 96.

U65-0108   Archie Shepp Quintet

January 8, 1965   Contemporary Center: 180 7th Av NYC

Archie Shepp (ts); *probably* Marion Brown (as); others unknown and probably similar to **U64-1230**.

Shepp's group played the first night of the Guild's debut weekend at its new home.

Advertised in *Village Voice* January 7, 1965, p. 14.
The photograph of a Shepp group in John S. Wilson "Dig That Free Form Jazz" New York Times January 24, 1965, p. II:13 may have come from this engagement, or possibly from a later Contemporary Center performance shortly afterward that is not otherwise documented.

U65-0109   New York Art Quartet

January 9, 1965   Contemporary Center: NYC

Roswell Rudd (tb); John Tchicai (as); unknown (b); Milford Graves (d)

The NYAQ (having changed its name from the Roswell Rudd-John Tchicai Quartet) played the second night of the Guild's debut weekend at its new locale. Advertising now mentioned the names of Rudd, Tchicai, and Milford Graves; the bass chair rotated frequently and may here have been filled by Walter Booker, Richard Davis, Eddie Gomez, Don Moore, Steve Swallow, Reggie Workman, Lewis Worrell (all of whom played with the group), or yet another player. Dixon: "Lewis Worrell was their standard bass player, and he was the best. He wasn't a virtuoso, but he had a solid presence they could hang their hats on."

Advertised in *Village Voice* January 7, 1965, p. 14.

U65-0115   Free Form Improvisation Ensemble

January 15, 1965   Contemporary Center: NYC

John Winter (fl); Gary William Friedman (as); Alan Silva (b); Burton Greene (p); Clarence Walker (d)

From the second weekend of Guild-sponsored events in 1965.

Advertised in *Village Voice* January 14, 1965, p. 10.

U65-0116 Paul Bley Quintet
January 16, 1965   Contemporary Center, NYC

Paul Bley (p); others unknown and probably similar to **U64-1229**

Dixon: "One of the first concerts that was supposed to happen there coincided with Ornette Coleman's Village Vanguard opening to end his retirement. That was downstairs while upstairs the Guild was to present Paul and Carla Bley. For whatever reason, someone disappeared and went to Florida (?); they didn't show. The audience came but there was no one to play. Paul was almost ejected from the Guild; we had a 'trial' and it ended up with whites on one side and blacks on the other side. It turned out that Paul didn't want to play opposite Ornette Coleman." Coleman apparently opened at the Vanguard January 8, when Archie Shepp's group was at the Contemporary Center; he returned January 22 and was held over into February. It seems likely that Dixon is referring to Bley's scheduled January 16 or 29 Guild concert.
Advertised in *Village Voice* January 14, 1965, p. 10.

U65-0122 Sun Ra and His Solar Music
January 22, 1965   Contemporary Center, NYC

Sun Ra (p); others unknown and probably similar to **U64-1231**

From the third weekend of Guild-sponsored events in 1965.

Although advertised using the name of the Jazz Composers' Guild, a gallery opening scheduled the same night at the Galaxy Art Center (52 W 58th St.) with a (possibly) Guild-approved musical presentation was not a formal concert presentation of the Guild. At the Galaxy paintings by "Mike Snow, Bob Thompson, William White, and Joyce Snow" were exhibited; poetry read by "LeRoi Jones, Ralph Lewis, and others", and the New York Art Quartet performed: Roswell Rudd (tb); John Tchicai (as); Eddie Gomez (b); Milford Graves (d).
8:30pm; $2.50 contribution with a discount for WBAI listeners.
The episode offers some of the earliest evidence of a splintering of the Guild's constituents as the organization lost cohesion, partially owing to conflicting allegiances to Dixon and the Guild on the one hand, v. LeRoi Jones and the Black Arts Repertory Theater on the other. See also **62-0526** and the text that follows.
Advertised in *Village Voice* January 21, 1965, p. 18; NYAQ in *Village Voice* January 21, 1965, p. 18.

U65-0123   Mike Mantler-Carla Bley Quintet
January 23, 1965   Contemporary Center, NYC

Mike Mantler (t); Carla Bley (p); Marion Brown (as); *possibly* Kent Carter (b);
Billy Elgart (d)

From the third weekend of Guild-sponsored events in 1965.
Advertised in *Village Voice* January 21, 1965, p. 18.

U65-0129   Paul Bley Quintet
January 29, 1965   Contemporary Center, NYC

Paul Bley (p); others unknown and probably similar **U64-1229**

From the fourth weekend (by this time they included three performances) of
Guild-sponsored events in 1965, as are the next two entries.
Advertised in *Village Voice* January 28, 1965, p. 12.

U65-0130   Archie Shepp Quintet
January 30, 1965   Contemporary Center, NYC

Archie Shepp (ts); others unknown and probably similar to **U64-1230**

Advertised in *Village Voice* January 28, 1965, p. 12.

U65-0131   Sun Ra and his Solar Orchestra
January 31, 1965   Contemporary Center, NYC

Sun Ra (p); others unknown and probably similar to **U64-1231**

The Sunday matinee ran from 6:00 to 10:00pm, with the same entrance contribution
of $2.00.
Advertised in *Village Voice* January 28, 1965, p. 12.

U65-0205   Free Form Improvisation Ensemble
February 5, 1965   Contemporary Center, NYC

John Winter (fl); Gary William Friedman (as); Alan Silva (b); Burton
Greene (p); Clarence Walker (d)

From the fifth weekend of Guild-sponsored events in 1965, as are the next two
entries.
Advertised in *Village Voice* February 4, 1965, p. 12.

U65-0206   Sun Ra and his Solar Orchestra
February 6, 1965   Contemporary Center, NYC

Sun Ra (p); others unknown and probably similar to **U64-1231**

Advertised in *Village Voice* February 4, 1965, p. 12.

U65-0207   New York Art Quartet
February 7, 1965   Contemporary Center, NYC

Roswell Rudd (tb); John Tchicai (as); unknown (b); Milford Graves (d)

See **U65-0109** for bass candidates.
Advertised in *Village Voice* February 4, 1965, p. 12.

U65-0212   Archie Shepp Sextet
February 12, 1965   Contemporary Center, NYC

Archie Shepp (ts); others unknown and probably similar to **U64-1230**

From the sixth weekend of Guild events in 1965, as are the next two entries.
Advertised in *Village Voice* February 11, 1965, p. 12.

U65-0213   Mike Mantler-Carla Bley Quintet
February 13, 1965   Contemporary Center, NYC

Mike Mantler (t); Carla Bley (p); Marion Brown (as); *probably* Kent Carter (b);
Billy Elgart (d)

Advertised in *Village Voice* February 11, 1965, p. 12.

U65-0214   Paul Bley Quintet
February 14, 1965   Contemporary Center, NYC

Paul Bley (p); others unknown and probably similar to **U64-1229**

This Sunday performance was scheduled for 9:00pm-2:00am.
Advertised in *Village Voice* February 11, 1965, p. 12.

U65-0219   Sun Ra and his Solar Orchestra
February 19, 1965   Contemporary Center, NYC

Sun Ra (p); others unknown and probably similar to **U64-1231**

From the seventh weekend of Guild events in 1965, as are the next two entries.
Advertised in *Village Voice* February 18, 1965, p. 18.

U65-0220   Burton Greene Quartet
February 20, 1965   Contemporary Center, NYC

Burton Greene (p); others unknown

With this concert, Greene further established his own groups away from the Free
Form Improvisation Ensemble (he had concertized as a leader in the Summer of
1964), despite a classified listing showed this as an FFIE event.
Advertised in *Village Voice* February 18, 1965, p. 18 and last page.

U65-0221   New York Art Quartet
February 21, 1965   Contemporary Center, NYC

Roswell Rudd (tb); John Tchicai (as); unknown (b); Milford Graves (d)

See **U65-0109** for bass candidates.
Advertised in *Village Voice* February 18, 1965, p. 12.

U65-0226   Paul Bley Quintet
February 26, 1965   Contemporary Center, NYC

Paul Bley (p); others unknown and probably similar to **U64-1229**

From the eighth weekend of Guild events in 1965, as are the next two entries.
Advertised in *Village Voice* February 25, 1965, p. 18.

U65-0227   Archie Shepp Sextet

February 27, 1965   Contemporary Center, NYC

Archie Shepp (ts); *probably* Marion Brown (as); others unknown

Advertised in *Village Voice* February 25, 1965, p. 18.

U65-0228   Jazz Composers Guild Orchestra

February 28, 1965   Contemporary Center, NYC

Mike Mantler (t); Joseph Orange, Roswell Rudd (tb); Steve Lacy (ss); Marion Brown, Lee Konitz, Jimmy Lyons, John Tchicai (as); Sam Rivers (ts); Fred Pirtle (barsx); Buell Neidlinger, Alan Silva (b); Lowell Davidson, Carla Bley (p); Paul Motian (d)

> Radio
>
> Communications no. 4 (Day)

A "special workshop performance" from the eighth weekend of Guild-sponsored events in 1965.

"Radio" was Carla Bley's composition; Mantler's piece "Day" was also known as "Communications No. 4"

Jazz Monthly reported that the orchestra for this concert comprised fifteen players, and, curiously, that it took place at the beginning of March; on the contrary, there is no evidence of JCG Orchestra concerts at the Center before this one, or between it and **U65-0409/10**. The article goes on to explain that "[t]he Contemporary Center concerts gained public recognition and so it was decided to invite guest composers to write and conduct pieces of their own [leading to **U65-0409**]."

Lowell Davidson's presence for this concert reflected a transition in his working situations. Dixon: "George Russell had introduced me to Lowell Davidson. I thought he was brilliant, though in another world. One of the best groups to come out of the new music of the Sixties was the quartet that Davidson led with Mike Mantler on trumpet--short, cryptic pieces. I had met them when they came down to play the Cellar at the October Revolution. Lowell Davidson was invited to join the Jazz Composers' Guild, not Mantler. But Lowell couldn't (or wouldn't) come down from Boston that much, so Mike came as a representative for Davidson, and subsequently he began to form the Jazz Composer's Orchestra."

Advertised in *Village Voice* February 25, 1965, p. 18; "The Jazz Composer's Orchestra" [uncredited article] *Jazz Monthly* July 1968, p. 7.

U65-0305   Burton Greene Quartet
March 5, 1965   Contemporary Center, NYC

Burton Greene (p); Joel Freedman (cello); others unknown

From the ninth weekend of Guild-sponsored events in 1965, as are the next two
entries. Freedman was identified by name in advertisements for this concert.
Advertised in *Village Voice* March 4, 1965, p. 18.

U65-0306   Sun Ra and his Solar Orchestra
March 6-7, 1965   Contemporary Center, NYC

Sun Ra (p); Pharoah Sanders (ts); Clifford Jarvis (d); others unknown and
probably similar to **U64-1231**

From the ninth advertised weekend of Guild-sponsored events in 1965. Sanders and
Jarvis were named in advertisements for the concert.
Advertised in *Village Voice* March 4, 1965, p. 18.

U65-0307   Daniel Nagrin-Cecil Taylor
March 7, 1965   Town Hall, NYC

Cecil Taylor (p);
not at this concert: Daniel Nagrin (choreography, movement)

        Careful Softshoe

A man named Don Kelman assayed to present Cecil Taylor in a Town Hall concert.
Dixon: "I suspected Kelman as not being what he represented himself to be. Going to
his house a few days before this concert and I found that he moved back to
Washington, D.C.--where he was from--and had left the preparations halfway done.
So I ended up picking up the pieces, including the advertising: I designed the poster,
with a photograph of Cecil.
" 'Careful Softshoe' is the piece he had been working on a long time with
[dancer/choreography] Daniel Nagrin, and I think he had been committed to Nagrin to
go out to the coast and do this piece. Instead, Cecil made a beautiful tape of the music
part of it, and at the same time he was performing it in Town Hall [5:30pm EST],
Nagrin was dancing with the tape. The concert was well attended."
In the end, Nagrin actually performed with a tape of another pianist performing a
transcription of Taylor's music. "Careful Softshoe" was apparently Taylor's name
for the musical element of the work (and/or the Town Hall concert), while Nagrin
performed it on this occasion at a theater in Los Angeles under the title "Not Me, But
Him". He also rendered the piece in Manhattan later under that title.
advertised in Village Voice February 11, 1965, p. 11; February 25, 1965, p. 24.

U65-0312   Sun Ra and his Solar Orchestra
March 12-13, 1965   Contemporary Center, NYC

Sun Ra (p); Eddie Gale (t); Marshall Allen, Marion Brown, Danny Davis (as);
Pharoah Sanders (ts); Pat Patrick (barsx); Roger Blank, Jimhmi Johnson (d);
others unknown and probably similar to **U64-1231**

From the tenth advertised weekend of Guild-sponsored events in 1965, as is the
following. Sanders and Clifford Jarvis were named in advertisements for the concert.
Advertised in *Village Voice* March 11, 1965, p. 15; personnel from "Strictly Ad Lib" *down beat*
April 22, 1965, p. 48.

U65-0314   New York Art Quartet
March 14, 1965   Contemporary Center, NYC

Roswell Rudd (tb); John Tchicai (as); unknown (b); Milford Graves (d)

See **U65-0109** for bass candidates.
Advertised in *Village Voice* March 11, 1965, p. 15.

U65-0320   Cecil Taylor Unit
possibly ca. March 20, 1965   Contemporary Center, NYC

Cecil Taylor (p); Michael Mantler (t); Jimmy Lyons (as); possibly Henry
Grimes (b); Tony Williams (d)

Though apparently not advertised, both Mantler and Williams point to this episode
having happened. Otherwise, Taylor is not known to have performed at the
Contemporary Center.

Michael Mantler and Alan Silva recall either similar episodes or the same incident
differently. Silva remembers his only musical encounter with Tony Williams at a
Cellar rehearsal for a late 1964 appearance of Cecil Taylor's Unit. The rehearsal
session included Taylor, Pharoah Sanders, Silva, and Tony Williams. This group's
planned performance was derailed when Miles Davis insisted that Williams (who was
then a salaried member of his quintet) not appear in other contexts.
Alternately, Mantler remembers a session at the Contemporary Center in which
Taylor, Jimmy Lyons, Sanders or possibly Makanda Ken McIntyre, Mantler, Silva or
Henry Grimes and Tony Williams took part.

U65-0321   Burton Greene Quartet
March 21, 1965   Contemporary Center, NYC

Burton Greene (p); Joel Freedman (cello); Jimmie Stevenson, Jr. (b); Gerry Tomlinson (d)

From the eleventh weekend of Guild-sponsored events in 1965. 9:00pm
Advertised in *Village Voice* March 18, 1965, p. 24.

U65-0326   Archie Shepp Sextet
March 26-27, 1965   Contemporary Center, NYC

Archie Shepp (ts); *probably* Marion Brown (as); others unknown

From the twelfth weekend of Guild-sponsored events in 1965.
Advertised in *Village Voice* March 25, 1965, p. 23.

U65-0402   Paul Bley Quintet
April 2-3, 1965   Contemporary Center, NYC

Paul Bley (p); others unknown and probably similar to **U64-1229**

From the thirteenth advertised weekend of Guild-sponsored events in 1965, as is the following. 9:00pm to 2:00am
Advertised in *Village Voice* April 1, 1965, p. 18.

U65-0404   Alan Silva Ensemble
April 4, 1965   Contemporary Center, NYC

Alan Silva (b); George Abend (perc, p); others (probably 2 musicians) unknown

From the thirteenth advertised weekend of Guild-sponsored events in 1965. 9:00pm to 2:00am

Silva's concert was cited in the *Village Voice* classified listings as "free form quartet", reflecting his ties to the now dissolving/ed FFIE.
Abend's environmental paintings were also exhibited on this weekend, as they had been at earlier 1965 Guild performances.
Advertised in *Village Voice* April 1, 1965, p. 18.

U65-0409   Jazz Composers Guild Orchestra
April 9-11,1965   Contemporary Center, NYC

Mike Mantler, Bob Zottola (t); Roswell Rudd (tb); Perry Robinson (cl); Steve
Lacy (ss); Ed Curran, Jimmy Lyons, probably Robin Kenyatta (as); Ken
McIntyre (as, bcl); Sam Rivers (ss, ts); Fred Pirtle (barsx); Kent Carter, Steve
Swallow (b); Carla Bley (p, cond); Barry Altschul, Tony Williams (d)

> Day (Communications no. 4)
> Radio
> Loose Latin
> Communications no. 5
> Unknown

10:00pm. The Guild's fourteenth weekend in 1965 was given over to a presentation
of works-in-progress by Dixon (see **R65-0409**) and Burton Greene, and repeat
performances of Carla Bley's "Radio" and Mantler's "Day", both premiered at
U65-0228. Bley also composed "Loose Latin". The Friday and Saturday
gatherings were advertised as "workshop performances", leading up to a more formal
concert on Sunday.
Jazz Monthly cited this as the final JCG Orchestra performance while the Guild was
still together, and also the group's final performance at the Contemporary Center.
Peter Sabino photographed the event.

"Strictly Ad Lib" *down beat* May 20, 1965, p.11; "The Jazz Composer's Orchestra"
[uncredited article] *Jazz Monthly* July 1968, p. 7.

U65-0416   New York Art Quartet

April 16-18, 1965   Contemporary Center, NYC

Roswell Rudd (tb, euphonium); John Tchicai (as); Steve Swallow (b); Milford Graves (d)

The Jazz Composers Guild's fifteenth weekend of programming in 1965 was also probably its last official act under that name. The program comprised:

Friday: *New York Eye and Ear Control* a film by Mike [Michael] Snow

Saturday: *"silent film by Don Kalfa"* [*sic*] *with sound to be improvised live by the NYAQ.*

Sunday: *Uncompleted ballet, "Hallelujah on Sunday" or "Death", by Judy Dearing with John Tchicai; "American Error", a tape by Paul Haines.*

down beat confirms after the fact that most of the above happened. Apparently George Abend's environmental paintings were part of the exhibit as well.

Snow's film was evidently being premiered at this event. Rudd and Tchicai had taken part in the July 17, 1964 recording that preceded and catalyzed the film and they also appeared on screen in it, though not performing and not in synchronized-sound footage.

Calfa's name is correctly spelled with a "C"; it was misspellesd in advertisements. He recalls the film as The Diner, in contrast to the report in *down beat* of a short known as Goofin' Off.

One eyewitness recalls being the only paying attendee at this concert not connected with the Guild or the presentation.

Advertised in *Village Voice* March 11, 1965, p. 15; "Strictly Ad Lib" *down beat* June 3, 1965, p. 10.

~~Newport 65~~

"A fringe group of the Guild's members later went to the Newport Jazz Festival--Cecil, Paul Bley, Archie Shepp, and the Jazz Composer's Orchestra. I had already informed [the festival's producer] George Wein that the Guild's structure was looking shaky, that these people coming to the festival were misrepresenting themselves, and that the Jazz Composers' Guild name should not be used. Very belatedly I heard from him, when there was a panel conference on which I spoke. For the next year's event, Wein said 'Those people represented themselves to me as members of the Guild, and I guess I owe you an apology.... I hereby extend to you an invitation to play Newport.' That's the only reason I played at that festival in 1966 (see **R66-0702**).

"These people--before the Guild was finally dissolved--went up there and got themselves in by calling themselves the Jazz Composers' Guild. So long before that I knew it was a lost cause."

described tangentially in John Wilcock "The Jazz Scene: Sinatra Is Not of This World" *Village Voice* July 8, 1965, p. 18.

Savoy

"The records I produced for Ed Curran, Bob Pozar, and Marc Levin were done as a cluster. I got along with Fred Mendelssohn; periodically, he would ask me if I wanted to make another record. Having done the first one **[R62-1000a/b]** and half of the other one **[R64-0204]**, that was enough of it for me. Savoy didn't have good distribution. It was difficult getting them played on the air. I had made my record and a half and found out that that wasn't going to do what it was supposed to do anyway: you needed a record in those days to be able to work in the clubs. Already people were talking about the music in a different way, so I didn't see any sense in going through all that trouble doing another record for them.
"But I had these people who were studying with me. Like practically everyone else, they all needed a record, so I assumed the responsibility. Mendelssohn said: 'We'll give you [as producer] the money that we would give you [as an artist]; any other money they'll have to raise themselves.'
"I wanted to write the liner notes, because I knew these people, and I wanted to do the design. I wanted the experience in A&R and how to engineer and edit a record. That was the reason I did it, and for these musicians to have a record, and I enjoyed doing that. The next thing I knew, everybody's asking me to produce a record for them, which was the furthest thing from my mind."
Bill Dixon "Jazz: Contemporary Dilemma" *Record World* April 27, 1968, p. 27 and 72.

U67-0300   Marc Levin
spring, 1967   Stereo Sound Studio, Newark

Marc Levin ("flutes and brasses"); Jonas Gwangwa (tb); Calo Scott (cello); Cecil McBee (b); Frank Clayton (d)

Morning Colors	16:30	Sav MGS12190
The Dragon and the Rainbow: Forum...	3:39	--
The Rainbow	7:28	--
Twilight Dance		--
Meditation:The Sea		--
The Fire		
The Earth	11:58	

Savoy MGS 12190 titled *The Dragon Suite*, probably issued in compatible stereo only. Jackets give the catalog number as "SMG-", while the record has a more typical "MGS-". Produced by Bill Dixon.

The second selection is titled "The Dragon and the Rainbow: Forum with the Modernmen"
reviewed in "Jazztrack" by Rupert Kettle: *DOWNTOWN*, through October 7, 1967. p. 8.

U67-0306   Bob Pozar

March 6, 1967   unknown studio, NYC area

Bob Pozar (d, tape); Mike Zwerin (bass t, tb); Kathi Norris (cello); Jimmy
Garrison (b)

-1 omit Pozar, Zwerin
-2 tape by Mike Sahl

The Mechanical Answering Service of...	3:30	Sav MGS12189
Robin Hood	2:58	--
Renfield	9:35	--
Keying in Your Bank	7:00	--
Sweet Little Maia -1	5:45	--
Good Golly Miss Nancy -2	4:36	--

Savoy MGS 12189 titled *Good Golly Miss Nancy*, probably a stereo-only issue.
Jackets give the catalog number as "SMG-", while the record has a more typical
"MGS-". Produced by Bill Dixon.
"Robin Hood", "Sweet Little Maia", and "The Mechanical Answering Service of Chris
and Martha White" were reissued on Savoy SJL 2235, titled *New Music: Second
Wave*.
Jimmy Garrison's composition (listed on Pozar's record as "Maia") was correctly
re-titled "Sweet Little Maia" on SJL 2235, and recorded elsewhere under the correct
title.

Engineer Jerry Newman is credited as a "tape consultant" on the project, though there
is no direct statement that he recorded it.
reviewed in "Jazztrack" by Rupert Kettle: *DOWNTOWN*, through October 7, 1967. p. 8.

U67-0310   <u>Ed Curran</u>

March 10, 1967   *probably* Savoy Studio, Newark

Ed Curran (as, cl-1); Marc Levin (c, flgh-2, mellophone-3); Kiyoshi Tokunaga
(b); Bob Pozar (d)

-4: omit Levin

Cire -3	6:10	Sav MGS12191
Why	3:43	--
Mid Tempo	3:42	--
Looking Back -1, -3	6:59	--
Duos	4:13	--
Lady A -1, -2	5:38	--
Nicole -2	7:40	--
Drac -4	3:16	--

Savoy MGS-12191 titled *Elysa*, probably issued in compatible stereo only.
Produced by Bill Dixon.
Jackets give the catalog number as "SMG-", while the record has a more typical
"MGS-".

The LP was named for Curran's daughter, Elysa, born March 13, 1967.
reviewed in "Jazztrack" by Rupert Kettle: *DOWNTOWN*, through October 7, 1967. p. 8.

U69-1009   Marzette Watts
c. October, 1969   Stereo Sound Studios, NYC

Marzette Watts (ts); George Turner (c); Marty Cook (tb); Frank Kipers (vln);
Cevera Jehers, Steve Tintweiss (b); Bobby Few (p); Patty Waters, Amy Sheffer
(voice); Tom Berge (d)

-1 *omit* Kipers and Sheffer

Lonely Woman -1	5:49	Sav MG 12193
Octobersong	6:59	--
Medley	8:56	--

Savoy MG 12193 titled *Marzette Watts Ensemble*. Produced by Bill Dixon.
"Lonely Woman" was reissued on Savoy SJL 2235, *New Music: Second Wave*
Jehers name is pronounced as "Jeffries".

This was the second of two sessions Dixon produced for Watts's Savoy record,
apparently held roughly ten weeks before Jerry Newman's death in early January,
1970. The other date is documented in **R69-0999**.
Dixon's composition "Octobersong" was premiered on Watts's record.

Personnel above is substantially revised--per the recollections of Watts, Dixon, and
Steve Tintweiss--from that given on SJL 2235. Tintweiss played arco bass on
"Lonely Woman", and the bassists appear in opposite channels of this stereo date.

According to the LP jacket, these may be the only pieces that came from Newman's.

Logically all of Dixon's activities in the Black Music Division at BCVT belong in this chapter alongside his work with the UNJS, JCG, and Savoy. Some of the details of concert events sponsored by Dixon without his participation--spring and fall festivals, senior concerts, etc.--are included in entries in chapters 1-10. Others must be left for a fuller exegesis of the activities of the Black Music Division as a whole.

In the days immediately following the thirtieth anniversary of the *October Revolution in Jazz* (1994), Dixon organized a three day festival of music at Bennington College. The *Three Days in October* coincided as well with the beginning of Dixon's seventieth year (his final year on faculty at the College), in addition to loosely marking a twenty-year anniversary since the Black Music Division was founded and the ten-year point since it was dissolved.
Participants included Bennington alumni of the distant and recent past and a number of players from the current musical cultures of Boston and New York.

The event was fully audio- and video-recorded.

U94-1006a　　*Three Days in October*
October 6, 1994 AFTERNOON　　　　Carriage Barn: BCVT

Duo-turned-trio of Arthur Brooks (t); Gregg Bendian (d, perc);
Glynis Lomon (cello)

See also **R94-1005**.

U94-1006b　　*Three Days in October*
October 6, 1994 EVENING　　　　Carriage Barn: BCVT

Jason Zappa Quintet: Zappa (barsx); Sabir Mateen (ts, cl, fl); Billy Stein (g);
Reuben Radding (b); Rashid Bakr (d)
Mark Leonard Trio: Leonard (b) John Blum (p); Nick Skrowaczewski (d)
Allen Shawn: (solo p)
Arthur Brooks Ensemble: Brooks, Alex Huberty, Bill Heminway (t); Glynis
Lomon, Mary Springer (cello); Link Smith, Jeremy Harlos (b); unknown (p)
Justin Perdue (el g); Gregg Bendian, Matthew Weston (d)
So-Called Jazz Sextet:Bill Heminway (t); Michael Chorney (ss, as); Ray
Paczkowski (p); Justin Perdue (g); Jeremy Harlos (b); Matthew Weston (d)
After hours impromptu duo of Scott Currie (barsx); Chris Cauley (as)

U94-1007a   *Three Days in October*
October 7, 1994 AFTERNOON   Carriage Barn: BCVT

Gregg Bendian solo (d, perc);
then add Stephen Haynes (t);
then add Lisa Sokolov, Rena Sokolov-Gonzales (voice)
Impromptu: Mark Hennen (p); Hal Onserud (b); Jackson Krall (d)
then Eric Zinman (p) *replaces* Hennen

EVENING
Lisa Sokolov (voice solo)
-1: William Parker Group: Parker (b); Patricia Nicholson-Parker (movement);
Rob Brown (as); Cooper-Moore (p);
Bill Dixon see **R94-1007**
-2: Vance Provey: Provey (p); David Bindman (ts); Glynis Lomon (cello);
Stephen Haynes (t)

     Air Pockets -1
     For Bill -2

All other titles unknown

U94-1007b   *Three Days in October*
October 7, 1994 EVENING   Carriage Barn, BCVT

-1: Gregg Bendian: solo percussion and vibes
Glynis Lomon: Lomon (cello); Dave Peck (ts, bcl); Sam Lobell (bcl, ts)
Trio+one: Hennen-Onserud-Krall (as **U94-1007a**); *add* Chris Cauley (as)
-2: Eric Zinman Trio: Zinman (p); Craig Schildhauer (b); Laurence Cook (d)
Zinman-Cook duo *follows after* Schildhauer *departs*
-3: Raqib Hassan Trio: Hassan (ts, shenai, wood flute); Larry Roland (b, recitation); Shino Kuchukildirim (d)
Bendian-Sokolov-Haynes: (as **U94-1007a**)
David Warren-Tor Snyder: Warren (elbg); Snyder (g); Jackson Krall (d)
-4: Molly McQuarrie: McQuarrie (ss) see **O94-1007**
Scott Currie Sextet: Currie (barsx); Molly McQuarrie (ss); Chris Cauley (as); Dave Peck (ts); Craig Schildhauer (b); Jackson Krall (d)

>   Billowing Segments (d, perc) -1
>   Untitled (?) (vib) -1
>   Unknown (EZ composer) -2
>   Stately (Lowell Davidson) -2
>   Unknown (EZ) -2
>   The Journey -3
>   Solo for Soprano Saxophone -4

Bill Dixon's appearance in this program is shown as **R94-1007a** and **b**.

CHAPTER THIRTEEN

Educator

X60-0699 Panel discussion: Lower Eastside Neighborhoods Association
before July 7, 1960 St. Mark's-in-the-Bowerie Church, NYC

Bill Dixon, Edith Stephen, Alan Polite

"LENA was very active. If I'm not mistaken, one of the first things I ever did there was a panel discussionabout the arts in general: Alan Polite and Edith Stephen were on it, and I was. He was a poet, she was a dancer, and I was a musician. That's how I met Edith."

Villager article mentions Dixon's work with the UNJS, but does not explicitly cite this as event as a function of the organization.
The Villager July 7, 1960.

X60-0999   "The Anatomy of Contemporary Jazz"
after September 15, 1960   Merryall Comm. Ctr: New Milford, CT

Dixon lectured on "The Anatomy of Contemporary Jazz" as a part of his activities at
the UNJS (Saturday, 9:00-11:00pm). Adjacent arts presentations at the facility were
given by composer Gunther Schuller and clarinetist/conductor Eric Simon.

Dixon gave similar presentations at the Industrial Recreation Directors' Association
in Manhattan and the Bayside Community Center (Queens) in roughly the same time
period.

Strictly Ad Lib *down beat,* September 15, 1960; *The Villager* [date unknown]; "Center features
Jazzman Dixon" *New Milford Times* [1960: date unknown].

X61-0397   Jazz Arts Society
early 1961   NYC

"There was a group formed in the early 60s called The Jazz Arts Society--this is when
I was getting ready to leave the UN, up until I began to work with Archie. A black
man and a white woman ran this thing."
According to a February announcement in *Metronome*, Christopher Elliott and Leona
Finestone, along with the attorney Miles J. Lourie founded the JAS, an
"incorporated, non-profit educational organization" in early 1961, "designed...to
'foster and promote the understanding, creation, research and study of Jazz as a unique
art form."
Dixon: "I met them by accident; they seemed to be sincere. They were the ones who
introduced me to John Mehegan. He was doing some teaching for them, and they got
me to do some teaching. I spent a lot of time with these people but eventually fell
out with them."
By June of 1961, John Handy, musical director of the JAS, Lourie, its secretary, and
Dixon all made clear (again in *Metronome*) that they no longer had any connection to
the organization. Afterward, the JAS apparently remained active in producing
concert and educational events, and continued to offer scholarships for youths 12 to
20 years of age to its New York School of Jazz until at least 1963.

"Jazz Arts Society" *Metronome* February, 1961, p. 8; "Life in the Arts" *Metronome* June, 1961, p.
4; "Jazz Arts Society Offers Scholarships" *Village Voice* June 6, 1963.

X62-0129   Introduction to an American Art: Jazz
winter term: late January, 1962 fwd   South Side Inst: Rockville Centre, NY

The senior high school's course brochure describes a "non-technical introduction to the international art form to be annotated with recordings played in class and guest artist, group presentations" taught by Dixon and attorney Miles J. Lourie (see also **X61-0397**).

Course guide for the Adult Education program; *down beat* "Strictly Ad Lib" February 15, 1962, p. 52.

X63-0899   *From the Musician's Point of View*
beginning August, 1963   WBAI Radio, NYC

"When I left the UN, I said to [radio executive] John Murray that I would like to have a
television program where five or six musicians could sit around and play records.
Now the idea wasn't original; in the late Forties, the trumpeter/bandleader Bobby
Sherwood had had a program similar to that, in the very beginning of television.
That appealed to me, even when I was just starting in music. I wanted to do that for
the new music--to have people come up and present things, play records, maybe have
a group play there, and present it the way that Leonard Bernstein had done his
television programs. So Murray thought it was an excellent idea, and arranged a
meeting with a television executive at the overseas press club.
"This man looked at me and said 'You're wearing a beard; you're black...' He was
telling me all of this negative stuff about what was and wasn't going to be acceptable
being transmitted into people's living rooms, and of course the idea never went any
further than that. This is about 1962."

Eventually a less broad version of this notion was applied in the format of radio, at
WBAI. "At that time, A.B. Spellman, Don Heckman, Gunther Schuller, and Henry
Cowell were all doing programs dealing with the music. Schuller was excellent,
really, doing his history of music programs. I did a regular program playing records
from my own collection."
Dixon initiated a second program of interviews with composers and musicians,
From the Musician's Point of View. "The substance of some of these was built around
'What do you listen to? How do you work? How do you compose? How does it occur
to you? Does it *need* to be done?' I know how to ask a question and get an answer."
Bill Dixon's 1964 *curriculum vitae* described the series as a weekly 1-hour program of
interviews with musicians and playing of their records, beginning in August, 1963.
The WBAI program guide showed the following six-part sequence on alternate weeks.
October 26, 1963: Rod Levitt
November 9: Teo Macero
December 7: Hale Smith
December 21: Lucas Mason
January 4, 1964: Carla Bley [Dixon: "I was supposed to do Paul Bley, but he was
going out of town. He suggested his wife, Carla, who at that time had not had a radio
interview."]
January 18: Hall Overton
cited in vita/resumé 1964; "Strictly Ad Lib" *down beat* December 19, 1963, p. 46.

X67-1218   Duke Ellington Jazz Society
December 18, 1967   Park 100 Restaurant, NYC

Details from concert program.

X68-0915   Dixon-Dunn Lecture/Demonstration
September 15, 1968   Jewish Community Center, Detroit

Dixon and Dunn performed, bringing audio-visual recordings of their work to this
two-day workshop. The event coincided with their appointments to the BCVT
faculty.

X70-0499   lecture
spring, 1970   Nassau County, Long Island [NY]

Dixon's topic was loosely described as "American Jazz" and more specifically as
"The Black Musician and Composer" sponsored by Nassau County Special programs
and BOCES [the Board of Co-operative Educational Services].
"Faculty Notes"? *Quadrille* Fall 1970.

X71-1214   The Cheeters
December, 1971 forward   Milwaukee, Wisconsin

"The University [UWM] had gotten a grant of a couple of thousand dollars to teach
professional black musicians in Milwaukee who were musically illiterate. [I had a
system of teaching people to read music fast. It was very simple: if you paid
attention I could have you reading in a month.] But because of the political climate
one particular group, The Cheeters, wouldn't come to the University.
"So I found out where they were performing and went to hear them. They were a very
good entertaining group. When I went backstage they were stunned that I had come
all of this way to talk to them. They explained that they wanted to be able to read and
write their own music. We arranged for a place in the University there in Milwaukee,
and I had them rehearse in front of me. I took David Moss, Steve Horenstein, John
Hagen, and probaby Jim Tifft.
"Here's the way they rehearsed: they had these speakers, and would put on a record,
and each of them would crouch in front of a speaker with the volume cranked up in
order to hear the parts off the record.
"So I started from the beginning: rhythmic subdivisions, etc. Then I would have each
one of the people that I brought with me take one of these guys into a corner and

drill them. I was doing two things: teaching [the Cheeters] and teaching my students at the same time, because I couldn't come over there every time, and they would have to run the thing. I had the students make tapes of the classes they led, and I would then correct them on their teaching. I didn't go the next two weeks, and the next time I was there, they were able to write lines down. At the end of about eight weeks, they were writing all of their own things and could set harmony for them."

X73-0228   lecture
February 28, 1973   University of Wisconsin at Milwaukee

From campus handbills :
At 2 pm, in Bolton 172, Mr. Dixon will discuss the black artist's adaptation to the urban environment, concentrating particularly on the music which has been called jazz. At 8 pm, in Room 175W in the Students' Union, Mr. Dixon will give a lecture/demonstration using video tapes of his own compositions, some of which were produced in cooperation with dancer-choreographer Judith Dunn. Sponsored by the Departments of Afro-American Studies, Anthropology, Music, Sociology, and Urban Affairs

X73-0615   commencement speech
June 15, 1973   Mt. Anthony Union H.S.: Bennington

Dixon was elected by the members of the high school class of '73 to speak at the commencement. His topic was "aspects of education as applied to responsibilities to students, to institutions, and the expectations of teachers".
"Bill Dixon to Speak at MAU commencement" *Bennington Banner* June 8, 1973, p. 14.

X74-0214   lecture
February 14, 1974   Fireside Lounge: prob UWMilwaukee

titled "Aesthetics As ____ ____ [illegible]".

X74-0614   lecture
June 14, 1974   University of Wisconsin at Milwaukee

Only known citation is from Dixon's explanation of **R74-0612**.

X74-0703   Newport in New York
July 3, 1974   Carnegie Hall: NYC

Part of the educational program of 1974's Newport/New York festival was a series of lectures by "The Jazz Professors" on the history of Jazz and Black Music--presented decade by decade. Dixon lectured on the music of the 1960s.

Shortly after this speaking engagement, Dixon was interviewed on WBAI Radio in New York by Clayton Riley.

X80-1003   Cannonball Adderley Jazz Festival
October 3, 1980   Moore Auditorium: Florida State Univ.

   "Jazz: A Historical Perspective"

Dixon was invited to give this lecture during the three-day festival in Tallahassee.
Florida Flambeau October 3, 1980, p. 3.

X83-0613   Judith Dunn Day
June 13, 1983   Paul Robeson House, BCVT

Dixon attempted to have Bennington College issue a formal declaration of the day in Judith Dunn's honor. Though administrative red-tape narrowed the project somewhat, Dunn's colleagues in Black Music and Dance carried out the plan.

Linda Dowdell presented a dance work; Phoebe Neville, Nadi Qamar, David Signorelli, and Arthur Brooks performed. Photographs, posters, reviews, artworks, and the video tape of "Relay" [see **R70-0428**]were shown; Martha Wittman, Neville and Dixon led a discussion of Dunn and her work.

X85-0206   Lecture: literarisches Quartier
February 6, 1985   Alte Schmiede, Vienna

Programm für Februar der Alte Schmiede.

X87-0607   Working With Dance: A Visit with Five Musicians
June 7, 1987   Martha Hill Dance Workshop, BCVT

BC Dance video

Dixon was one of five musicians taking part in a public panel discussion (in honor of composer Josef Wittman's retirement) on dance collaborations. The entire event was videotaped.

X91-0304   On the Nature of Making Things
March 4, 1991   Southern Vermont College, Bennington

The full title of Dixon's lecture was "On the Nature of Making Things: Creative and Artistic Survival; A Personal Point of View".

Ensemble Members by Academic Term

Following are listed names of particpants in the Black Music Ensemble, Ensemble III, IV and VI and their descendants that Dixon led at UWM and BCVT, derived from class rolls, recordings, and information from the participants.

The Bennington ensembles for most of the first ten years of Dixon's appointment there encompassed many players who were not enrolled students at the college; all regular members are listed here, whatever their status. Likewise, not all of the following were at every convening of the ensemble, but all apparently had something to do with the groups' rehearsals at one point (at least) in the term. While they are intended to gather all possible names, these accountings are not complete.

Fall, 1971 [Madison]

Pat Lagg, Jim Tifft, John O'Brien (t)
Jeff Hoyer, M. Tim Verbich (tb)
John Cole (tu)
Les Edwards (fl)
Unknown (afl)
Tom Lachmund, Lee Rust (as)
Steve Horenstein and one other (ts)
John Hagen (ts, ss, E-flat contralto cl)
Virgil Jackson, Elaine _____ (bcl)

Jay Ash, DeSayles Gray (barsx)
Hal Onserud and one other (b)
Kent Taylor (elbg)
Mark Hennen, Jeff Hoyer,
  Eric Schoenbaum (p)
Joel Parker, Basil Georges,
  and one other (g)
David Moss, Chris Billias, Russell
Allen, Henry Letcher (d, perc)

Spring 1972 [Madison]
Pat Lagg, Jim Tifft, Jeff Borchardt (t)
Jeff Hoyer, M. Tim Verbich (tb)
John Cole (tu)
Les Edwards (fl)
Tom Lachmund, Lee Rust (as)
Steve Horenstein (ts)
John Hagen (ts, ss, E-flat contralto cl)
Virgil Jackson (bcl)
Jay Ash, DeSayles Gray (barsx)
John Illingworth (cello)
Hal Onserud (b)
Kent Taylor (elbg)
Mark Hennen, Eric Schoenbaum (p)
Joel Parker, Basil Georges (g)
David Moss, Chris Billias,
  Russell Allen (d, perc)
Mara Herskowitz, Irvin A.
  McAllister (voice)
Charyn A. Simpson, Debby Holmes,
  Jackie Banks (movement)

Fall 1972 [Bennington]
David Appel, Susan Feiner,
  Roger Kay (fl)
Nora Nissenbaum (oboe)
Doug Cumming (saxophone)
Thomas Guralnick, John Hagen (ts)
Roxanne Richter (cello)
Henry Carnes, Baird Hersey (g)
Leslie Winston, Steve Riffkin (p)
Julian Gerstin (d)
Mara Purl (koto, voice)
Doug Houston (voice)
Cris Compton, Alexandra Hughes,
  Donna Light, Sarah Sawyer,
  Medora Waldman (voice, movement)
Steve Brooks, Neal Richmond (unk)

Spring 1973
Jim Tifft, John O'Brien (t)
Jeff Hoyer (tb)
Laura Dubetsky, Charles Morgan (fl)
Sue Feiner (afl)

Don Kaplan (as)
Doug Cumming (saxophone)
John Hagen (ts, ss, bassoon)
Thomas Guralnick (reeds)
Bill Baumen, Stephen Horenstein (ts)
Jay Ash (barsx)
Roxanne Richter (cello)
Baird Hersey (g)
Leslie Winston (p)
Mara Purl (koto, voice)
Medora Waldman (voice)
David Moss, David Copeland (d, perc)
Alexandra Hughes, Madora Waldman,
  Cris Compton, Laurel Sprigg
  (voice)
Doug Ludwig (unk)

the critical writing student Susan B.
MacGregor also was enrolled in the
class as an observer

Fall 1973
Arthur Brooks, John O'Brien, Jim
Tifft (t)
Susan Feiner (afl)
Dominck Messenger (as)
Doug Cumming, Steve Simon (ts)
Jay Ash (barsx)
John Squires (elbg)
Michael Klein (p)
Henry Letcher, Sydney Smart (d)
Thomas Matthews, Linda Raper,
  Alex Wilkerson (unknown)

Spring 1974
Jim Tifft (t)
Jeff Hoyer (tb)
John Hagen, Stephen Horenstein,
  John Love (ts)
Susan Feiner (afl)
Henry Letcher, David Moss (d)

Fall 1974
Jim Tifft (t)

Jeff Hoyer (tb)
Marc Long (fl)
Susan Feiner (afl)
George Menousek, Don Kaplan (as)
John Hagen, Stephen Horenstein,
John Love, Nick Stephens (ts)
Jay Ash (barsx)
Glynis Lomon (cello)
Larry Jacobs (g)
Leslie Winston (p)
Prent Rodgers (b)
Henry Letcher, David Moss,
   Dennis Warren, Sydney Smart,
   Bill Eldridge, Jackson Krall (d)
John Clink (cga)

Spring 1975
BD ON SABBATICAL NO
ENSEMBLE

Fall 1975
Jim Tifft (t)
Jeff Hoyer (tb)
Adam Fisher (fl)
Don Kaplan (as)
Stephen Horenstein (ts)
Jane Weiner (cello)
Dor Ben-Amotz, Gregory Brown (g)
Buddy Booker, John Squires,
   David Warren (elbg)
Leslie Winston (p)
Henry Letcher, Dennis Warren (d)
Lisa Sokolov (voice)

Spring 1976
Adam Fisher (ss)
Jeff Hoyer (tb)
John Love (ts)
Susan Feiner (afl)
Leslie Winston (p)
Larry Jacobs (g)
Glynis Lomon (cello)
Don Kaplan (as)
Henry Letcher, David Moss,

Dennis Warren, Jeff Locklin,
   one unknown (d)
John Clink (cga)
Lisa Sokolov (voice)

Fall 1976
see note after **R76-0807**

Spring 1977

Fall 1977
Leslie Winston, Diedre Reckset (p)
Stephen Horenstein, Steve Simon (ts)
Larry Jacobs (g)
Buddy Booker (elbg)
Kevin Campbell (d)
Holly Markush (cello)
Charlie Townsend (vln)
Rob /Shu/
Stephen Haynes, Arthur Brooks (t)
Rick Hogarth (frh)
Beth Kanter (afl)

Spring 1978
Jean Barnet (vib)
Buddy Booker, Xtopher Faris (b)
Leslie Winston, Diedre Reckseit (p)
Stephen Horenstein, Steve Simon,
   John Love (ts)
Larry Jacobs (g)
Kevin Campbell (d)
Holly Markush, Charlie
   Townsend (cello)
Paul Austerlitz (bcl)
Stephen Haynes, Devon Leonard (t)
Rick Hogarth (frh)
Lulu Nelson, Lorraine Steiner,
   Ellen _____ (voices)
Beth Kanter (afl)

Fall 1978
Stephen Haynes (t)
Rick Hogarth (frh)

Beth Kanter (afl)
Paul Austerlitz (bcl)
Unknown (as)
Stephen Horenstein (ts)
Jay Ash?? (barsx)
Larry Jacobs ??,
  Robert Lavin-Flower (g)
Carl Landa, Linda Dowdell,
  Leslie Winston (p)
Dana Goode [and others] (b)
Amanda Degener (voice and
  possibly fl)
Laurie Steiner (voice)

Spring 1979
Stephen Haynes (t)
Rick Hogarth (frh)
Beth Kanter (afl)
Paul Austerlitz (bcl)
probably Stephen Horenstein (ts)
Jay Ash?? (barsx)
Larry Jacobs,
  Robert Lavin-Flower (g)
Holly Markush (cello)
Carl Landa, Linda Dowdell,
  Noah Rosen (p)
Spin Dunbar (b)
Kevin Campbell (d)

Fall 1979
Stephen Haynes, Arthur Brooks (t)
Rick Hogarth (frh)
Beth Kanter (afl)
Dan Froot, Steve Albahari (as)
Stephen Horenstein (ts)
Holly Markush (cello)
Larry Jacobs (g)
Susan Barry, Linda Dowdell,
  Noah Rosen (p)
Ed Buller (b)
Kevin Campbell (d)

Spring 1980
DIXON ON SABBATICAL;

NO ENSEMBLE

Fall 1980

Spring 1981
Vance Provey (t)
Holly Markush (cello)
Spin Dunbar (b)

Fall 1981

Spring 1982

Fall 1982

Spring 1983
3(d)
2(t)
(fl)
(p)
(cl b g)
5 (voice)?

Fall 1983
Vance Provey, Robert Miller (t)
Johnathan Bepler (as)
Ian Gittler (g)
Dan Gorn, David Warren (elbg)
Linda Dowdell (p)
Rick O'Neal, Whitney Dickey (d)
Jane Harvey (voice)

Spring 1984
Jeff Taylor (ts)
Dan Gorn (elbg)
probably Andy Dillon (d)

Spring 1985
Dan Gorn, Joel Stillerman (g)
Pilar Castro, Kenneth Dell[?] (elbg)

Melinda Castriota, Eric Zinman (p)
Andy Dillon (d)

Fall 1985
BD ON SABBATICAL; NO
ENSEMBLE

Spring 1986
Mark Nye (tb)
Magnus Peterson (fl)
John Schenck (cl)
Rachel Neill (as)
Emory Creel (ts)
Matt Henderson, Joel Stillerman,
  Tony Wilson (g)
Alex Fattoruso (elbg)
_____ Gauthier (p)
Tony Widoff (d, p)
William Engstrand (unknown)
Claudia Friedlander (*probably* voice)

Fall 1986

Spring 1987
Rachel Neill (ss)
Johnathan Staufer (as)
Josh Kirsch and
  possibly Mark Nye (tb)
Marty Albion, Emory Creel, Jay
Knapp, Evan Sornstein (ts)
Tony Wilson (g)
Kenneth Dell (elbg)
Jared van Dongen (p)
Jeremy Harlos (b)
Ehran Elisha (d)
Shawn Brice (tb) was in ensemble(s)
for this and/or proximate term(s)

Fall 1987
Josh Kirsch and
  possibly Mark Nye (tb)
Rachel Neill (ss)
Evan Sornstein, Jay Knapp (as)

Marty Albion, Emory Creel (ts)
Kathryn Brandt, John Keugel (vln)
Lorelei Bond (vla)
Tony Wilson (g)
David Sechy, Kenneth Dell (elbg)
Jared van Dongen (p)

Jeremy Harlos (b)
Ehran Elisha (d)

Spring 1988
Josh Kirsch (tb)
Rachel Neill (ss)
Evan Sornstein (as)
Emory Creel (ts)
Kathryn Brandt (vln)
Tony Wilson (g)
David Sechy (elbg)
Ehran Elisha (d)

Fall 1988
Josh Kirsch (tb)
Rachel Neill (ss)
Marty Albion (ts)
Kathryn Brandt, John Keugel (vln)
Tony Wilson (g)
David Sechy (elbg)
Jeremy Harlos (b)
Jared van Dongen (p, barsx)
John Blum (p)
Mark Pennington, Bill Dobrow (d)

Spring 1989
Josh Kirsch (tb)
Paul Opel (bcl)
Jared van Dongen (barsx)
Jeremy Harlos (b)
John Blum (p)
Mark Pennington (d)

Fall 1989
Arthur Brooks (t)
Rebecca Rodriguez (bcl)
Seana Gamal (cello)

Justin Perdue (g)
Jeremy Harlos (b)
John Blum, Michael Johnson (p)
Jodi Berggren (p, vib)
Rich Hauver (vib)
Mark Pennington (d)

Spring 1990
BD ON SABBATICAL;
NO ENSEMBLE

Fall 1990
Rebecca Rodriguez (bcl)
Jason Zappa (barsx)
Justin Perdue (g)
Xtopher Faris, Mark Leonard,
   Jeremy Harlos (b)
John Blum, Michael Johnson (p)
possibly Rich Hauver (vib)

Spring 1991

Fall 1991
Jason Zappa (barsx)
Mark Leonard (b)
Shawn Gould, Kristin Dispaltro (p)
Rich Hauver (vib)
Shannon Jones (voice)

Spring 1992
Mollie McQuarrie (ss)
Jason Zappa (barsx)
Vincent Carte (g)
Mark Leonard (b)
Shawn Gould, Eric Zinman (p)
Kristin Dispaltro (voice, p)

Fall 1992
Mark Sutton (t)
Mollie McQuarrie (ss)
Laura Henze (as)

Jason Zappa (barsx)
Vincent Carte, Kip Mazuy (g)
Chris Lightcap (b)
Shawn Gould (p)
Matthew Weston (d)
Shannon Jones (voice)

Spring 1993
Alex Huberty (t)
Laura Henze (as)
Eric Bauer (g)?
Mohamed Ali (perc)
Matthew Hutchinson (p)
Kristin Dispaltro (p, voice)
Matthew Weston (d)
David Brandt (d, perc)
Shannon Jones (voice)

Fall 1994
Nick Skrowaczewski (vib)
2 (voice)?

Spring 1994
Alex Huberty *or* Mark Sutton (t)
Laura Henze (as)
probably Matthew Weston (d)

Fall 1994
Alex Huberty and *possibly*
   Mark Sutton (t)
Mary Springer (cello)
Linc Smith (b)
Hong Ting (p)
Matthew Weston (d)

Spring 1995
Alex Huberty (t)
Mary Springer (cello)
Linc Smith (b)
Hong Ting (p)
Matthew Weston (d)

APPENDIX II

Known Class Recordings

"(2)" or "(3)" added to a date indicates that the episode was recorded across two tapes or three, respectively.

Fall, 1970 [Bennington]: October 6.

Fall, 1971 [Madison]: September 16, 21, 22, 24, 28, 29, 30; October 1, 5, 7, 8, 10, 12 (2), 13, 14, 15, 19, 21, 22, 26 (2), 27, 28, 29; November 2, 3, 4, 5 (2), 9, 10, 11, 12, 17, 18, 23, 30 (2); December 1, 2, 7, 8, 12, 15 (4).

Spring, 1972 [Madison]: January 4, 11, 12, 13, 31; February 1 (2), 2, 4, 7, 8 (2), 11, 14 (2), 15, 16, 18, 23, 24, 29 (2); March 4 (3?), 5, 13, 14 (2), 17, 20 (2), 22 (2), 24, 27, 28 (2), 29 (+?); April 9, 11, 14, 16 (3), 17, 18, 24, 25 (2), 26, 28; May 1, 2, 3, 8, 9 (2), 10;
and up to 10 other undated reels from Madison.

Spring, 1973 [Bennington]: April 19; May 3, 10.

Fall, 1973: September 20, 23; November 2, 29; December 6.

<u>Spring, 1974</u>: February 1.

<u>Spring, 1975</u>: **Sabbatical--no ensemble**

<u>Fall, 1975</u>: See **R75-1207**.

<u>Spring, 1976</u>: March 11, 12, 18, 22 (2), 25 and one unknown; April 1, 2, 9, 15, and one unknown; one May unknown; **R76-0507**.

<u>Fall, 1976</u>: October 7; November 5.

<u>Spring, 1977</u>: April 7; May 7, 19 (2).

<u>Fall, 1977</u>: September 14 (2), 15 (2), 22, 23, 30; October 6, 7, 14, 20, 21; November 8, 9, and two unknowns; December 12; 3 unknowns for the term.

<u>Spring, 1978</u>: March 10, 16, 17, 23, 24, 28, 30 (2), 31; April 2, 6, 7 (2), 13 (2), 14(2), 19 (2), 20 (2), 21; May 3, 4, 5, 9, 11 (3), 12, 18, 29; June 1.

<u>Spring, 1979</u>: April 20; June 7.

<u>Fall, 1979</u>: September 20, 21, 29; October 5, 6 (2), 18, 25 (2), 26; November 1 (2), 2 (2), 8 (2), 9, 10 (2), 13, 15, 17, 29, 30 (2); 3 unknowns for the term.

<u>Spring, 1980</u>: **Sabbatical--no ensemble**

<u>Spring, 1981</u>: March 5, 6 (2), 11, 12 (2), 13 (2), 24, 25 (2), 27; April 3, 9, 10, 16, 21; May 1, 14, 15, 18.

<u>Spring, 1983</u>: March 25; May 5, 19, 20, 26.

<u>Fall, 1983</u>: September 22; October 14 and 15, and one unknown; November 4, 8, 10, 11, 18; December 4, 7, 8, 15; 4 unknowns for the term

<u>Spring, 1986</u>: May 26, 28, and 4 unknowns.

<u>Fall, 1985</u>: **Sabbatical--no ensemble**

<u>Fall, 1986</u>: October 3 and 1 unknown.

<u>Spring, 1987</u>: March 27 (2); April 3; 3 unknowns for term.

<u>Spring, 1988</u>: 1 March unknown; 4 April unknowns; May 12, 13, 26 and 4 unknowns; June 2, 3.

<u>Fall, 1988</u>: September 15, 16; October 27, 28; November 3; 1 unknown for the term.

<u>Spring, 1990</u>: **Sabbatical--no ensemble**.

<u>Fall, 1991</u>: September 6, 7, 12, 13, 19; October 17, 31; November 1; 3 unknowns for the term.

Bibliography

The "Bill Dixon Story" has been most eloquently set forth--for all of time--by Dixon himself. His autobiography, *Born on the Fifth of October*, has remained all-but-published for most of two decades, except for chapters and excerpts used in liner essays (in *Considerations I*, for example). Further sections from it and similar autobiographical pieces can be found in *L'Opera Volume One*, the most thorough compendium yet printed of Dixon's written works. Subtitled "A Collection of Letters, Writings, Musical Scores, Drawings, and Photographs (1967-1986)", *L'Opera Volume One* offers an indispensable perspective on Dixon that is not otherwise captured in the available reportage. With Dixon as compiler and editor, it may be the only work to show the significance of correspondence for all of Dixon's undertakings. A second volume of *L'Opera* and a revised edition of the first are in the offing as *Dixonia* goes to press.

Beyond Dixon's book(s), the most direct window on his art and philosophy, there exists a universe of short, topical pieces published piecemeal over a period of forty years. John Gray's *Fire Music: A Bibliography of the New Jazz, 1959-1990*, a cornerstone for all research in the field, provides the most comprehensive list of these articles. The myriad citations there to articles about

Bill Dixon--most relating to a specific phase or facet of Dixon's work--have been digested into the main text of *Dixonia*, where they are appended to relevant individual entries. (See *BIBLIOGRAPHIC CITATIONS* under "Using this Volume" in the Preface to *Dixonia* for further explanation.)

The first time Dixon was offered a platform in any major journal to describe his own musical activity was his 1967 article, "To Whom It May Concern." Dixon's printed briefing on the state of his work was reprised in "To Whom It May Concern Nineteen Years Later." The next most available forum continues to be Dixon's notes to his own recordings, beginning with the scarce *Archie Shepp-Bill Dixon Quartet* recording (Savoy), and including *Considerations 2*, *The Collection*, and *Vade Mecum*. All his essays for these records were designed to offer some insight into his aesthetics as well as an understanding of the state of the music in that time. The same is true of Dixon's notes for the Savoy recordings by Marc Levin, Ed Curran, Bob Pozar, and Marzette Watts that he produced: they apply both to Dixon's experiences with those musicians (his students) and his relationship to some of the then upcoming "third" wave of young, creative players. Dixon's essay on Sunny Murray intended for *In the Sign of Labyrinth* [FORE Records, unissued] and his book reviews for *Freedomways* show him again in the role of commentator on the artform's current developments (or lack thereof) and its documentation. Dixon's printed exchange of letters with magazine publisher Taylor Castell provides another very pointed example of this interaction with the press.

The most articulate comments about Dixon's career written by others have come from artists inside his work, or from journalists very close to that work and to the scene at large. Dancer/choreographer Judith Dunn was literally a part of all of the creative collaborations that Dixon undertook in the last half of the Sixties. Her liner essay accompanying the *Intents and Purposes* LP was arguably the earliest text to probe the method and substance of Dixon's work, and the insights she had as the only "informed" eyewitness to those recording sessions are succinctly presented with all relevant details. Dunn's letters from the same period, published in "A Letter to Helen" and her interview given to the *Village Voice* offer further information about how she viewed their collaboration. Ten years later, saxophonist Stephen Horenstein had a similar proximity to Dixon's life and work; he wrote copiously about those in his journal account of the winter term, 1975 in the Black Music Ensemble at Bennington College. Part of that chronicle was published in French in *Jazz Magazine*.

Perhaps the earliest journalist to cover Dixon's work thoroughly was columnist Robert Levin, whose major article on the subject remains unpublished. His relationship to Dixon is represented by a small group of *Village Voice* articles from the Dixon-Shepp period. Poet Ted Joans wrote his eyewitness article on the Festival D'Automne sympathetically, compromising neither his listener's objectivity nor his mission of support for Dixon's philosophy. Roger Riggins's *down beat* feature, "Professor Bill Dixon: Intents of an Innovator," despite severe editing and the magazine's neglect of even listing the article on the cover, conveys his close perspective on a transitional period of Dixon's career as educator and musician.

Among the treatments of Dixon's work by journalists in the music, Bob Rusch's *Cadence* interview is notable, as is Thomas Mießgang's nearly unnoticed interview in the collection *Neue Musik im Gespräch* , and the extensive interview by Angelo Leonardi published in *Musica Jazz* and later among the notes to both volumes of *Bill Dixon in Italy.* Where these pieces were geared toward a career overview or retrospective, Dixon's interview for the Bennington College journal, *The New Paper*, delivers a more specific and timely perspective on the founding stages of the Black Music Division. Valerie Wilmer's profile of Dixon in *As Serious As Your Life*, like her *Melody Maker* article compromises some exactitude in her sociological approach to the music. The Dixon segments of her book (Chapter 13 and *passim*), however, amount to the most substantial critical assessment of the Jazz Composers' Guild, although the more fundamental information for study of the Guild is to be found in the only major article published during its existence, "The Jazz Composers' Guild: An Assertion of Dignity."

The quantifiable part of Dixon's career--his issued recordings--has been adequately charted by Keith Thompson and in cyberspace by Robert Stubenrausch. Thompson's obscure discography, probably the earliest to deal exclusively with Bill Dixon, suffers from predating most of Dixon's active recording career, but it was commendable for its time, identifying several film scores that continue to be ignored by Dixon researchers, including Stubenrausch. Not surprisingly, the latter has the most thorough documentation to date. As a kinetic, "virtual" documentation, Stubenrausch's Internet discography has potential to keep pace with all future issues, outstripping even *Dixonia*. Innumerable thumbnail sketches of Dixon's career on records (encompassing various handfuls of the information that Thompson and Stubenrausch provide) have been appended to several profile articles and performance programs, but none of these truly merit further discussion.

For statistical completeness, the first known appearance of Bill Dixon's name in print was occasioned by his early success in the theater arts and public oratory; his elementary school paper carried a cover story calling attention to his achievements in that area. Dixon's earliest public recognition in music (related to the United Nations Jazz Society) include the Associated Press piece by the late William Otis and *The New York Times* articles described in the text segment on the UNJS.

Anderson, Jack. "Judith Dunn and the Endless Quest." *Dance Magazine* (November, 1967): 48-51 and 66-67.

"Black Music: An Interview with Bill Dixon." *Quadrille* (Fall, 1975): 6-11.

Briançon, Pierre. "Entretien avec Bill Dixon." *Jazz Blues & C°* (November, 1976): 4-5.

Cerutti, Gustave. "Discographie: Bill Dixon." *Jazz 360°* (December, 1981): 12-14.

Dixon, Bill. autobiographical response to questionnaire in "Jazzmen Nouveaux à la Question" *Jazz Magazine* [date uncertain; ca 1966].

Dixon, Bill. "Collaboration 1965-1972; Judith Dunn-dancer/choreographer, Bill Dixon-musician/composer." *Contact Quarterly* (Spring/Summer 1985): 7-12.

Dixon, Bill. "Contemporary Jazz: An Assessment" *Jazz & Pop* (November, 1967): 31 et seq. [submitted to *Freedomways* for publication alongside Dixon's book reviews in the Spring, 1967 issue. When that publication declined to print all three parts together, it was taken up by *Jazz & Pop*.]

Dixon Bill. "Jazz: Contemporary Dilemma." *Record World* (April 27, 1968): 27 and 72.

Dixon, Bill. "Jazz Through Four Innovators." (review of *Four Lives in the Bebop Business*) *Freedomways* Spring, 1967.

Dixon, Bill. In "Judith Dunn 1933-1983." *Contact Quarterly* (Fall 1983): 52.

Dixon, Bill. *L'Opera Volume One: A Collection of Letters, Writings, Musical Scores, Drawings, and Photographs 1967-1986*. Bennington, Vermont: Metamorphosis Publishing, 1986.

Dixon, Bill. "The Music of Harlem." In *Harlem USA*, John Henrik Clarke, ed. New York: Collier Books, 1971. Dixon's essay was included in some but not all editions of this collection, also printed as *Freedomways*.

Dixon, Bill. "Some Explanations of the Materials Thus Far Used in Contemporary Improvisation." *SILO* (Fall, 1987): 36-39.

Dixon, Bill. "Sunny Murray." essay intended for *In the Sign of Labyrinth* [FORE Records, unissued].

Dixon, Bill. "Thoughts." *Cardinal Monday Magazine* (March 30, 1972): ca. 4-5.

Dixon, Bill. "To Whom It May Concern." *CODA* (Volume 8, Number 4: October/November, 1967): 2-10.

Dixon, Bill. "To Whom It May Concern Nineteen Years Later" *CODA* (Number 211: December 1986/January 1987): 24.

Dixon, Bill. "Valuable But One-sided Collection." (review of *The Encyclopedia of Jazz in the Sixties*) *Freedomways* Spring, 1967.

Dixon's interview for the Bennington College journal, *The New Paper* [date uncertain; ca. 1977].

Dixon, Bill and Taylor Castell. "Bill Dixon." *Sounds and Fury* (July/August, 1965): 38-40.

Dunn, Judith. "A Letter to Helen." *Dance Perspectives* (Number 38: Summer, 1969): 44-49.

Endress, Gudrun [?]. "Bill Dixon." *Jazz Podium* (October, 1968): 306-09.

Farnè, Libero. *Vedere Il Jazz: Relazioni fra Jazz e Arti Visive nelle Esperienze del Dopoguerra a Oggi* . Milan: Gammalibri, 1982: 152-54 and *passim*.

Farnè, Libero. "Bill Dixon." *Musica Jazz* (June 1987): 20-25, and (July 1987): 20-23.

Goddet, Laurent. "Bill Dixon." *Jazz Hot* (Number 300: December, 1973): 6-11; continued in (Number 301: January, 1974: 15-17.

Gray, John. *Fire Music: A Bibliography of the New Jazz, 1959-1990*. Westport, Connecticut: Greenwood Press, 1991.

Horenstein, Stephen. "Les Leçons de Bill Dixon" *Jazz Magazine*: printed in segments in sequential issues: (November, 1975): 18-19; (December, 1975): 24-25; (January, 1976): 16-17; (February, 1976): 14-15.

Joans, Ted. "Bill Dixon: The Intransigent Black Musician Arrives Very Much Alive in Paris." *CODA* (Number 152: December, 1976): 10-11.

Johnston, Jill. "Dance Journal: Interview with Judith Dunn." *Village Voice* (November 17, 1966): 14-15.

Leonardi, Angelo. three-parted interview whose first two installments were published with *...in Italy* volumes 1 and 2. The third section appears in "Bill Dixon Ha Molte Cose da Dire." *Musica Jazz* (March 1981): 3-6.

Levi, Paulo. "Paulo Levi Talks to Bill Dixon." *The Badger Herald* (May 15, 1972): 14-15.

Levin , Robert. "The Jazz Composers' Guild: An Assertion of Dignity." *down beat* (May 6, 1965): 17-18.

Levin Robert. *Village Voice* articles cited *passim* in Chapter 2 of this volume.

Mießgang, Thomas. *Neue Musik im Gespräch.* Hofheim: Wolke Verlag, 1991.

Peremartí, Thierry. "Bill Dixon." *Jazz Hot* (April, 1993): 34-37.

Riggins, Roger. "Professor Bill Dixon: Intents of an Innovator." *down beat* (August 1980): 30-32.

Rusch, Bob. *Cadence* Volume 8, Numbers 3, 4, and 5; also reprinted in *JazzTalk: The Cadence Interviews* (Secaucus, New Jersey: Lyle Stewart: 1984), p. 121-75.

Stubenrausch , Robert. "Bill Dixon Discography." (rojac@iicm.tu-graz.az.at).

Thompson , Keith. "Bill Dixon--Too Long in The Background." *Pieces of Jazz* 1970, p. 106-108.

Wilmer, Valerie. "Bill Dixon the Loner." *Melody Maker* (January 13, 1973): 30.

Wilmer, Valerie. *As Serious As Your Life.* (London: Quartet, 1977).

Zuffery, Maurice. "Bill Dixon." *Jazz 360°,* (March, 1982): 5-8.

Index

Page numbers shown in boldface type refer to Dixon performances in which the named person materially took part (i.e., where that artist is shown in the personnel section). Paleface page-number listings indicate other text references to that person, and/or "U-" events in the non-Dixon chapter (13) in which s/he took part. Titles of compositions performed in Chapter 13 entries are not indexed.

The last names of the composers/lyricists/choreographers/directors who wrote or created a given piece next to the name of the work in the index. Their full names and further specifics are available in the respective entries. Many proper names of persons, institutions, and compositions mentioned in the text but not immediately relevant to Dixon performances are not indexed. Record titles also are not indexed.

About the Compiler

BEN YOUNG is a research coordinator in the catalog development department of Verve Records.

ISBN 0-313-30275-8

90000>

EAN

9 780313 302756

HARDCOVER BAR CODE